A HUNDRED YEARS OF

JAPANESE FILM

A HUNDRED YEARS OF
JAPANESE
FILM

A Concise History, with a Selective Guide
to DVDs and Videos

DONALD RICHIE

Foreword by Paul Schrader

KODANSHA INTERNATIONAL
Tokyo • New York • London

Dedicated to the memory of
Kawakita Kashiko
(1908–1993)

NOTE: Personal names are romanized in their original order: family names first.
Still captions list actors left to right.

Distributed in the United States by Kodansha America, Inc., and in the United Kingdom
and continental Europe by Kodansha Europe Ltd.

Published by Kodansha International Ltd., 17–14 Otowa 1-chome, Bunkyo-ku, Tokyo 112-8652,
and Kodansha America, Inc.

ISBN-13: 978-4-7700-2995-9
ISBN-10: 4-7700-2995-0

First edition, 2001
Revised edition, 2005
05 06 07 08 09 10 11 12   10 9 8 7 6 5 4 3 2 1

Library of Congress Cataloging-in-Publication Data available.

www.kodansha-intl.com

C O N T E N T S

II—A SELECTIVE GUIDE TO DVDs AND VIDEOS

Over the last forty years Donald Richie has written and rewritten not only the history of Japanese film but also a history of critical methodology. Whatever we in the West know about Japanese film, and how we know it, we most likely owe to Donald Richie.

He arrived in Japan in January 1947 as a civilian staff writer for the *Pacific Stars and Stripes*. His initial motivation was "more to get out of Lima [Ohio] than to go to Tokyo," but he was soon gravitating toward Japanese culture—cinema in particular—and writing film reviews for the *PSS*. It was an extraordinary time to be an American civilian in Japan. Richie made the most of it, and it made the most of Donald Richie.

His studies of Japanese film began in 1959 with *The Japanese Film: Art and Industry*, which he coauthored with Joseph Anderson. For me, a film student, it was a seminal instructive work. As with Borde and Chaumeton's *Panorama du Film Noir Américan*, a door opened to a world of fascinating rooms. Richie's first history used a humanistic model: the film director struggling to be an individual while, at the same time, moving toward what was presumed to be the realistic norm. ("Realistic" or "representational," as opposed to "presentational"—a critical distinction central to Japanese aesthetics as well as to Richie's writing.)

The amazing—absolutely unique—nature of Richie's accomplishment is that he has not simply updated his history (like most other film historians) by appending new chapters every decade or so. Instead, in every later work he has chosen to approach his subject from another angle, rescreening the films and rethinking his assumptions, acknowledging that as history evolves so does the historian and his methodologies.

Richie, writing alone, published his second history, *Japanese Cinema: Film Style and National Character*, in 1971. This volume emphasized a cultural point of view: the struggle of Japanese filmmakers to be Japanese in a non-indigenous medium. It also subscribed to the critical *Zeitgeist* of the time—auteurism, the notion that the director is responsible for everything that appears on screen. Also, at this time, Richie wrote the initial and still defini-tive books on Kurosawa and Ozu.

The third of his histories, *Japanese Cinema: An Introduction* (1990), turned its atten-tion to how films were actually made: the multitude of practical considerations that define a single film and its contemporaries: politics, economics, morality, intermedia competition, technological advances, personality conflicts. To achieve this, *An Introduction* emphasized reporting over theory.

In this new book, *A Hundred Years of Japanese Film*, Richie relies even less on theory. He has refined and amplified the approach of the 1990 volume, retained his sensitivity to the actual circumstances of film production (something filmmakers consider important but his-torians often overlook), renounced his previous methodologies and proposed a new one, one which seeks to oppose then reconcile the *unconsidered* assumption of a native Japanese accent and the demands of a cinematic lingua franca. He desires to show the interweave of filmmaking (the contributions of directors, writers, cinematographers, actors, composers, art directors, as well as financiers). Decline-and-fall modalities are found too simplistic, as is the infancy-maturity model. Film's unspoken assumptions, the hows and whys of filmmaking, the laws of supply and demand—these are now central concerns.

Fascinating issues arise: Japanese assumptions about "realism," the growing respecta-bility of the "representational," the merging of high and low cultures, the evolution of the genre, as well as the demise of the period-film and the emergence of the dominant contem-porary theme, in Ozu as elsewhere, of the failing family.

Stepping ashore in 1947, Donald Richie, the Commodore Perry of Japanese film history, was given a unique opportunity. Still in Tokyo more than half a century later, he has—in response as it were—given film historians a model of the modern critic: a man of restless, evolving intellect.

Paul Schrader

In 1896, when film was first seen in Japan, a fifty-year-old member of this initial movie audience would have been born into a feudal world where the shogun, daimyo, and samurai ruled. He could not have left his archipelago or, if he did, he could not have returned upon pain of death. His manner of dress and way of speech were regulated by his status, and his ignorance of the outside world was general. It was still the epoch of the Tokugawa clan which ruled Japan from 1600 through 1867, encompassing much of what we now know as the Edo period.

During the ensuing period, the Meiji era (1868–1912), this kimono-clad viewer would not only have seen the Meiji Restoration (when the sixteen-year-old emperor was brought from Kyoto to Edo—now Tokyo—to become the nominal head of the new government), but also the Meiji "Enlightenment."

Here, under the slogan "A Rich Country and a Strong Military" (*Fukoku Kyohei*), he would have seen the abolition of the feudal socioeconomic system under which he had grown up, the adoption of modern (Western) production methods, and universal conscription. Under another of the many colorful slogans of the period, "Civilization and Enlightenment" (*Bummei Kaika*), he would have experienced the official urging of Western clothes and meat eating, the abolition of sword carrying and *chommage* (topknots), and eventually the disbanding of the samurai themselves.

This hypothetical fifty-year-old would have also witnessed the forced adoption of the Western (Gregorian) calendar, the emergence of a nationwide public school system, the inauguration of telephone and postal services, and the construction of railways.

And through it all, he—now perhaps in a three-piece suit and wearing a bowler hat—would have been told to somehow hold on to his Japaneseness. Yet another slogan indicated the way: "Japanese Spirit and Western Culture" (*Wakon Yosai*)—in that order. The national ineffables of Japan were to illuminate Western materialism. In this manner, it was hoped,

Japan might avail itself of the ways of the modern West and, at the same time, retain its "national entity." It was a difficult task, one which Japan is still trying to carry out.

When film came to Japan, the country had only allowed foreign imports for a few decades. The nation's culture—which means its way of accounting for, of constructing, of assuming—was still its own. Whatever early debts were owed to China and Korea, they had long been canceled by an appropriation which rendered their influence "Japanese." The nontraditional, the modern, the Western, was not even half a century old. The traditional, though eroding swiftly, was still centuries deep.

In Japan, film arrived as a commercial product. Though it might eventually be illuminated by native ineffables, proving that film was a uniquely national art was not a Japanese issue. Nor was there a need to discover paradigms—to trace a path from simple to complex, from infancy to maturity and beyond. Indeed, it was not necessary to treat film history as destined to fill any of the various categories of an aesthetic system.

In time, however, a need to account for a certain Japanese tradition in Japanese films developed, a need which still remains. And though "Japaneseness" is not a concept which ever much interested the Japanese filmmaker (though it has occasionally fascinated the Japanese politician), filmmakers remain Japanese, and the international language of film is even now locally spoken with a native accent. As director Ozu Yasujiro once put it: "We are Japanese, so we should make Japanese things."

Histories of the Japanese film (both in Western languages and in Japanese itself) have most often chosen a *volksgeist* theory where the culturally specific can be used as a vehicle for historical reorienting and aesthetic inquiry, and where the uniqueness of the Japanese film may be insisted upon. In actuality, however, there are more similarities than differences among the films of Europe and America, and those of Japan. Though each country creates a national cinema (and hence a national cinematic style), it is only through the most common, pragmatic, and universal of means. A film history is a search for a way through which narrative can be presented more efficiently.

Conventionally, the historian is given several choices. He or she can arrange the material to form a kind of narrative, one which stretches from primitive beginnings toward something like present perfection. Or, another ploy, the events can be arranged to assume a familiar pattern—birth, maturity, decline. Or, again, the historian may postulate as primary a country's culture and character. The method adopted here is more eclectic and less concerned with any single theory. It follows the mechanics of cause and effect and it believes, along with Alexis de Tocqueville, that "history is a gallery of pictures in which there are few originals and many copies."

Further, this narrative insists upon the importance of importation. While all countries incorporate culture from elsewhere—the process is called "progress"—Japan does so with a certain finality. Any definition of Japanese style has to face the fact that most Japanese are usually unable to handle anything without swiftly nationalizing it. Or, perhaps better put, the Japanese have a particular genius for assimilation and incorporation. Thus any influence—be it *gagaku* court dancing from medieval Korea, punk rock from modern America, the narrative patternings of European sophisticate Ernst Lubitsch, or the made-in-U.S.A. attitudes of Quentin Tarantino—is swallowed, digested, and turned into something sometimes rich, often strange, and always "Japanese." All of these choices, moreover, are purposeful: identity is, in the process, more constructed than discovered.

In Japanese cinema, there was thus no Japanese essence awaiting liberation by a few individual directors. Nor was a storytelling narrative there from the first. This rose from the needs, often commercial, to regularize production. The storytelling cinema was not so much the result of cinematic discoveries as that of a consolidation of techniques, many of them old, some of them new, all of them depending upon circumstances. Narrative rose from regularization; style from standardization.

The enormous if rapidly shrinking weight of the traditional certainly informs Japanese culture, but so does the mass of all its imports. Balancing all this, not succumbing entirely to *volksgeist* theory on one hand, nor, on the other, completely subscribing to the effects of foreign influences, is the task of the historian.

One of the ways in which I have attempted to identify the demands of an assumed native culture is by presupposing a polarity between what I identify as a presentational ethos, which I find more in Asia than in the West, and a representational ethos, which I find more in the West than in Asia.

The representational intends to do just that, represent: It is realist and assumes that "reality" itself is being shown. The presentational, on the other hand, presents. This it does through various stylizations, with no assumption that raw reality is being displayed. The West is familiar with some of these stylizations (impressionism/expressionism), and the Japanese cinema will introduce us to more. Film "realism" is itself, to be sure, just one stylization among many, but its position is in the West privileged. It is not so traditionally privileged in the East. And, though I believe my generalization is largely true, we can still think of presentational European and American films, and representational Japanese ones.

My use of this presentational-representational axis is not original. It is a concept familiar to many historians of the Japanese film. I am, however, perhaps alone in so stressing it. Though it remains a schema, it is a powerful one, because through it one can discover a basic assumption governing the shape of the Japanese film. It provides a base upon which to build.

The idea of presentation also welcomes an expanding tradition. Japanese tradition now includes much that was originally foreign. Ozu made *Our Gang* his own, and group-minded Japanese descendants have become the attractive gangs of rascals in the films of Kitano "Beat" Takeshi and others of his generation. At the same time, presentation as a dominant assumption makes possible the creation of individual directorial styles. This is true in all cinema; the gestural camera in Mizoguchi Kenji and Max Ophüls, the precision of detail in Kurosawa and Hitchcock, the narrowly selective realism of Ozu and Robert Bresson. One might say that a representational ethos results in a less individual style.

This said, one must also add that commercial film is a collective effort, and tracing responsibilities is not all that easy. The auteur theory conventionally assigns such responsibility to the director himself, under the assumption that the captain is responsible for the ship. However, contributions to a finished film are various, perhaps particularly in Japan, where harmonious contribution is encouraged and single-minded determination is not. In this work I may not have entirely solved the many problems of attribution but, at least, I have indicated some of those—producers, writers, photographers, art directors, actors—who have contributed. In so doing, I hope to have emphasized something about the nature of this joint product.

Anyone attempting a history of Japanese film is at something of a disadvantage in that so little Japanese film is left. Even in a world medium where two-thirds of all silent cinema is lost and perhaps a quarter of all sound films as well, the destruction of the Japanese cinema is extraordinary. Except for a few known titles, there is little fully extant from the period of 1897 to 1917 and only somewhat more from 1918 to 1945. The 1923 earthquake, the 1945 fire-bombing of the major cities, the postwar Allied Occupation torching of banned films, and the later indifference of the industry itself have meant the destruction of ninety percent of all Japanese films made before 1945. I have noted such missing films in the text with the designation "n.s." (not surviving).

There is now a large amount of scholarly work on the Japanese film. Since one of my aims in writing this new account is to accommodate film students, I have purposely availed myself of it, calling attention in the bibliography to its availability. For the same reason I have compiled a guide to English-subtitled film on DVD and videocassette to assist both teacher and student, as well as the interested reader.

Finally, in writing this book I am grateful, as always, to the Kawakita Foundation, the Japan Foundation, and the National Film Center, and to their generosity in allowing screenings and lending stills. I want to acknowledge my debt to the late Earle Ernst who first introduced me to the presentational/representational paradigm which has become central to this book. I am as well indebted to David Borwell, Arthur Nolletti, Keiko McDonald, and Mark Schilling, all of whom took time to read the manuscript and make suggestions; to the input of Aaron Gerow; to Paul Schrader, who not only read the manuscript but wrote the foreword; and to my Kodansha editors, Barry Lancet, Uchiyama Michiko, and Cathy Layne.

Donald Richie

I

A CONCISE HISTORY
OF JAPANESE FILM

"One need only compare American, French, and German films to see how greatly nuances of shading and coloration can vary in motion pictures. In the photographic image itself, to say nothing of the acting and the script, there somehow emerge differences in national character."

Tanizaki Jun'ichiro, *In Praise of Shadows* (1933) (*In'ei raisan*, translated by Thomas J. Harper and Edward G. Seidensticker, 1977)

BEGINNINGS AND THE *BENSHI*

Film began in Japan, as in most countries, during the last few years of the nineteenth century. The Cinématographe Lumière made its Osaka debut in 1897. Within weeks, Thomas Edison's Vitascope was also seen there and, shortly after that, in Tokyo as well. In the same year the first motion-picture camera was imported by photographer Asano Shiro of the Konishi Camera Shop, and he was shortly shooting street scenes around the capital. At nearly the same time the Mitsukoshi Department Store formed a photography department and its cameramen, Shibata Tsunekichi and Shirai Kanzo, began taking shots of the Ginza and of geisha.

By early 1899, Asano had turned to geisha as well, capturing a series of dances. Komada Koyo, also originally with the Konishi Camera Shop and soon to be one of the leading *benshi* (silent-film narrators), later remembered the trouble they had with the focus and with keeping the dancers within the sight-lines they had drawn on the floor. Nonetheless, after much struggle, they finally produced a Japanese motion picture.

Geisha were chosen as subjects not because they were quintessentially Japanese but because their appeal was so strong. Asano and Komada had both noticed that among the various popular photographic postcards their stores sold, those of geisha outsold any other. Geisha were therefore a commodity popular enough to warrant the necessary cinematic outlay.

By the middle of 1899, Komada had acquired enough capital to leave the camera store and form the Association of Japanese Motion Pictures. This organization now sponsored an entire program of such geisha dances, all newly filmed, all in focus, at the Tokyo Kabuki-za, and the event was well attended even at the inflated admission prices common to that venue. Thus inspired, other camera-wielding businessmen began producing their own programs.

Shibata, at the request of a local dramatic troupe, filmed a scene from one of its plays, *Armed Robber: Shimizu Sadakichi* (Pisutoru Goto Shimizu Sadakichi, 1899, n.s.), and later in the year he approached kabuki itself and filmed excerpts from *Maple Viewing* (Momijigari, 1899) and *Ninin Dojoji* (Two People at Dojo Temple, n.s.). The latter was tinted (another Japan first) by the Yoshizawa Company, later one of the first film production companies.

Maple Viewing, 1899, Shibata Tsunekichi, with Onoe Kikugoro V, Ichikawa Danjuro IX.

Originally, the leading kabuki actor Ichikawa Danjuro IX was against the idea of motion pictures, dismissing them as (apparently unlike kabuki) merely vulgar amusement. In fact, kabuki actors—though not Danjuro himself—had already appeared before the Lumière cameramen when they visited Japan, but this apparent contradiction was acceptable since those performances were for export. However, Danjuro was eventually won over by the argument that his appearance would be a gift for posterity.

Consequently, joined by Onoe Kikugoro V, Danjuro went through three short scenes for the camera. Shibata had decided to shoot in a small outdoor stage reserved for tea parties behind the Kabuki-za, but that morning there was a strong wind. Stagehands had to hold the backdrop, and the wind carried away one of the fans Danjuro was tossing. Reshooting was out of the question, and so the mistake stayed in the picture. Later, Shibata remembered that some viewers remarked that the accident gave the piece a certain charm. As one of the earliest Japanese films to survive, *Maple Viewing* can still be appreciated today, with the "flying fan" scene intact.

In the same year, the active Komada appeared at the Kinkikan, a small theater in Tokyo's Kanda district where Vitascope premiered. Dressed in formal evening wear and carrying a silver-headed cane, he greeted his guests and began explaining what they were seeing—in this case, a series of American Vitascope shorts.

Although this benshi lecturer-commentator had his counterparts in most early cinemas, the role was retained longer in Japan than elsewhere. The need for a live narrator had faded in the United States by 1910, but in Japan the benshi survived well into the era of sound, and was not really challenged until 1932. Eventually, the profession was done in by the enormous popular success of Josef von Sternberg's early talkie, *Morocco* (1930).

The reasons for the long life of the benshi were various. Since Japan had only some forty years before been "opened up to the West" (a phrase invented in the West), ignorance of much of the outside world was common. The benshi filled in the gaps of knowledge Western viewers had acquired long before. They were "a reassuring native presence with a presumed acquaintance of the foreign object," a necessity which might even now "explain the Japanese affection for teachers, tour guides, sommeliers, and other conduits for the acquisition of new experience." [1]

In addition to his educational role, the benshi was essential to the film-viewing experience. In part, this was because the early cinema of Japan was, as elsewhere, a cinema of short, often unrelated clips—initially films from abroad: in the Lumière collection, one saw babies being fed, gardeners being squirted, and so on. A commentary connecting these clips not only made a short program longer but more coherent. Later, when longer programs became available, story links were created by the benshi. Still later came the illusion of a self-contained story-world. Until then, the benshi was all that these little glimpses had in common.

The benshi was also required to fill the time. This he accomplished in various ways. Besides talking, he sometimes lengthened the viewing time. Many films were quite short, and so a number were shown on a single bill. Sometimes, as was common in early showings in France and the United States, films were repeated. Since the audience had not yet developed what has been called a "linear response," no one minded a second viewing as it gave one a chance to catch new things the second time around.

In recalling the films he had seen around 1898, as a child of about ten, novelist Tanizaki Jun'ichiro said: "The ends of the reel would be joined together so that the same scene could be projected over and over. I can still remember, endlessly repeated, high waves rolling in on a shore somewhere, breaking and then receding, and a lone dog playing there, now pursuing, now being pursued by the retreating and advancing waters." [2]

Another example of the need for length occurred during the initial Japanese showing of the Edison film, *The May Irwin/John Rice Kiss* (1896). Though the film was seen by Western spectators but once, in Japan, with the ends joined together, John approached May and kissed her some dozen times. This repetition had consequences. Suspicious police appeared, but the quick-minded commentator—one Ueda Hoteikan—explained that Westerners customarily greeted each other with a full-mouth kiss and that the ladies and gentlemen of the audience ought to be edified by this documentary footage of what in America was an everyday courtesy.

The technique of repetition has a proper Japanese name, *tasuke* (continuous loop), and its use remains common on Japanese television and in the movie theaters, where advertising clips are repeated several times. The aim now is not to make a short program longer, but the argument holds that anything short may be twice savored. After all, repetition seemingly for its own sake is so accepted an element in Japanese dramaturgy that its cinematic equivalent seems quite natural. Perhaps those Western viewers who, even during a Mizoguchi Kenji or an Ozu Yasujiro film, sigh and hope the director will soon get on with it are responding to this tradition of repetition.

The benshi mostly filled in the time with lengthy explanations, a time-consuming rhetoric, and drawn-out, often moralizing conclusions. It was the benshi who created the narrative for the audience to follow, and even today, when the narrator's performance has been reduced to a more or less scholarly reconstruction, a plethora of explanations, repetitions of information, and voice-overs remains in Japanese commercial film. This was what the uninformed audience required and consequently wanted. "What to filmgoers in the West might seem an overdetermined, annoying repetition was for Japanese audiences constitutive of meaning."[3]

From the Western perspective, it could be said that the benshi delayed the cinematic development of narrative in Japan. However, this line of thought is valid only if one believes that the development of narrative was a "natural" development of the film and that there were no other alternatives. Actually, as Japanese film itself indicates, there were.

In the West, cinema was evolving into a self-sufficient narrative. It seemed the most practical and efficient way to entertain increasingly sophisticated audiences. A series of short clips gave way to lengthier, more coherent stories. The audience's involvement in more detailed stories increased attendance. It was thus possible to find in the narrative film the most suitable cinematic form if the industry required films to be quickly and cheaply made.

In Japan, however, the perception of narrative was different. It was the benshi and not any self-contained cinematic narrative which made sense to the audience. He not only explained what was being shown on the screen but also was there "to reinforce, interpret, counterpoint, and in any case to intercede."[4]

The role of the benshi was a very traditional one. From the earliest times, Japanese drama had required an informing voice. The chorus in noh drama, the *joruri* chanter in bunraku puppet drama, the *gidayu* narrator in kabuki—all premodern Japanese theater is a pictorial expansion of verbal storytelling. Joseph Anderson has indeed defined the Japanese drama as a presentation "in which actors do not autonomously enact events for spectators; dialogue spoken by actors is not the primary speech modality; and basic plot structure is not based on conflict, crisis, climax, resolution, and dramatic unity."[5]

Rather than being presented as an occurrence, drama is presented as a recounted occurrence. Although many national dramas have entertained like assumptions, the Japanese theater (and its descendents, movies and television) has remained remarkably faithful to the authoritative voice. As one early critic expressed it, the film itself was like the bunraku puppet and the benshi was the gidayu reciter.

Initially, the benshi merely told the story before the performance—the *setsumei* (summing up), or an explanation provided before the fact. Soon, however, he was telling the story during the screening itself. In those first years, the images had been sometimes accompanied by the actors (if available) who voiced their lines behind the screen. Hence the name of this technique—*kagezerifu* ("shadow dialogue"). Such presentations were somewhat like another early cinematic form called *rensageki* (joined drama), where scenes from a play with real actors were interspersed with filmed scenes, the actors stationed behind the screen to voice their roles. Eventually, the benshi assumed all the lines. To do so, he often resorted to using a variety of voices. This technique, which was an earlier method taken over from the puppet drama, was called *kowairo* ("voice coloring").

A surviving outline of a typical stage-inspired film, *The Golden Demon* (Konjiki yasha, 1912, n.s.), suggests how this worked. This film version of the stage adaptation of Ozaki Koyo's popular novel became a vehicle for Tsuchiya Shoju, a benshi noted for his mastery of "seven separate and distinct voices." This scene of an argument requires three voices:

Kowairo (for the heroine, Omiya): If I marry Tomiya, what will you say?
Kowairo (for the hero, Kanichi): Then you're all set to marry him! What a fickle flirt you are!
Narrator (the benshi voice): Kanichi, overcome with rage, kicks the fragile Omiya . . . [6]

The many-voiced benshi also developed a vocabulary of styles. The historical film was thought to demand an inflated, somewhat nasal delivery; films about modern life were more colloquial, and the tone for foreign films was sententious and didactic.

When the vocal demands were too great, benshi often shared films, just as bunraku sometimes switches gidayu narrators in mid-play. There were also benshi "contests," which drew spectators attracted to particular benshi rather than to the film itself. Benshi even made recordings, which sold well and were listened to without the accompaniment of film. One of the later benshi constantly rendered his big hit, Robert Wiene's *The Cabinet of Doctor Caligari* (1919), on the stage, but without the film; he even made a 78-rpm recording of part of it that sold quite well.

The benshi were employed in many other ways. One of their number, for example, solved a serious censorship problem. This concerned a French Pathé feature, *La Fin du Règne de Louis XVI—Révolution Française* (ca. 1907, n.s.), a film considered incendiary since Japan had proclaimed its own ruler to be of divine descent. "On the day before it was to be shown, the French film was withdrawn as a menace to public peace." In its place appeared another film, *The Cave King: A Curious Story of North America* (Hokubei kiden: Gankutsuo, 1908, n.s.). This was in fact the same film, only now Louis XVI was the "leader of a robber band," and the rabble storming the Bastille became "a band of citizens loyally joining the police to suppress the outlaws, all this action taking place in the Rocky Mountains."[7]

The benshi affected the growth and development of the Japanese cinema in other ways. His preference tended toward simple stories—the better to exhibit his own talents. No narrative function other than his own was welcomed. Given his skills, he also preferred that each scene be a little drama, a *mise-en-scène*. With the benshi present, there was no need to construct the illusion of a scene-to-scene development, since he himself provided the necessary narrative. He was in this way much like his theatrical predecessors.

The influence of the benshi continues even today. Joseph Anderson remembers listening to a modern Japanese television soap opera from another room in the house and discovering that "voice-over narration not only recaps previous episodes but every so often talks about things that are happening right now on the tube. I don't have to look at this television drama. I hear it."[8]

FILM, THEATER, AND ACTORS

The Japanese audience perceived film as a new form of theater and not (as in, say, the United States) a new form of photography. It is not surprising then that nearly all of the early Japanese story films were in some manner or other taken from the stage. Though this is no longer true, the Japanese film audience still behaves much as it does at the theater. Like the audience of the latter, the moviegoer takes his seat at the beginning of the session. Film-viewing is not seen as a circular entertainment that one may enter and leave at will. Rather, it has its own narrative rules, and these are to be respected. Members of the Japanese audience rarely leave the theater during the projection and often remain seated until all the credits have been viewed and the lights go up. For whatever reason, the film is watched in silence, in marked contrast to film-viewing habits elsewhere, but much in keeping with Western theater-going behavior.

The subjects of the early Japanese cinema were equally theatrical—scenes from kabuki classics or sections of *shimpa*. These two genres were thought of as separate. Kabuki was "old school" (*kyuha*) and shimpa (which had first appeared around 1890) was the "new" (*shin*) "school" (*ha*).

This latter drama was originally designed as a typically Meiji-era compromise. It was written for a rapidly modernizing Japan which had thrown off feudal rule. The language was colloquial, the topic was largely concerned with the contemporary scene, and the performance was acted out not through the strictly stylized movements of kabuki but through movement thought closer to life itself. Still, shimpa retained many kabuki accouterments, including males in female roles.

It was this distinction between old and new school that shaped the forms taken by the nascent cinema: kabuki-based films became *jidaigeki* (more commonly, *jidaimono*), a rubric which now defines all period-films; and the shimpa-based pictures were the beginnings of *gendaigeki*, or contemporary films.

Kabuki-based movies continued to be constructed of various snippets—scenes abstracted from popular stories long part of the collective consciousness—but adaptations from the more dramatic shimpa provided a stronger narrative and thus generated longer films. Yet both kyuha and shimpa were constructed, photographed, and presented in much the same way. Not only was the narrator present, but there were also *oyama* (male actresses) in place of women, and the film itself was usually comprised of full-frontal, long-running stagelike shots.

When Konishi Ryo shot the first film version of the kabuki classic *Chushingura* (The Loyal Forty-Seven Ronin, 1907, n.s.)—an extremely popular subject, with over eighty-five film versions to date—the camera was fixed at a spot about thirty feet away and, since the film was intended to be just like a play, the view was strictly frontal. There was even a curtain between scenes.

The film frame was commonly considered the equivalent of the theatrical proscenium. Regarding his *My Sin* (Onoga tsumi, aka One's Own Sin, 1909, n.s.), the first shimpa screen adaptation, cameraman-director Chiba Kichizo recalled that he erected poles on the beach and strung a curtain between them. The curtain could be raised to reveal the drama taking place. This dramaturgy "indicated the direction early Japanese cinema took: it captured stage action as a picture, rather than as a moving image."[9]

Though many films from other countries were still constructed of extended long-shots, early Western directors were finding new ways to direct the viewer's attention within this frame. They integrated shorter scenes with the camera set closer to delineate the action, and close-ups to call attention to characters. None of this occurred in Japan, however, because of the pervasive theatrical influence.

Early Japanese filmmakers clung to the idea of the film frame as stage. On the stage itself, audience attention was directed by the dialogue, a convention which continued with benshi-dominated cinema. But as the benshi's voice was divorced from the actor on the screen, it was sometimes difficult to see just whom among those distant flickering figures was doing the talking.

One means of effectively directing attention was to focus on a privileged person: the hero or heroine. Spectators could follow a story shot at a considerable distance if they had someone to follow about. Stars became necessary, and were soon created.

Among the earliest stars was a provincial actor, Onoe Matsunosuke. He was discovered by Makino Shozo, a former kabuki-troupe manager and, it was later said, the first person to deserve the title of director in the Western sense of the word. Onoe, who had met Yokota Einosuke (head of the company which later became the Nikkatsu motion picture company), began acting in kyuha films featuring *tachimawari* (kabuki-style sword-fighting). Makino, impressed by Onoe's ability to handle the physical rigors of his trade, made the actor the star of *Goban Tadanobu* (1909, n.s.). Onoe became so popular that by the time he died in 1926 he had made hundreds of films, many based on kabuki stories, such as his popular *Sukeroku* (1914, n.s.).

Sukeroku, 1914, Makino Shozo, with Onoe Matsunosuke.

Despite the competition of the new shimpa product, these kabuki-based kyuha remained popular for decades to come: nearly six thousand jidaigeki were made between 1908 and 1945, and their descendants still grace the tube. The audience for a sword-wielding star was large. It is said that during Onoe's period of greatest fame, when Japanese schoolboys were asked to name the greatest man in Japan, they always named him second. (The emperor was, of course, first; third was one of the reigning benshi.)

Onoe has said that during this period of early filmmaking, neither actors nor directors used a script. Instead, Makino carried the plot in his head and called out the lines for the actors while they were on camera, just like the joruri chanter in bunraku. Onoe also recalled what hard work it was. He was required to make nine or more features a month, which meant that he was working on three separate features at any one time. Sometimes, he said, he was so exhausted that he mixed up his parts. And, indeed, overworked, he died on the set.

Seen today, these Makino-Onoe films indicate how necessary such a central figure was to the audience's understanding. Even in an inferior print (and by any standard, all extant prints are inferior), the star is always plainly visible. So, too, even when the film is projected at the wrong speed (most of Onoe's films were undercranked in order to save on film), his athletic vitality is apparent. He alone comprised the narrative upon which the benshi commented.

At the same time that Makino's films were becoming star-based attractions, something similar was occurring in the West, though for different reasons. In an effort to create stars (in this case, to win respectability and raise ticket prices), both the French *film d'art* (Sarah Bernhardt, among others, like kabuki actor Ichikawa Danjuro before her, having been induced to allow selected stage scenes to be filmed for posterity) and, in America, Adolph Zukor's self-explanatory "Famous Players in Famous Plays" were introduced.

These static stage presentations, one scene sedately following another, may have brought a better class of people into the theaters in the West, but Japan did not have to worry about respectability. Film was by now an art popular with all classes, no matter what their income. Indeed, the Crown Prince was induced to attend an early film showing and later the Emperor Meiji himself was sat down and shown one.

One of the results of the Western films d'art—with all their scenes from famous plays passing before the viewer—was that they prepared audiences for longer films. By 1910, the film d'art, as well as the Italian epics and some of the longer American movies, set a precedent for length. Longer running times, in turn, required detailed and developed scripts.

In the West, the emergence of scripts led to scenic construction, to early expository intertitles, and to greater visual communication. Later, the intertitles were more commonly devoted to dialogue, and these eventually evolved into a screenplay, which attempted to show as much as it told.

None of this, however, initially occurred in Japan. Nor was there any reason for it to. Onoe bounced from scene to scene capturing attention, while the consequences of the slender narrative were still assumed by the benshi. Whereas the Western script incorporated more complex stories plus innovations in shooting and editing, the Japanese benshi had no use for any of this.

Nor need the benshi concern himself with an assumed fidelity to what in the West was becoming known as cinematic "realism." In Europe and America, this child of photography was expected to obey the laws of appearance. And since realism was a photographic virtue, the film became a document. This did not occur in Japan—for a number of reasons.

REALISM AND REALITY

To most Japanese, the Western idea of "realism," particularly in its naturalistic phase, was something truly new. All early Japanese dramatic forms had assumed the necessity of a structure created through mediation. The same was true for Japanese culture in general: the wilderness was natural only after it had been shaped and presented in a palpable form, as in the Japanese garden, or flowers were considered living (ikebana) only after having been cut and arranged for viewing. Life was thus dramatically lifelike only after having been explained and commented upon. Art and entertainment alike were presentational, that is, they rendered a particular reality by way of an authoritative voice (be it the noh chorus or the benshi). This approach stood in marked contrast to the representational style of the West in which one assumed the reality of what was being shown.

Indeed, Japan had no tradition of the common style known as realism, the style that Susan Sontag has defined as "that reductive approach to reality which is considered realistic." [10] Though Hokusai's sparrows are thought realistic in Japan, this kind of realism is seen as partial when contrasted with the claims of "cinematic realism" in the West. Thus, what passes for realistic in Japan, elsewhere is thought highly stylized. These inherent differences may also explain why the Japanese were puzzled over what Degas and Monet could have found so special in ordinary Japanese prints.

The national inclination toward the presentational did not mean that certain realistic aspects of the moving picture were neglected. It was rather that they were not insisted upon and that, when included, they appeared compromised (to Western eyes) by a stagey artificiality. The documentary, with its almost ostentatious lack of presentation and its tacit assumptions of representation, became influential in Japan much later than it had in other countries. Indeed, it was not until the Russo-Japanese War of 1904–05 that newsreels of an event showed large audiences documentary footage, thereby preparing the way for a wider reception of a more representational and less presentational cinema.

Even early newsreels retained an unusual amount of presentation. A theater showing such newsreels had Japanese flags, a band, and a benshi. Komada Koyo's wartime offerings in Tokyo's Asakusa district in 1905 included high claims of authenticity—every foot of film, he said, had been shot right where Japanese blood had sanctified the soil. And, in truth, some of it was. Yoshizawa Shokai had dispatched a camera crew to capture some scenes. Shibata Tsunekichi and another early cameraman, Fujiwara Kozaburo, were sent to the front. Authentic material shot by Pathé and the Charles Urban Company was also included.

Still (as was common in the newsreel footage of some other countries as well), there was much fake footage added. Though this fakery was detected and reports of derision from the audience did surface, the Japanese, as a rule, acknowledged, even enjoyed, the charm and entertainment value of the falsified newsreels. As has been wisely said: "Originality was never a primary value in Japan." [11]

In the West, on the contrary, faked newsreels caused concern. An American attempt to cash in on the San Francisco earthquake of 1906 was sternly refused distribution in that country. This regard for realism was to lead to a cinematic style that was almost ostentatiously representational. In Japan, one might say that newsreels were expected to be "fake," that is, as presentational as anything else. If early Western newsreels defined, and to an extent created, narrative film in the West, nothing of the sort occurred in Japan until much later.

When Japan's first war drama, *The Cherry Blossoms of Japan* (Yamato zakura, n.s.), was finally filmed in 1909, realism was not among its values: Ridge 203 in Port Arthur was obviously the studio lot, and firecrackers were used—kabuki-like—to create the bursts of smoke from fired rifles. The realism of newsreels was thus turned into nonrealistic theatricality.

In Japanese film, as on the Japanese stage, actuality was one thing; theatricality was another. *Armed Robber*, based on a scene taken from a play which in itself is based on "a real-life happening," was using a standard ploy of the topical bunraku and kabuki vehicles of such early Edo playwrights as Chikamatsu Monzaemon and Tsuruya Namboku. The actuality of the event might be a selling point, but theatricality, not fidelity, was the goal. Though a robbery may have occurred last month, the scenery, acting style, and lighting would have come from a century before.

Realism as a style concerned with appearances was nevertheless slowly influencing the emerging Japanese film. Wartime newsreels were, in part, responsible for this, as was the growing importation of Western films. A third reason for change was a new form of theater, *shingeki* (literally, "new drama"), which was also foreign, consisting as it did of a Japanese version of Western proscenium theater.

The Japanese audience was now ready for something besides shimpa melodrama and Onoe's kabuki-like cavortings. What in ten years had become the "traditional" Japanese film was losing its audience. Sato Tadao has said that at that time, around 1910, it was "common knowledge that Japanese films were rubbish compared to foreign films. People who went to Japanese films were snotty-nosed little kids." [12] While the audiences may have included a grown-up or two, the narrative means of these early films were juvenile, or what the foreign critic would call primitive. Early Japanese film thus contained a paradox: It was a new means of expression, but what it expressed was old.

WESTERN INFLUENCES

Compared to the perceived staleness of the Japanese film, new films from the West were freshness itself. Imported in numbers after 1915, foreign cinema offered new perspectives to the Japanese moviegoer. Initially, in the 1890s, these films were seen as educational. When the early Japanese audience watched the waves at Deauville rolling toward them, they were enjoying their first glimpse of the outside world, a thrilling experience to a people for centuries isolated from the world at large.

As might be expected, given the audience, the appeal of these early films was at least partially didactic: the audience went to be educated as well as entertained. Since Japan, like the rest of Asia, lacks entirely the antipathy for being taught that is so common in the West, these early films found a ready and enthusiastic following, for whom learning what the French cavalry looked like and how Fatima danced were matters of the most lively interest. Ozu Yasujiro recollects how "the [Japanese] movies at that time did nothing more than follow the plot . . . but when an American film, *Civilization* [1916] by Thomas Ince, was shown . . . that was when I decided I wanted to be a film director." [13]

Though he was speaking of a slightly later period, Ozu was obviously impressed by a narrative intricacy different from that of the simple, static Japanese film. When American movies began appearing in greater numbers, many Japanese would have agreed with Ozu, who confessed, "film had a magical hold on me." Now films were not only educative, they also offered a new way of looking at the world.

After Universal Pictures opened a Tokyo branch, among the first films to enter Japan was a modest group of hour-long program pictures called Bluebird Photoplays. The series had no influence on filmmaking in the United States, but it certainly left its mark in Japan. One critic remarked that when a Bluebird film was compared to a Japanese film it was like suddenly moving from the early playwrights of the Edo period to the literature of the modern naturalists (Shimazaki Toson, Tayama Katai).

These "photoplays" had shots of nature, determined young heroines, and a dose of sentimentality. Though the settings were mainly rural, much of the story found the young people coping with new urban ways, just like young folks in Japan. In addition, there was a novel kind of narrative: scenes were not only shorter but shot from various angles, and the camera moved in closer. The audience was actually shown what it was expected to see.

In the face of this fresh approach, the benshi changed their habits. For the Bluebird films, they dropped their didactic ways and turned lyrical. A benshi "script" for the conclusion of a Bluebird film called *Southern Justice* (1917) ends with: "Stars strewn across the sky, blossoms falling like snow on the green earth. It is Spring—romance is in the South. Spring, ah, Spring!"

Western films were warmly welcomed. In his autobiography, Kurosawa Akira drew up a list of over one hundred foreign films he had seen between 1919 (when he was nine) and 1929. Many were American. At the age of eleven, the future director saw Charlie Chaplin's *The Kid* (1921); at twelve, D. W. Griffith's *Orphans of the Storm* (1922); and at thirteen, Chaplin's *A Woman of Paris* (1923). He had begun watching serials even earlier. Favorites included William S. Hart in *The Tiger Man* (1918). Remembering how impressed he was as a child, Kurosawa wrote: "What remains in my heart is that reliable manly spirit and the smell of male sweat," [14] qualities which he was later to reproduce in his own work.

Foreign film was popular not only with the audiences but also with those in the industry itself. The 1919 showing of D. W. Griffith's *Intolerance* (1916) was a sensation, and many of those who later became directors, scriptwriters, or cameramen remember attending and being impressed by this and other foreign-film showings—impressed, often to the point of imitation. Sato Tadao has listed some later American films which have been "repeatedly imitated": Ernst Lubitsch's *The Marriage Circle* (1924), F. W. Murnau's *Sunrise* (1927), Frank Borzage's *Seventh Heaven* (1927), and Frank Capra's *Lady for a Day* (1933).[15]

Among those many professionals attending showings of new foreign films was Makino Shozo, who had by then discovered there were better ways of making films than shouting directions at Onoe. Indeed, he was the first Japanese director to realize the importance of having a scenario.

The first two decades of Japanese film history had already passed before scenarios were used: Makino's original *The Loyal Forty-Seven Ronin* (1912, n.s.) was shot from a mere outline, a simple list of the forty-five scenes held in the hand of the director. Now this same director saw that this was not sufficient. His production philosophy, when he got around to phrasing it, was: first, the story; second, a clear picture; third, action. This differs from the director's previous stance, in which getting a picture focused and lit was as important as having something to film. The story had not been the first priority. Makino's next version of *The Loyal Forty-Seven Ronin* (1917, n.s.), by contrast, had a proper script, matching cuts, and reframing pans, along with other indications of advanced planning.

Earlier films had often been a procession of postcardlike scenes, or an assemblage of bits from kabuki or shimpa, their continuity assured not by the filmmaker's skill but by the audiences' familiarity with the basic narrative. What story there had been was rigidly formed to fit into the requirements of the benshi. Now, however, something more complicated was about to be discovered. This was a more revealing and hence engaging kind of storytelling, an ordering which would make emotion more palpable. Rather than a simple assemblage of separate scenes, there would be a series of linked scenes—each of which commented on the other, forwarded the story, and revealed cause and effect. In short, this was finally narration since (in Sontag's words, applicable everywhere) "only that which narrates can make us understand."[16]

SHINGEKI AND NEW NARRATIVE TACTICS

Just as the shimpa had made possible the beginnings of a more complicated kind of cinematic narrative, so it was that a newer form of Japanese drama, shingeki—along with contemporary Western films—enabled the Japanese cinema to further evolve.

Like shimpa, shingeki, the Japanese version of Western realist theater, was regarded as reformative. The narratives were those of Ibsen, Chekhov, Gorky, and O'Neill, and the rhetoric was that of the European (particularly Russian) proscenium theater, or what was understood of it. If shingeki later became as standardized as shimpa, initially—from 1909 on—it had a great reforming influence.

Looking at the popularity of the new shingeki on the stage, those in the film industry decided that a motion picture with a self-contained story along more realistic lines would win back the former audiences who had been supplanted by "snotty-nosed little kids." One of the first shingeki adaptations indeed proved popular. *Resurrection* (Kachusha, 1914, n.s.) was Hosoyama Kiyomatsu's filming of a portion of a shingeki dramatization of the Tolstoy story. It was "realistic"—at least to the extent that it used "authentic" Russian costumes—and, though it used oyama instead of actresses and stuck to other stagey conventions, it nonetheless impressed many moviegoers. Playwright Akimoto Matsuyo described the picture as magnificent, adding that he had truly felt whatever it was that so agitated the heroine Katsusha, an emotional response presumably not afforded by prior Japanese films.

Resurrection, 1914, Hosoyama Kiyomatsu, with Tachibana Sadajiro, Sekine Tappatsu.

Hosoyama's success encouraged others. Since audiences flocked to both the "foreign" shingeki as well as American and European films, producers were soon drawing up lists of popular foreign techniques: short scenes, closer shots, a more thorough narrative, and an editing process more complicated than that of pasting one tableau to the next.

A favorite foreign film of the period, the German *Gendarme Möbius*, became *The Lieutenant's Daughter* (Taii no musume, 1917, n.s.) in Inoue Masao's adaptation, which was quite "Western" in its use of flashbacks and close-ups. Large close-ups were also employed in the director's *Poisoned Herbs* (Dokuso, 1917, n.s.), but since these shots were of oyama rather than actual female actresses, the producers decided that in the future female impersonators would be best appreciated at a distance.

In all of these experiments, enlarging the audience was a major concern. The nascent Japanese industry was also looking to export its work. Japan had been the only country to thus far successfully resist the American cinematic invasion. (India's film industry had not yet begun, while in France and Italy, production was suffering.) Though foreign influence was everywhere and its products were well regarded, the Japanese industry itself was slowly expanding. With a firm home audience that would support a local product if it were sufficiently updated, the Japanese industry saw no reason why it, in turn, could not push into foreign markets. This was the idea behind the encouragement of some of the early companies to produce "Western-style" films.

Such tactics were so successful that by 1914 the movies had become a big business in Japan. As early as 1908, the means to insure steady profits had already been sought. Kawaura Kenichi of Yoshizawa Shokai (provider of the 1904 footage of the Russo-Japanese War and the first production company to have an in-house "story department") returned in 1908 from a fact-finding world tour and proceeded to construct in Tokyo's Meguro Ward a studio like Edison had in the Bronx and, behind it, a villa like Georges Méliès's in Paris, an indication of big-business intentions.

In the same year, Umeya Shokichi decided that exploitation was one of the ways to make money. An indication of this surfaced when he formed his M. Pathé Shokai, borrowing both name and reputation without Pathé's knowledge or permission. In the appellation, Shokichi also chose to flagrantly ignore the fact that rival Yokota Einosuke's company, the original importer of Cinématographe Lumière, was the actual importer of Pathé films into Japan. Shokichi's originality confined itself to the addition of the "M," which he later claimed was for "distinction."

The director-producer's costume spectacular *The Dawn of the Soga Brothers' Hunting Grounds* (Soga kyodai kariba no akebono, 1908, n.s.) was designed to showcase the attractions of both East and West. The Soga brothers themselves were a staple in kabuki repertoire, and the film starred an unprecedented all-girl kabuki troupe, apparently put together for the occasion. Added, too, were dialogue titles, attempted speech synchronization on discs, and a kind of wide-screen process. To top things off, the film was shown in a large theater usually used for drama, with attractive usherettes, a higher admission price, and all the hype that such a venture usually demands.

Though the film appears to have been financially successful, there were technical difficulties as well as the jealous ire of the benshi to contend with. Also, competition was increasing. There were now four motion picture manufacturers, all trying to turn a profit.

Having heard that similar circumstances of overcrowding had led to the creation of the Motion Picture Patents Company in the United States—seven companies that formed a cartel and monopolized the entire industry—Shokichi now approached his Japanese rivals with an attractive offer. The result was the creation, in 1910, of the Greater Japan Film Machinery Manufacturing Company, Limited, though all such machinery was actually being imported from abroad. Yokota became the director of the new cartel, Kobayashi Kizaburo became the head of the business department, and Yoshizawa backed out and sold his shares. All told, the new company owned three studios, including the former Yokota studio in Kyoto, and seventy permanent theaters.

In 1912, having made his profits, Umeya decided to leave as well, and the large cartel changed its unwieldy and inaccurate name to Nippon Katsudo Shashin Kabushiki Kaisha (Japan Cinematograph Company), which was in turn soon shortened to Nikkatsu. The three smaller studios were sold, and a large new studio was built in Mukojima, on the east side of Tokyo. By 1914, the company was producing fourteen films a month.

The Mukojima studio initially turned out the expected shimpa product—one of the resident oyama was Kinugasa Teinosuke, later director of both *A Page Out of Orderp* (Kurutta ichipeji, aka A Crazy Page/A Page of Madness, 1926) and *The Gate of Hell* (Jigoku mon, 1953). By 1915, the average Nikkatsu film was rapidly changing: it was about forty minutes long and comprised fifteen to thirty camera set-ups.

Tenkatsu (Tennenshoku Katsudo; Natural Color Motion Picture Company), a nonmember film company, run by Kobayashi Kizaburo, was making films of the same length with some fifty to seventy camera set-ups, some of which utilized Charles Urban's Kinemacolor, whose rights Kobayashi had acquired. His were, it was thought, the more "modern" product.

Nikkatsu and Tenkatsu thus largely controlled the creation and exhibition of Japanese motion pictures. In 1917, they overtook foreign companies as the main source of income for all Japanese screens. By 1921, Nikkatsu alone owned over half of the six hundred motion picture theaters in Japan.

Despite novelties from Tenkatsu and others, Nikkatsu continued to control most of the market. For one thing, the theater owners were satisfied with Nikkatsu's contracts (double bills: one kyuha film, one shimpa) and, for another, the larger Japanese audience was not all that certain that it really liked what it had glimpsed of further cinematic innovations in foreign films.

Though this same audience had originally embraced the novelty of movies with even more enthusiasm than that of some other nations, they were now in phase two of what is perhaps a peculiarly Japanese pattern of behavior: first an indiscriminate acceptance of a new idea, then a period of reaction against it, and finally its complete assimilation, whereby the idea is transformed and tailored to Japanese tastes.

THE *GENDAIGEKI*

In 1917, Tenkatsu hired Kaeriyama Norimasa, a man who was to have a decisive influence on the development of the Japanese film. In 1913, Kaeriyama began Japan's first film magazine. Three years later, he wrote *The Production and Photography of Moving Picture Drama* (Katsudo shashingeki no sosaku to satsueiho), a book in which he roundly criticized the product of that time. Since film was a silent medium, he argued, a narration was necessary in order to make the result comprehensible. Yet, if a script could be designed for a purely cinematic presentation (that is, without benshi) and titles were inserted only where necessary, films would be widely understood by everyone. In his opinion, films that needed off-screen narration were devoid of any value, nor was the capturing of stage dramas from an unmoving frontal position what he considered cinema.

In line with his more elevated estimation of the motion picture, Kaeriyama changed his terminology. *Katsudo shashin*, which means "moving photographs" (as in the company's original name), had already taken on the nuance of "the flickers." To counter this antiquated image, Kaeriyama introduced the modern term *eiga*, which is still used today. It was contemporary sounding and could mean (depending upon how it was read) "descriptive pictures," "reproduced pictures," "projected pictures," even "attractive pictures."

Believing, like Makino Shozo, in the necessity of a script, he wrote that the scenario was the foundation of the motion-picture drama, and that the value of this drama depended on the script. The director would use it to decide the actions of the actors and all other aspects of the film. This made the scenario very different from the text for a stage drama.

Kaeriyama's dissatisfaction with Japanese film was echoed by Tanizaki Jun'ichiro, already a well-known writer, who said, as though in answer, that not only did he enjoy nothing more than going to see Western films, but that he believed the difference between them and Onoe Matsunosuke's films was the difference between the West and Japan.

The Living Corpse, 1917, Tanaka Eizo, with Yamamoto Kaichi, Kinugasa Teinosuke.

Tanizaki and Kaeriyama also believed that not only would a good script produce a good modern film—a gendaigeki which could compete with rivals and thus win a larger audience—but that such a product, being self-explanatory, would eliminate the need for benshi.

The idea of winning larger audiences appealed to the producers. Thus, the twenty-four year-old Kaeriyama convinced Tenkatsu that he and his associates—actor Murata Minoru and shingeki dramatist Osanai Kaoru—could come up with a product that would win audiences both in Japan and abroad. Besides, Nikkatsu—the competition—had already profitably allowed Tanaka Eizo to make a "Western-style" picture, *The Living Corpse* (Ikeru shikabane, 1917, n.s.), which contained a larger number of shots, some dialogue titles, and realistic costumes. At the same time, reassuringly, there were oyama in the cast (Kinugasa played the heroine), the benshi talked through the dialogue titles, and shimpa was imposed over Tolstoy's storyline. It was a winning combination of elements: a tried-and-true shimpa formula plus lashings of novelty from abroad.

Kaeriyama's first film was *The Glory of Life* (Sei no kagayaki, aka The Glow of Life, n.s.), released in 1919. It was the story of a country girl (Hanayagi Harumi) who falls in love with an urban aristocrat (Murata Minoru). In a playful moment, the girl asks him the meaning of life. He lightly responds that it is to do whatever one likes. When he does just that and abandons her, she attempts to drown herself but is saved. The aristocrat reappears, repents, and the films ends with the sober statement "Life Is Effort," superimposed upon a shot of the dawn of a new day.

One critic called the movie shimpa with imitation Western titles. With its desertions and betrayals, it was indeed quite shimpa-like. Still, there was much that was new. Kaeriyama, like everyone else, had studied the Bluebird Photoplays with their simple, understandable structures. He had his heroine read Ivan Turgenev, while her little brother imitates Charlie Chaplin. In addition, the whole picture was tinted in the manner of the fashionable Italian product.

Kaeriyama and his associates added so many new touches that the company became suspicious during the shooting. In his defense, Kaeriyama claimed the picture was something like an experiment and that he therefore needed room to be creative. Further, he argued, as he was actually making the picture for export, he needed to cater to the foreign audience's appreciation for things like editing, short shots, and close-ups. As final justification, Kaeriyama explained that he intended to make a statement with the work, which he described as "an ambitious attempt to unravel the meaning of life in four reels."[17]

The company accepted the argument that the requirements of an overseas audience were distinct. Then, as now, products made for the foreign market were conceived differently from products made for local consumption. Kaeriyama's film was thus shown in a theater specializing in foreign pictures, where it experienced a modest success. More importantly, it proved inspirational to other filmmakers. Yamamoto Kajiro, later himself a film director (and mentor of Kurosawa Akira), saw it when he was a student. The picture's hyperbolic advertisement had caught his eye: "the first filmlike film made in Japan." Since he had, in fact, never seen a Japanese film, he decided that this would be a double first. Yamamoto was favorably impressed. He later wrote: "Japanese dialogue, titles of a modern design; close-ups and moving camera work; the actors' faces untouched by elaborate stage make-up; the plain, unaffected presence of a real woman; and the slightly awkward yet straightforward and sincere acting—this was a genuine film." [18]

The Glory of Life, despite its failure to draw a large audience, was considered successful enough that the industry as a whole, scenting future profit, grew more reform-minded. Even conservative Nikkatsu, which had by then absorbed Tenkatsu, allowed Tanaka Eizo to make *The Kyoya Collar Shop* (Kyoya eri mise, 1922, n.s.), which, though traditional in content and structure, contained some innovation. Reassuringly and decidedly traditional was the picture's shimpa story: the proprietor of an old business marries his favorite geisha, only to have his children leave him, while his new wife continues to see a younger lover; in the end, the old man's shop is destroyed by fire. The film was among the last to use oyama in all the female roles. (Later that year there was a mass walk-out of all the female impersonators, frustrated over the fact that the new directors were not using them.)

The Kyoya Collar Shop, 1922, Tanaka Eizo, with Azuma Takeo, Miyajima Kenichi, Fujino Hideo, Koizumi Kasuke.

Other traditional elements included a four-part structure that emphasized the seasons (with titles indicating Spring, Summer, Fall, and Winter—somewhat haiku-like seasonal references) and a melodramatic finale (during the fire, the distraught merchant grabs the geisha's hair, is next shown carrying a bloody swath of it, and then stabs her in the stomach with a butcher's knife). Shindo Kaneto, later a director himself, long remembered the "sinister smile fixed on his [the merchant's] face."[19]

Among the innovations was the attention paid to set design. Kamehara Yoshiaki, the first real art director in Japanese cinema, provided unusually detailed sets. The entire shop, for example, was constructed in the Mukojima studio, with walls that could be removed to accommodate the camera. The assistants (including young Mizoguchi Kenji) were all familiar with the latest Western products. Their knowledge combined with the director's sensibilities resulted in a cinematic experience apparently traditional and yet contemporary enough to please all audiences.

In the meantime, some companies had again gone foraging in the West in order to return with modern methods and people familiar with Hollywood know-how. Taikatsu hired "Thomas" Kurihara, then just twenty-five years old, and an actor, part of the entourage of the popular matinee idol, Hayakawa Sessue. With him returned "Henry" Kotani and "Jackie" Abe (later better known as Abe Yutaka), as well as young Tokunaga Bunroku, who had changed his given name to "Frank."

Taguchi Oson, another Japanese who had studied abroad, returned with many ideas for what he called modern methods. He introduced a system whereby all Japanese scripts were to be phonetically transcribed into the Western alphabet, thus rendering them foreign looking. The actors were never to be shown the script, nor allowed to develop a character—this was the job of the director. They were merely told to laugh or to cry without being given any hint of motivation. In addition, what instruction they received was to be indirect. Henry Kotani, one of this group, is famous for having attempted to create fear by announcing that a lion was preparing to pounce, though there was nothing about any such animal in the script.

Though anecdotes such as these may indicate cultural misapprehension, some of the methods matched Japanese examples. Except for the biggest names, actors are often treated in just such an unsympathetic manner. Some of the finest performances in Japanese cinema were given by the actors working for Ozu Yasujiro, a director who famously used the Taguchi-Kotani approach. When the actress Sugimura Haruko, weary of endless takes, asked what her motivation was for playing her role in *Tokyo Story* (1953), the director is supposed to have answered: money—you are getting paid for it.

Taikatsu went on to make a number of new films, of which nothing remains but a few stills. One of these films, *Amateur Club* (Amachua kurabu, 1920, n.s.), an American-style comedy written by the newly appointed Tanizaki Jun'ichiro and directed by returnee Thomas Kurihara, was about a bunch of young enthusiasts trying to stage a kabuki play by the seaside. Another was *The Lasciviousness of the Viper* (Jasei no in, aka The Lust of the White Serpent, 1921, n.s.), a Kurihara film, based on the Ueda Akinari story, in which Kaeriyama's concepts were first seen in a historical setting. Playing one of the extras was future director

Amateur Club, 1920, Thomas Kurihara, with Kamiyama Sango (left).

The Lasciviousness of the Viper, 1921, Thomas Kurihara, with Okada Tokihiko (left), Benizawa Yoko (right).

Uchida Tomu. The same story was later used as the basis for Mizoguchi's better known *Ugetsu* (Ugetsu monogatari, 1953).

Despite or because of these innovations, Taikatsu ran into such financial difficulties that only a few years later it merged with the Shochiku Cinema Company, a new concern which had been organized by Shirai Matsujiro and Otani Takejiro. Both of these entrepreneurs had started their careers as peanut vendors (nowadays it would be the popcorn franchise).

Shochiku, already an entertainment entity, had its own kabuki and shimpa troupes, but both men were eager to enter the film industry. Shirai had returned from a successful overseas fact-finding trip, and Otani, who had stayed in Japan, watched *Intolerance* playing to packed houses at ticket prices higher than those of the best Japanese drama.

The two men saw that the old-style Japanese movie was probably on its way out and that something new was perhaps coming in. Consequently, the new cinema arm of Shochiku built its own studio. Looking for a place a bit like Southern California, it settled on Kamata in the southern suburbs of Tokyo and adjacent to the Pacific, or at least to Tokyo Bay.

Since the company had to train all of its employees, a Shochiku Cinema Institute was inaugurated, and Osanai Kaoru, one the founders of shingeki, was put in charge. Osanai had worked with stage director Max Reinhardt and had introduced the Stanislavsky acting method into Japan. His Jiyu Gekijo (Free Theater), named after the Théâtre Libre and founded in 1909, had staged some critically successful productions but had failed financially, and its founder was now grateful for movie work.

Cast complete, Shochiku released a manifesto which read in part: "The main purpose of this company will be the production of artistic films resembling the latest and most flourishing styles of the Occidental cinema; it will distribute these both at home and abroad; it will introduce the true state of our national life to foreign countries. . . ." [20]

Critics complained of a perceived Americanization, but such complaints ceased when it became apparent that Japanese cinema, far from being assimilated, had itself assimilated a studio system not only very like that of Hollywood, but also promising to be just as successful.

An early Shochiku picture—one of the few prewar Japanese films that can still be seen— was *Souls on the Road* (Rojo no reikon, 1921). Its reconstructing from various prints, following World War II, was the work of Ushihara Kiyohiko, who not only helped write the script but also played the comic butler. He later became one of Japan's most popular directors. (Another future director of note, Shimazu Yasujiro, was listed as lighting director.) The direction of the picture itself is credited to Murata Minoru, though Osanai (who plays the uncompromising father in the picture and is also billed as executive producer) certainly had a hand in its making. It was he who sometimes spoke of this film as the first "realist" picture in Japan.

As is often the case with such ideas, the concept of film realism has evolved over time. In any event, there is also the peculiarity of what various cultures call "realistic." Today, of course, the film does not strike the viewer as "realist," but then few 1921 films, regardless of origin, would. What strikes the contemporary viewer is the eclecticism of influences on the film and the emotional power which, despite or because of these, the film retains.

Souls on the Road was originally viewed as a picture "in the foreign manner," and one sees why. It is composed of a number of stories, taken from foreign sources, which are then

Souls on the Road, 1921, Murata Minoru, with Minami Komei, Tsutami Takeo.

recombined in a style similar to that of profitable *Intolerance*. The main story, two ex-cons on the road, was culled from the shingeki adaptation of Maxim Gorky's *The Lower Depths*; the wastrel son who returns home with wife and child is from a story called "Children of the Streets" by a once-popular German author named Wilhelm Schmidtbaum; and the pastoral romance between the daughter of the house and a working-class youth owes much to the Bluebird Photoplays.

The title that opens and closes the picture is a pious quotation from the Gorky drama: "We, as human beings, must have pity for those about us. Christ had this quality and we also must cultivate it. There is a time for us to express this—this we must watch for." There are other titles as well: 127 of them in what was originally a ninety-one-minute film—an extremely high average, much more in line with the American than the Japanese pictures of the time.

The film's other influences from abroad include an enactment of that exotic holiday, Christmas; the conscious decision to have the daughter (played by the actress Sawamura Haruko instead of an oyama) dressed to look like, and apparently instructed to act like, Mary Pickford; plus a plethora of optical effects, including wipes, fades, dissolves, and irises. There are also panoramic shots (the camera swiveling), dolly shots (the camera on wheels), close-ups, flashbacks, and moments of parallel editing. In its use of these innovations, however, the film's discourse reveals its local accent.

Earlier films had given many indications that Japan's use of Western techniques was going to be different. Japan's first pan shot, said to have occurred in the previously mentioned *The Golden Demon* of 1912, was filmed during the beach scene when the brutal

Kanichi kicks the fragile Omiya. The director, it is claimed, noticed the peaceful mountain range across the bay and (having an articulated head on his tripod) decided to film it first, only then panning the camera to the principles. Ordinarily, pan shots in early Western films were more narrative in intent: two acting areas were connected, making for a tighter and more "realistic" story. In Japanese films, as one might expect, the focus was initially aesthetic. Thus, in *The Golden Demon*, the director called attention to the beautiful mountains simply because they were beautiful. There is also a kind of narrative connection: dramatic contrast—the mountains are peaceful, the kick on the beach is not. The assumption that character can be defined by similarities or contrasts to the physical surroundings is likewise an old Japanese narrative technique seen in many a scroll and screen. In all, the pan was not initially used to the same effect as it was in the West.

The close-up, which had gained a prominent role early on in Western cinema, was also applied differently in Japan. In the West, the close-up brought the audience nearer to the face of the protagonist so that moments of high emotion could be observed. The theory was that this created empathy, enabling the viewer to "feel" more. Yet the first Japanese close-up (there are several contenders for the honor) was not used in this manner at all. It—*Resurrection* (1914) being a typical example—merely permitted a closer view of a character who was doing a bit of business that would complicate appreciation of the anecdote unless closely observed.

Even now, close-ups are not nearly as common in Japanese films as in Western pictures, and some directors (notably, Mizoguchi) employed a scarcity of close-ups as a part of their mature styles. Indeed, the Japanese audience was very late in accepting the assumptions of the technique. There is some evidence that the close-ups in Henry Kotani's *Island Women* (Shima no onna, 1920, n.s.) actually provoked laughter in Japan.

In the same way, the initial Japanese flashback—usually ascribed to a 1909 M. Pathé film called *The Cuckoo: A New Version* (Shin hototogisu, n.s.)—was used not so much to explain as to decorate the storyline. In *The Cuckoo*, the viewer need not know that the heroine had been previously victimized by a man. The flashback is not employed to elucidate the present by reference to the past but rather, as in Japanese poetry, to suggest a parallel.

Similarly, in *Souls on the Road* the flashbacks explain nothing at all, nor are they intended to. In general, the editing in the film insists upon an aestheticization of time and space. Each of the several stories stops after a certain portion is viewed. When we return to it we find it just where it was when last we saw it. There is no elapsed time in this universe, just as there is none in traditional Japanese dramaturgy.

The editing is unusual as well. Those who complained they could not follow the single simple flashback in *The Cuckoo* would have been truly confused by *Souls on the Road*. There is, however, no record that anyone actually was, and this fact is sometimes used to suggest that Ushihara, when he put together the single 84-minute print we now have, was to a degree influenced by all the pictures he had seen between 1921 and 1951, including not only those by Griffith but also some by Sergei Eisenstein as well.

A more likely explanation for the "erratic" editing patterns in many Japanese films of this period is provided by David Bordwell in his discussion of "decorative tendencies." The critic speaks of "flashy transitions" and maintains that the Japanese filmmaker is more likely to take the transition as a pretext for stylistic embroidery."[21] Bordwell's example is the dissolve (one image appearing over another): in the West it suggests the passing of time, while in Japan it is simply decoration. Through the dissolve, the filmmaker—intentionally or not— insists on the theatricality that remains so much an aim in any Japanese entertainment.

The editing in *Souls on the Road* is certainly not put to any of the putative uses of "realism." A particularly "unrealistic" use is seen in the final sequence of the film. A title announces, "If he [the father] hadn't forgiven them; if he had forgiven them," and we see what would have perhaps happened had things been otherwise. Unlike a similar construction in the double ending of F. W. Murnau's *The Last Laugh* (1924), this decorative flourish proceeds from nothing inherent in the film itself. It is used for its own innocent sake.

In *Souls on the Road*, as in many other films of this and later periods, one is struck by the free use of what in the West would be considered advanced, even avant-garde techniques. This held true for the most commercial of Japanese films as well. One reason, undoubtedly, was that the presence of any kind of narrative (in the Western sense) was an imported idea. And while Japanese have always discriminated among imports as to their usefulness, there are often no other criteria for their use.

Even in today's media this phenomenon can be observed. An FM radio program of Western music is likely to contain Anton von Webern alongside Leroy Anderson. The reasoning is not that one is avant-garde and one is not, or that one is serious and one isn't, but simply that both are Western.

Thus, even routine Japanese program-pictures of the twenties and thirties contained shots or sequences which the West associated with only the most advanced art films. Usually, however, such techniques were used solely for effect and played a negligible part in the structure of the picture. The combination of traditional (East) and modern (West) formed the patterns that gave the prewar Japanese film both its traditional base and its modernist patina.

That such a mélange of influences as those creating *Souls on the Road* should have produced a film still enjoyable after eighty years indicates something about the Japanese aesthetic and its universality. What one sees and retains in *Souls on the Road* are parallels, not conflicts. This is true not only of the characters and their problems but also of their very position within the cinematic world they inhabit. The interest is in the emotional overtones of a situation, one which creates an overall mood or atmosphere.

Creating a sturdy narrative is all well and good, but just as important is the careful construction of a context, a nexus. Love within a family, for example, or comradeship among men—these themes are not to be shown through the uncommon moments of high emotion usual to a carefully plotted story. Rather, they are to be appreciated within a context of winter landscapes and overcast skies, where "the men and women move as though aimless, harshly outlined, sharply defined, against the somber mountains and the dark forest." [22]

During the first years of its history, the Japanese film was thus evolving in its own eclectic manner. But the manner was truly pragmatic—only what worked for the audience was used. The aim was popularity, film being the commercial business that it was (and still is).

There is a theory that the conventions of the Japanese theater—the appearance of men acting as women; the presence of that presentational agent, the benshi—all somehow served to preserve the "Japaneseness" of this cinema, protecting it from rapacious Hollywood. Such a theory, however, fails to take into account the fact that achieving Japaneseness was never an ambition, and that any Hollywood "takeover" was a highly selective and invitational affair. If anything, it was Japanese companies that took over the ways of the California studios. It is probably safe to say that Japan has never assimilated anything that it did not want to.

TAISHO DEMOCRACY AND SHOCHIKU

The 1923 Kanto Earthquake continued what the Meiji Reformation had begun, the erosion of the Tokugawa-period foundations upon which traditional Japan had rested. Though "feudal" elements remained, the assumptions of the Tokugawa government were hardly useful in a world where many of its creations had vanished.

Actually, the erosion had been going on for decades—the earthquake merely provided a sense of closure. Upon the death of the Meiji emperor in 1912, the major oligarchies which had effectively ruled the country reluctantly withdrew from positions of direct political leadership. Though they continued to oppose many progressive ideals, including the idea of parliamentary rule, their influence gradually lessened. The modern, the new, and the foreign thrived in the new Taisho era, posthumously named after the emperor Meiji's third and only surviving son, Yoshihito. The Taisho era was a period of lively artistic progress, severe economic stress, and a series of military crises that eventually culminated in the disaster of World War II.

The decade is now characterized as the period of "Taisho democracy," a term coined by post–World War II Japanese historians to imply a contrast with the much less democratic Meiji period and the plainly repressive Showa era which was to follow. A period of social unrest and major change—particularly in media, education, and cultural matters—Taisho also saw the relaxation of governmental surveillance and censorship, those Tokugawa techniques adopted by the Meiji rulers. New emphasis on the individual and on addressing social inequalities meant that the traditional position of women was questioned, unions were formed to protect workers, parliamentary procedure was introduced, and big business was encouraged.

The cinema was hard hit by the earthquake. Many of the studios and theaters in the capital were destroyed or badly damaged, and the structure of the film industry was seriously shaken. Many old concepts had to be abandoned and many new methods and ideas had to be adopted.

One major change the earthquake hastened was the division of production. Jidaigeki production was now firmly centered in Kyoto, where there were still studios standing, and *gendaigeki* were exclusively made in Tokyo. This made sense. Kyoto was thought conservative and old-fashioned; it was also believed to embody traditional Japanese virtues. Tokyo, on the other hand, was seen as modern and new, and attractively Western. Whether anyone ever intended a division this complete or not, it occurred, and, until the collapse of the genre fifty years later, most jidaigeki continued to be made in Kyoto. Even today, historical television serials are still often shot in the old capital.

Post-earthquake Tokyo took to the movies and, as did Tokyo, so did Japan. Before long, new features were being turned out, eventually some seven hundred a year. By 1928, five years after the disaster, Japan produced more films annually than any other country, and would continue to do so for another decade, until World War II curtailed production.

Movies made money. As public entertainment, films had no rivals. Almost everyone in Japan, it would seem, went. This audience watched Japanese films, foreign films, and perceived all cinema, old-fashioned or newfangled, as mass entertainment.

This new post-earthquake cinema, as Komatsu Hiroshi has said, "virtually destroyed the long-standing and traditional forms on the one hand by assimilating American cinema and on the other hand through the imitation of avant-garde forms such as German expressionism and French impressionism."[1]

Tradition was thus challenged in late-Taisho and early-Showa movies, and no one more firmly flung down the gauntlet than did Kido Shiro when he became head of the Kamata Shochiku Studios in 1924. "There are two ways to view humanity . . . cheerful and gloomy. But the latter will not do: we at Shochiku prefer to look at life in a warm and hopeful way. To inspire despair in our viewer would be unforgivable. The bottom line is that the basis of film must be salvation."[2]

This represented a new kind of bottom line. Usually, finances dictate the bottom line, and this eventually proved to be true at Shochiku as well, but initially, at least, the company was attempting to make a new kind of product. This it did—though not always an excessively cheerful one.

In fact, though Kido gathered around him some of the best directorial talent of the post-earthquake era, he could not, despite many efforts, impose such facile restrictions on directors as varied and as talented as Gosho Heinosuke, Shimazu Yasujiro, Shimizu Hiroshi, Ozu Yasujiro, and then Naruse Mikio, Yoshimura Kozaburo, Oba Hideo, and Kinoshita Keisuke. These directors all went on to make serious films, and by no means did most of their work fit the ideals of the "Kamata style," that sobriquet under which Kido envisioned his salvationist product.

Actually a light and cheerful style was not a Shochiku monopoly. Attractive modern ways

The Girl Who Touched His Legs, 1926, Abe Yutaka, with Okada Tokihiko, Umemura Yoko.

of presenting attractive modern experiences were by now fairly common. Even the more conservative Nikkatsu made a few modern *modan-mono* ("modern pieces"). Examples are found in the films of Abe Yutaka, a director who trained in Hollywood under Ernst Lubitsch and created such successful satirical comedies as *The Girl Who Touched His Legs* (Ashi ni sawatta onna, aka The Woman Who Touched the Legs, 1926).

Kido might not have been able to fully enforce the ideals he wanted but he was able to prevent what he did not want: "The shimpa style . . . failed to portray real people. Some immutable moral code of the times was taken as a point of departure, the character's actions were considered to move within the confines of the code as though utterly ruled by it. We wish to resist blind acceptance of some banal moral rule, to use a criticism of morals as a point of departure to grasp the reality of human beings."[3]

What was being criticized was nothing less than traditional Japan and those attitudes (a repressive kind of pessimism, a bleak spirit of self-sacrifice, etc.) which were still being fostered in some corners of the bright new Taisho world. However, the cheerful Kamata style could turn just as sober, as is indicated by the fate of several of its pictures. When Ozu Yasujiro's *I Was Born, But . . .* (Umarete wa mita keredo, 1932) "came out very dark," as Ozu himself phrased it, Kido delayed its release by a number of months and remained famously unmollified when this uncheerful film won the Kinema Jumpo First Prize that year. And when Oshima Nagisa made the grave *Night and Fog in Japan* (Nihon no yoru to kiri, 1960), Kido ordered it yanked out of the theaters three days after its release.

He and Life, 1929, Ushihara Kiyohiko, with Tanaka Kinuyo, Suzuki Demmei.

Some directors, however, if they were cheerful enough, experienced no such difficulties. Ushihara Kiyohiko, one of those on the staff of *Souls on the Road*, returned effortlessly optimistic in 1927, from a year of study with Charlie Chaplin. Such consequent films as *Love of Life* (Jinsei no ai, 1923, n.s.) and *He and Life* (Kare to jinsei, 1929, n.s.) earned him the nickname "*senchimentaru* [sentimental] Ushihara," a title considered more complimentary than not. An example would be *The Age of Emotion* (Kangeki jidai, 1928), nineteen minutes of which still exist, a maudlin but cheerful romance, starring the "love team" of Suzuki Demmei and Tanaka Kinuyo.

Though Kido proclaimed optimistic intentions, he also spoke of "the reality of human beings," and this not always cheerful quality found its way into the films he produced. Here his better directors were with him. They were young, they were equally sick of the dour shimpa product, and they did not approve of official repressive measures such as the "understood" moral codes the government was beginning to suggest. Having now glimpsed the outside world (even if only through American productions), these young directors were no longer satisfied with "traditional" Japan.

Since the Shochiku brand of gendaigeki was both pro-modern and pro-Western (that these two are not identical remains a major theoretical argument in Japan), anyone examining Japanese cinema must look beyond the storylines. One must inquire into the assumptions of the directors and their associates as well as examine their conjectures and surmises.

THE NEW *GENDAIGEKI*: SHIMAZU, GOSHO, SHIMIZU, OZU, AND NARUSE

A director who first—and some maintain best—exemplified the aims of the new Kamata style was Shimazu Yasujiro. Shimazu had worked on *Souls on the Road* and would become the mentor of Gosho Heinosuke, Toyoda Shiro, Yoshimura Kozaburo, and later, Kinoshita Keisuke, Nakamura Noboru, and Kawashima Yuzo—all directors who were at one time or another in their careers associated with Shochiku. He made nearly one hundred and fifty films and had a strong influence on those who worked under him.

Shimazu's first notable picture, *Father* (Otosan, 1923, n.s.), was a light comedy about a baseball champion and a simple country girl. It apparently resembled American comedies of the period except that it seems to have relied more on character and mood than upon plot and slapstick. It also exposed class differences in a way unusual for Japanese films.

Father, 1923, Shimazu Yasujiro, with Masakuni Hiroshi, Mizutani Yaeko.

In the old-school kyuha, the samurai class was assumed to be on top and everyone else on the bottom; in the shimpa-based film, the distinction was not so much socialized as gendered—it was the men who were on top (however insecurely) and the women (however undeservedly) who were on the bottom. In the films of Shimazu and those who worked with him, issues of social class long apparent in Japanese life now became discernible on the screen as well.

The simple country girl in *Father* struggles with her rural, low-class social standing as does the hero of *A Village Teacher* (Mura no sensei, 1925, n.s.). This interest in "people just like you and me," one of Kido's original dictates, had the effect of emphasizing "the lower classes" in a manner hitherto rare in Japanese films. People liked the novelty of seeing "themselves" on the screen and the result was a genre usually called *shomingeki* or *shoshimingeki*. Such films about the "little people," which would later turn pathetic or political or both, began in these light comedies of Shimazu and those who worked under him.

Our Neighbor, Miss Yae, 1934, Shimazu Yasujiro, with Aizome Yumeko, Takasugi Sanae.

The picture by which Shimazu is best remembered, *Our Neighbor, Miss Yae* (Tonari no Yae-chan, 1934), shows how the director and his associates portrayed everyday people and at the same time satisfied modern expectations.

The two neighboring families featured in the film, though lower middle-class, have enough income to be noticeably Westernized (the kids sing "Red River Valley," for instance, and they all go to the movies and see a Betty Boop cartoon), but these lives are presented in a context very different from that of, say, Frank Capra's *It Happened One Night*, the big foreign hit of the same year.

In *Our Neighbor, Miss Yae*, there is no social subtext as there is in the Capra film, where the heroine is an heiress, spoiled and snobbish, and the hero a workaday reporter, poor but honest. And certainly, there is no comparable melodramatic plotting. Instead we have an anecdote and, in the place of an assumed social text, we have aesthetic patterning, in the Japanese manner. The daughter (Miss Yae) of one family fancies the son of the other; Yae's sister, too, has her eye on the boy, but it is Yae who moves in with the neighboring family to finish her high-school studies when her own family moves away. Her last line is: "I'm not a neighbor anymore."

Though there is a degree of social commentary (one father says to the other: "If the boys knew how we talk about our jobs, they wouldn't have much hope for the future"), the interest is in the design of the narrative. The film opens, for example, with a slow dolly shot showing two houses with boys playing baseball on the lot in the middle. A missed ball breaks a window (one family has intruded upon the other) and the story begins. The opening scene thus encapsulates the entire plot. Throughout, highly selective realism reveals how a director can make things lifelike while retaining control through that very selection.

One of Shimazu's assistant directors was Gosho Heinosuke, who went on to enlarge the shomingeki tradition, to deepen an interest in character, and, at the same time, continue to suggest ways in which the Western techniques of cinema could accommodate the Japanese audience.

Though some have said that Shimazu's was the first and only influence on Gosho, there were others as well. First, the younger director was an even more avid student of Western cinema than most of his contemporaries. He said he had seen Lubitsch's *The Marriage Circle* (1924) at least twenty times and named it (along with Chaplin's *A Woman of Paris*, 1923) the greatest Western influence on his work.

This influence is quite apparent in the earliest of Gosho films extant, *The Neighbor's Wife and Mine* (Madamu to nyobo, 1931). Usually referred to as "Japan's first talkie," though there were other earlier part-talkies, it remains interesting because of its deft use of sound. The film recounts how a struggling low-class journalist—one of the "little people" to be found in such shomingeki as this—is kept from concentrating by the jazz-band racket coming from the house next door. Going to complain, he remains to be seduced by the noisy "madame" of the Japanese title. Along the way are various jazz selections, all of them quite loud, and a number of aural jokes—meowing cats, squeaking mice, crying children.

Like the later Lubitsch, Gosho found a way to incorporate sound as a structural element in this early film and to comment on the "all-talkie" as he simultaneously established its conventions. There is even a Lubitsch "touch" at the end, where a couple take their baby out for some air to the sound-track accompaniment of "My Blue Heaven" (a great favorite in

The Neighbor's Wife and Mine, 1931, Gosho Heinosuke, with Watanabe Atsushi, Tanaka Kinuyo

Japan). At the lines "and baby makes three," the happy couple find that they have wandered off and left the baby carriage behind.

Another influence from foreign films was an unusual number of close-ups and the relative brevity of separate shots. As early as 1925, Gosho became known (in contradistinction to, say, Mizoguchi Kenji, already working at the Nikkatsu Studios) as the director who used three shots where others would use one. A later film, *An Inn in Osaka* (Osaka no yado, 1954), is composed of over one thousand separate shots, and the following year's *Growing Up* (Takekurabe, 1955) contained, in its now-lost integral version, even more. Other contemporaneous American films averaged only three hundred to seven hundred shots. Only rare films, such as *Shane* (1953) or *Rear Window* (1954), had one thousand.

Gosho was one of the Kamata directors most interested in literature—as differentiated from popular reading matter. As we have seen, early Japanese film was much indebted to drama. Many of the popular shimpa dramas had been adapted from popular novels. Consequently, films came more and more to rely upon the same type of source material. Some critics have justifiably maintained that the Japanese cinema is singular in its closeness to popular literature.

But melodrama (which is what most popular literature was and is) lends itself to stock situations and stereotypes. In the 1930s, those not satisfied with such limitations turned to another kind of reading. In Japan, this resulted in the genre known as *jun-bungaku* (pure literature), books more closely resembling real life, considered also as "serious" literature. Almost all Japanese novels known through translation in the West belong to this genre. Gosho and those who wrote his scripts were among the many in the Japanese film industry who were dissatisfied with stock plots and characters. In striving for something more approaching truth, they also—perhaps without intending to—prepared for a cinema which was more representational than presentational.

Gosho, however, the fastest cutter on the lot, was also a haiku poet. There is no contradiction in this. Even now, many Japanese (and back then, most Japanese) included in their modern (Western-influenced) lives a traditional pastime such as penning these short lyrics. Here is a haiku that Gosho sent to his friend Ozu Yasujiro as a seasonal greeting on January 2, 1935:

> Hot springs here,
> and there goes
> my first New Year crow. [4]

His composition is conventionally expert, as it includes a seasonal reference, a definite place, and a movement—in this case the felicitous way that first things are awaited on the New Year: the first rice, the first hot bath, even the sight of the first crow. Note the Gosho-like touch of humor since, unlike the nightingale, this common bird is not pleasurably awaited.

Gosho's double-aesthetic heritage (Japanese and Western) naturally affected his cinematic style, which combined "the haiku and Lubitschian découpage—and how they function." [5] He sometimes used what we might call a haiku-like construction. One of the best known examples is in *Growing Up*. In one scene the young heroine, destined for a life of prostitution but never fully aware of it, innocently enters into a conversation with the adults, who avoid divulging her precise fate. As the scene closes, Gosho cuts to a bird in a cage. We have noticed this caged bird before; there was even a bit of business built around it. Now, however, Gosho makes a comment through cinematic metaphor. Brevity and lack of emphasis restore to the trite symbol much of its original freshness and power, just as in a haiku.

During his long career, Gosho made a total of ninety-nine films. These were of various genres: farces, light comedies, romantic melodramas, family dramas, social dramas. Most rewardingly, these genres are eclectically mixed. Just as he combined Western techniques with an often haiku-like construction, so he could infuse comedy with unexpected emotion.

This creative blending of genres was not thought well of in the West. Sergei Eisenstein once had an opportunity to see Gosho's early *Tricky Girl* (Karakuri musume, 1927, n.s.) and disliked it, saying that it began like a Monty Banks comedy but ended in the deepest despair. What he objected to was the mixing of genres. Indeed, over and over, the films of Ozu, Naruse Mikio, Toyoda Shiro—even Kurosawa Akira—have disconcerted the rigid West by successfully combining elements assumed to be antithetical.

The Japanese audience felt no such compulsion to adhere to strict categorizations. In fact, "Gosho-ism," which became an accepted critical term often used by Japanese film critics, was defined as a style incorporating something that makes you laugh and cry at the same time. Chaplin was often mentioned as the single foreign example.

There are other similarities between Gosho and Chaplin besides the deliberate mixing of humor and pathos. Both directors—Shimazu Yasujiro as well—make much of the kind of humanism which the shomingeki encouraged and which is perhaps best expressed at the end of *An Inn in Osaka* when the hero, finally transferred to Tokyo, says: "None of us can say he is happy or fortunate, yet things still seem promising . . . we are able to laugh at our own misfortunes, and as long as we can laugh we still have the strength and courage to build a new future." And so it goes in Gosho's films. There is a sense of release—the circumstances remain the same but the outlook has changed. In his work we can clearly see the familiar pattern of joining modern methods to traditional assumptions.

Shimizu Hiroshi, a contemporary of Gosho's at Shochiku, made more than one hundred and sixty films in his long career, though many of the earliest works are now lost. From the first, Shimizu seems to have fit the Kamata style well. Kido recalls that, even in his melodramas, "Shimizu composed his effects, not in terms of the facial expressions of the actors, but in terms of the story itself. His composition became the expressive media. This was his new method."[6]

Even melodrama itself was apparently reformed in these early Shimizu films. At Nikkatsu, directors such as Uchida Tomu and Mizoguchi Kenji were at the time still staging shimpa drama, relying on stage sets and stage-trained actors. At Shochiku, on the other hand, directors such as Shimazu Yasujiro and Shimizu were using natural locations and young actors who had never been on the stage.

Shimizu's early *Undying Pearl* (Fue no shiratama, 1929), based on a melodrama by popular writer Kikuchi Kan, used natural settings, such as harbors and stations, in conjunction with sets. *Mr. Thank You* (Arigato-san, 1936), a film about a bus driver, was shot in its entirety on real streets and roads.

Such methods affected the style of the films themselves. It has been suggested that one of the reasons for Mizoguchi's signature long-held shots was that the actors needed time to generate their performances. If this is so, perhaps the shots were often short in Shimizu films because the actors could not handle long takes. Kido noticed this when he said: "Instead of using facial expressions to draw the drama out, [Shimizu] dissolves the actor's movements into several fragments, each shot in a short take. This mounting tension of short shots becomes the propelling force of the story."[7]

Indeed, acting had little to do with a Shimizu film. Oba Hideo remembers that when he was assisting Shimizu, the director rarely, in any usual sense of the word, directed his actors. Rather, he treated them as props, saying that if they acted, they would overdo it. If an actor asked what kind of feeling was needed, the directive would be to just do the scene without any feeling.

Such treatment of actors was already a tradition—the "Taguchi method," as we have seen being much practiced by directors such as Ozu. Though down at the Nikkatsu studios Mizoguchi was being equally difficult with his more famous actors, his motivations were different. He wanted outstanding performances and would go to great lengths to achieve what one critic has called the mainstay of Mizoguchi's films: a grand display of the will of a woman who endures her fate in tears.

However indifferent Shimizu might have seemed to his actors, he was not so with the films themselves. If his treatment of his actors was untraditional (most Japanese directors, then as now, willingly accept whatever emotional interpretation the actor offers), he was much more traditional in his structuring. His films consist of a series of scenes in which the narrative is simply their common mutuality. Each episode comments upon and extends the story, but there is no heavily plotted narrative story to be told. Rather the content is (in the Japanese manner) shaped by the form.

In *Japanese Girls at the Harbor* (Minato no nihon musume, 1933), the story is both anecdotal and mundane: three high-school girl friends all like the same boy; when one of them marries him, the other two go bad and start working in a dance hall. He, no better than they, begins to dally with one of them; she, however, turns noble and leaves. The film opens as it ends: with scenes of an ocean liner leaving a port. This is followed by a patterned sequence of scenes showing two of the girls walking home from school, with the ship in the dis-tance. A boy on his bike

Japanese Girls at the Harbor, 1933, Shimizu Hiroshi, with Oikawa Michiko, Inoue Yukiko, Sawa Ranko.

joins them. The next sequence is structurally identical, including the same pattern of scenes, but this time the boy appears only in the girls' conversation. At the end of the film, it is to this same location that the boy and one of the bad girls (now married man and fallen woman) come. Again, the patterning is identical. This kind of structuring does indeed render matter subservient to the form.

In one sequence, the spurned girl finds the boy with another woman. Having just taken his gun, she now uses it. The way in which this is shown is formalized to an unusual degree.

There are four camera shots, each progressively closer (from frontal long-shot to frontal close-up). There is a shot of the girl, shot of the gun, shot of the boy and other woman (unhurt), and a reverse of the girl in long shot. Later in the movie, the girl finds the woman she aimed at in her bed (the boy having perhaps just left), and the structure is the same. Four short shots of the woman in bed, from long shot to close-up, recall in patterned and formalized form the former sequence.

Though the film has several exaggeratedly Western elements (art-deco dialogue titles, characters with names such as Dora and Henry, the boy listed in the credits as a "half-breed"), the style is not at all Western, though the cutting does perhaps owe something to whatever experimental cinema Shimizu might have seen.

The many parallels—the use of objects to contain emotion (the wife's knitting becomes a motif almost Wagnerian in its permutations), the ellipses (the boy's marriage is not shown, it is simply assimilated, after the fact), and the use of startling simile (when a person is no longer needed, he simply vanishes, visibly fading out)—all point to something other than Western models.

This is equally true of *Undying Pearl*, the earliest extant Shimizu film. The appearance of the film is so modernist that one wonders if the director had not viewed the Robert Mallet-Stevens decor for Marcel L'Herbier's *L'Argent* (1929). In the Shimizu film, the cocktail lounge where two sisters disport themselves is all frosted glass and exposed structure; the dance hall is all spotlights and geometrical furniture. At the same time, this kind of minimalism was not only on display in modern Japanese coffee shops, it was also present in traditional Japanese architecture. Though the hero writes "I Love You" (in English) in the sand with the tip of his companion's parasol, the elaborate playing with the curves of its opening and closing, employed to flesh out the composition and provide continuity, calls to mind the visual and structural strategies of the traditional Japanese artist.

One is also reminded in this and in many of Shimizu's films of a kind of structure seen in Japanese fiction—Kawabata Yasunari, for example, particularly in his "modernist" phase, around 1930—where the work is filled with ellipses, unexpected metaphors, and a conclusion which merely stops when the pattern is complete rather than effecting a conclusion. One might say that Shimizu's "new method," where composition becomes the dominant expressive medium, can be seen as an assumption about narrative design and as an echo of Japanese literary heritage.

If this is true, then particularly "Japanese" is an eleven-minute episode in *A Star Athlete* (Hanagata senshu, 1937), where thirty consecutive dolly movements are used: "forward or backward along a country road, with the camera always preceding or following the students." Of this sequence, Allen Stanbrook has also said that "by subtly varying the angles, now dollying forward, now dollying back, now marching at the double or letting the camera break free to follow, Shimizu here created a sequence close to pure cinema in which the matter of the film is almost subservient to the form."[8] It is also an example of the usage of space as ancient as that of the *e-maki*, the painted handscroll where space is unrolled (unreeled) before us. It is also during this sequence that two of the marching students compare their situation with that of Gary Cooper in *Morocco*—an example of Shimizu's fusing of Eastern and Western concerns.

The "modernist" aspect of the Kamata style found its fullest expression in the work of Ozu Yasujiro, who in his thirty-five-year directing career made fifty-four films, some thirty-three of which survive, though several of these are incomplete. From the first, Ozu was interested in Western films. He once proudly said that when he had his Shochiku interview he could recall having seen only three Japanese films.

Ozu was thus ideal for Kido's purposes. Though Ozu was originally made merely an assistant cameraman and forced to lug the heavy machine around the set, he was later apprenticed to Saito Torajiro, known as something of a specialist in Western-style comedy. Thus, he soon met his Shochiku contemporaries (Shimizu Hiroshi, Gosho Heinosuke, Naruse Mikio) as well as his future scriptwriter, Noda Kogo, and his future cinematographer, Shigehara Hideo. All were involved in forging the new Kamata style, one which was more progressive than that emerging from Nikkatsu and other studios.

Japanese filmmakers borrowed extensively from native popular literature, from the theater's reworkings of Western narrative principles, and from foreign (particularly American) films' conventions of style and structure. It was traditions both native and foreign that gave a basic linear unity to early Japanese films.

New genres also emerged. One of the most engaging of these flourished under the euphonious designation of *ero-guro-nansensu*. None of these three components were new. All were characteristic of late Edo literature, especially *ero*, the erotic. The *guro*, or grotesque, was something often seen in art or drama, and *nansensu*—comic exaggeration or farce—had been a Japanese staple for centuries.

It was this latter characteristic which appealed to the young Ozu. When he was given his chance, he asked to work not under Ushihara Kiyohiko or the other prestigious directors, but under Okubo Tadamoto, a specialist in nansensu productions who called himself a truly vulgar director, a term which—with necessary qualifications—could be applied equally to Ozu and later to Kawashima Yuzo, who also worked under Okubo.

Ozu later explained that his choice of Okubo may have been due to his own laziness and Okubo's notorious laxness—Okubo's assistants never had to work very hard. Certainly another reason, however, was the commonness of Okubo's material and its complete lack of pretensions. The difference between the two directors is that Okubo created from vulgar material; Ozu, from mundane material.

David Bordwell has discerned three principal tendencies at work in the creation of Japanese-style cinema narrative during the period when Ozu was emerging as a director. First, the "calligraphic" style, associated with *chambara* (Japanese sword-fighting), was flamboyant, full of fast action, rapid editing, and bravura camera movement, and had as its chief exponent Ito Daisuke. Second was the "pictorialist" style—derived from shimpa and influenced by Hollywood's Josef von Sternberg—where each shot was a complex composition with long shots predominating, in a style later exemplified by Mizoguchi. Finally, there was the "piecemeal" style (one bit of information per shot). In this style, the average shot length ranged from three to five seconds, and the narrative, comprised of neat, static shots, was associated with gendaigeki and derived mainly from Lubitsch. No doubt Ozu was drawn to this style because of Kido's partiality to it, but also in part because of the style's generic predisposition, including the fact that Okubo used it. Likewise, Ozu responded favorably to the style "because of the possibilities it holds for mixing playfulness and rigor." [9] Finally, this resulted in a clean, transparent structure, something which Ozu admired both because it reflected Japanese tradition and defined modernism.

One of the reasons for this was that modernism as an international style was much indebted to Japan. Its continued use, now that it had become internationally fashionable, seemed but natural. The Bauhaus, a school which codified many modernist assumptions, sponsored a style which was comfortable to the people who had created the Katsura Detached Palace, that single structure which influenced the construction of the Bauhaus itself.

Ozu himself never paid close attention to theory. Nonetheless, he did, from film to film, incorporate a number of assumptions about structure. Such assumptions may be viewed as operating within the larger cultural nexus. One of Japan's structural assumptions has always been that visible structure is permissible. Thus, there are no façades in traditional Japanese architecture. In traditional drama, such as noh, anecdote takes the place of scenery and a *kata*-like structure takes the place of a plot. Whereas early cinema worldwide revealed its structural elements, false fronts were soon erected to hide these. In Japan, structure long remained visible, and not only because modernism insisted upon it. Thus Japan's visible structural assumptions contributed to the West's definition of modernism, just as Japan's later lack of consistent aesthetic theory contributed to postmodernism. Ozu looked at modernism and identified with what he saw there.

Many other Japanese at the time also related well to modernism. For most, however, modernism merely meant being up-to-date. All periods are "modern," though not all of them so label themselves. For traditionally-minded Japanese, modernism was a way of working with what they already knew. In the West, modernism questioned temporality, reevaluated it, opposed it, and thus defined itself against tradition. This was very difficult for Japanese, including Ozu, to comprehend. In any event, modernism in Japan was not the polemical affair it was in the West. It was merely one of a plurality of styles, though one which somehow reaffirmed traditional notions, reinforced earlier methods of construction.

Modernism as a Western style also shared with traditional Japan a freedom from accepted realism, a tendency to the formally complex, and a fondness for the elliptical. What is left out of noh and of the typical Ozu narrative can, in this case, be equated with what is left out in the stories of Gertrude Stein and the novels of Henry Green.

There is also in Western modernistic narrative a certain openness of structure. These works show how they are made. Even in Ozu's earliest pictures, so influenced by the conventional Western film, there is a like transparency of structure which is Western only in that some modernist Western films had inadvertently appropriated Japanese ideas. Despite all the American paraphernalia, even the early Ozu films show the pellucid structural exposure which we associate with both the traditional ethos of Japan and modernist foreign cinema.

I Graduated, But ..., 1929, Ozu Yasujiro, with Takada Minoru, Tanaka Kinuyo.

There are many examples of such visible construction. In the eleven minutes that remain of *I Graduated, But* . . . (Daigaku wa deta keredo, 1929), a character is introduced in analytical manner: first a foot in a door, then the upper frame of the door, then a hat. In *A Straightforward Boy* (Tokkankozo, 1929), nine minutes of which are preserved, a series of gags is shown, each one scene long, with cause and effect plainly visible. *Fighting Friends, Foreign Style* (Wasei kenka tomodatchi, 1929), fourteen minutes of which still exist, announces itself as a Japanese version of an American film, *Fighting Friends*. The Japanese flavor was to be enjoyed more in the parallel sequences and the visible

I Was Born, But ..., 1932, Ozu Yasujiro, with Sugawara Hideo (left), Tokkankozo (right).

linkage of like scenes rather than in the exotic buddy-bonding inherent to the original story.

When in Ozu's *I Was Born, But . . .*, the camera dollies past bored boys at their school desks, then cuts to a similar dolly maneuver past the boys' bored fathers at their office desks, the film reveals its construction through parallels. Its structure becomes visible; its content becomes its form and vice versa. At the same time, the origin of this particular type of sequence was not to be found in traditional examples of Japanese structural exposure but in René Clair's *A Nous la Liberté* (1931), a film released a year before the Ozu film in which parallel dollies connect and contrast bored prisoners in jail and bored factory workers on the job.

Ozu formed his style from all sorts of sources. By appropriating and then using or discarding as necessary, Ozu offers something of a paradigm for the way that Japanese directors often work. There is a great openness about influences. Not only did Ozu learn from Lubitsch, as did everyone else, but often from Mack Sennett and from the Hal Roach *Our Gang* comedies. He took from whatever he saw around him.

Thus Naruse Mikio's film *Flunky, Work Hard* (Koshiben gambare, aka Ode to a Salesman, 1931) was also a source for *I Was Born, But . . . .* The Ozu film, though made in 1931, was released a year later. The two films shared the same milieu, the Kamata suburbs, and the same indications of social inequality. In Naruse, the employee's son beats up the boss's son, and the aggressor's father implores the boy to go and apologize. In Ozu, the sons say they can beat up the boss's son so why does their father have to work for his.

The way in which Ozu combined influences created his methods. For example, Kihachi, the lovable no-good hero of a number of pictures—*Passing Fancy* (Dekigokoro, 1933), *The Story of Floating Weeds* (Ukikusa monogatari, 1934), *An Inn in Tokyo* (Tokyo no yado, 1935), and *An Innocent Maid* (Hakoiri musume, 1935, n.s.)—is based on a real person. Ozu said that when he was growing up he knew just such a person. Ikeda Tadao, his scriptwriter, knew the same fellow, so they created the character together.

Kihachi was also Ozu. In his journal entry for August 8, 1933, the director addresses himself: "Kiha-chan! Remember your age. You're old enough to know it's getting harder to play around with [in English] 'sophisticated comedy!'"[10] At the same time the character is most certainly based on Wallace Beery in King Vidor's *The Champ* (1931). Later, Kihachi was to be metamorphosed in like fashion by another director, Yamada Yoji, in the popular Tora-san series.

The Story of Floating Weeds, 1934, Ozu Yasujiro, with Yakumo Rieko, Sakamoto Takeshi.

Kihachi may serve as an amalgam of the various influences that formed Ozu's way of doing things. In *Passing Fancy* one notices how Wallace Beery's eminently naturalistic performance has been choreographed and structuralized by Ozu and his actor, Sakamoto Takeshi. Their Kihachi could be seen as a modernist construction. His personal characteristics are surmised from his behavior: he always scratches himself in the same way, he stomps his way out of his trousers in the same manner, his typical gestures are typical. The result is humorous, since repetition is one of the techniques that comedians use, but at the same time, the spectator is allowed to see into the character, just as visible structure allows one to see into a film or, architecturally speaking, to peer into a building.

Ozu went on to further refine his means. He made some emerging techniques, such as color, his own. Others he abjured—the wide screen, he said, reminded him of a roll of toilet paper. In general, he minimalized his technique: "While I was making *I Was Born, But . . .*, I decided to never use a dissolve and to end every scene with a cut. I've never used a dissolve or fade after that. They aren't elements of film grammar or whatever you want to call it, but simply physical attributes of the camera."[11] He later said that he had fully intended "to film the last fade-out of the silent cinema."[12]

Such modernist sentiments created the traditional Ozu style, comprised of low-angle shots, a stationary camera, arrangement of characters in the scene, avoidance of movement, full-face shots of the speakers, stability of the size of the shot, linking by means of cutting alone, a prevalence of curtain-shots, performance-based tempi, and choreographed acting. In a completely contemporary setting, using the most modern and mundane of materials, Ozu was also using the tools of the earliest Japanese cinema.

Though the same can be said of some other directors, Ozu was much more rigorous. He is also emblematic of Japanese filmmakers of his generation, directors able to avail themselves freely of both national past and foreign future. Perhaps for this reason, critical opinion can even now find Ozu not only a conservative ("the most Japanese of all directors") but also a radical modernist.

Looking more closely at Ozu's stylistic characteristics, we might inquire into their origins and nature. Ozu once told his cameraman that it was very difficult to achieve good compositions in a Japanese room, especially in the corners, but that by keeping the camera position low, the task was made easier. As for the veto on dolly shots, there were no dollies that could accommodate such a low camera position.

The majority of Ozu's stylistic means had a single end in view: the creation of a composition which satisfied him. This most traditional of aims he gratified through the most modernist of methods. Experimenting and refining, watching Western films, absorbing influences everywhere, Ozu was also, in his own way, concerned with a kind of traditionalism. This is not only true of his subject matter (throughout his career he only had one serious theme: the dissolution of the traditional Japanese family) but also of his way of working with it.

Ozu, like many Japanese directors (Mizoguchi, Kurosawa, Ichikawa Kon), was a draughtsman. His pictures (usually still lifes, all in that rustic manner typical of the traditional amateur aesthete, the *bunjin*) are highly competent. Whether he so regarded them or not, his sketches, watercolors, and ink drawings are the opposite of modernist—they are deeply traditional.

Perhaps the most traditional aspect not only of Ozu's films but also of Japanese cinema as a whole is its long-lived and still-continuing concern for composition. Dictionaries define composition as the combining of distinct parts to create a unified whole, and the manner in which the parts are combined or related. This presentation of a unified view is one of the elements in Japanese culture—the garden, ikebana, the stage—and it is not surprising that an acute compositional consciousness should be part of the visual style of the country.

In Japanese film the compositional imperative is so assumed that it is the rare director who fails to achieve it. (If he so fails, as in the films of Imamura Shohei, it is intentional.) Usually, a concern for a balanced composition, symmetrical or asymmetrical, has become an identifying mark of Japanese films—right up to the films of, say, Kitano Takeshi, and beyond.

If Ozu's compositional interests can be seen as traditional, so too, can his thoughts on construction. Critic Nagai Tatsuo once mentioned that many of Ozu's titles refer to the seasons and asked Ozu if that meant he was interested in haiku. The director replied that he wrote maybe three haiku a year, although, in truth, his journals are filled with them—one a week or so. He would at times be self-critical, such as with the following haiku, after which he wrote, "What a bad poem."

> Spring rain
> Begins to fall
> Poor *kotatsu*.[13]

The seasonal reference is certainly there. The fact that the foot-warmer is no longer needed now that the warm spring rains are falling is, true, a bit mawkish. Nonetheless, Ozu himself thought haiku of relevance to film: "Since *renga* [linked classical verse] is similar to film editing, I found it a good learning experience."[14]

Among the less traditional of the new gendaigeki directors at Shochiku, and perhaps consequently the last to be promoted, was Naruse Mikio. Naruse eventually made eighty-nine films (forty-four of which have survived), though he was not allowed to begin directing until 1930.

One of the reasons for this relatively late start was Kido Shiro's antipathy. Kido later told Audie Bock that he had disliked Naruse's "absence of highs and lows," his "monotone pace," characteristics, he believed, endemic to the director's style. [15]

Light, cheerful, diverting comedies that looked on the bright side were not characteristic of Naruse. The director is famous for having later said that "from the earliest age I have thought that the world we live in betrays us—this thought remains with me." He used to speak of his characters as being caught in this betrayal: "If they move even a little, they quickly hit the wall." [16] He felt the home was simply too narrow a place, yet almost all Japanese gendaigeki films dealt with mainly the home, something which the director found a major fault. Perhaps he was influenced in this view by his reading of such novelists as Shimazaki Toson, Tokuda Shusei—whom he would adapt in *Untamed* (Arakure, 1957)—and Hayashi Fumiko, a number of whose works Naruse made into movies.

Naruse's mature style was probably more formed by the books he read rather than (as it was with most of the other young directors at Shochiku) the films he saw. His style, realistic yet carefully banal and devoted to the ordinary lives of ordinary people, was achieved through simplified scripts in which superfluous lines were cut. Location work, which he disliked, was avoided, as were elaborate sets (which he called nuisances); his camerawork was simple, even severe. The scripts themselves were usually adaptations from serious books, jun-bungaku.

This economy would later stand Naruse in good stead with his producers (when he went to work at Toho, his producers praised him for never exceeding the budget), but the earlier films were praised only by Ozu. After seeing Naruse's *Pure Love* (Junjo, 1930, n.s.), a film Naruse later thought a presage of his mature style, Ozu said that someone who could do that well on only his second film had real directorial strength.

Kido had also noticed, with disapproval, this affinity between Naruse and Ozu. As he later told Naruse, he didn't need two Ozus. In any event, the director's Shochiku days did not long continue. Among the last of the first group of directors to be taken on, Naruse was the first to leave. In 1931, fed up, he went to say goodbye to Gosho, the single director, besides Ozu, who had fought the company on his behalf. Gosho scolded him, saying he was still young and that he would never succeed by giving up.

Naruse did not give up. He went to another studio. In 1934 he joined the Photo-Chemical Laboratories (PCL) which later, under the leadership of Mori Iwao, became Toho. Originally concerned with developing and printing, PCL was by now producing films as well. Here Naruse fared much better. In his words: "At Shochiku I was *allowed* to direct; at PCL I was *asked* to direct. A significant difference." [17] Working considerations were much less structured, producers were much closer to directors, and just one year after Shochiku had seen the last of Naruse, Kido suffered the embarrassment of this dismissed director's winning the prestigious Kinema Jumpo first prize with his *Wife, Be Like a Rose* (Tsuma yo bara no yoni,

Wife, Be Like a Rose, 1935, Naruse Mikio, with Chiba Sachiko, Fujiwara Kamatari, Ito Tomoko.

1935). Naruse's film was also one of the first Japanese pictures to achieve a long-held Japanese ambition of playing commercially (under the title of *Kimiko)* in the United States.

The picture came from a shimpa drama named *Two Wives* (Futarizuma; a more accurately descriptive title and one retained for the original release of this film). Naruse himself adapted the drama to film. In it, a daughter desires marriage but, as her mother has been deserted by her father, she must find him to get his consent. The girl's father is supposed to be disreputably living with a geisha, but when she locates him, she discovers that the ex-geisha is not only supporting him but also sending money to her and her mother. The ex-geisha is opposite in all ways from what the daughter had feared and contrasts starkly with the cold, selfish, poetry-writing intellectual woman whom her father deserted. Two wives—the one supposedly good is in reality bad, the other supposedly bad is actually good. And the father, brought back to give his blessing, returns to the good one, leaving the bad one to rue her fate. It is to the latter that the studio-selected title directs its pointed imperative: Hey, wife. Be like a rose! The daughter, Kimiko, has learned a lesson about life and she, too, becomes a better sort of wife.

The play from which the film was made, the work of Nakano Minoru, was a *shinsei* shimpa, or "new drama." The melodrama is toned down and the heroines are much more modern than usual. Kimiko (the daughter) certainly is. She wears the latest Western fashions of 1935, walks independently in front of her fiancé rather than respectfully behind, and is outspoken with her estranged parents. She has what was then called an "American" personality. Yet she is able to sympathize with the more traditional elements of Japan: she respects her parents and, at the end, defers to her fiancé.

When the film opened in New York in 1937, one critic understood it as an example of modern trends in that the heroine is a typical modern Japanese girl with a story that unfolds against a background of the old traditional and the newly Westernized Japan. Unlike Mizoguchi Kenji's *Sisters of the Gion* (Gion no kyodai, 1936), the film does not contrast these two elements at work in society so much as it makes a distinction between the modern (Kimiko) and two aspects of the traditional (the two mothers).

Tradition in its ordinary sense is belittled. Mother's classical poetry is made fun of and uncle's gidayu bunraku singing frightens his pet birds and makes Kimiko giggle. Later during kabuki, the father falls asleep to the scandalized irritation of his art-loving wife. At the same time, however, tradition in its better sense is seen in the generosity of the ex-geisha, the sincerity of the traditional father, and Kimiko's gradual awakening to the moral worth around her.

Modernity in this film is consequently not a foil to be encountered but a kind of modish decoration. An office boy whistles "My Blue Heaven," which is—transition—the very tune the boyfriend is whistling. Kimiko is a modern American-like girl who, initially at any rate, competes with her man. Also, she has seen American films. This she indicates when they cannot get a taxi and she says that she knows how to stop one, that she's seen how it's done in the movies. She then steps into the street and repeats Clark Gable's thumb-in-the-air gesture from *It Happened One Night*, a film released in Japan the year before. (She does not repeat Claudette Colbert's more successful gambit in that film, showing a bit of leg. This would have been impossible, even in the modernized Tokyo of the time.)

Other lessons Naruse learned from American films are evident in the plethora of sound effects (often used as bridges, as in the talkies of Ernst Lubitsch) and the constant use of background music. Equally "American" is a super-active camera which is always seeking ways to express itself. One of the most singular examples is a very high shot from over a wisteria trellis, by way of an elaborate aerial dolly, which shows the interiors of several rooms, in succession, of Kimiko's house, but has no other justification. There are also numerous dollies in and out which are not used for the emotional emphasis Westerners would expect, but as ornamentation.

All of this is decidedly unlike the mature postwar Naruse. Still, there is a moral concern present in all of his better films of that time (the quality which made Shochiku-style comedies an impossible genre for him) and a talent for simplicity, lending the films their emotional persuasiveness.

Film critic Iwasaki Akira has said "every Japanese film shows signs of the director's struggle with his Japaneseness—his identity, his tradition. Apart from the few directors such as Kurosawa and Yoshimura [Kozaburo] who try to avoid or go beyond this, there are two who are the most Japanese in both the good and bad senses: Ozu and Naruse."[18] Though Iwasaki did not stipulate what the bad is, Naruse did when he said: "We've continued living a life of poverty on these small islands . . . our aesthetics reflect this poverty. Plain tastes like green tea over rice are regarded as authentically Japanese and since the people are like this, a film-maker has to resign himself to the limitations of this way of life. There's no other way to work." [19]

Nonetheless, though Naruse would not have expressed it this way, it is only within limits that creative freedom can be found. Further, the Japanese aesthetic has always found this rewarding—nothing but mud and, consequently, perfect pottery; too poor for furniture, and so *ma*, a geometry of space.

Kurosawa has left an account of how Naruse (whose assistant he once was in 1938) coped with temporal poverty: "His method consists of building one very brief shot on top of another, but when you look at them all spliced together in the final film, they give the im-pression of a single long take. The flow is so magnificent that the splices are invisible. This flow of short shots that looks calm and ordinary at first glance then reveals itself to be like a deep river with a quiet surface disguising a fast-raging current underneath." [20] Okamoto Kihachi (also a former assistant) tells about Naruse's *nakanuki* ("cutting out the middle") technique "where an entire [dialogue] scene is shot with only one person's lines, then the camera angle is reversed and the other actor's responses are filmed." [21] This frugal method of work (to be encountered in the West mainly in films with smaller budgets) is, as Okamoto points out, very efficient for the director and his crew but terrible for the actors. Even Ozu, often cavalier about his actors, usually filmed his dialogue scenes as written, changing the camera position for each actor as the lines were spoken.

Such a technique might be likened to the attitude of traditional Japanese craftsmen: the carpenter observes the grain of the wood, the mason, the texture of the stone, and both work-ing swiftly and economically with few tools and much skill.

One of the attributes of this attitude is also a tenet of the aesthetic tradition, something which Iwasaki recognized when he said that "Naruse Mikio, in both personal temperament and artistic vision, is totally and purely *mono no aware*, the essence of Japanese tradition, the most Japanese element of Japaneseness." [22]

This much misunderstood if venerable quality of mono no aware was perhaps first dis-cussed in the work of Ki no Tsurayuki, a tenth-century theorizer of poetry, and is later men-tioned fourteen times in *The Tale of Genji*, and to be evoked many times since then. There have also been many attempts at definition. All are agreed that mono no aware connotes a kind of contented resignation, an observance of the way things are and a willingness to go along with them. It advocates experiencing the basic nature of existence, savoring the comforts of being in harmony with the cycles of the universe, an acceptance of adversity, and an appreciation of the inevitable.

The novelist Kawabata Yasunari has been called the purest exponent of mono no aware in modern Japanese fiction, just as Naruse has in Japanese film. The director, in fact, worked often with the novelist. Kawabata is listed as "script supervisor" on *Repast* (Meshi, 1951), though it was based on a Hayashi Fumiko novel. Naruse adapted three of Kawabata's works: *Three Sisters with Maiden Hearts* (Otomegokoro sannin shimai, 1935), *Dancing Girl* (Mai-hime, 1951), and *Sounds of the Mountain* (Yama no oto, 1954). All are contemporary, all are to some degree modernist, and all are, in their own way, deeply conservative in essence—mono-no-aware–esque oeuvres.

Perhaps it is this combination of the contemporary with the conventional, modern frosting on the traditional cake, that appealed to the appetites of the 1935 audience and which won Naruse his coveted Kinema Jumpo prize. The additions from the West are apparent, and retentions from the East are there to be discovered.

THE NEW *JIDAIGEKI*: ITAMI, INAGAKI, ITO, AND YAMANAKA SADAO

During the same period that the gendaigeki was being developed from, among other things, the shimpa, the new jidaigeki was being fashioned from the old kabuki-based kyuha. And just as the Shochiku contemporary-life films were much indebted to the shingeki, so the impetus for the new period-film was yet another recent theatrical form—the *shinkokugeki*, or "new national drama." When the shinkokugeki appeared in 1917 and featured a more literal violence in substitute for the dancelike duels of the kyuha, this, in turn, created in the jidaigeki a kind of realism new to Japanese period-drama.

One of the first of these new jidaigeki, based on a popular shinkokugeki play, *The Purple Hood: Woodblock Artist* (Murasaki zukin: Ukiyoe-shi, 1923, n.s.), was important in determining the future of the genre. The film was directed by Makino Shozo, who had by now broken with Onoe Matsunosuke and founded Makino Motion Pictures, and was written by Suzukita Rokuhei, a young shingeki director and playwright whose subsequent scripts would come to define the period-films of the 1920s. Suzukita's major contribution to the genre was the application of what he called "realist" principles to period-films: "I gave Makino a script filled with real violence, real combat scenes, thoroughly realistic. He said it would have to be done with real weapons . . . what happiness I felt. Several of the actors were actually hurt by the flailing swords."[23] Equally inspired by American action films and by such swashbuckling local novelists as Nakazato Kaizan and Hasegawa Shin, the Suzukita scripts, and the subsequent films of both the Makinos—Shozo and his son, Masahiro—were soon popular.

It was the apparent, if selective, realism that probably appealed to audiences. And realistic these films appeared, at least by comparison with earlier period-films. Onoe certainly had not depicted such desperate emotions as are to be found in these new heroes—all determined jaws and defiant gazes. Perhaps this was because he had come from kabuki while these new heroes were drawn from the illustrations in popular novels. None of the sources of the new period-film had anything to do with any other kind of literature. It is estimated that some seventy percent of these films drew their ideas from serializations in newspapers and magazines.

The placement of the actors (as distinct from their acting) was, however, still stage-oriented. Makino's *The Loyal Forty-Seven Ronin: A True Account* (Chukon giretsu: jitsu-roku chushingura, 1928), a portion of which still exists, indicates the reforms he intended. The acting style was "realistic," that is, the gesticulation was toned down and even the oyama were persuaded to curb their more extreme mannerisms. Stagelike two-dimensionality was often abandoned, and some use was made of depth, particularly during the various processions, arrivals, and evacuations which stud the story. At the same time, Makino ("the D. W. Griffith of Japan") retained the dancelike patterns of the shinkokugeki (referred to as "shimpa with swords") with heavily and unrealistically choreographed blocking of action.

This combination of "realistic emotion" and formalized dueling distinguished the genre through its entire career: one may compare the period-films of Ito Daisuke, Yamanaka Sadao, and Kurosawa Akira and find them, in this respect, similar. One remembers an earlier ideal, *wakon yosai* ("Japanese spirit, Western culture"), a concept which continued to emerge during the Showa era, including this new kind of hero who was very much his own individual but was restrained by the national group-choreography imposed upon him.

This new hero was played by such popular period-film actors as Tsukigata Ryunosuke, Kataoka Chiezo, Okochi Denjiro, Hayashi Chojiro (later to become even more famous as Hasegawa Kazuo), and the most popular of them all, Bando Tsumasaburo. These were young, streetwise toughs who had about them nothing of the noble warrior as portrayed by Onoe. The sword fights of the new genre, as choreographed by Bansho Kammori, were heroic, but the heroism was that of the intrepid fighter of popular fiction: fast and calculated.

Also, as the director Masumura Yasuzo has stated, from the 1920s on, some directors self-consciously set out to study popular literary techniques, after which they incorporated their own findings. He mentions *kodan*—with its abbreviated statements, curt dialogue, and swift shifts of scene—a storytelling format which exerted a major influence on the structure of these new jidaigeki. The restrained kodan narrator was not, however, emulated. Instead, the acting consisted of lots of facial gestures plus influences from the fair and high-minded William S. Hart, and the daring and insouciant Douglas Fairbanks. This new sword-fighting samurai was thus an individual, even a nonconformist, a kind of kimonoed cowboy—as epitomized by Mifune Toshiro in one of his later appearances, in Kurosawa Akira's *Yojimbo* (1961).

When the young Bando began playing this kind of hero in 1924, the popular image of the young masterless samurai (*ronin*) as an intrepid but suffering rebel quickly became established. This type has been identified as the *tateyaku*, a term taken from kabuki to

characterize idealized samurai, warriors who are not only victorious in fights but also saga-
cious men, with strong wills and a determination to persevere. This new hero, however, was
also often dispossessed. Though brave and occasionally victorious, he had begun to doubt the
idealized code of conduct which had created him.

In the 1930s, another scriptwriter, Mimura Shintaro, extended the self-conscious tateyaku
character. His heros were malcontents in an age of repression. Though Mimura favored the
Edo period as his setting, his screenplays also reflected the results of the so-called Showa
"Restoration" (1933–1940), that period during which governmental repression began to
push back Taisho "democracy."

While the traditional-minded (including those in the government) criticized and eventually censored or banned works featuring the antisocial heros of Mimura and others, figures
of this sort obviously spoke to the larger audience. The popularity of the new jidaigeki was
such that the hero's role grew to encompass not only samurai and ronin, but also itinerant
gamblers (presumed the early ancestor of the present day *yakuza*, Japanese organized gangsters) and the various hoodlums who loitered outside society. The post–World War II gang
genre, one which continues even now on television and in the films of Kitano Takeshi,
among others, has its roots in the jidaigeki of the 1920s and 30s.

Early ronin, those in Makino Shozo's *The Loyal Forty-Seven Ronin* (1912), for example,
were bound by awful oaths to their former lords. But the ronin in the films of the later 1920s
were loyal to no one. Not only did they lack feudal faith, they seemed to lack any faith at all.
Indeed, "nihilistic" was a term applied to *Orochi* (1925), written by Suzukita, directed by
Futagawa Buntaro, and starring Bando. In this film the ronin—one man against a whole
gang of samurai—lives a misunderstood life. To his constant query as to whether there is
justice in this world, the answer is always no. In fact, titles appear at the beginning and end
of the film asserting that "there is no justice, society judges only by appearances, it is a world
of lies." This may have reflected the view that in turbulent modern Japan, an equally mind-
less authoritarian government was again emerging.

The multipart *The Street of Masterless Samurai* (Ronin-gai, 1928–29, n.s.), directed by
Makino Masahiro, Shozo's son, and scripted by Yamagami Itaro, was about two men who
questioned the feudal code. It went so far that, even though it won the Kinema Jumpo award
for 1928, it was much cut before release. Nonetheless, it proved of lasting influence on the
work of Yamanaka, Kurosawa, Kobayashi, and later filmmakers. The film was remade (sight
unseen, though the original scenario exists) by Kuroki Kazuo in 1990, and the original
director is listed in the credits as advisor.

Another film so outspoken that it ran into trouble was Ito Daisuke's *Man-Slashing,
Horse-Piercing Sword* (Zanjin zamba ken, 1929, n.s.). A young samurai is hunting for his
father's murderer—a common enough opening to the ordinary historical film. But, unlike

The Street of Masterless Samurai, 1928–29, Makino Masahiro, with Minami Komei.

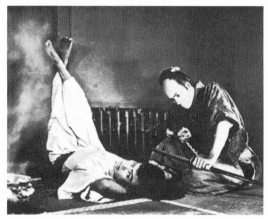

Man-Slashing, Horse-Piercing Sword, 1929, Ito Daisuke, with Tsukigata Ryunosuke, Amano Jun'ichi.

the typical hero who always battles his way to the top, this samurai meets only reversals. Eventually, in order to live, he must steal from the farmers, who are just as poor as he is. When he learns that the reason for their poverty is the oppression of the local government, he joins them in their revolt, an act further motivated by his discovery that his father's killer is the local overlord.

Itami Mansaku further enlarged the role of the period-protagonist. A boyhood friend of Ito Daisuke, he later, along with Inagaki Hiroshi, became assistant to the older director. Itami's first films were for Kataoka Chiezo, who not only owned his own production company, but was an actor as well, capable of projecting the type of hero the new jidaigeki needed. He was heroic without being a superman; he portrayed an ordinary person who happened to do the right thing at the right time. For him, Itami created a series of ironic and sometimes satirical historical films.

Peerless Patriot (Kokushi muso, aka The Unrivaled Hero, aka A Dreamy Patriot, 1932) was a typical film with this new hero. In the existing twenty-one minutes, a decidedly irreverent young swordsman impersonates his high-born samurai fencing teacher. The situation was developed in a manner which ridiculed many of the feudal traditions, particularly those which had survived in modern Japan. That the imposter could not be distinguished from the lordlike teacher and bested him in a parody finale openly questioned basic feudal precedents.

Itami furthered his radical humanization of the samurai in *Kakita Akanishi* (Akanishi Kakita, 1936). In this adaptation of a Shiga Naoya story, the good-hearted hero joins other like-minded samurai to defeat the bad retainers who surround an essentially stupid lord. Itami Juzo, the director's son (who preserved this film and even made an English-titled print), maintained that the film was a political allegory. The bad retainers represented the militaristic government, and the intellectually challenged lord, the emperor. Good-hearted samurai Akanishi cleared the way for those later, postwar heroes who so resemble him. When Kurosawa's "yojimbo" first appears on the screen, swinging his shoulders in that characteristic manner, he is walking straight out of this tradition.

Kakita Akanishi, 1936, Itami Mansaku, with Sugiyama Shosaku, Kataoka Chiezo.

Along with new dramaturgy and characterization came new cinematic techniques. They exemplified the iconoclastic intentions of the new jidaigeki. Itami wrote (bravely, in wartime 1940) that "the first thing we learned from American movies was a fast-paced lifestyle . . . the next, a lively manner and a readiness to take decisive action . . . we learned to take an affirmative, purposeful, sometimes even combative attitude toward life." [24]

In 1928, Itami, in collaboration with Inagaki Hiroshi, made *Tenka Taiheiki* (1928) one of the first *matatabi* ("drifters") movies. The dialogue titles used colloquial speech, and the heroes were contemporary with their audience. It was Inagaki who regarded the jidaigeki as

"*chommage o tsuketa gendaigeki* [gendaigeki with a samurai topknot])." [25] He consequently availed himself of all the new cinematic techniques coming from the West as had his
mentor, Ito Daisuke (often called "Ido Daisuki" ["I Love Pan-Shots"] on the set because of
his predilection for the latest imported cinematic styles).

Nonetheless, much of the dramaturgy of the traditional drama was somehow retained in
jidaigeki. This was particularly evident in the sword-fight scenes, choreographed with details
shown in sudden close-up: visual compositions which held the eye. Like the traditional prints
upon which they were sometimes based, these compositions dramatized scene and encapsu-
lated story. And, as in the traditional drama, one scene followed the other, impelled not so
much by storyline as by aesthetic spectacle. As Donald Kirihara has noted: in, say, *The Red
Bat* (Beni komori, 1931) by Tanaka Tsuruhiko, all that flashy tracking, panning, spinning,
canting, and fast cutting "is there for just that reason: flash." [26]

This combination—guided narrative and unleashed spectacle—is seen at its most spectacular in the films of Ito Daisuke. In *Jirokichi, the Rat Kid* (Oatsurae Jirokichi goshi, 1931),
Okochi Denjiro, a Robin Hood–like robber ("a life rich in nothingness" says one of the
titles), has a series of adventures which lead to a completely decorative finale. Festival
lanterns in one compositionally perfect tableau after another stud the sequence, culminating
in, not dramatic revelation, but aesthetic enjoyment.

A fine example of Ito's prowess with regard to the pictorial is seen in *Diary of Chuji's
Travels* (Chuji tabi nikki, 1927), a film thought entirely lost until part of it (one hour and
thirty-six minutes) was discovered in 1991. Its gambler-hero (Okochi Denjiro), predecessor
of modern yakuza-movie heroes, is caught in the perceived opposition between *giri* and
ninjo, the traditional conflict between duty to society and duty to oneself, rendered in terms
easily recognized by the audience.

Diary of Chuji's Travels, 1927, Ito Daisuke, with Okochi Denjiro.

Much of the film looks like a modern—specifically American—movie. Yet it often segues into a decidedly Japanese sensibility. The dialogue scenes are in medium close-up, there are two shots with a forty-five degree shift of viewpoint, and eyelines follow international standards. Yet, in the sequence at the saké brewery, we follow a downward pan from darkness to patches of sunlight, beams, ropes, and finally to the men manning the works. A written title appears in this initial darkness and continues all the way through the pan—in effect turning the screen into a calligraphy surface, a two-dimensional page.

The following sequence, in the saké brewery yard, is Japanese aesthetic bravura. The area is littered with enormous empty barrels, some on their sides, and so the scene is filled with circles. Shot after shot emphasizes ceaselessly the resulting circular compositions. A girl wanders in circles; children play circular games: the design has become the story. And during the remainder of the film, scenes return to the compositions of this sequence, reminding us of it. The heroine goes to sit in the circle of a big, empty vat; later, children form a dancing circle around the distraught samurai hero.

Such apparent design-as-narrative reminds one of traditional printmakers, particularly Hokusai, and brings to mind the printmaker's insistence that visual schemes can take the place of plot. We can readily understand the role that traditional composition plays in Japanese cinema. At the same time, decorating this pictorial balance are details of a quotidian realism. One of Ito's characters is shown realistically brushing his teeth, realistically spitting. After all, the director had originally been a scripter for Osanai Kaoru, one of the first "realistic" shingeki authors.

The joining of concern for aesthetic design and realistic ("undesigned") acting in Ito's film is evident in the stylization of the sword fights which ornament the storyline. These are striking combinations of movements, both those of the actors and those of the camera. Long, racing dollies, flashpans all over the place, close-ups of the various deaths, and lots of shinkokugeki extras scampering about. The last of these fights concludes with a slow march through the forest, the survivors bearing the fatally wounded Chuji through the (blue-tinted) night, the water glistening, the leaves softly moving. This procession is far more beautiful than it need be and it is beautiful for its own sake: an aesthetic display which enhances the charm and pathetic vulnerability of our dying hero.

Set in contrast to this is the finale sequence, in which the hero in his hidden fortress holds a long dialogue through which the mysteries of the plot are unraveled (a conclusion typical of this genre), while elsewhere the authorities search for him. After the open-air excitement of the fight, and the nocturnal beauty of the journey, the close-ups are now tight. A gun is produced to ward off the attackers who have forced open the door; we turn and look at the dying hero, his breath visible in the cold. All the exhilarating choreography has brought him to this, a close-up which chronicles his last moment. He smiles acceptingly—

this is what the feudal world has done to him and he (a modern man in Edo times) smiles. The End.

Perhaps the finest of the directors of the new jidaigeki was Yamanaka Sadao, though, dying at twenty-nine, he made the fewest films. He completed twenty-three pictures in seven years, only three of which have been preserved. Yamanaka's ambition was to further modernize the period picture. Such modernization was the stated manifesto of a group of eight young Japanese filmmakers who called themselves the Narutaki-gumi [Narutaki gang], after the area in Kyoto where they lived and where they jointly wrote under the collective pseudonym of Kimpachi Kajiwara.

Yamanaka, who worked with the Nikkatsu studios, was not interested in a nihilistic hero nor in a savior of the common man. Rather, he wanted "to shoot a jidaigeki like a gendaigeki,"[27] the kind of picture that Inagaki called contemporary drama with a topknot.

The differences between Yamanaka and the more representative Itami can be seen in a comparison of their separate versions of the same story. In 1935, they both made a film about Kunisada Chuji. Itami's was *Chuji Makes a Name for Himself* (Chuji uridasu, 1935, n.s.) and Yamanaka's was simply *Chuji Kunisada* (Kunisada Chuji, 1935, n.s.). The former picture was oriented toward social criticism and dealt only with the young Chuji after he had abandoned farming because of oppressive taxes and a despotic government. That a farmer had turned into a gambler was the concern of the picture. Yamanaka, on the other hand, was interested only in character. His Chuji, under an obligation to a man who hid him from the authorities, must kill to pay back his moral debt. This moral dilemma was used to create an atmosphere. Yamanaka was not specifically concerned with social criticism but with emotional problems and the way in which they reflect character.

Humanity and Paper Balloons, 1937, Yamanaka Sadao, with Suketakaya Sukezo, Kawarazaki Chojuro, Nakamura Gan'emon.

Yamanaka's finest film was his last, *Humanity and Paper Balloons* (Ninjo kamifusen, 1937). In the opening sequence, a former samurai has committed suicide. His neighbors talk about the death and one says: "But he hung himself, like a merchant. Where was the man's spirit of *bushido*? Why didn't he disembowel himself like a real samurai?" To which another replies: "Because he no longer had a sword—he sold it the other day for rice." This is the familiar death-theme opening, so typical of the conventional period-drama, with its reference to bushido, "way of the samurai." But there is an enormous difference. In the conventional product, the hero would have come to a glorious end. Not so, however, in this critical, contemplative, and contemporary film. The sword, which supposedly symbolizes a samurai's life, has been sold so that the samurai, ironically enough, might live.

Sato Tadao has said that this film is "a consistent endeavor to shatter old stereotypes."[28] The characters speak modern Japanese instead of the thees and thous of sword-fight melodramas; the samurai behavior is no longer ritually stylized; there are no conventional generalizations, and those that do appear are used for ironic purposes. The result is a freshness, a freedom, in which serious problems are treated lightly.

In the first of Yamanaka's surviving films, *The Million Ryo Pot* (Tange sazen yowa: hyakuman ryo no tsubo, 1935), the hero is a chambara (sword-fighting) character as famous as Kunisada Chuji. Tange Sazen is meant to be a superhero despite his missing eye and lopped-off arm. Here, as played by Okochi Denjiro, however, he is a shambling swordsman, slow to think things through and incorrigibly lazy.

Yamanaka's hero does not realize just where the priceless pot is, though this has been obvious to the spectator since the beginning of the film, and his attempts to find it are consequently amusing. Like Kurosawa's *Sanjuro* (Tsubaki Sanjuro, 1962), a picture in many ways indebted to this Yamanaka film, he is limited as well as skillful, and therefore completely human. Such was not Nikkatsu's original intention. *The Million Ryo Pot* was to have been a film by Ito Daisuke, who would have created a much more serious and heroic picture had he not left the company to go to Dai Ichi Eiga. Yamanaka was a very different director from Ito.

The second of Yamanaka's surviving films is the Nikkatsu feature, *Soshun Kochiyama* (Kochiyama Soshun, 1936). Written by Mitsumura Shintaro, it was originally conceived as a period-melodrama, after a kabuki play by Kawatake Mokuami. In the rewriting and directing, Yamanaka changed the underworld thugs

Million Ryo Money Pot, 1935, Yamanaka Sadao, with Okochi Denjiro (right).

into warm-hearted, good-natured people. He did the same thing to Mitsumura's kabuki-based script for *Humanity and Paper Balloons*. The original version has intrepid villains fighting each other, but in the finished film there is little of such action: the people are quite ordinary, incapable of such heroic resolve. Among the reasons Yamanaka so humanized his scripts at the very time when there was a governmental call for heroics is that he valued ninjo rather than giri, personal rather than institutionalized feelings.

In Yamanaka's last scenario, *Sono Zenya* (1939), which he did not live to direct, ninjo becomes something like bravery. A family running a Kyoto inn during the Meiji "revolution" is caught in the midst of the Shinsengumi uproar. The Shinsengumi, a pro-government army usually portrayed as a benevolent band of Boy Scouts, is here depicted as something approaching the Red Guard. When one considers the date of the work, one realizes what Yamanaka is doing. The wonder is that he could have gotten away with it—implicitly comparing a violent and destructive Shinsengumi with a violent and destructive contemporary Japanese army. Maybe he did not get away with it after all. He was drafted shortly after.

Yamanaka had much in common with Ozu, one of his closest friends. Both were what we would now call liberals, both inculcated unpopular truths, and both used what we now recognize as minimalist techniques. They stripped sets of all but essentials; they limited gestures; they expressed ideas indirectly through jokes, asides, and short, suggestive conversations. Like Ozu, the younger director began early on gathering about him actors with whom he could work. Though Yamanaka used such stars as Arashi Kanjuro and Okochi Denjiro, he also cultivated his own group. In his later films, he used members of the Zensen-za, the Progressive Theater, in addition to such new actors as the now famous Hara Setsuko, who appears in *Soshun Kochiyama*.

The acting in both *Soshun Kochiyama* and in *Humanity and Paper Balloons* is noteworthy. There is an ensemble quality which is rare on the Japanese screen and was only duplicated in such perfect form in Kurosawa's later films, such as *The Lower Depths* (Donzoko, 1957). In Yamanaka's films, there is also a reliance upon performance which is rare in Japanese films of the 1930s. For example, in *Soshun Kochiyama*, the entire sequence in which two of the minor characters attend an auction consists of a medium shot of the two alone. We never see the rest of the crowd, and we have no idea what they are bidding for, but the ensemble acting, one actor playing off the other, allows us to follow the action with interest and amusement.

Equally minimal are the interiors, often filmed from slightly below (just as Ozu's films were being shot), showing limited period-detail as well as ceilings. Story structure is also kept to what is necessary, and only that. Series of scenes (younger brother in a fight, elder sister in trouble, complications over a fake sword) are kept separate, with many purposeful ellipses in the story. In one such scene, the younger brother takes his knife and creeps into the house of one of the bad men. The camera stays outside the closed *shoji* door. We hear voices and see shadows against the paper panes. There is a glimpse of the knife silhouetted. The light is suddenly extinguished. We hear an exclamation. That is end of the sequence. We are never directly told the outcome (though we learn it from the context of the rest of the film), nor what it might mean.

Plot in its causal sense is missing, but all the story strands are forcibly pulled together in the action-filled finale during which repressed anger erupts and the full panoply of chambara swordplay is displayed. The whole town, all those sets we have been obliquely viewing, is now used as the men battle up and down the narrow alleys. Though the pace is very fast, the editing never loses us. From a narrowly framed alley we are turned forty-five degrees to a bridge crossing a ditch, a perspective that affords a view of three different fights (on three different bridges) going on in town. In the end, the main ruffian dies a samurai's death as he allows the unhappy younger brother to escape.

Action leads to resolution, though that is not its only purpose in the film. This violence (like so much Japanese blood-letting) is an aesthetic spectacle. The patterns of disorder are composed into compositions which filter the excitement and render beauty from chaos. By simplifying action, reducing it to its individual elements, excitement may not be enhanced, but appreciation is.

We recognize this forced simplicity in the concluding night sequences. This is expressionism (of which more will be said later), the nominally German style for indicating a single frame of mind through everything the artist shows. By the 1930s, the style had been completely Japanified. Expressionism no longer contained any deranged *Doctor Caligari* connotations and was used, instead, as one more element of a complete presentation—the mind of the viewer made visible.

There are many other Western influences in the work of Yamanaka, particularly in story development. Hasumi Shigehiko has discovered elements from an American comedy *Lady and Gent* (1932) by Stephen Roberts in *The Million Ryo Pot*, and sections of Jacques Feyder's *Pension Mimosa* (1934) in the final shots of *Humanity and Paper Balloons*. Yet there is also much that indicates earlier Japanese models. For example, Yamanaka uses a narration technique, taken from both kodan and the balladlike *naniwabushi*, where the authoritative voice, at first anonymous, is later revealed as a character in a subsequent segment. The first scene of *The Million Ryo Pot* is a castle, whole and in some detail, which we examine as a voice begins the tale. When the director finally cuts inside the castle, the voice is revealed as that of a retainer telling the daimyo the secret of the pot.

At the same time some of the dialogue might have come out of Lubitsch. Bride turns to groom and says: "That old pot is going to look pretty strange to our wedding guests," a remark which sets the desirable container on its adventures, just as firmly as the loss of the lottery-ticket-carrying coat sends that garment on its journeys in René Clair's *Le Million*, a 1931 film that was enormously popular in Japan. Like the Clair film, this Yamanaka piece is also conceived as an operetta. There are festival dances and songs—"Just a pinwheel turning in the wind" sings the entertainer heroine, presumably of herself.

There is also much ridicule of the foolish paraphernalia of the old-fashioned kyuha plot, often concerned with military secrets. One such secret is hidden in a pot, hence its apparent value. The samurai searching for the important container says that all the fuss "makes it sound like a vendetta," a line repeated twice in the film, lest differences from ordinary period films not be noted by the viewer.

And since the ordinary period picture is about decision and intrepid action, we have Yamanaka's hero absolutely refusing to do something and in the next scene doing it. This adamant refusal—followed by an inexplicable reversal indicating something less than a resolutely courageous decision—is used on three different occasions in the film, attesting to its satirical usefulness. The film is, in effect, a loving parody of the chambara. That Kurosawa learned much from this film is evident in *The Hidden Fortress* (Kakuishi toride no san akunin, 1958), where the adventures of the gold bars parallel those of the missing pot.

Technically, Yamanaka melded native and foreign influences into a most persuasive style. In speaking about his technique he said that once he found where to put his camera, his problem was solved. "As regards this position," he added, "I do the reverse of what Pudovkin taught." [29] (What Pudovkin taught was that montage was "the highest form of editing . . . the foundation of film art.") [30] Yamanaka, like most Japanese directors, edited relatively little, at least in comparison with the Russians. Editing usually simply involves découpage, nothing like what Pudovkin meant by montage. Yamanaka's concept of space was different, hence the prime importance of the camera position, his vantage point.

In *Humanity and Paper Balloons*, Yamanaka presents a contrast of two areas of space—the only ones shown. One is the world inside the gates of a tenement quarter, the other is the world outside them. The difference between these worlds, the demonstration of their separateness, is emphasized in both the opening and closing sequences. In the first, the gates are closed and the residents confined while the authorities investigate a suicide. In the last, the gates are again closed, this time to check the deaths of the hero and his wife. This reticulation of space—a network of scenes describing a specific area—is fitting in other than cinematic terms. The film is based on *Kamiyui Shinzo*, a Mokuami kabuki drama that, like most in its genre, is geometrical in its use of space.

The concern for the concepts of inside and outside is also a very Japanese one. *Uchi* (inside) and *soto* (outside) are considered much more defining, and limiting, than they are in the West. There is also a Japanese assumption that the former is safe and the latter is not. The assumption therefore fittingly delineates a story where the outside is a repressive governmental area distinguished by its lack of ninjo, the quality of human feeling so touchingly depicted inside the tenement, the closed quarter.

In the second sequence of the film—a lane outside the tenement—we find that the camera is placed level with the human eye and that all shots are economically edited along a single axis. In this, Yamanaka was certainly influenced by Ozu. Though there are asides during the length of this sequence (one of them is to introduce Unno, the masterless-samurai hero of the film), in the main the camera placement of each scene during the progress along the alley varies not at all—the angle coinciding with the axis.

This way of working is not often seen in American or European films of the period because these scenes could be said to "not match," also because their sequence violates one of the assumptions of international cinema style, namely, that a film progresses by opposing shots. Shots which are compositionally similar are thought to confuse, though this Yamanaka sequence is proof that this is not necessarily so. The theory about opposing shots seems to be based upon a Western assumption that narrative can proceed only through conflict and confrontation, compositionally as well as otherwise. The idea of a narrative proceeding through harmony and similarity, not often encountered in Western cinema, is seen again and again in Japanese movies.

What this sequence does provide, and this would seem to be Yamanaka's concern, is a literal depiction of the alley. Once we have been led so carefully along it, we become thoroughly familiar with it, and we believe in it. One is reminded of the old Japanese studio rule that in the initial seven cuts the whole house, or main location, must be established. Such ritualized rules were commonly disregarded when the exigencies of production took over, but in some pictures, such as those of Yamanaka, something like the old rules prevailed, and overall concepts as to how space was to be depicted remained.

In showing us the tenement alley, the director moves along its length, shot after shot. A precise rendering of the street is given, a believable accounting of its space, a logical introduction of the characters, and the setting up of half of the spatial metaphor. This is the closed and crowded alley itself which, though invaded by officials from time to time, is really the safer part of the world.

When the outside world (the town outside the tenement district) is delineated, we are given no such spatial grounding. We do not know the location of the pawnbroker's house in relation to our alley, nor the location of the bridge where one of the main characters will be killed. The temple gate, the fairground, all those "outside" locations are separate, distinct, cut off from each other. They lack the continuity of the tenement, which we were shown whole and complete. Consequently, it is the tenement which feels safe, like home, and it is the outside which is dangerous, or alien. "Spatially, Yamanaka—having set up this opposition of spaces, having fully reticulated one and left the other carefully and threateningly unreticulated—has created for himself a bipolar structure."[31]

Among these new jidaigeki, these "gendaigeki with topknots," it was commonly thought that Inagaki Hiroshi's works were sentimental but lyrical, that Itami Manasaku's were intellectual but ironic, and that Yamanaka's, with their minimal elegance and beautifully flowing rhythms, were in a class all by themselves—the highest. It is also conceded that with his early death (sent to the front as a common private, he died of dysentery) Japanese cinema lost one of its finest directors.

NIKKATSU AND THE *SHIMPA*: MIZOGUCHI KENJI

Though the kyuha had been effectively transformed into something more complicated, shimpa-based films continued (and indeed still continue today in the daytime serials of contemporary television) in their established pattern. Nevertheless, some changes were taking place.

Nikkatsu, home of the shimpa-film, allowed Suzuki Kensaku to make a more involved kind of drama in *Human Suffering* (Ningen ku, aka Human Anguish, 1923, n.s.), a multi-stranded story, with nocturnal photography, dialogue titles, faster editing, and a kind of realism: since the film was about the hungry poor, Yamamoto Kaichi, the leading actor, was not permitted to eat before and during his performance.

Murata Minoru, who had directed *Souls on the Road*, left Shochiku and went to Nikkatsu, where, in 1924, he made *Seisaku's Wife* (Seisaku no tsuma, n.s.), the first of several "new style" films. In it a young wife, unable to tolerate her husband's return to the Russo-Japanese front, deliberately blinds him. After prison she returns to her sightless mate, begs his forgiveness, and drowns herself. When Seisaku learns this, he forgives her, then jumps in after her.

This was all very shimpa-like, but there were differences. For one thing, the unhappy wife was played not by a man but by one of the first Japanese actresses, Urabe Kumeko, an amateur shortly to become a star. Here, too, was a heroine who was active and forceful, if in a subversive manner. Also, since the story is that of a soldier about to go to the front to fulfill his sacred duty to the divine emperor, the picture would become, in the eyes of some critics, one of the first antiwar films.

To create this movie, Murata used what he called "symbolic photographicism," a realism in which all the characters were lifelike, yet their actions had symbolic, almost allegorical meanings. In her final sequence, for example, Seisaku's wife is shown, or rather displayed, bound in fetters—both a real character and an abstract symbol. That this particular image had been borrowed from Karl Heinz Martin's film *Von Morgens bis Mitternacht* (1920), and would again be borrowed for the final scene of Kinugasa Teinosuke's *Crossroads*

(Jujiro, 1928), did not affect its usefulness. Whether or not much of the allegorical message was appreciable on the screen, the intentions were progressive. Masumura Yasuzo has said that cinematic psychological realism in Japanese cinema had its origins in this Murata film, as well as in Tanaka Eizo's *The Kyoya Collar Shop*, adding that "it strikes me as more than coincidence that the main characters in these realistic films were women."[32]

One of the results of *Seisaku's Wife* was more real females playing women on the screen. The oyama had by now all but disappeared, and actresses were becoming popular. Among these were Umemura Yoko, Sawamura Haruko (who had appeared in *Souls on the Road*) and—most popular of all—Kurishima Sumiko, whose photographs were best-sellers. Perhaps consequently, more women were going to the movies, and this meant a new audience to be satisfied. Shortly, a separate genre evolved, one which was loosely called the "women's picture," perhaps to differentiate it from men's pictures, the jidaigeki.

Among the new directors enlisted for the new product was Mizoguchi Kenji, who has said that "when I was working for Nikkatsu, the company already had Murata Minoru making films featuring heroes, so for balance they made me do films featuring heroines. Also, I'm very quarrelsome, and so when I work there is always the possibility of a fight, but I can't very well slug an actress."[33]

Mizoguchi made over eighty-five films from his first in 1922 to the year of his death in 1957. So many are about women that this is often seen as the director's preferred subject matter. Indeed, the Japanese call Mizoguchi a "feminist," though in Japanese the term means not one who believes in women's rights but merely one who likes and concerns himself with women—by extension, a womanizer might be called a feminist in Japan.

There are other reasons, of course, for Mizoguchi's making the kinds of film he did. One was studio practice. Shochiku's Kamata studio was emphasizing a shot-by-shot construction, and it was from this that Ozu, for example, derived his style. Nikkatsu, on the other hand, was using a sequence-by-sequence approach. Yoda Yoshikata, later Mizoguchi's major scenarist, remembered that Murata had him analyzing sequences in foreign films and then considering them "as basic elements in the construction of a scenario . . . Every director was expected to more or less construct a scenario in this fashion, including Mizoguchi."[34]

Though this director's choice was for the sequence, not the shot, he made a number of early films (all of them now vanished) which seem to call for a method perhaps more dynamic than that for which he is now famous. *Tokyo March* (Tokyo koshinkyoku, 1929, n.s.), for example, was a *keiko-eiga*, what would later be called a tendency (leftist) film. Written by popular novelist Kikuchi Kan, it proved a box-office success, prompting the company to order more of the same. The result was *Metropolitan Symphony* (Tokai kokyokyoku, 1929), a "people's film" of which five minutes or so still exists. The script was not by a popular author but by several "proletarian" writers, something the company did not know, or else it might not have allowed its production. Nikkatsu wanted a fashionably liberal picture, not leftist propaganda.

Metropolitan Symphony was shot on location in Tokyo's Fukagawa area, where, as Mizoguchi later remembered, it was so dangerous that cast and crew alike smeared their faces with dirt and dressed like laborers. He himself went around hiding the camera under his coat. The danger, it should be added, was not from the proletariat but from the police, already looking for dissidents. Later Mizoguchi made *And Yet They Go On* (Shikamo karera wa yuku, 1931, n.s.), shot in Tamanoi, another tough place. Not only did the police again investigate, but the crew was threatened by gangsters as well. This was not the first and certainly not the last instance of gang activity in Japanese film production.

Popular though these films were, Mizoguchi did not believe them to be successful. He was interested in the "new realism" but, at the same time, this style was never one he made his own. Masumura has said that Mizoguchi simply "couldn't adapt to the realism of Osanai Kaoru and Murata Minoru," and gives an interesting reason: "because it was too contaminated with Westernization."[35]

So, though Mizoguchi made many different sorts of film, it is his sequenced "woman's pictures" which distinguish him. The first of these of which a print still exists is *The Water Magician* (Taki no shiraito, aka Taki of the Waterfall/White Threads of the Waterfall/Cascading White Threads, 1933). Scripted mainly by Tateoka Kennosuke and based on an Izumi Kyoka shimpa play, the film is fraught with coincidence and melodrama illustrating the burden of the woman's plight—her silent suffering at the hands of men. Taki, an entertainer, falls in love with a young man whose education she pays for. Unfortunately, the money has been borrowed from a loan shark who eventually becomes so importunate that she has no recourse but to kill him. The presiding judge at the trial turns out to be the young man whom Taki has educated. He upholds the law of the land and condemns her to death. Taki eludes this fate by biting off her tongue; he, in remorse, commits suicide.

The Water Magician, 1933, Mizoguchi Kenji, with Irie Takako, Okada Tokihiko.

Redeeming such shimpa-like excesses is the physical beauty of the film's images. The asymmetrically balanced sequences—each of which increases our understanding of the characters—carry along with them the subtext of their own aestheticism. The bridge where the lovers meet is used to comment upon their relationship: they meet there, she wanders alone there, he kills himself there. During the seduction scene, the camera writhes almost as much as does Taki. Later, in prison, jail bars cast perfectly placed shadows across Taki's face.

Mizoguchi, initially a painter himself, was, like most Japanese directors, much concerned with the beauty of his scenes and the aesthetics of his sequencing. Because of his pictorial interests, he was also drawn to a view which focused on the big picture, rather than its subject. He disliked subtitles because they interrupted the sequential flow, and consequently rather preferred the benshi.

The director himself has said, "When I was finally able to learn how to show life as I see it, it was also from about that time that I developed a technique of shooting an entire sequence in a single cut, the camera always remaining at a certain distance from the action."[36] This technique is indeed paramount to the Mizoguchi style. Yoda Yoshikata, who scripted a number of Mizoguchi's later films, said: "The deepest beauty must be recorded with a long, continued shot . . . I take this single-shot technique into account in all my scripts."[37]

The effect of this technique has often been commented upon, but its strength has been perhaps best described by Shinoda Masahiro, when he compares the long shots of Mizoguchi with the short shots of Ito Daisuke and stresses "the tremendous increase in emotional impact which [Mizoguchi] gained by exchanging the manipulations of short multiple shots for the objectivity of the long single shot."[38] One such sequence in *The Water Magician* opens with the autumn sky, the camera moving to a tree, panning down with the leaves as they fall, watching them. The camera then moves to theater posters being taken down, on past this scene to inside a theater, where it records the actors packing, glides past, and, finally, stops—all this in one shot—only to catch one of the characters saying what we have already seen, that this is the end, that the season is over.

Sato has remarked upon the close relationship between Mizoguchi's style and traditional performing arts. "His characteristic 'one scene equals one cut' technique, for example, is like the musical accompaniment in traditional dance, in bunraku puppet theater, in noh . . ."[39] Sato also draws attention to the moments called *kimaru* in classical dance, that is, poses or gestures which emphasize the beauty of shape. Mizoguchi's cutting, Sato continues, emphasizes this. Motion is sequential, "changing from one exquisite shape to another. Short shots cannot capture this subtle flow, which can be caught only by complex camera movements such as panning or craning."[40] The director's long shots are thus seldom static, though they are often of a singular duration. The aesthetic structure of any single scene is the result of a balance within an asymmetrical composition.

Sato cites in a later film, *The Life of Oharu* (Saikaku ichidai onna, aka The Life of a Woman by Saikaku, 1952), a concluding kimaru-like moment, a long shot showing the place of execution, and the hero (Mifune Toshiro), bound. After his last words ("May there come a time when love is not a crime."), the camera pans swiftly up to the executioner's sword. "The movement is comparable to a stroke in calligraphy, when pressure is applied at the point where the moving brush stops . . . In the next instant the sword flashes down without a sound, but the camera remains immobile, staring out into space. Unwaveringly, the kimaru movement has been resolved."[41]

This style can lead to a static, superficial kind of beauty—Sato here mentions such late films as *Lady Musashino* (Musashino Fujin, 1951) and *Miss Oyu* (Oyu-sama, 1951)—and Mizoguchi was indeed often criticized for just this. Also, refined though the director's technique was, critics felt that it was not progressive, that it looked back to the formalized aesthetics of the classical theater and that his slow tempo indicated old-fashioned sentiments, things that a modern Japanese should regard with ambivalence.

One critic has derided the director's well-known antiquarian tastes and found his contemplation of old porcelains a strange devotion to meaningless trivia. Another critic has called Mizoguchi's use of long shots a rather rudimentary technique, one which is most common in countries producing second- and third-rate films. Yet another critic has gone further, calling Mizoguchi so old-fashioned, his views on aesthetics so premodern, that in many ways his pictures are just like "primitive" Japanese films.

Mizoguchi himself was aware of these aspects and began to turn away from such obviously pictorial structures as that of *The Water Magician*. In later films, such as *Osaka Elegy* (Naniwa ereji, 1936) and *Sisters of the Gion* (1936), he began to reflect the very cultural dichotomy that made this kind of criticism possible: the pull of the traditional and the equally strong impetus toward things new.

Osaka Elegy, 1936, Mizoguchi Kenji, with Shindo Eitaro, Yamada Isuzu, Hara Kensaku.

Sisters of the Gion, 1936, Mizoguchi Kenji, with Umemura Yoko, Yamada Isuzu.

Many Japanese of Mizoguchi's generation were necessarily of two minds—mutually incompatible to the West—about their world. Just as there was a presumed gulf between Japanese kimono and Western dress, between a native fish diet and the meat victuals received from abroad, between jidaigeki on one hand and gendaigeki on the other, so there was a perceived antagonism between these two different images that Japan had of itself.

This divide had been reflected in much Japanese art and in film, too, it became a major concern. Emotionally, the present was a simple and understandable continuation of the past; at the same time, the contrast between old and new was so problematical that it led to complications. This became a major Mizoguchi theme.

The director has said that he didn't begin portraying Japan realistically until *Osaka Elegy* and *Sisters of the Gion*, and both films clearly indicate Mizoguchi's accommodations to a selective realism. In the first picture, a dilemma is presented on its own terms—that is, realistically—and the audience judges the situation for itself. A young telephone operator (a modern occupation) is ruined because of an innocent desire for money. Her boss takes advantage of her and her family stands helplessly by—a traditional element presented in a lifelike manner. Realism was apparently an aim. After making Yoda Yoshitaka rewrite the scenario ten times, Mizoguchi was still dissatisfied because he said it failed to portray people so real that the audience could smell their body odor.

In *Sisters of the Gion*, the heroines are traditional Kyoto geisha sisters. The elder possesses all the virtues of the legendary Gion entertainer, while the younger is modern and inclined to ignore the traditions of her profession, and Japanese traditional society in general. Despite the geisha code which authorizes only one patron per woman—a man who is wealthy enough to afford her—the younger geisha jumps from man to man in search of ready cash. She also decides that the elder sister needs a new patron as well, since the first one has lost all of his money. The contrast between tradition and modernity is embodied even in the casting: the elder being played by a now established traditional star, Umemura Yoko, and her younger counterpart, by newcomer Yamada Isuzu.

One of the younger geisha's rejected suitors jealously pushes her from a moving automobile, but even when she lies in the hospital, unable to interfere with her sister's life any longer, the elder is still too encumbered by tradition, too much the geisha to rejoin her now impoverished lover. She will always be afraid of going against custom. The younger, however, with every chance of recovery, will take up where she left off.

The director went to great pains to create the uniform background against which these extremes are viewed. The opening sequence is an example. Shinoda Masahiro has given a description of it: "The Furusawa household, the possessions of a bankrupt textile merchant are being auctioned. The camera begins with a medium shot of the fast-talking auctioneer behind a podium, then slowly pulls back. On the sound track the dialogue of auctioneer and bidders. As the bidding continues, the camera slowly reveals that the store had been a large one. Then, as the auctioneer enters the final bid in his ledger, the camera slowly moves into the living quarters in the back of the house. As the off-screen bidding resumes, the camera discovers three forlorn people seated in a room stripped of all but the barest furnishings: the owner Furusawa, his wife Omie, and his elderly manager Sadakichi, who says: 'Depressing, isn't it, watching them sell the things we've lived with our whole life. Almost like they're slicing us up and selling us off.' " [42]

The film ends with the celebrated hospital sequence. The camera dollies along a corridor and then pauses for a very long time on the other side of a screen, behind which are the sisters—a period of stasis in which the director seems to ask us to reflect on what we have seen. Only then does the camera move to the protagonists. Eventually, it slowly tracks toward the younger sister, to end with a close-up that Donald Kirihara has called "a visual as well as a didactic climax." [43]

Mizoguchi used the close-up, when he used it at all, in a manner all his own. For example, at the end of *The Downfall of Osen* (Orizuru Osen, 1935) there is a full close-up showing the heroine deranged in a railway station. But this shot is not for easy identification with Osen. It is for us, like her, to ignore the crowds, to more readily understand rather than to experience her situation. Likewise, the close-up of the younger Gion sister, Omocha, is for us to regard and contemplate her own final question: "Why are there such things as geisha in this world?"

If Mizoguchi's sentiments occasionally, and almost by default, go to the elder sister, his ending questions these. The problem suggested by the film admits no easy answer and, by implication, goes far beyond the narrow world of the geisha, to the shifting pendulum of Japanese society itself.

The problem of choice is one which animates many films and much Japanese modern literature. In noh, the choice has already been made before the play begins, and if the choice is made for personal indulgence over social duty, one may be certain that ghostly revenge is not far behind. In kabuki, the choice itself constitutes the plot: will the lovers neglect duty because they love each other? Can the hero bear to decapitate his own son, as duty plainly demands, so that his lord's child may be saved? Even lyric poetry reflects the theme of choice. The elegiac quality of much Japanese traditional verse is occasioned by the poet's regrets that he followed the path of personal inclination, or that he did not. In Japanese films, often the choice between the old and the new, the traditional and the modern, becomes the theme itself. In world cinema as well. All directors find themselves facing the force of the traditional. Producers are often conservative, so are audiences—the director is in the position of having to modernize his traditions or traditionalize his modernity.

Nonetheless, timely though it was, *Sisters of the Gion* was not a financial success. The director has said: "Though it didn't take long to finish, certainly less than a month, Daiichi [where Mizoguchi continued to make films after leaving Nikkatsu] went bankrupt because of it. Actually, it was Shochiku [the distributor] that gave us a raw deal by refusing to show a good film like this in a first-class theater."[44] In any event, Daiichi Eiga broke up in 1937, and Mizoguchi moved to Shinko Kinema, originally a part of Shochiku. Here he began making a different kind of film, starting with *The Story of the Last Chrysanthemum* (Zangiku monogatari, 1939).

EXPRESSIONISM, KINUGASA TEINOSUKE, AND THE LEFTIST FILM

Mizoguchi's concern for a realism so extreme that he could smell the characters' body odor represents one end of the realistic spectrum. At the other end are the stereotypes of early film, the clichés and patterns of shimpa-based melodrama. Yet, what the Japanese mean by realism is not what is usually meant elsewhere. According to Erich Auerbach, the Western definition of realism is "to represent phenomena in a fully externalized form, visible and palpable in all their parts, and completely fixed in their spatial and temporal relations."[45] As previously suggested, however, realism as a style is always partial—one chooses from life to make that simulacrum which is film. The degree is marked by the openness with which the choice is displayed. The United States—a land where realism was thought a virtue and where reality itself was not only defined but endorsed—produced films the realism of which was assumed, as though there were no other stylistic possibilities.

According to Auerbach, in realism nothing was to remain hidden or unexpressed, nothing was left fragmentary or half-illuminated, never a lacuna, never a glimpse of unplumbed depths, all events in the foreground. Though even American films were rarely this realistic, their makers often assumed that they were. However, other countries—France, Germany, Japan—gave early evidence of the possibility of film styles reflecting different concepts of reality.

Cinematic impressionism, for example, offered another kind of realism (as in the films of Jean Renoir and other French directors) where, following the example of the impressionist painters, a way of seeing more natural to the eye was approximated. Things were painted as they "looked," not as convention suggested. That Japan did not avail itself of the impressionist style might be because there were no close ties between it and France (nothing approaching those between Japan and Germany), and because many impressionist films (those of Dimitri Kirsanoff and Jean Vigo, for example) were not locally shown until much later.

On the other hand, expressionism played an important role in early Japanese cinema, and traces can be found even now. Historically associated with German literature and graphics, expressionism was a style in which the writer—or painter, composer, filmmaker—sought to avoid the representation of external reality and, instead, to project a highly personal vision of the world.

In drama, this style was seen as a reaction against naturalism and, consequently, a number of plays imported into shingeki were expressionist: those of August Strindberg, Franz Wedekind, Ernst Toler. The film *Von Morgens bis Mitternacht*, so popular in Japan, was originally an expressionist play by Georg Kaiser. It was also thought fitting that expressionist plays imported into this far archipelago should be performed in what was understood to be an expressionist style, one which it was discovered, meshed so satisfyingly with the Japanese assumption of presentation as a dominant mode.

A further reason for the preponderance of expressionism in Japan was that there had long been a definite, if undefined, disinclination toward naturalism—that variety of realism which expressionism was definitely not. Though some Japanese authors, such as Tayama Katai and Nagai Kafu theoretically emulated Emile Zola and the other early "naturalists," when these methods were put to use in the first-person *shishosetsu* novels they became projections of a vision of the world so personal that it colored whatever the author looked at. It was in itself a kind of home-made expressionism.

Hence, though it was considered avant-garde in other cultures, expressionism found a ready home in mainstream art in Japan. And, as formula had long been a Japanese preference, expressionism à la *Doctor Caligari* offered a new and novel formula. In addition, and most importantly, expressionism did not pretend to be representation, it was not "realistic"—it was pure presentation, and this was something the Japanese knew all about.

Finally, this imported expressionism contained an urban prejudice which made it seem, in the eyes of the Japanese, truly modern. The works of early expressionism in Europe were "typically, situated on the edge of the specifically modern context, the megalopolis of industrial capitalism . . . Beneath a rigid asphalt crust, man-made and controlled by the authoritarian father-figure, chaotic forces, ungovernable by man, are destructively active."[46]

The typical expressionist product made criticism of the social status quo both impossible to avoid and easier to voice. Social criticism was traditionally expressed in what Carl Zuckmayer called the major expressionist theme, the revolt of son against father, a theme implied in many Taisho-era films, *Souls on the Road* among them. Challenging authority was implicitly a political act, and it is for this reason that Japanese expressionism could so easily and quickly turn leftist.

Ambitions were similar in both expressionistic and leftist literature. Plays and films often presented the negative effects of authority. Mizoguchi Kenji's first picture, *Blood and Spirit* (Chi to rei, 1923, n.s.), about the masses downtrodden by authoritarian capitalism, was said to have been noticeably expressionist. So was Murata Minoru's *Eikichi, Chauffeur*

(Untenshu Eikichi, 1924, n.s.), with an added touch of class consciousness. Social criticism found a natural discourse in expressionism.

The work of Uchida Tomu, a director originally much influenced by expressionism, indicates this. From his expressionist social satire, *A Living Puppet* (Ikeru ningyo, 1929, n.s.), Uchida went on to refine this style (threatening capitalist city, sinister goings on) into its close relative, what we now know as film noir, in *Police* (Keisatsukan, 1933, n.s.). He also engaged in social criticism in his naturalistic-seeming *Earth* (Tsuchi) of 1939. This film, a full print of which was discovered in the Russian archives in 1999, recounts the plight of a poor farmer under the capitalist heel. The theme is taken up again in many of Uchida's later pictures, such as the *Hunger Straits* (Kiga kaikyo, 1965), where the whole of social justice is questioned.

Expressionism as a style is seen in its fullest and most extreme Japanese form in two early pictures by Kinugasa Teinosuke, the former oyama turned academic director, who later became famous for the Kikuchi Kan–scripted *The Gate of Hell* (Jigoku mon, 1953). Between 1920 and 1966, Kinugasa made over one hundred and ten pictures of varying quality. Number thirty-five in his prolific output, however, was utterly unlike anything before or after. This was *A Page Out of Order* (aka A Page of Madness/A Crazy Page), the negative of which was discovered in 1971. Made to be shown in a commercial theater (though one usually reserved for foreign films), it is—among other things—an illustration of how styles considered advanced or difficult in the West were readily accepted into the Japanese mainstream.

A Page Out of Order, 1926, Kinugasa Teinosuke, with Inoue Masao (right).

Expressionism was regarded as the latest entertainment import from the West, and that in itself made it welcome. Also, it was from Germany, a country from which Japan had adopted a number of products, such as an army based on the Prussian model. Early expressionist German films proved popular in Japan. Tanizaki Jun'ichiro very much liked the Paul Wegener films *Der Student von Prag* (1913) and *Der Golem* (1920), and Kinugasa had seen a good many as well, including F. W. Murnau's *Der Letzte Mann* (1924)—his "ideal film"—which he viewed five times.

Much of the artistic ferment of the Taisho mid-1920s was occasioned by literature and films from abroad. Miyoshi Masao has spoken of the wholesale interest in "bits and dollops of Paul Morand, Andreyev, Croce, Bergson, Futurism, Cubism, Expressionism, Dadaism, Symbolism, Structuralism, Realism, Strindberg, Swinburne, Hauptmann, Romain Rolland, Schnitzler, Lord Dunsany, Wilde, Lady Gregory, and a lot else."[47]

By 1925, the two major literary schools in Japan were the proletarian-literature movement and the expressionist-like Shinkankakuha, or "Neo-Perceptionist School," a group which included Kawabata Yasunari, now in his experimental phase, and Yokomitsu Riichi, whose *The Sun's Corona* (Nichirin, 1925) had already been filmed by Kinugasa. Though finished in 1923, this film's release was held up by the Ministry of the Interior. The story of an aristocratic woman who runs off with the family chauffeur was thought to contain veiled references to the imperial family.

Kawabata had early pointed out that German expressionism, as opposed to the realistic naturalist view, was the best vehicle for perceiving the primacy of subjectivity. He compared the new German style to old Asian-style Buddhism, which—as in Zen—had among its aims the breaking down of subject and object. The subjective view of expressionism was, he thought, much like the preliminary stages of this breakdown. Kinugasa agreed, so did Yokomitsu, and it was decided that they would attempt a self-consciously expressionist independent film.

Originally, Kinugasa wanted the film to be about an amusement park, like *Caligari*, a film he had not seen but which Kawabata had. Later, scouting for ideas, he went to a mental hospital and discovered his subject. This location appealed to the other two Neo-Perceptionists—after all, *Caligari* had also taken place in a mental hospital, and the hallucinations of someone institutionalized would be an ideal vehicle for expressionist treatment. Apparently the entire group wrote the script, and Yokomitsu named it. Kawabata subsequently wrote a short story about the filming called "Warawan Otoko" (translated as "The Unsmiling One") and eventually included the script in his complete works.

A Page Out of Order is about a man who abandons his wife, causing her to drown her baby and go insane, or else to go insane and drown her baby. The older daughter holds her father responsible and he, feeling guilty, attempts to make amends by getting a job in the asylum where his wife is incarcerated. His memories and hallucinations occupy him as they do his unfortunate spouse. In the end, his surviving daughter's marriage having been happily arranged, he stays on—now as much a part of the asylum as his wife is.

Such a story would have equally suited the demands of shimpa, but the scriptwriters purposely scrambled time and space. In addition, Kinugasa complicated any easy reading by leaving out all the dialogue titles that Kawabata had provided and by cutting any scenes that could forward a recognizable plot. He also urged the inclusion of logically irrelevant but emotionally evocative scenes—a broken rice bowl, a rain-soaked cat—and interrupted the narrative so often that the audience had to bring its own subjectivity to assist in any interpretation.

Among the opening scenes is the following sequence:

13. The rain falls outside. Flashes of lightning appear in the sky, one superimposed on the other.

14. A dancing girl.

15. The sound of a *taiko* drum and other musical instruments is heard in the rain.

16. The dancing girl, exhausted from dancing, suddenly collapses on the floor. Her feet are bleeding.

17. Musical instruments are heard in the rain.

18. The dancing girl on the floor listens intently. Then she gets up and starts dancing again.

19. Blood stains here and there on the floor.[48]

This is a translation of the Kawabata script rather than a reconstruction of the actual film, but its "expressionism" is obvious. It is the author's intent that the dancer should "hear" music during a rainstorm in a silent film (by double-printing the musical instruments over her image), that her impressions should be ours, and our experience of the asylum be hers. Kinugasa also seeks to increase this visual impact. He turns this seven-part scene into a sequence made up of over fifty cuts.

A Page Out of Order was photographed by Sugiyama Kohei, the cameraman who also went on to win Kinugasa his various prizes for *The Gate of Hell*. Visually, it owes much to the German expressionist product: nighttime lighting, lots of reflections, rain-soaked sets, shadows, and urban menace.

In place of the steady, sober pace of the German expressionist films, however, *A Page Out of Order* is a mosaic of small scenes, the pattern of which must be inferred by the viewer. There is enough of a plot line to assist the benshi (who must have been otherwise baffled by the film), but its tempo is often as fast as possible, making one wonder if Kinugasa had not also seen films by Dimitri Kirsanov or Sergei Eisenstein. But Kirsanov's *Menilmontant* (1924) was never shown in pre–World War II Japan, and Kinugasa saw neither Eisenstein's *Strike* (1924) nor his *Potemkin* (1925) until he went to Russia several years later.

There is also no Japanese precedent for such fast cutting. And fast it is. Though it lasts under an hour, the film usually exhausts its audiences. Yet, it is certainly part of the expressionist ethos to give all angles of an object and to include in the subjective experience of the film everything about the space and time it encompasses. Expressionist film is not so much about anecdote as it is about being inside the anecdote.

The writers chose to enter the story at a typically odd angle, since the insane dancer is neither the wife nor central to the story. More important than story, however, is atmosphere—something Japanese audiences early detected—in this case, the subjective experience of the asylum itself. This means that the narrative, what there is of it, is reassuringly atmospheric and at the same time takes on a near allegorical importance. This is all there is, but this is enough because this is what the world is.

As Iwasaki Akira said in his review of *A Page Out of Order*: "Directors like Kinugasa who can make use of the camera freely, independently, and effectively are not so common in Japan. They are rare even in other countries. The camera becomes almost an organism which grasps the object naturally and perfectly. The operation is not simply a mechanical one. Hence they [Kinugasa and Sugiyama] succeed in producing an original creative work."[49] When the picture opened, the press was attentive and respectful. Though not enough money was made to finance a second experimental film (one of Kinugasa's stated ambitions), it was still thought of as a commercial film, if a rather advanced one.

The film was thus financially successful enough to attract the attention of Shochiku. Always interested in novelty, the company agreed to distribute Kinugasa's next picture. The director later remembered that "during this period there was a clamor among a section of moviegoers to take away the swords from the chambara film: in other words, to remove the fighting scenes from samurai films in order to elevate the artistic quality of Japanese cinema. Accordingly, our next film was a conscious attempt to exclude a historical plot with its colorful incidents and to include a simple story describing the affection between a brother and sister, poor, living in an obscure corner of the city."[50]

Crossroads (Jujiro, aka Shadows of the Yoshiwara, 1928) is a more commercial film than *A Page Out of Order*. Its expressionism as well as the pace are considerably toned down. At the same time, *Crossroads* illustrates how an imported style can come to be nationalized. The film's expressionist intentions are conveyed mainly in the sets—huge, cavernous UFA-type settings, which recreate Japan's feudal era with lots of night

Crossroads, 1928, Kinugasa Teinosuke, with Chihaya Akiko, Bando Junosuke.

shots, shadows, smoke, and steam. The wounded and thirsty hero crawls from his bedding only to find himself in a Fritz Lang–like space with enormous half-buried casks full of water. Yet, when he tries to drink, the water boils. Pain becomes steam. The hero is particularly chambara-like and strikes a variety of poses. This is in contradistinction to the acting in *A Page Out of Order*, where the actor playing the remorseful husband (well-known lead, Inoue Masao) gives an intensely realistic performance. Overall, the acting in this film is more "Japanese" than it was in Kinugasa's earlier picture.

On a deeper level, the linkage between scenes in *Crossroads* is often, in the Japanese manner, neither logical nor causal, but emotional. A woman is concerned with her brother's safety, so the scene cuts directly to the two of them in their childhood, which establishes her memories and her concerns. A cut is determined not by the convolutions of the story, but by the visuals of the scene—the round shape of a sedge hat suggests the round shape of a teacup.

Foreign viewers seeing this picture, which was among the first Japanese films shown in Europe, appreciatively noted its "realism," for example, how the character's breath was visible in some sequences. Such realism was not, however, among the aims of the picture. Actually, this particular effect was unintended—the studio was unheated and it was winter.

The difference between these two Kinugasa films is most easily exemplified by the treatment of their respective cats. In *A Page Out of Order*, the wet cat is just there, and nothing much is made of it. Consequently, its misery intensifies the horror of the asylum. The cat in *Crossroads*, on the other hand, is one of the actors. Its role is to creep up to the hero, attracted by the wounds, and lick the blood.

———

Films which expressionistically showed the menace of city life and the prevalence of insane asylums were, intentionally or otherwise, criticizing society itself, finding fault with the status quo. Since fault is inevitably found with the status quo, such criticism merely expresses the equally inevitable popular aspirations of certain elements in society, and this offends the authorities. Perhaps this is even more evident in Japan, where historically the status quo has been less regularly challenged.

Literature, drama, and film in the "democratic" Taisho-Showa 1920s tended to criticize. The keiko-eiga, or "tendency" films—films which tended toward leftist sympathies but avoided overt political commitment—eventually became numerous enough to form a genre. Usually these films took a stance against some repressive government-backed political action. As the authorities looked more and more closely at the liberties taken during the decade of the 1920s, increasing efforts were made to curb this license, resulting frequently in ever more overt expressions of criticism.

Many directors contributed to the keiko-eiga genre, including Mizoguchi, Itami Mansaku, and Tasaka Tomotaka, whose *Look at This Mother* (Kono haha wo miyo, 1930, n.s.)—a look at a proletarian mother sacrificed to society's cruel hypocrisy—was one of the most popular. Uchida's expressionist *A Living Puppet*—written by popular proletarian writer Kataoka Teppei (who also wrote the script for Mizoguchi's *Metropolitan Symphony*)—was a keiko-eiga as well. Its protagonist is a man who begins to fight against the capitalist system but ends up playing into its hands. Later the genre included films from such nominally conservative directors as Shimazu Yasujiro, his *Lifeline ABC* (Seikatsusen ei-bi-shi, 1931, n.s.), about striking workers, being an example.

The most popular of these keiko-eiga was a film which became something of a sensation and thus attracted the direct attention of the government. This was *What Made Her Do It?* (Nani ga kanojo wo so sasetaka, 1930), the work of Suzuki Shigekichi, based on a novel by a well-known proletarian writer, Fujimori Seikichi. In it, a poverty-stricken woman turns arsonist. What made her do it was the miseries of capitalism.

The film was found so persuasive that there were (claimed the press) local riots. It became the highest-grossing picture in Japanese silent-film history. With it, the government began taking an even stronger interest in the industry, particularly when it became apparent that the film was scheduled to run in the Soviet Union.

In 1994, a partial print of this picture was discovered in the Goskino film archives in Moscow, and thus a new generation could finally see this notorious film. *What Made Her Do It?* is a melodrama in which nothing good is allowed to happen to the downtrodden, and anything bad that can happen to the heroine does. At the same time, it surprises.

What Made Her Do It?, 1930, Suzuki Shigekichi, with Hamada Kaku, Takatsu Keiko.

Though a melodramatic potboiler, from the Western point of view, it is also extraordinarily film literate.

If a narrative this well designed had appeared in Europe, the film would have become as famous as, say, E. A. Dupont's *Varieté* (1926), a melodrama which it somewhat resembles.

When, for example, the hungry heroine is being fed, the meal is encompassed in an unusual series of dissolves, and the articulation of space around the hearth is a piece of experimental geometry resembling the works of Man Ray, except that it is instead a product of the Japanese mainstream of 1930. Such was the acceptance of the latest in film techniques; such was the ignorance of their original purposes.

It was not the aesthetics of the film that roused the government, of course, but its critical message. The 1920s had been a period not only of "license" and relative freedom but also of economic setbacks and widespread poverty. Many Japanese were dissatisfied and made this known. The authorities were quite prepared to act against such dissidence. Director Suzuki, feeling threatened, retreated to safer ground and three years later was making patriotic documentaries for both the Japanese army and navy. Nonetheless, the suspicions of the government, never actually dormant, were now rekindled.

From the age of the Tokugawa shogunate through the Meiji and Taisho governments, an oppressive governing body had been the rule rather than the exception. One might charitably call the system paternal but, in fact, it plainly sought to exert control to a degree uncommon in other countries. The frivolities of the 1920s did not much concern it, but the growing dissidence of the 1930s did.

Movies had long been under a kind of semiofficial control. Early on, Victorin Jasset's very popular *Zigomar* (1911), about a successful robber, was singled out for investigation and censorship. Eventually, it and its various Japanese emulations were banned. By 1917, a film-control regulation law was on the books, and in 1925 its stringencies were tightened. Oshima Nagisa later noted that at first there was only postproduction control, followed by a loose system of general control; then, in 1939, "total control." [51] This 1939 law, modeled after the Nazi Spitzenorganisation der Filmwirtschaft, was a result of the militaristic and nationalistic political climate, which had grown much stronger after the 1937 invasion of China by Japan, and the need to control opinion.

Consequently government supervision became more frequent and more severe. Censors deprived the script for Ozu's *College Is a Fine Place* (Daigaku yoi toko, 1936) of a seemingly innocent bit of comedy, when two students try to avoid their military training class. Once the teacher calls the class to order, what was to have followed was a parody of military training, at the end of which the two rebellious students were to be upbraided in the overblown, rhetorical style of General Araki.

Later, scissoring became even more frequent. Naruse Mikio's *Traveling Actors* (Tabi yakusha, 1940), about fellow workers (who between them played the front and back half of a horse) had a whole section cut, apparently for reasons of excessive levity. A drinking scene in Yamamoto Kajiro's *Horses* (Uma, 1941) was cut because it was thought to encourage alcohol consumption on the job. Yamamoto's pupil, Kurosawa Akira, had a love scene taken out of his debut picture, *Sanshiro Sugata* (1943), and Kinoshita Keisuke, Kurosawa's contemporary, almost lost the final sequence of *Army* (Rikugun, 1944).

Army, 1944, Kinoshita Keisuke, with Tanaka Kinuyo.

In *Army*, a distraught mother (Tanaka Kinuyo) runs alongside the train which is taking her young son away to the front. She is so plainly upset by this event that the censors demanded that it be cut; mothers were supposed to be smiling proudly as sons were sent off to battle, the kind of scene which occurred with some frequency in other pictures. Kinoshita's sequence was saved because it could be argued that the mother's stress was caused by the conflict between her knowing what was socially correct (sending the boy off) and her own selfish and possessive nature in loving him (the old dramatic kabuki standby—giri versus ninjo). Many other films, though, were hacked up, or else banned completely. Kurosawa's *Sanshiro Sugata*, based on the popular Tomita Tsuneo novel, and bafflingly called an insult to Japan as well as "Anglo-American," was saved only by a timely remark by Ozu, who was on the committee and was a man whose opinion carried some weight. He said he knew nothing about Anglo-Americanism but that he thought this was a very fine film.

Foreign movies as well, particularly those dealing with the military, were similarly censored. Lewis Milestone's *All Quiet on the Western Front* (1930) suffered nearly three hundred cuts, amounting to about twenty percent of the screening time. Anything showing war as it was had to go. This included scenes of those dead in battle, scenes where men were killed, and the climactic sequence where Lew Ayres bayonets a French soldier and is stunned at what he has done. Other war films were completely excluded. When a print of Jean Renoir's *La Grande Illusion* (1937) arrived in Japan, it was confiscated and sent back home.

Naturally, the government also looked after public morals and the possible threat to them by foreign products. Kisses were routinely removed, with the result that foreign actors and actresses approached each other tenderly only to recoil with inappropriate suddenness. And there were many other reasons as well for cutting the foreign product. The Mongol prince was not left hanging by his queue in Raoul Walsh's *The Thief of Bagdad* (1924) because he was, after all, a prince. René Clair's *Le Dernier Milliardaire* (1934) was ordered deprived of all scenes that seemed to profane a royal family.

There remained for a time several genres where protest could covertly continue. One of these was the jun-bungaku film, film adapted from the better class of fiction. Companies usually accepted the proffered script because directors were at least showing serious intentions to work with pretested material that had already found something of an established audience. This could also hold off the censors, the argument being that since the work was already known, the film was not responsible for the ideology contained. In addition, there was ample precedence for the genre. Japanese cinema, perhaps more than any other, is close to all forms of literature.

The resulting films were called *bungei-eiga*, "literary films." In the early 1930s, the genre appeared frequently: Gosho's adaptation of Kawabata's *Dancing Girl from Izu* (Izu no odoriko, 1933); Shimazu Yasujiro's *Okoto and Sasuke* (Shunkinsho: Okoto to Sasuke, 1935), based on a Tanizaki novel; Gosho's *Everything That Lives* (Ikitoshi ikeru mono, 1934), based on a Yamamoto Yuzo novel. Later, Yoshimura Kozaburo adapted Kishida Kunio's *Warm Current* (Danryu, 1939), and newcomer Shibuya Minoru came to popular attention with *Mother and Child* (Haha to ko, 1938), based on a Yada Tsuneko novel.

A director who gave the literary-film movement much of its vitality was Toyoda Shiro. His *Young People* (Wakai hito, 1937), based on a novel by Ishizaka Yojiro, proved popular, and he went on to make many other distinguished adaptations, among them *Crybaby Apprentice* (Nakimushi kozo, 1938), based on a famous novel by Hayashi Fumiko, and *Nightingale* (Uguisu, 1938), after an Ito Einosuke work.

Though bungei-eiga were generally protected from the censors, some ran into trouble. Uchida Tomu's *Earth* (1939) was based on a serious novel by Nagatsuka Takashi, but the message was too keiko-eiga–like for the conservative censors. Nikkatsu did not like the idea. The book was highbrow realism which criticized the existing order. Furthermore, as the story took place over four seasons and was all location work, it would be costly to make. In addition, there was the feeling that the government would not take too kindly to a film which shows a poor widow forced into poverty by the system.

Earth, 1939, Uchida Tomu, with Kosugi Isamu, Miake Bontaro.

Nevertheless, despite this opposition, Uchida and his devoted staff and cast went ahead and made the picture. Facilities, money, and film from other productions were slipped to the *Earth* production unit. The studio heads, never too close to what was going on under them, did not notice this activity until the picture was almost complete. Presented with the finished film, Nikkatsu was annoyed but finally agreed to release it as a gesture of good will toward its obviously devoted employees. To the company's embarrassment, the picture won the main Kinema Jumpo prize that year and consequently (since no costs had ever been credited to the unit) earned an unprecedented return on the investment.

Though the government indeed disliked the Uchida film, the general public made it a success. The reason, said one critic, was that audiences were weary of melodrama. Bungei-eiga were more faithful to real life, and by using them, filmmakers could move closer to the lives of ordinary people and achieve more realistic portrayals. Borrowing from literature thus moved the Japanese film closer to what the West would recognize as realism.

Another genre which could register protest was films about children. As Iranian cinema was to later discover, a repressive government often does not notice implicit criticism if it is offered, as it were, by kids. Further, even watchful censorship is apt to see such films as innocent, just like the young actors appearing in them. Such films were rarely censored, and all were notably realistic.

Typical of these films was Tasaka Tomotaka's *A Pebble by the Wayside* (Robo no ishi, 1938), scripted by Ikeda Takao, who had earlier worked on Ozu's various "children's" pictures. Here the trials of the little boy hero are directly caused by brutal authority: a drunken, abusive father; a system that apprentices youngsters to adult trades; a government completely uncaring. The picture was enormously popular, and the censor's scissors never touched it. Toyoda's *Crybaby Apprentice* was another example of this strategy, as was Shibuya's *Mother and Child*, a film in which a young girl sees a repressive society through her disrupted family—an authoritarian father and his mistress.

A Pebble by the Wayside, 1938, Tasaka Tomotaka, with Kosugi Isamu, Katayama Akihiko.

None of these films were overtly sentimental, perhaps because the child's point of view was preserved, and children—rarely sentimental about themselves—are often pragmatically realistic. This was certainly true of several such pictures made by Shimizu Hiroshi in a successful attempt to escape having to make government-sponsored films. His *Children in the Wind* (Kaze no naka no kodomo, 1937) and *Four Seasons of Children* (Kodomo no shiki, 1939) ignore the adult world until it collides head-on with the kids themselves. It is then that, just like the two little boys in Ozu's *I Was Born, But ...*, they compare themselves with grown-ups, only to find their elders wanting.

Four Seasons of Children, 1939, Shimizu Hiroshi.

CRITICISM AND CRACKDOWN: WORLD WAR II

Attempts to make individualistic films waned as the 1930s drew to a close. The government had decided upon a course which was to preclude the freedom of such personal expression for some time. As one high-ranking government official put it: "Films are our bullets and there is not a foot of film to give to the private sector."

It was, after all, wartime. Japan's conflict with China was not unsought, and a pretext for invasion had occurred in 1937. Three years later the entire archipelago was being mobilized, and by 1941 the country was at war with, among others, the United States. The government needed to mobilize everything it had, including films.

The problem was that the profit-oriented film industry was not initially prepared for wartime sacrifices. Its films were making money just as they were and, besides, there was a shortage of executive personnel. Kido of Shochiku, for example, was out helping organize film activities in occupied lands. Others were making pictures in China and Korea. There was little leadership and no one at all to direct a change in production policies.

By 1941, the industry had run into real trouble with the military because of its failure to produce a sufficient number of national-policy films. Though some companies made token efforts—Mizoguchi Kenji's *The Loyal Forty-Seven Ronin*, for example, was a film which indeed stressed the military's conception of bushido—it was officially decided that the industry had to be entirely reorganized.

The ten major film companies then operating (Nikkatsu, Shochiku, Toho [ex-PCL], Shinko, Daito, Tokyo Hassei, Nan-o, Takarazuka, Otaguro, and Koa) were told that they had to form themselves into two companies, and that each company was to make two films a month. Raw film stock would not be available unless the studios made the kind of pictures the state required.

Nagata Masaichi, earlier at Nikkatsu and later a major player in the postwar film industry, maintained that this plan was really designed by Kido to consolidate his personal power and Shochiku's strength. It was certainly true that under this plan Nagata's own Shinko Kyoto studios would have been closed and he himself would have been out of a job. Consequently, he countered with a new proposal: make three companies instead of two. The government was pleased. A new third company, composed of firms with weak management, would have little power to oppose government policy.

So, Shochiku and Koa composed one company; Toho, Otaguro, Tokyo Hassei, Nan-o, and Takarazuka made up a second; and the third comprised Nikkatsu, Daito, and Nagata's own Shinko. This pleased everyone except Nikkatsu, which owned a large chain of theaters and would now have to show non-Nikkatsu films in them. Nikkatsu president Hori Kyusaku tried to defend his company and thus earned the displeasure of the higher powers. When joining time came, Nikkatsu found itself purposely undervalued, while Nagata's Shinko was padded to the extent that it became dominant in the combine. Shortly the company took a new name—Dai-Nihon Eiga, or, as it was soon called, Daiei. Nagata as managing director was, of course, appointed as the new president. The government, having orchestrated a major upheaval in the film industry, could now order the kind of film it desired.

A problem remained. Japan had never developed a war genre. The occasional newsreels of thirty years before had done little other than celebrate the glory of victory. Now that a war-film genre was contemplated, it was felt that emphasis should be placed upon the sacrifice demanded and the discipline required. War was to be fully supported.

Construct a realistic film about war; but so far there had not been any. Shochiku's big production of 1925 had been *Fatherland* (Sokoku), which featured three thousand extras and four airplanes; Ushihara Kiyohiko's *The Army Advances* (Shingun, 1930), a romantic Shochiku comedy, had combined whole sections of King Vidor's *The Big Parade* (1925) and William Wellmen's *Wings* (1927), and featured the top box-office duo, Tanaka Kinuyo and Suzuki Demmei, but offered nothing that would raise national consciousness. Others were even less bellicose.

The existing genre of war-related films would not do if the audience was to believe what it saw. A compromise was suggested by the *kultur-film*, a recently imported German genre which allowed for greater manipulation than did the assumptions of the British or American documentary. A combination of kultur-film "realism," mainstream feature narrative, and less apparent propaganda ought, it was thought, to be a proper recipe for an acceptable war film.

Japan's initial wartime films seemed to Western eyes to lack propaganda. The first and best of these (from the viewpoint of aesthetics, if not that of the war effort) was Tasaka's *Five Scouts* (Gonin no sekkohei, 1938). A company commander calls on five men. They are to reconnoiter, but on their way they are attacked. Only four of them return. While his companions mourn, the fifth straggles back. Soon after comes the order to move out for a general attack. The men know that this time there will be no returning.

Five Scouts, 1938, Tasaka Tomotaka, with Kosugi Isamu.

Only at the film's end comes something the West might recognize as propagandistic. The field commander quietly speaks to his soldiers: "The battalion is now about to move out into action. There is nothing I can say to you at this time since I know each of you has prepared himself . . . From now on I want you to entrust your lives to me as you would to your own fathers. Let us all join together in the glorious death of the warrior hero. *Tenno Heika Banzai* [Long live the emperor!]." Yet despite this closing address, from the Western point of view, the film's attention to detail, its refusal to generalize, and its lack of melodramatics did not make very good wartime propaganda. It is also without the fervent nationalism then being pushed by the government, and lacked the warrior heroism of the ordinary period-drama. The soldiers seem without any sense of mission—divine or otherwise. The enemy is never seen; all that the scouts experience is the terrifying effect of enemy fire.

When not being shot at, the soldiers' lives are made up of just what they would be otherwise: searching for flowers they knew at home, trying to find something that could be used as a tatami mat, waiting for the mail, boredom. The men, of course, realize their danger, but this danger is not objectified. It might be argued that in a Japanese wartime propaganda film, enemy objectification was not necessary. In a nation where obligation, rather than feeling or reason, now defined the social order, it was not crucial to dramatize, identify, or present a rationale for war. It was necessary only to show people what was required of them. In any case, the Office of Propaganda took no exception to *Five Scouts*; rather, it encouraged the production of others like it.

Critic Hazumi Tsuneo has argued that the ubiquity of newsreels, no matter how edited, accustomed the public to "documentary realism," and that this in turn molded popular taste. Literature turned to the "reportage" novel, while illustrative art became photographic. It was but natural, Hazumi reasoned, that film now had to accommodate realism as well. People had to be shown things as they more or less really were. Tasaka, along with the Office of Propaganda, however, had to find, as he phrased it, a way to achieve some degree of independence from the authority of the documentary. He thought *Five Scouts* did this well. Tasaka followed this success with *Mud and Soldiers* (Tsuchi to heitai, 1939), a work that created a model for many other early wartime films.

One of the more interesting of these variations on the theme was Yoshimura Kozaburo's *The Story of Tank Commander Nishizumi* (Nishizumi senshacho-den, 1940), written by Kikuchi Kan, who, with the changing times, was now obviously regretting his earlier keiko-eiga affiliations. The film's hero is shown going about winning the war by being friendly with enemy civilians and fraternizing with his own men. Yoshimura later explained: "I really didn't want to make the film into some rousing war-support piece. I wanted some kind of battlefield Good Buddies Club, something in the mode of a typical Shochiku home melodrama, and featuring Nishizumi as a fairly ordinary character."[52] To do so, however, he would have had to trash a script which already had a message of racial superiority over the

The Story of Tank Commander Nishizumi, 1940, Yoshimura Kozaburo, with Uehara Ken.

Chinese built into it. Shimizu Hiroshi, by now thoroughly adroit and to whom the script was originally handed, might have pulled that off, but he said it was time to give the younger directors a chance, and went back to making films about children.

The Story of Tank Commander Nishizumi was typical of the new war product. It was based upon the life of an actual soldier, a man who had received one of the Japanese government's highest posthumous honors, being designated a *gunshin*, or "military god." And, indeed, the young officer is godlike in his military devotion to both his country and his men. Still, by international standards, the propaganda level is low.

Such quasi-humanistic expression, for a time, was encouraged because it did not violate the rules laid down by the Home Ministry. According to these, one ought not to make light of military matters, but one also ought not to exaggerate the horror in scenes dealing with war. One should avoid scenes of close fighting and do nothing to lower the morale or destroy the fighting spirit of the conscripted men, which was indeed something which might occur if the full horror of war was revealed.

Among the other stipulations, later enforced by the Office of Public Information (created by the Cabinet in 1940), was that films should display the beauty of the peculiarly indigenous family system, show the spirit of complete sacrifice of the nation at large, and reflect "the Japanese national philosophy."

This meant, of course, that a national philosophy had to be invented before it could be displayed. At this the Japanese had had some experience. A similar goal had been pursued since the Meiji Restoration in 1868. With the ending of Japan's isolationist policy, Japan felt it necessary to define what it was that made the Japanese people and their life so Japanese. There is an entire literature on the country which does nothing else. It is called *nihonjin-ron*, which might be translated as "studies on being Japanese." The vast majority of these studies are more prescriptive than descriptive, and many seek to defend as much as to define. Their partiality is now so notorious that the better books on Japan show no ambition to be considered nihonjin-ron.

After 1936, however, real efforts were made to express a national essence. The military-led government needed to define "Japaneseness" since its expansionist policies (first in China and Manchuria, eventually in the entire East Pacific) depended upon the durability of the imperial Japanese aura. This led to a state-sanctioned ideology of Japanese identity and the necessary resulting mystique. The search for this amalgam of characteristics had been going on for some time. It had continued beneath the liberality of the prewar period and lurked under modernism. Now, however, with war as both reason and excuse, there was new need for an agreed-upon "Japaneseness."

Little remained untouched during this new period of Japanification, and Japanese film was no exception, particularly as it was now notorious for importing not only new techniques, fads, and fashions but also new attitudes and ideas. It was Japanese film which had created the questionable shomingeki, the suspiciously critical jidaigeki, and the dissident keiko-eiga, and it was now importing a dubious "realism." Film, in particular, needed to be de-foreignized.

The government, with its home ministries and offices of censorship, called for a cleanup, one which, as they might have phrased it, would return the cinema to the people. The result was the fostering of a style which restored to Japanese film many of its original most "Japanese" elements.

The first order of business, since Japanese film style had moved toward Western realism, was to correct this. Repressive regimes do not favor realistic films. It is said that a 1949 Egyptian film-censorship law equated realism with social subversion. The Japanese government (despite earlier approval) now thought along these lines. It had in hand an alternative: the new governmentally approved style, which adapted the language of classical Western cinema to accommodate a presumed classical Japanese design. Darrell William Davis describes the resulting product: "In technique as well as subject matter . . . the films enact a canonization of history, an emphasis on indigenous art forms and design, and a corresponding technical repertoire of long takes and long shots, very slow camera movements, and a highly ceremonial manner of blocking, acting and set design." The wartime style set out "to transform Japanese traditions from a cultural legacy into a sacrament."[53]

Among Davis's examples of culture as sacrament is *Story of the Last Chrysanthemum* (Zangiku monogatari, 1939), a Mizoguchi Kenji film about a Meiji-period kabuki family, which Davis calls "a sacramental depiction" of the Japanese family-system. It functions as "an admonition to the Japanese people to return to their rightful place in the imperial lineage . . . the purer, straighter lines of the *ancien régime*," the picture itself becoming "a strange, wonderful amalgam of moral tract and aesthetic rigor."[54]

Story of the Last Chrysanthemum, 1939, Mizoguchi Kenji, with Kawarazaki Gonjuro, Umemura Yoko, Hanayagi Shotaro, Kawanami Ryotaro.

Among the other films Davis lists as defining this monumental style are Kumagai Hisatora's *The Abe Clan* (Abe ichizoku, 1938), Kinugasa Teinosuke's *The Battle of Kawanakajima* (Kawanakajima gassen, 1941), Makino Masahiro's *Shogun Iemitsu and His Mentor Hikozaemon* (Hasegawa to Roppa no Iemitsu to Hikoza, 1941), and—since the line continues—Kinugasa's *The Gate of Hell* (1953), Kurosawa's *Kagemusha* (1980) and *Ran* (1985), Teshigahara Hiroshi's *Rikyu* (1989) and, of course, Mizoguchi's *The Loyal Forty-Seven Ronin* (Genroku chushingura, 1941–42).

This last named picture is yet another version of the celebrated morality tale from bunraku and kabuki, in this instance taken from the 1937 governmentally "approved" version by Mayama Seika. Here action is reduced to static reenactment, and the hierarchical quality of Japanese court life is presented, by inference, as a contemporary possibility. The framing and camera movement, the distant scenes, and the long takes self-consciously revert to the means of early Japanese cinema—something from which, despite his occasional close-ups and fast cutting, Mizoguchi was never far.

The Loyal Forty-Seven Ronin, 1941–42, Mizoguchi Kenji, with Ichikawa Utaemon, Nakamura Gan'emon.

The film also reflects, perhaps not so intentionally, the sparse techniques of the early Japanese film. Some scenes in this late version would not have been out of place in the very first one. The difference is, of course, that here the slowness, the severity, and the use of classical aesthetics are all conscious and intentional, aimed at creating an official and canonical Japaneseness for nationalist ends. Or at least so it appears.

After World War II, when nationalistic excesses were being called to account, Mizoguchi implied that in actuality he was escaping into history (*Story of the Last Chrysanthemum* is about a Meiji theatrical family, *The Loyal Forty-Seven Ronin* is about mid-Edo-period court life) in order to avoid the demands of the troubled present.

As the war progressed, however, it became apparent that neither movies which grandly asserted Japaneseness nor those which showed the joys of soldierly comradeship were enough. What was needed was something akin to what the West recognized as wartime propaganda. The solution was the so-called *kokusaku-eiga* ("national-policy film").

Among the most representative national-policy films were those of Yamamoto Kajiro, an actor, scenarist, and director who had begun his career under Murata Minoru. *The War at*

Sea from Hawaii to Malaya (Hawaii-mare oki kaisen, 1942) was sponsored to commemorate the first year of the "Greater East Asian War," to dramatize "the Navy Spirit as culminated at Pearl Harbor." To this film Yamamoto brought documentary techniques, already used in his *Horses* (Uma, 1941), plus the resources of his studio. A huge model of Pearl Harbor was constructed on the Toho lot, and exact scale models of warships were floated here and there. The results were so effective that, after the war, Occupation authorities mistook some of the studio shots in *The War at Sea* for the real thing.

The War at Sea from Hawaii to Malaya, 1942, Yamamoto Kajiro, with Fujita Susumu, Kiyokawa Soji.

Horses, 1941, Yamamoto Kajiro, with Takamine Hideko.

Yamamoto, now remembered chiefly as Kurosawa's mentor, was perhaps typical of those directors who made unquestioning wartime propaganda films. Though a liberal person, he joined most Japanese in finding that the war, particularly after the Pearl Harbor attack, filled him with a mixture of euphoria and apprehension. In his memoirs he is honest enough to record what he felt that December morning in 1941: "Upon hearing the news I felt a subtle pleasure at everything becoming clear at last . . . the ten years leading up to this morning had been filled with uncertainty. Now something was certain."[55]

With its combination of apparent probity and absolute propaganda, *The War at Sea* pleased everyone: it recuperated at once the entirety of its enormous investment, the government was happy, and Toho was jubilant. It is interesting, however, that the monumental style played no part in this success. The picture is completely realistic, fast, and intimate. It is, in fact, much like an American wartime film. It was also partial. Sato Tadao, who later wrote a scathing analysis of it, says that its tacit claim to being an accurate portrayal of recruit life was an absolute lie, since nowhere does the film show the brutality which was a daily, very real ingredient in the lives of these young men.

Such an anomaly escaped notice in 1942 and, in any event, the film was clearly intended as celebratory. Other pictures which tried to tell more of the truth fared less well. One of these was Kamei Fumio's documentary *Fighting Soldier* (Tatakau heitai, aka Soldiers at the Front, 1939). It was so honest, so open in its depiction of the soldiers' routine and boredom that critics said it should have been named "Exhausted Soldiers" (*Tsukareta heitai*), and the government banned it.

That the government ban came as such a surprise to Kamei indicates the narrow terrain that the film industry was required to traverse. According to the original plan, the picture was supposed to have been a grand war spectacular, sponsored as it was by the Public Information Section of the army. However, after looking at the actual war, Kamei remembered: "We threw out our spectacular plan to show groups of 'fighting soldiers,' and began to depict . . . the honest life of the soldiers which fully showed the most beautiful humanity with a pure and simple consciousness." [56]

Kamei's aims were ostensibly those of Tasaka and Yoshimura, yet his efforts were met with protests. The Metropolitan Police Board's chief, head of the so-called thought police, is reported to have shouted: "These aren't fighting soldiers, they're broken soldiers!" The difference in reception had much to do with the difference in orientation among these directors. Tasaka and Yoshimura came from commercial film and could make use of accepted realist conventions. Kamei was a documentarist and could not. He says in his autobiography: "I did not have any intention of making an antiwar film . . . My greatest concern was to thoroughly describe the pain of the land and the sadness of all the people, including soldiers, farmers, and all living things . . . Horses, even plants suffered during the war." [57]

For his efforts, Kamei was eventually imprisoned, one of the few filmmakers to suffer incarceration. Since he was also to suffer severe censorship under the Supreme Commander of the Allied Powers (SCAP) censors after the war was over and the Allied Occupation Forces became the authority, many have pointed out that the real reason behind such treatment was that Kamei was an unrepentant Marxist, something frowned upon by both the wartime Japanese and the American Occupation censors.

Laws supporting censorship were viewed in different ways by different critics. While most echoed the words of one of them, that "the law intends to urge the qualitative improvement of the motion picture," the outspoken Iwasaki Akira, for years Japan's only independent critic, said of the same law that "it strikes out the creativity and spontaneity of film authors; limits the themes and contents; and atrophies, even kills, the film itself." [58] Iwasaki was taken into custody for this offense among others (he was also accused of being Marxist), was prosecuted, jailed, and beaten to the extent that he carried facial scars to his death.

Escaping governmental demands was something that few in the film industry could manage. Some, of course, directly joined the military. One such was Kikuchi Kan, a very powerful literary figure, who also wrote scripts and was editor-in-chief of the influential publication *Nippon Eiga*. He supported the "Spiritual Mobilization" (*Seishin Sodoin*) the government spoke of and said that it was necessary to turn away from the artistic darkness and negativity one associates with realist-tinged works.

Clearly one of Kikuchi's targets was realistic films such as Uchida Tomu's *Earth*, a picture he particularly disliked. He also included Shochiku shomingeki films, even *Horses*, a picture which the army had originally admired. With a determined administration and spokesmen like Kikuchi, governmental demands became more and more difficult for directors to withstand. A kind of passive resistance was the most they could hope for. Shimizu Hiroshi was forced to make a documentary about the capital of Japan-occupied Korea, *Seoul* (Keijo, 1940). Though it was supposed to illustrate "Korean Unification with the Homeland," it did nothing of the sort. Shimizu contributed twenty minutes of pan shots showing little except how Japanified the city had now become.

Among the few directors who retained any integrity was Ozu. He was twice inducted into the army, the second time explicitly to make films, and on both occasions he managed to do nothing at all. It is true that under pressure he sketched out an overseas wartime comedy, *Far from the Land of Our Parents* (Haruka nari fubo no kuni)—something like "Kihachi Goes to War"—but it was never submitted to preproduction censorship and was, perhaps at the director's instigation, abandoned.

Though both of Ozu's completed wartime films, *The Brothers and Sisters of the Toda Family* (Toda-ke no kyodai, 1941) and *There Was a Father* (Chichi ariki, 1942), were warmly praised by critics and the government, there is nothing of the national-policy film about either. Indeed, the only wartime concession is that the Toda family decides to move to Manchuria—something which many Japanese families were then actually considering.

Mizoguchi was less adroit. However unwillingly, he did make a number of national-policy films. The best, as film, was *The Loyal Forty-Seven Ronin*, and the worst were

There Was a Father, 1942, Ozu Yasujiro, with Ryu Chishu, Tsuda Haruhiko.

very bad indeed. Other directors, less accommodating, were less fortunate. Gosho Heinosuke's *New Road* (Shindo, 1936) had nearly a fifth of its length cut because it showed the decay of the family system. Though Kinoshita Keisuke had managed to make a satirical comedy out of his debut film, *The Blossoming Port* (Hanasaku minato, 1943), he was, as we have seen, heavily criticized for *Army*, the final scene being called deplorable and an unnecessary stain on an otherwise fine film. The censors kept their eyes on Kinoshita until the war was lost.

Kurosawa Akira, too, had difficulties. Though he made his national-policy films like everyone else—*The Most Beautiful* (Ichiban utsukushiku, 1944) and *Sanshiro Sugata, Part Two* (Zoku Sugata Sanshiro, 1945)—he also ran into trouble with his new version of the kabuki play, *Kanjincho*, which he called *They Who Step on the Tiger's Tail* (Tora no o wo fumu otoko-tachi, aka The Men Who Tread on the Tiger's Tail, 1945). The idea sounded good on paper: a great, stately, slow Japanese classic, done under the most limited of means.

It would have only one set, one camera, and some locations in the forest next to the studio. Kurosawa's script, however, though true to the letter of the play, included a new character—a porter, played by the comedian Enomoto Kenichi, better known as Enoken, whose thoroughly modern concerns completely altered the meaning of the drama.

Even while *They Who Step on the Tiger's Tail* was in production, the censors were getting ready to ban it, but since

They Who Step on the Tiger's Tail, 1945, Kurosawa Akira, with Enomoto Kenichi, Okochi Denjiro.

its production terminated more or less with the war itself, there was not much they could do. Nonetheless, by leaving it off a list of films sent to the new censorship office of the Allied Occupation, the censors made certain it was not released. Later, reviewed by the American censors, this film which the Japanese censors had found too democratic, too American, was discovered by the Americans to be too feudal, too Japanese. This instance of double censorial blindness meant that the film was not released until after the Americans left in 1952.

As the war continued and Japanese losses began to be apparent, the national-policy product turned more and more crude until its hate-the-enemy films became just as primitive as their equivalent everywhere else. All villains were now Western (mostly Japanese actors in sunglasses and moustaches), spies were everywhere, mothers were eternally brave, soldiers died happily, and everyone cried.

Nonetheless, Japan lost the war, an unimaginable calamity for the country. All major cities with the exception of Kyoto, Nara, and Kanazawa were destroyed; hundreds of thousands of civilians were killed in fire-bomb raids; the atomic bomb was dropped not once but twice, and Hiroshima and Nagasaki along with most of their inhabitants were obliterated. The defeat was total. Still the populace had been schooled in enduring the unendurable, and there was now an opportunity to demonstrate this ability.

THE OCCUPATION OF JAPAN

After the defeat of World War II, movies were among the few forms of entertainment left to a hungry yet hopeful population. Since Japan was now under Allied Occupation, most aspects of its wartime civilization were under scrutiny, and this included the cinema. Viewers were therefore seeing a new kind of Japanese film.

Within four months of Japan's surrender to the Allied Powers, in August 1945, the film law of 1939 was revoked, and in its place were new formulations issued by General Douglas MacArthur himself, the Supreme Commander of the United States–led Occupation.

SCAP announced a list of prohibited subjects: anything infused with militarism, revenge, nationalism, or antiforeign sentiment; distortion of history; approval of religious or racial discrimination; partiality toward or approval of feudal loyalty; excessively light treatment of human life; direct or indirect approval of suicide; approval of the oppression or degradation of wives; admiration of cruelty or unjust violence; antidemocratic opinion; exploitation of children; and opposition to the Potsdam Declaration or any SCAP order.

Along with the taboos came a list of subjects to be favored. Filmmakers were to show all Japanese of every walk of life endeavoring to construct a peaceful nation; soldiers and repatriates being rehabilitated in civilian life; those in industry and farming in the process of resolving the problems of postwar life; labor unions being peacefully organized; the hitherto bureaucratic government casting off and adopting true governmental responsibility; the free discussion of government problems taking place; every human being and every class of society being respected; individual rights being upheld; and historical personages, too, struggling for government representation of the people and for freedom.

Judicious prohibitions were balanced by utopian stipulations, and a special office was ordained, the Civil Information and Education Section (CI&E), among whose duties was the examination of new screenplays and the review of finished products. As for wartime and prewar films, such prints and negatives as were extant were reviewed and sentenced.

A total of over five hundred movie titles was compiled, and about half of these were burned. It was announced that these were simply extra copies, that original prints and negatives had been placed in storage by the Eighth Army before being turned over to the Signal Corps, and that eventually these would be transferred to the Library of Congress. In fact, no one knows just what was destroyed in the 1946 bonfire. Original prints and negatives were probably consumed along with the "extra copies." Title lists were not kept, and some companies (Toho and Daiei) had already destroyed what they thought might be incriminating. (One film, however, was saved. A single print of Yamamoto Kajiro's *The War at Sea from Hawaii to Malaya* was secretly buried at the Toho studios and later resuscitated.) The Occupation ended in 1952, and by 1967, all of the still extant prints and negatives had been returned to Japan by the Library of Congress. The collection now reposes at the National Film Center.

After the bonfire, it was then the turn of those who had made these films to be punished. The Japanese government, under pressure from SCAP, requested the All-Japan Motion Picture Employees Union to draw up a list of "war criminals" within the industry. There were three kinds, labeled A, B, and C. The first category included those to be "permanently" removed. Besides governmental officials concerned with films, this category included Kido Shiro of Shochiku; Osawa Yoshio, former head of Toho; Hori Kyusaku, head of Nikkatsu; and both Kikuchi Kan and Nagata Masaichi, of Daiei, among the twenty-three individuals listed in this category. Class B was devoted to those presumably less criminal, and included Kawakita Nagamasa, head of Towa; Mori Iwao, production head of Toho; the director Kumagai Hisatora; and others, totaling ten in all. Class B "criminals" were to be removed from the industry for a fixed period of time. Those who stood accused of class C crimes were ordered to perform "self-examinations" of their past actions. Included in this category were Yamamoto Kajiro and Yoshimura Kozaburo as well as a number of others.

The crime, of course, was that all had made wartime films. Kawakita, for example, had been head of the China Motion Picture Company and had worked with Germany in 1937 on an ill-fated German-Japanese production. The picture was to have been codirected by Arnold Fanck and Itami Mansaku, but differences soon developed and eventually two films evolved. In *Die Töchter der Samurai* (1937), the heroine nearly expires in a volcano, while in *The New Earth* (Atarashiki tsuchi, 1937) she goes off to the new lands—Manchuria—recently conquered by her countrymen. What the two versions had in common was their actress, Hara Setsuko.

The New Earth, 1937, Itami Mansaku, with Hara Setsuko.

Such collaboration was now deemed a crime, though by the same reasoning, had Japan won the war and the United States lost, John Ford, Frank Capra, and John Huston would also have been "war criminals." In any event, however, none of the "criminals" was hanged and a number were soon sprung. Among those listed in class A, charges against Hori, Kikuchi, and Otani were dropped. Though Kido, Osawa, and Nagata were still among the "criminals," the latter two were "rehabilitated" early in 1948.

For whatever reason, Kido was not granted clemency, and it was commonly said that his rancor at being labeled a "war criminal" stemmed at least in part from the fact that he was consequently kept out of the industry while his rival, Nagata, was fully reinstated and busy with big ideas. Later, in his autobiography, Kido was still furious about the affair, though his motivation was now political. If he was to be banished by the order of someone as insignificant as Iwasaki Akira (who headed the committee to name war criminals), then it was indeed a glorious thing to have been banished.

Criminals having been taken care of in the brave, new democratic world that the United States was constructing, it still remained necessary to root out "feudalism," a more difficult task. For example, there was the issue of Mount Fuji. This venerable volcano had been used by the wartime government as a sacred, mystical image, one strongly associated with the birth of the nation and hence the ruling imperial house. Fuji was plainly feudal.

Consequently, when Makino Masahiro wanted to depict Mount Fuji in *A Fashionable Wanderer* (Ikina furaibo, 1946), he was told that he couldn't. Since his story was about cultivation on the mountain's slopes, Makino claimed that it was not a symbol of nationalism but of the people themselves. CI&E refused. Irritated, Makino said that in that case they ought to have bombed Fuji instead of Hiroshima and Nagasaki. Eventually the Americans admitted that maybe he was right about Fuji but told him that he still could not put it in the film.

The new censors were faced with many similar cultural obstacles on screen. Bowing posed another problem for the authorities. It obviously displayed feudal tendencies yet, at the same time, it was an ingrained and omnipresent custom of salutation in Japan. It could scarcely be banned but it could be countered. Kissing, for example, was also a salutation and, further, one which implied a sort of equality.

When this decision became known, there was some rivalry among filmmakers as to who would make the first film with a real kiss in it. It was typical of the new political adroitness that the first was by the same man who had earlier made the bellicose *Songs of Allied Destruction* (Gekimetsu no uta, 1945), Shochiku's Sasaki Yasushi. He recorded the "first kiss scene" for his *Twenty-Year-Old Youth* (Hatachi no seishun, 1946); however, he was obliged to share the honor with Daiei's Chiba Yasuki, whose *Certain Night's Kiss* (Aru yo no seppun, 1946) opened the very next day.

One of the more curious aspects of the CI&E was its highly selective approach to wartime facts. The script for Ozu's *Late Spring* (Banshun, 1949), for example, had two lines changed quite arbitrarily. The line describing the daughter's health as bad "due to being conscripted by the navy during the war" was amended "due to forced work during the war." The other line ordered changed is that of the father, who says that Tokyo is "so dusty." Originally he said the city was filled with bombed-out sites.[1]

Not only was American damage to Japan to be minimized, there was also a standing order that members of the Occupation were not to be shown on film. When Shimizu Hiroshi was making *Children of the Beehive* (Hachi no su no kodomotachi, 1948) and had to shoot on location at railway stations, where many of the homeless loitered, he had to reframe constantly to avoid including the GIs gathered there. Yamamoto Satsuo, making *War and Peace* (Senso to heiwa, aka Between War and Peace, 1947) in downtown Tokyo, was told to avoid not only GIs but also jeeps, English-language signs, and burned-out areas. Even the term "burned-out," as Ozu was to discover, was not allowed in scripts. As John Dower has noted: "The 'occupied' screen did not merely offer a new, imagined world. It also made things disappear."[2]

Despite such vagaries most Japanese filmmakers thought that things were much better under the Occupation Forces than they had been under their own military. And many would have agreed with Kurosawa when he said of the U.S. Army censors: "Not a single one among them treated us as criminals, the way the Japanese censors had . . . Having lived through an age that had no respect for creation, I recognized for the first time that freedom of creation could exist."[3]

For all the improvement, the postwar film industry was not without its problems. It was almost impossible to make jidaigeki. While Meiji-period settings were perhaps permissible, anything before that was, by definition, feudal, and hence suspect. This meant that much Japanese drama (some bunraku, some kabuki, most kodan) was banned. *The Loyal Forty-Seven Ronin* could not even be staged, much less filmed.

There were ways around the difficulty. Mizoguchi Kenji, for example, wanted to make a movie about the Edo-period woodblock-print master, Utamaro. Though originally discouraged, he did not despair. He himself called on the Occupation authorities, giving them cogent reasons for his making the film. The common man, he averred, loved Utamaro—he was a great cultural object. A mollified CI&E, given a reason to agree, gave him permission, and the result was *Utamaro and His Five Women* (Utamaro wo meguru gonin no onna, aka Five Women around Utamaro, 1946).

Utamaro and His Five Women, 1946, Mizoguchi Kenji, with Iizuka Toshiko, Bando Minosuke.

On the other hand, if making jidaigeki had become more difficult, making gendaigeki had now become much easier than before and during the war. Here was a genre—films about contemporary life—in which the Occupation authorities were interested. These could include instructions for the future as well as recriminations for the past.

An early success was Kinoshita Keisuke's *Morning for the Osone Family* (Osone-ke no asa, 1946), about a family during the war. Written by Hisaita Eijiro, who had been active in the prewar proletarian literary movement, the film depicts a militarist uncle involved in shady deals. The uncle's dubious activities are detected by the mother of the family, prompting her to make a long speech condemning military evils. With the

Morning for the Osone Family, 1946, Kinoshita Keisuke, with Miura Mitsuko, Sugimura Haruko, Osaka Shiro, Tokudaiji Shin, Tanaka Haruo.

coming of peace, the family is brought together again. The allegorical "morning" of the title refers to this new life occasioned by the end of the war. The film concludes with the family celebrating, a sequence whose final shot is that of the sun rising as if to hail the coming of democracy.

CI&E, which had insisted upon that final shot despite Kinoshita's resistance, was pleased by the film as it was by Kurosawa's *No Regrets for Our Youth* (Waga seishun ni kui nashi, 1946). Here the subject was academic freedom: a democratic-minded teacher is silenced by the military, and one of his students is arrested as a spy. The teacher's daughter (Hara Setsuko in an untypical role), who is married to the student, endures great hardships. After his death she works with his peasant parents. And, once the war is over, she stays on—through suffering she has become a real individual, she has no regrets for her youth.

No Regrets for Our Youth, 1946, Kurosawa Akira, with Hara Setsuko, Fujita Susumu.

The scenario, another by Hisaita Eijiro, went through a number of transformations, none of which Kurosawa wanted and all of them dictated by Toho's own Scenario Review Board, a leftist organization formed between the two Toho labor strikes, a time when the number of Communist Party members had much increased. Nonetheless, the film showed what Kurosawa wanted it to show. "I believed then that it was necessary to respect the 'self' for Japan to be reborn. I still believe it. I depicted a woman who maintained such a sense of 'self.' Those who criticized would have approved if the protagonist of the film had been a man."[4]

Another film which looked seriously at the new freedoms was Yoshimura Kozaburo's *Ball at the Anjo House* (Anjo-ke no butokai, 1947). Written by Shindo Kaneto, and much indebted to Anton Chekhov's *The Cherry Orchard*, it was about an aristocratic family who, having lost both peer status and fortune in the postwar era, are forced to close down the family mansion. On the last night together, a party is held by both family and servants—the occasion serving as a reflection of their thoughts and reactions concerning the family's prosperous military past and its penniless but hopeful future. Toward the party's end, the father is about to end it all, but his daughter (Hara Setsuko) takes away the gun, puts on a phonograph record, and leads him in a dance. This, she says, is the way to start a new life.

Ball at the Anjo House, 1947, Yoshimura Kozaburo, with Aizome Yumeko, Mori Masayuki, Takizawa Osamu, Hara Setsuko.

There were many other postwar pictures which looked forward to a bright future. While occasionally casting a backward glance at the darker past, most of their creators earnestly, if sometimes naively, aspired to a future of peace, prosperity, and equality. Among these were new directors from within the ranks of the industry itself who were able to profit from the postwar changes which had so shaken the industry's organization. Producers turned to directing, as did scriptwriters, photographers, and even actors.

No matter where this now directorial talent came from, in postwar Japan all directors were confronted with a stylistic problem. Until August 1945, Japanese directors had been required to make national-policy films, ones which favored Japaneseness. In the period after August 1945, Japanese directors were required to make films which were specifically American. There were also, naturally, continuations. Imai Tadashi, who had been forced to make such national-policy films as *The Numazu Military Academy* (Numazu heigakko, 1939, n.s.) and *The Suicide Troops of the Watchtower* (Boro no kesshitai, 1943, n.s.), could now revive the concerns of the prewar keiko-eiga and, in so doing, define the new social film. In 1946, he directed *An Enemy of the People* (Minshu no teki), a picture which had nothing in common with Ibsen save its title, being about "the wartime oppression of the masses by the capitalists, and labor's heroic opposition to capitalism, militarism, and imperialism," to quote from the original précis of the picture.

Imai later remembered that since "no one had the guts to make a film critical of the emperor, [we] made films that fitted into permitted categories. The organization of unions was one of the major recommendations of the CI&E, so I had guidelines." The guidelines were delivered in the form of "several officers [who] . . . made a few long speeches. They threatened us, saying if we didn't cooperate [within the permitted territories] they would immediately shut down the place. We cooperated."[5]

Written by leftist authors Yasumi Toshio and Yamagata Yusaku, *An Enemy of the People* was about corrupt capitalists who in collusion with the military make enormous profits by exploiting the workers. It easily passed the Occupation censors. Not only was it anti–big-business/government combines, it was also critical of the emperor system. Though Imai later said that he did not want to make an ideological diatribe, the film could also be seen as anti-capitalist. It was a postwar keiko-eiga—a genre about which the postwar American authorities would eventually have as many second thoughts as had the wartime Japanese.

Another picture with an apparent political orientation was Toho's *War and Peace* (Senso to heiwa, 1947), directed by Yamamoto Satsuo and Kamei Fumio. Though based on the Griffith film *Enoch Arden* (1911), the hero was now politically committed to the left. Thought dead by his family, he returns from China, where he had learned the evils of Japanese militarism. Approved though the script had been, the picture was eventually censored and about half an hour removed before it was released. The reasons were various, but one of them certainly

War and Peace, 1947, Yamamoto Satsuo.

was that Kamei was involved. Kamei had been heavily criticized, as will be remembered, for his *Fighting Soldier*, a film deemed too sympathetic to China and, in any event, failing to glorify Japanese aggression. The film was banned and the director jailed. Yet here was this man again, once more saying that the Chinese treated their Japanese POWs well, and teaching collective peace and prosperity.

At the beginning of the Occupation, anything that Kamei had wanted to make would have been welcomed by the authorities, so plainly was he a martyr to feudalism. When he announced plans for *A Japanese Tragedy* (Nihon no higeki) in 1946, to be produced by Iwasaki Akira, he received ready permission. A documentary highly critical of the imperial system (a shot of the emperor held the commentary: "This is the man who should be punished"), it was also unfriendly to capitalism. The film spared no one: the emperor, the militarists, the politicians, the financial moguls. Also, a Marxist historical analysis underlay the film's focus on the economic factors behind the Japanese leaders' now notorious exploitation of domestic labor and their plainly expansionist policy in Asia.

The film's underlying political currents were, of course, nothing new in Occupied Japan, but Kamei did not stop there. Rather, he went on to name names and to denounce the "war criminals," some of whom had not been apprehended, or even suspected, and this at a time when there were indications that the Occupation was not long going to continue in the liberal way it had begun.

Kamei was not a member of the Communist Party, but he had studied in Russia, admired Eisenstein and Pudovkin, involved himself with leftist concerns, and was friends with many party members. Other directors had similar interests, but they did not make films attacking capitalism and openly labeling men who, though former militarists, were now friends of the Occupation.

There was also the growing suspicion in Washington that many of the Occupation policies were leftist (as, indeed, they were) and that "Communists had infected" an operation which had begun by inculcating democracy in Japan. By 1947 it was also becoming apparent that communist Russia and the democratic United States were beginning to square off in what would become the Cold War, a scenario in which Japan now had to play the role of "bastion of freedom."

Though *A Japanese Tragedy* was actually released, a second review found that it really should have been banned—and so it was. All negatives and prints were ordered to be submitted to the CI&E within the week. What seems to have happened was that Premier Yoshida Shigeru had complained about the film and asked General Charles Willoughby to convey to General MacArthur, SCAP himself, his request that something be done about it. Something was.

The American report on the film said the banning was in the interests of public order because "its radical treatment of the emperor" might "well provoke riots and disturbances."

This fear was congruent with MacArthur's decision that the imperial institution should be protected. After all, not only had the emperor supported the Occupation, but abolition of the imperial system could threaten the nation's stability. Thus, the single most feudal object of all, the imperial system, remained unpurged.

So sudden was the change of direction, members of the Occupation itself found themselves being purged by Washington and the new House of Un-American Activities Committee. Senator Joseph McCarthy, who was becoming interested, discovered that the Japanese film industry was a nest of Communists. There were certainly a number of party-member insiders—Imai, for example—yet their presence could be explained by an Occupation policy which, up until then, had upheld liberal aims. The new policy caught the industry's most active players unawares. Such aims could now be construed as leftist. Hirano Kyoko notes this in her discussion of this period. The suppression of *A Japanese Tragedy*, she says, "resulted from an intrinsic contradiction within occupied Japan: the Americans decided to rule the country by means of the existing Japanese governmental and bureaucratic system rather than destroying it, as they did in occupied Germany. The most vocal Japanese critics of the emperor were Communists, and the Americans thus equated anti-emperor feelings . . . with Communism, in many cases without justification."[6]

This change of direction taken by the Occupation was to have many results. While some of the improvements, such as land reform, were implemented, others (the intended destruction of big-business *zaibatsu* combines, for example) were not. Though the United States had taught Japan all about labor strikes, Toho's third major strike, in 1948, was settled by a show of Occupied force. As the *New York Times* reported the event: "Communist-led sit-down strikers agreed today to leave the ground of Toho movie studios after United States tanks and troops were called out in the first serious labor demonstration since General Douglas MacArthur banned strikes."[7] Talk of individuality and democracy became less common, though the attractions of capitalism were rendered no less inviting.

Directors and screenwriters were thus, as the Occupation deepened, no longer so interested in subjects which advertised the rosy future and their country's changed ways. The Japanese no longer needed to regard themselves as model citizens of the future. It was now possible to return to being "Japanese" in the traditional sense.

POSTWAR DEVELOPMENTS

Though the Occupation of Japan was not officially terminated until the spring of 1952—having lasted almost seven years, a period nearly twice as long as American involvement in World War II—Japanese filmmakers had already begun to occupy themselves with again defining who they were. To do so, they wished to avoid, on one hand, the rhetorical and monumental Japaneseness imposed by the wartime government and, on the other, the facile copying of American program-pictures as required by the late Occupation. Thus began a period in which films reflected the harsher realities of postwar life.

The same transformation was occurring in another defeated country, Italy, where in the *neo-realismo* films of Roberto Rossellini and Vittorio De Sica audiences were recognizing themselves on the screen: an image accepted because it was true. In Japan, for the first time, a majority audience was now accepting and encouraging films which showed themselves as they truly were, rather than as they were told to be or as they wished to be.

One of the results was indeed a new kind of realism. This style, as Erich Auerbach reminds us, is always for its own sake. Anything moral or religious or psychological lessens it, because reality is only that which can be made real to the senses. Postwar Japanese film became realistically detailed and nuanced, looking more like life itself.

Drunken Angel, 1948, Kurosawa Akira, with Mifune Toshiro, Shimura Takashi.

The bombed-out set for Kurosawa Akira's *Drunken Angel* (Yoidore tenshi, 1948)—economically reused from Yamamoto Kajiro's *New Age of Fools* (Shin baka jidai, 1947)—looked precisely like many of Tokyo's bombed-out sections; the dark, ruined Osaka streets of Mizoguchi's *Women of the Night* (Yoru no onna-tachi, 1948) were identical to those surrounding the theaters where the film was initially seen; the makeshift homes and squalid rooms of Ozu Yasujiro's *Record of a Tenement Gentleman* (Nagaya shinshi-roku, 1947) looked just like those in which the majority of moviegoers lived.

Women of the Night, 1948, Mizoguchi Kenji, with Urabe Kumeko, Tanaka Kinuyo.

Record of a Tenement Gentleman, 1947, Ozu Yasujiro, with Iida Choko, Kawamura Reikichi.

In a sense, all Japanese cinema became, for a season, shomingeki. All films were about the "little people" because, for the time being, everyone was "little," poor, just scraping by. As Arthur Nolletti reminds us, "The shomingeki was actually a broad, all-inclusive genre . . . as such it was able to accommodate an often wide and disparate range of material and moods, among them farce, light comedy, lyricism, social criticism, and melodrama . . . The genre exhibited remarkable variety in structure, thematic emphasis, and, most of all, style." [8] Amid this variety, the postwar audience was happy looking at what it thought was itself.

The movie which is said to have launched the shomingeki revival is Naruse Mikio's *Repast* (Meshi, 1951). Based on Hayashi Fumiko's last and unfinished novel, and written by

Ide Toshiro and Tanaka Sumie, it is about a poor white-collar worker—the average Japanese "salaryman"—and his wife. The couple decides to break up because they cannot make a go of it. In the end, they realize they are not alone in their plight, that there are many others just like them.

Repast, 1951, Naruse Mikio, with Hara Setsuko, Uehara Ken

A Japanese Tragedy (Nihon no higeki, 1953), written and directed by Kinoshita Keisuke (no relation to Kamei's unfortunate documentary of the same name), was another film which told about the difficulties of the little people. It began with postwar newsreels (the emperor, May Day riots, disasters, crimes), then a title ("Life isn't easy"), followed by another ("All over Japan there is darkness"), and a cut to the main title. The tragedy is personified by a mother who makes every sacrifice for her children, only to have them reject her.

A Japanese Tragedy, 1953, Kinoshita Keisuke.

Though experimental in form (documentary footage, newspaper clips, flashbacks), the picture was seen as an accurate reflection of society at large. It was also seen as fitting into the various subgenres now appearing. If *Repast* was said to be among the first films about wives (*tsuma-mono*), *A Japanese Tragedy* was seen as one of the earlier postwar films about mothers (*haha-mono*).

All these films make use of "American" devices: fast cutting, big close-ups, expressive camera movements. At the same time there was an avoidance of anything hitherto officially identified as "Japanese." The monumental style had been swept away: all was now movement, lightness, novelty. In a way, it was Taisho all over again—new ways of showing, new ways of viewing, and, instead of Lubitsch, there were new, realistic, American directors: John Ford, William Wyler.

Gosho Heinosuke, whose style had always been eclectic, handled this latest accent with great skill and created perhaps the most popular of the new shomingeki in *Where Chimneys Are Seen* (Entotsu no mieru basho, aka Three Chimneys/From Where Chimneys Are Seen, 1953). Written by Oguni Hideo (the "humanist" on the Kurosawa Akira writing team) after a Shiina Rinzo novel, the script was purposely episodic in structure. Though centering around

the anecdote of an unwelcome baby, the film could be seen as a "comedy," a "romance," or a "tragedy." Gosho's gift for blending genres was never more apparent, and each event related to the central philosophy of the film.

In *Where Chimneys Are Seen*, the factory chimneys under which the residents of an industrial suburb of Tokyo live become symbolic of an attitude toward life, one which had long been

Where Chimneys Are Seen, 1953, Gosho Heinosuke, with Tanaka Kinuyo, Uehara Ken.

identified with Gosho himself. The protagonist looks at the chimneys, positioned so that from different directions they never appear the same, and says that life is as each person sees it: "It can be sweet or it can be bitter—whichever you are."

Though the postwar Japanese audience found the new films realistic, Japan, as we have seen, was never enthusiastic about mimesis. Indeed, this particular Gosho film has itself been

found typical of the ambiguity generally characteristic of the Japanese approach to a "slice of life." Raw "reality" is always tempered, and it is a rare Japanese film which attempts anything more.

Imai Tadashi's *And Yet We Live* (Dokkoi ikiteru, 1951), Japan's first independently produced film—made outside the major studios by the newly formed Kindai Eiga—was one such rare film. The film's inspiration was De Sica's

And Yet We Live, 1951, Imai Tadashi. The Ueno Station sequence.

The Bicycle Thief (1949). Imai shot on the streets of Tokyo, around the major downtown railway terminal of Ueno. His camera was often hidden, and the characters were sometimes placed in real situations. At the same time, the actors included stars, members of the Zen-shin-za, and a famous left-wing drama troupe; Imai even engaged a production designer. Japan's documentary-like realism was always tempered. Similarly, Kurosawa had Matsu-yama So design *Stray Dog* (Nora inu, 1949), though it too was shot mainly on the streets of downtown Tokyo. Like Imai, he did this to create a realism independent of reality.

To be sure, all film directors, regardless of nationality, temper their realism, but a number (the postwar Italians, for example) also make realistic fidelity an aim. In Japan, the goal was elsewhere. Even though realism as a style became much more realistic, postwar film was still thought of as a presented experience, one which was controlled and did not simply represent whatever occurred in front of the camera. Perhaps because realism can be felt but not interpreted, Japanese directors made few naturalistic experiments, seeking rather for the means to infuse further meaning into realism.

Stray Dog, 1949, Kurosawa Akira, with Mifune Toshiro.

OZU AND NARUSE

The postwar films of Ozu Yasujiro and Naruse Mikio are examples of the ways in which influences both traditional and modern were blended and the means by which "realism" retained its Japanese accent. Early on Ozu had both consolidated his influences and minimalized his means. Now, after World War II, these two characteristics became further refined.

Unlike many foreign directors, but not unlike a number of Japanese, Ozu usually worked with the same crew and often the same cast: his cowriter Noda Kogo, his cameraman Atsuta Yuharu, art director Hamada Tasuo, and editor Hamamura Yoshiyasu. This staff stayed together for nearly fifteen years—from *A Hen in the Wind* (Kaze no naka no mendori, 1948) to *An Autumn Afternoon* (Samma no aji, 1962). In addition, his actors were often the same: Hara Setsuko, Ryu Chishu, Tanaka Kinuyo, Sugimura Haruko, to name a few.

Likewise, Ozu's methods remained the same. The scripting, for example, was almost invariably begun by inventing the dialogue (it was sometimes only later that the writers assigned the speakers and the setting), and it was often a typical phrase that was the genesis of a film. Though this way of working was not consistent, it does suggest an assumed cast of characters to whom such typical phrases were likely.

This was the Japanese family, and this initial core dialogue led to further situations and often developed into anecdotes—but not, Ozu maintained, a plot. "Pictures with obvious plots bore me. Naturally, a film must have some kind of structure or else it is not a film, but I feel that a picture is no good if it has too much drama." [9] Later, Ozu would be famous for saying that plot used people, and to use people was to misuse them.

We can only infer that it was his characters' singular likeness to complicated life that attracted him to them and that he had no use for the simplified characters so often demanded by plotted drama. Certainly the situations in which Ozu's characters were placed made no such demands. In *Late Spring* (Banshun, 1949), the interest is in the muted relations between father and daughter; in *Late Autumn* (Akibiyori, 1960), the relationship is duplicated between mother and daughter; and in *An Autumn Afternoon*, the focus is again upon father and daughter. In *Tokyo Story* (Tokyo monogatari, 1953), Ozu and Noda examine the relations between the generations, a theme which resurfaces in *Equinox Flower* (Higanbana, 1958).

Ozu was aware of this narrowness of focus (or, if one prefers, this depth). Of *An Autumn Afternoon*, he said: "This film, as usual, is about a man with a daughter soon to be married. I've always said I don't make anything besides tofu." [10] He later, upon another occasion, elaborated: "I'm like a tofu shop—so even when making a brand

Late Spring, 1949, Ozu Yasujiro, with Ryu Chishu, Sugimura Haruko, Hara Setsuko.

Late Autumn, 1960, Ozu Yasujiro, with Hara Setsuko, Tsukasa Yoko.

An Autumn Afternoon, 1962, Ozu Yasujiro, Nakamura Nobuo, Kita Ryuji, Ryu Chishu.

new film, I can't suddenly change to something completely different. It has to be something like maybe fried tofu or stuffed tofu, but certainly not pork cutlets." [11]

Ozu and Noda would render their anecdotes even more laconic. It sometimes seems that the Ozu picture leaves out more than it includes. One critic stated that Ozu was a director for whom "unintentional information was unwanted noise." *Late Spring* leaves out the entire finale, the wedding ceremony; *An Autumn Afternoon* cuts out both the arranged meetings and the courtship, as well as the wedding. In these films we know the daughter has left only because the following scenes finds the father alone. In *Late Spring*, the father returns home, sits down, and, not permitting himself even a sigh,

Tokyo Story, 1953, Ozu Yasujiro, with Yamamura So, Hara Setsuko, Sugimura Haruko, Kagawa Kyoko, Higashiyama Chieko.

Equinox Flower, 1958, Ozu Yasujiro, with Tanaka Kinuyo, Saburi Shin.

begins to peel a piece of fruit. We watch his face, we look at his hands, and we feel his solitude. The ensuing final scene, waves breaking on a nearby beach, suggests that this solitude is permanent. The reasons for leaving out that great plot-closure, the wedding, becomes apparent. Ozu wishes us to consider something more truthful—we are rarely together, we are usually alone.

The ellipses of Ozu films always have this purpose. At the conclusion of *Early Summer* (Bakushu, 1951), we are not shown the wedding but there is a nuptial reference, and the suggestion is made that one such ceremony is much like another. As the anecdote fades away we feel what Ozu intended when he said that "I tried to portray the cycle of life [*rinne*]. I wasn't interested in action for its own sake . . ." [12]

Such traditional ambitions always worked well with Ozu's modernist

Early Summer, 1951 Ozu Yasujiro, with Miyake Kuniko, Nihonyanagi Kan, Hara Setsuko.

structure, perhaps because both were so obviously a part of the country's identification. Speaking of *Equinox Flower* and the conflict among generations, Ozu said that today's young people will become just like their parents. "They'll instinctively behave the same way. Feudalism hasn't really disappeared from the Japanese heart." [13]

Among the ways that Ozu accomplished the creation of such a highly cohesive body of work was that he was able to control the way the film looked. During his career Ozu worked with two cameramen only, Shigehara Hideo and Atsuta Yuharu. He worked with Shigehara from the start, in 1928, up until the cinematographer's retirement, in 1938. Atsuta had been Shigehara's apprentice and was already his assistant on *Dreams of Youth* (Wakodo no yume, 1928). Thus, the Ozu "look" they had created could be continued. Later Ozu would speak with appreciation of Miyagawa Kazuo and his work on *Floating Weeds* (Ukikusa, aka Drifting Weeds, 1959), during the course of whose filming he apparently taught the director all about color photography.

But cameramen have to have something to photograph, and this is usually the actor. Yet, as has been mentioned, Ozu was not actor-friendly. Of his later films he once said: "You won't find any particularly new techniques except for the elimination of acting. When laughs and tears are as inflated as they are in most films today, trained monkeys would be perfectly adequate as actors. Actually moments of joy and sorrow are times when we keep our emotion most to ourselves. I minimize the acting in my films because life is like this." [14]

From the actor's perspective, there are many horror stories, one of the least harrowing of which is that of Ryu Chishu, so often the archetypal Ozu father. "Once I followed Ozu's precise instructions more than twenty times, but each time I went before the camera, I failed to convey the proper feeling and so we finally gave up." [15]

Everything was rigidly controlled. Shinoda Masahiro remembers that when he was an assistant director on the set of *Tokyo Twilight* (Tokyo boshoku, 1957), Ozu told him to put down an extra cushion in a scene they were filming. The young assistant was puzzled: no other character would be entering to sit on it, and it ruined the continuity. When he asked its function, Ozu told him to look through the viewfinder and see if he saw anything different. He didn't. Ozu then said that something was obstructing the composition. " 'It's that black border on the tatami mats that ruins it,' explained Ozu. The cushion was produced and the borders covered." [16]

Tokyo Twilight, 1957, Ozu Yasujiro, with Hara Setsuko, Arima Ineko.

Ozu's sense of composition remained paramount throughout his career. It was so extreme that it led some critics to press charges of formalism during a time when such charges held unfavorable implications. In actuality, Ozu's modernist-inspired formalism was intrinsic to a system of aesthetics which depended much upon the traditional view.

The traditional view is the view in repose, commanding a limited field but commanding it entirely. It is the attitude for watching, for listening, even for learning. Some have consequently compared this position with that of the haiku poet, the tea master, even the priest. Ozu would perhaps have smiled at these comparisons, but it could be said that such a view is inextricable from Buddhist precepts. This vantage point puts the world at a distance and leaves the spectator uninvolved, a recorder of impressions which he may register but which do not necessarily involve him.

Empty rooms, uninhabited landscapes, objects (rocks, trees, beer bottles, tea kettles), textures (shadows on paper-paneled *shoji*, the grain of tatami)—all play a large part in Ozu's later films, and a studied simplicity of view is matched by a like simplicity of construction.

The sequence is near invariable: usually a room in a home is shown, someone enters, the anecdotal point is made in conversation, someone leaves, the room is shown empty. These sequences are arranged in an order which is typically punctuated by shots on the way to the new location. These, as it were, move us there, sometimes accompanied by a bridge of music, sometimes not.

Formalistic as such a procedure might seem, it is never rigidly presented. For example, the opening sequence of *Late Spring*—three shots of Kita Kamakura Station, a temple roof, Enkaku-ji temple as seen from the station, then a shot of Noriko at a formal tea ceremony. Noriko's aunt appears with a pair of trousers she wants Noriko to mend. In particular, she would like her to "reinforce the seat." The higher aspirations of spatial geometry and the tea ceremony are purposely contrasted with such mundane efforts as reinforcing the trousers' seat. The structure is highly formalized but the presentation is decidedly informal.

Besides such spatial formality, another influence on Ozu's presentation of selected reality was the shishosetsu, the autobiographical novel, particularly the work of Shiga Naoya, the sole author Ozu revered and whom, in his journals, he reverently refers to as Master (*sensei*), a term the director otherwise abhorred and forbade in reference to himself. It has been pointed out by critic Imamura Taihei, among others, that both Shiga and Ozu share what he called a typical Japanese attitude. The observer simply tries to recall details of a phenomenon instead of analytically reconstructing it.

While Western plot stresses occurrence, causality, and responsibility, Japan's traditional narrative means, the *suji*, emphasizes sequential flow, connection, association. The presumed Japaneseness of Ozu's approach—his emphasis upon effect rather than cause, upon emotion rather than intellect—coupled with his ability to metamorphose Japanese aesthetics into terms and images visible on film—is what makes him, as is so often said, "the most Japanese of all directors."

Ozu's postwar "Japaneseness" was, from Shochiku's point of view, precisely the reason the director was given such freedom: he was allowed to make any film he wanted, and his films' often large production costs were unquestionably accepted. Not only did Ozu's films do fairly well at the box office, they were also, somehow, "Japanese" in the sense that Kido Shiro understood it.

Such traditionalism, however, is not to be seen as opposed to the director's modernism. Ozu's career followed a pattern which has long been noticeable in the lives of many Japanese: a period of early exploration among things Western, followed by a slow and gradual return to things more purely Japanese. There is another pattern his career paralleled, this one still more universal. When younger, one is more radically individualistic; older, one often becomes more conservative, and individual style merges with what is more commonly accepted.

These very patterns are in turn celebrated in Ozu films. Dramatic tension is obtained by the confrontations among various individuals who are in different sections of the pattern: a father who has "returned," for example, stands in contraposition to a daughter who is on her "way out." This is the pattern of *Equinox Flower*, and it is this film, as already mentioned, which Ozu saw as a demonstration of the survival of the traditional.

In the later films there is never much doubt as to where in the overlapping patterns Ozu's sympathies lie. For this reason there was a period after the director's death when the young disliked his work, calling it old-fashioned, reactionary. This attitude is also reflected in the writings of those Western critics who find the late films merely formalistic academic exercises.

Indeed, Ozu would appear reactionary, since he so continually celebrated those very qualities against which young Japan was in revolt: the traditional virtues of their country. Also, as he himself moved up the social ladder, from the "little people" to the upper bourgeoisie, so did his characters. The fathers of *Passing Fancy* (Dekigokoro, 1933) and *An Autumn Afternoon* display vast social differences, and this, to a certain mentality, is difficult to forgive.

That these traditional Japanese virtues are mainly theoretical in everyday Japan in no way lessens the criticism, nor does it undermine Ozu's position. Restraint, simplicity, and near-Buddhist serenity are qualities which still remain as ideals in the country, and Ozu's insistence upon them as well as the public feeling for or against them make these more than empty hypotheses. Or did. Now that the Japanese have reached the point where they have ceased to be so acutely aware of the distinction between what is Japanese and what is foreign, the entire argument becomes academic. Nonetheless, in accounting for what occurred, one must consider forces no longer vital. While it is true that Japanese tradition has ceased to be an issue, its role in helping form Japan is unequivocal.

Interestingly, following the traditional surmise results in a shared intimacy. Once we join the family in *Tokyo Story*, we do not want the film to end because we would have to leave these people whom we have come to understand. Ozu's assumptions are based upon the perceived fact that all of us are together in this big mess called life.

Among the many affecting and telling exchanges in this film is the one in which the old couple, on their way back home from their disappointing Tokyo trip, sum up their lives.

Tomi: Koichi's changed too. He used to be such a nice boy.

Shukichi: Children don't live up to their parents' expectations. (They both smile.) But, if you're greedy then there's no end to it. Let's think that they are better than most.

Tomi: They are certainly better than average. We are fortunate.

Shukichi: Yes, fortunate. We should consider ourselves lucky. [17]

We are lucky because we can still compare ourselves to others in our group and find that we are not wanting. This is a traditional assumption and one which Ozu maintained until the end. On his deathbed and still capable of irony, the director is reported to have said during a visit by his producer: "Well, Mr. Kido, it looks like home-drama to the end."

Ozu's later traditional assumptions can be more clearly understood when compared with those of a less traditionally-minded director. Sato Tadao has compared Naruse's assumptions with those of Ozu. "Naruse assumes the free attitude of observing his characters as strangers, himself as an outsider, while Ozu assumes the limited attitude of meeting his [characters] as both an acquaintance and a host. This is why the range of Ozu's observations is so remarkably narrow." [18] Naruse certainly meditates upon traditional problems, but these are not just the accepting reflection of Ozu. Naruse seems to imply, in most of his films, that his characters are right to fight against tradition, to attempt to escape, even when they cannot.

It is true that the traditional Japanese outlook is limiting, for better or for worse, and that the majority of Japanese film directors considering these values (and almost every Japanese director had to, so much were they a part of Japanese life) agreed that this limitation was for the worse, though the dismissal of tradition is not always as abrupt as in that of a Kurosawa or an Imai.

In a Naruse film, the family is usually held together by bonds so strong that no single member can break them. "My films deal exclusively with the home. So do most Japanese films. It is in this fact that we find a major fault of Japanese pictures—the home is simply too narrow a place in which to set everything . . . I've been filming small Japanese rooms for so long that wide screen doesn't end up being anything especially different."[19] If a family member does manage to break free from this domestic prison—as does the heroine of *Untamed* (Arakure, 1957)—she (or he) will remain outside the system and be more or less free. This is unlike an Ozu film, where the dissolving of familial bonds (the director's perennial theme) is seen as a distinct loss. The couples in Naruse's *Repast*, *Husband and Wife* (Fufu, 1953), and *Wife* (Tsuma, 1953) are locked up together, as are the siblings in *Older Brother*, *Younger Sister* (Ani imoto, aka Frère et Soeur, 1953.) The older geisha in *Late Chrysanthemums* (Bangiku, 1954) attempts to break free and reunite with an old lover only to face disappointment. The geisha in *Flowing* (Nagareru, 1956) are already at the end of their economic freedom, though they don't yet know it. For Naruse, traditional life is a daily round of fixed customs. Even the ways of expressing emotion are formalized. Thus the slightest personal emotional reaction has major and often unfortunate consequences.

Wife, 1953, Naruse Mikio, with Takamine Mieko.

Flowing, 1956, Naruse Mikio, with Yamada Isuzu, Kurishima Sumiko.

So, too, in *Mother* (Okasan, 1952), which Naruse called his "happiest" film, the mother, unable to support her family now that her husband is dead, has only the alternative of sending off her youngest daughter to relatives who can afford her. For the daughter this may mean freedom, but for the mother it means loss. Though the director had no say in the creation of the script ("it was never an idea or a proposal, I was offered the finished script, an original screenplay by Mizuki Yoko"), he accepted it at once because it was "about hardships in the family, which is the thing I understand best of all."[20]

Mother, 1952, Naruse Mikio, with Kagawa Kyoto, Okada Eiji.

Tragedy is constantly hanging over Naruse's characters, and they are never more vulnerable than when they for once decide upon a personal course of action. In Ozu a similar tragedy is averted through acceptance. In Naruse, if averted at all, it is because the protagonists find a kind of freedom in their mere resolve. The heroine of *Wife, Be Like a Rose* (1935) sees her father find contentment in the midst of unhappiness. In *Evening Stream* (Yoru no nagare, 1960), the young daughter—loving her mother's lover—consciously turns toward the traditional: she becomes a geisha. In *Repast*, the wife decides that the differences between her and her husband constitute a bond. "My husband here, asleep beside me," she says at the end of the film. "Perhaps I am happy . . . maybe my happiness, my happiness as a woman—doesn't it lie here?"

For Naruse, the relativistic optimism of Ozu's films is impossible. That fine study of postwar despair, Naruse's *Floating Clouds* (Ukigumo, 1955), is a tragedy precisely because the heroine unsuccessfully decides to get from life what she wants, even if only this once. The director embraced a similar resolve: "My object was the same as hers—to pursue the problem between men and women to the very end, no matter how painful. Mizuki's script [after a Hayashi Fumiko novel] was something great, and after I had finished shooting I knew I'd portrayed exactly what I wanted in exactly the way I wanted." [21]

Floating Clouds, 1955, Naruse Mikio, with Takamine Hideko, Mori Masayuki.

The heroine (Takamine Hideko) fights against the hopelessness of poverty-stricken postwar life and achieves a kind of recognition only after she dies. The man she loved (Mori Masayuki) realizes, too late,

When a Woman Ascends the Stairs, 1960, Naruse Mikio.

that he loved her as well and, in a touching scene, makes up—literally: he applies lipstick to her dead face before the funeral. In *When a Woman Ascends the Stairs* (Onna ga kaidan wo noboru toki, 1960), a Ginza bar madame (Takamine again) is profoundly dissatisfied with her empty life. Yet when she makes one gesture toward freedom, everything goes wrong. She retreats. Again she climbs the stairs to her bar—the motif which appears over and over in the film with its ironic suggestion of "getting to the top"—and in the final scene we watch as her face once more assumes the mask of the entertainer.

Yet Naruse also shows us from time to time that the characters' ignorance of approaching doom, their fortunate innocence, constitutes a kind of beauty, a sort of strength. Though happiness is impossible, contentment—however unwisely based—may yet be achieved. Such is the case in the long, unfolding final sequence, a kind of coda without dialogue, at the conclusion of *Flowing*. Only the elderly maid (Tanaka Kinuyo) knows what will happen in the geisha house where she works—that the house has been sold, that there are only a few more weeks left in which to enjoy a seemingly secure life. The others continue as they always have. The daughter (Takamine Hideko), who will never again try to escape, contentedly works her sewing machine; the mother (Yamada Isuzu) hoping for the future, practices her samisen.

It would have been out of the question for directors to make such coherent statements as Ozu and Naruse did had they not enjoyed the full backing of their studios. Most film directors had no choice in what they directed. They took what they were given. Increasingly, in postwar Japanese cinema, directors had been refused the status given Ozu, Naruse, or Mizoguchi. Newer directors had fewer options, and such auteur-like "statements" become rarer. It was only a very strong-willed director, such as "Emperor" Kurosawa Akira, who could achieve this control.

Naruse, once he had left Shochiku, found company support. Originally PCL extended this because of the money-making novelty of such films as *Wife, Be Like a Rose*. Contemporary-looking, with willful heroines, filled with the latest techniques from Hollywood, these pictures were seen as modern, untraditional, even attractively "Western." In a rare moment of humor, Naruse dubbed PCL (Photo-Chemical Laboratories) "Pork-Cutlet-Lard," a reference to its Western-tinged output that also reflected the Japanese perception of foreign food.

Yet, as the traditional returned during the prewar years, Naruse's pictures came to be seen as conservative and hence equally bankable. When PCL was incorporated into Toho, Naruse was a part of the package. And though he was given a number of scripts uncongenial to him, he was nonetheless often allowed to make those he really wanted to. In this way, with the writers, actors, and technicians he had in his unit, he was able to build an "oeuvre" and become what would later be known as an auteur.

Naruse's vision became, as he grew older, more and more traditional. While tradition itself was seen as one of the major impediments to a happy life, it was precisely these fought-against views that informed his view of life. Naruse's means, perhaps consequently, also became highly traditional.

Like a Zen master, Naruse refused to define. Tanaka Sumie, with whom a large part of *Repast* was written, said the director would demand "hundreds of pages of rewrites" without clarifying what it was he wanted. According to Mizuki Yoko, "Naruse always refused to discuss, or even mention, meaning or theory. Sometimes I would say, 'The theme should—'

and he would gently but firmly cut me off by saying: 'It will come out by itself.'"[22] Many are the stories of actors driven to despair by the director's unwillingness (or inability) to describe what he wanted. Nakadai Tatsuya (who played the bartender in *When a Woman Ascends the Stairs*) said that he had never in his entire career suffered such frustration.

Naruse's filmmaking methods themselves became more and more conservative. "I moved less and less until I finally stopped altogether. *Repast* contained very little camera movement, you couldn't find a single instance in *Mother*, and the only camera movement in *Lightning* [Inazuma, 1952] was necessitated by an actor's movement."[23]

It is singular to find Naruse drawing so close to Ozu but, as we have seen, they had never been far apart. They liked each other's films, and Kido was acknowledging a certain resemblance when he said that he didn't need another Ozu. Yet in fact, Naruse is an alternative to Ozu. The difference is in their attitudes toward the traditional. Ozu more or less accepted it and Naruse more or less did not.

On the other hand, the directors' means are close, and at times their attitudes toward the traditional, toward "Japaneseness," can seem identical. They even come together on a major theme of Japanese classical literature, the celebration of evanescence, mono no aware, which they see in purely cinematic terms. Ozu has said he felt early on that all films were ephemeral nonsense and that he still believed "the attractive thing about film is this transience, this mistlike vanishing quality."[24] Similarly, Naruse was of the opinion that films "always vanish a few weeks after release. Perhaps this is what films should be, things that live on only in the audience's memory or else vanish into thin air."[25]

MIZOGUCHI AND THE PERIOD-FILM

The traditional view is not the only one, and a concern with traditional problems is not the Japanese director's only concern. The country is as contemporary as it is traditional, as forward-as it is backward-looking, as radical as it is conservative. If a concern for the traditional might suggest a similarity among those directors who interest themselves in it, there is, at the same time, the greatest divergence and dissimilarity among those directors who interest themselves in the less traditional.

Naturally, all good directors, traditional-minded or otherwise, are individualists. This is as true for Ozu, Naruse, and Mizoguchi as it is for Kurosawa, Ichikawa Kon, and Imamura Shohei. The only directors who are not individualists are those not seriously interested in making good films. Ozu cherished his self-imposed limitations; Kurosawa would not tolerate limitations. One might even arrange this tolerance of limitations on a kind of scale in which Ozu would represent the extreme right and Kurosawa the extreme left.

Mizoguchi might be placed in the middle of the spectrum, since his films partake of both extremes. Indeed, in such a picture as *Sisters of the Gion* (1936), both extremes are personified: the elder sister is from a world which Ozu knows well, the younger might eventually fit into the world of Kurosawa. Mizoguchi himself perhaps thought so. Apropos of his attitude toward limitations and his use of realism he once said to Shimizu Hiroshi: "I portray the extraordinary in a realistic way. Ozu portrays the ordinary in a realistic way—which is even more difficult." [26]

Certainly one finds in Mizoguchi, particularly in the postwar films, a balance between classic poles: the acceptance of traditional values (the affirmation of the home, the joy of finding freedom in restraint) and the vindication of the individual (the impatience with restraint, the criticism of older values, the joy of overcoming obstacles and enlarging horizons). This is especially apparent in a single but important aspect of Mizoguchi's later films: his treatment of women. The director's major theme (in spite of his eclecticism, all of Mizoguchi's pictures can be seen as arranged around a theme) is women: their position, or lack of it; their difference from men; their relations with men; and the intricate relationship between women and love.

Ugetsu (Ugetsu monogatari, 1953) presents the theme in perfected form. A potter (Mori Masayuki), caught between opposing forces in the sixteenth-century civil wars, leaves his wife (Tanaka Kinuyo) and small son behind, and goes to sell his wares. There, a beautiful lady (Kyo Machiko) buys his stock, takes him home, and seduces him. He stays on only to awaken and find both mansion and lady gone. He has been enchanted; the lady was a ghost. When he finally reaches home, he discovers his wife waiting for him. When he awakens the next morning, he discovers that she, too, already dead, was also a spirit.

The two women might represent the opposite ends of Mizoguchi's theme. This is more than simply profane versus sacred love. Rather, both women died wanting love. The spirit in the haunted mansion is to be equated, not contrasted, with the loyal and loving wife. They are equal, and it is this parallel that interests Mizoguchi.

Likewise, in *Utamaro and His Five Women*, the point is that these women, despite their differences, are equated by their love for the artist. In *Women of the Night*, and in the director's last film, *Red Light District* (Akasen chitai, aka Street of Shame, 1956), the women, dissimilar in all else, are the same in their hunger for love in the midst of mercantile sex.

Red-light District, 1956, Mizoguchi Kenji, with Kyo Machiko, Mimasu Aiko, Wakao Ayako, Urabe Kumeko, Sawamura Sadako, Shindo Eitaro.

The Life of Oharu, 1952, Mizoguchi Kenji, with Tanaka Kinuyo.

Some films contain within them the extremes of Mizoguchi's richly ambivalent attitude toward the traditional, while others insist upon but one extreme. *The Life of Oharu* (Saikaku ichidai onna, aka The Life of a Woman by Saikaku, 1952) shows the heroine (Tanaka Kinuyo) falling from court lady to common prostitute. It does so with such close regard that the feudal institutions under which she labors are revealed as responsible. In *A Story from Chikamatsu* (Chikamatsu monogatari, aka The Crucified Lovers, 1954), a woman (Kagawa Kyoko) is forced into adultery by the very suspicion of it. It is only after her jealous husband drives her, innocent, from his house that she becomes "guilty." In *Sansho the Bailiff* (Sansho dayu, 1954), mother and daughter (Tanaka Kinuyo and Kagawa Kyoko, respectively) are brutally separated and never reunited. When the son finally discovers his aged, blind mother, she does not ask what happened to him, but rather she only asks after her daughter—another woman. In *The Princess Yang Kwei Fei* (Yoki-hi, 1955), the Chinese concubine (Kyo Machiko) so loves her emperor (Mori Masayuki) that she lives on after her execution. The final scene finds the aged ruler listening to the sound of her loving ghostly voice.

It might be thought unwise to categorize a director judging merely by "content analysis," since most directors have no control over their content—their producers do. In the case of Mizoguchi, however, content goes far toward describing character. The director was so eminent within Daiei that, like Ozu at Shochiku and Naruse at Toho, he not only chose his own material but his cameraman (Miyagawa Kazuo), his writer (Yoda Yoshikata) as well as the actors with whom he wished to work.

It is through the manner in which Mizoguchi made his films that the traditionalist in him is more clearly viewed. He was found old-fashioned—that is, traditional—because he was both literary and painterly: he thought in terms of character rather than camera, and he composed his scenes in a pictorially pleasing manner. Indeed, to remember Mizoguchi's films is often to remember a series of beautiful stills: the lovers on the lawn in *Ugetsu*, the couple in the boat in *A Story from Chikamatsu*, the aged woman sitting in the sun in *The Life of Oharu*, the mother and her children in the forest in *Sansho the Bailiff*.

Ugetsu, 1953, Mizoguchi Kenji, the lawn scene, with Kyo Machiko, Mori Masayuki.

A Story from Chikamatsu, 1954, Mizoguchi Kenji, the boat scene, with Kagawa Kyoko, Hasegawa Kazuo.

Sansho the Bailiff, 1954, Mizoguchi Kenji, the forest scene, with Tanaka Kinuyo (left).

It is perhaps indicative of Mizoguchi's growing concern with tradition that half of his postwar films were jidaigeki while most of his prewar films were not. The director might have disagreed with this statement. He has said that he only began making his prewar historical features because military censorship had become so strict that, though he wanted to continue developing the realistic contemporary experiments he had began in *Osaka Elegy*, the authorities forbade it. And as for his *The Loyal Forty-Seven Ronin*, he said: "We were virtually forced to make it." [27]

Once the Occupation was over, however, Mizoguchi became interested in the genre, which he saw as having suffered severe attrition. In 1952, Mizoguchi said that "since the deaths of Yamanaka Sadao and Itami Mansaku, the period-film has become an utter shambles. Both Ito Daisuke and Kinugasa Teinosuke are no longer active—they might as well have retired. It oughtn't to be this way." [28]

About the former director, Mizoguchi was later particularly stern: "Ito Daisuke, who more than anyone had defined the period-film's conventions for decades—giving [the films] a dazzling vitality, found that his only recourse was to repeat his initial innovations with increasing monotony and sterility." [29] He was equally harsh about the general standardization of jidaigeki: "This descent into rigid stylization can be seen [even] in the yakuza-film genre and the outlaw heroes portrayed by Tsuruta Koji and Takakura Ken." [30]

Mizoguchi would, in effect, create the style of the postwar jidaigeki, something which the other great period-film practitioner, Kurosawa, was happy to affirm when he said that Mizoguchi was the Japanese director he most admired and respected, that he liked his period-pieces, particularly *A Story from Chikamatsu*.

Kurosawa, however, did not think Mizoguchi was particularly good with samurai: "For example, *Ugetsu*, the battle scenes and swordfights. He couldn't really express samurai emotions. I suspect these scenes would have been better if he'd allowed me to direct them. After all, when he did *The Loyal Forty-Seven Ronin* he left out the final climactic scene—the samurai attack." [31] Indeed, Kurosawa's idea of "samurai emotions" was not compatible with the kind of pictorial traditionalism toward which Mizoguchi was moving. Samurai needed fast editing—as Kurosawa would go on to demonstrate in *Seven Samurai* (Shichinin no samurai, 1954)—not the one-scene, one-shot method, the subject long held from far away.

Mizoguchi's realistic patterning of history, on the other hand, needed just this kind of detailed distance. One long remembers, from *Ugetsu*, the potter and the princess almost lost in a field of superlative beauty; the little boy at the film's end who places the offering on his mother's grave while the camera, with the gentlest, most reverent of motions, begins to climb until finally the entire settlement by the lake is seen in a long, still shot which matches the slow pan from lake to village at the beginning of the film.

Mizoguchi's balancing of traditionalism's demands—condemning the moral consequences while, to be sure, availing himself of the aesthetic means—has resulted in films which illustrate the very dynamic which created them. As the director Masumura Yasuzo, no friend to tradition, has said: "Most filmmakers feel a need to keep up with the latest fads by riding the crest of each 'new wave.' But if 'modernization' is the standard of excellence, then Mizoguchi is at the bottom of the barrel. He never worked with new-wave ideas. In fact, he portrayed the world of shimpa, which was outdated before he began . . . His rigid abstinence may seem stupid to those who value the benefits of Westernization, but this stupidity is just what led him to the truth."[32]

NEW MEANS: *JUN-BUNGAKU*, COMEDY, AND SOCIAL ISSUES

As the Occupation ended and a more independent Japan was envisioned, directors increasingly searched out alternate roads to truth, beyond the traditional one. Concomitantly sought were the means to express these. The postwar emphasis upon the individual rather than the group occasioned a number of changes, among them the very way in which a craft such as filmmaking was learned.

The traditional method was no longer possible. Until the 1950s, established directors had under them a stable of assistant directors. These were trained both directly and by example in the proper ways to make a film. Complementing these were like groups in which the chief cameraman had his pupils and the chief scriptwriter had his apprentices. In essence, tradition was taught—though very often older directors (Yamamoto Kajiro was a famous example) gave his youngsters very free rein.

Some have seen the break in tradition occurring because of the Toho strikes. Kurosawa has said that "it was actually at that point, with the firing of these young assistant directors, that the Japanese film industry began its decline . . . I don't know if the older people stayed on in the movie industry because young people weren't trained, or if young people weren't trained because the older ones were staying on—in any event, no one took time for training young people."[33]

So, increasingly, the young people were forced to learn their trade as best they could. Some found that (just as in the early days of Japanese cinema) the best school was a theater showing Western films. The new young directors, particularly after the Occupation was over, learned the lingua franca of cinema, what has been called the "Hollywood codes," by watching foreign pictures. Here, along with the new freedoms occasioned by both the end of World War II and the conclusion of the Occupation, were new subjects and new attitudes as well as new genres—or old genres newly viewed.

One of the most important developments, along with the recently invented genres of postwar comedy and the social-issue film, was the revival of the jun-bungaku movement. If it had helped forestall the prewar censors, it now offered in postwar Japan a way to counter the commercialism of a growing number of postwar films—concerned as most of them were with capturing on film the first kiss or the new sensation of the boogie-woogie.

Gosho Heinosuke had long felt that "pure literature" offered better prospects for cinema than commercial fiction. Here, he and Toyoda Shiro had presented a more or less united front. They were able to interest their studios in their plans by pointing out that the audience, already familiar with the book, would hence more readily go see the film.

Gosho's interest in classic Japanese literature began long before the war, with his adaptation of the Yamamoto Yuzo novel *Everything That Lives* (Ikitoshi ikeru mono, 1934). After the war he turned a number of distinguished novels into distinguished films. Takami Jun's work was the basis for *Once More* (Ima hitotabino, 1947), Higuchi Ichiyo's for *Growing Up* (Takekurabe, 1955), Oda Sakunosuke's for *Fireflies* (Hotarubi, 1958), and Yasushi Inoue's for *Hunting Rifle* (Ryoju, 1961).

Gosho always tried to get from his literary originals the best possible scripts, sometimes by writing them himself. His aims were deceptively simple. He elaborates: "The purpose of a film director's life is to describe the real life around him and create works which express the true feelings of human beings."[34] Perhaps that is one of the reasons why he preferred to work with serious novels—the novelists' goals and his were one and the same.

The methods were also similar. A Gosho film sometimes begins like a book. In *Where Chimneys Are Seen*, a voice-over in first person presents himself and his wife to the camera. ("This is where we live, and here is my wife. And this"—shot of the bare foot of a man still asleep in the futon—"is me.") Later on in the film, Gosho, in novelist-like fashion, changes viewpoint. The opening voice is that of Uehara Ken, playing the husband. At the climax, the voice-over is that of Akutagawa Hiroshi, playing a tenant concerned about the baby.

There is a sequence in *An Inn in Osaka* (Osaka no yado, 1954) which owes much to the contrasts more often seen in fiction than in film. It begins with a scene where the maid looks at the drawing of a cow her son has sent her. Then comes a scene of cruelty involving the callous landlady and the cow drawing. This is followed by a funny scene showing the landlady's remorse. Then comes the real heartbreaker. The mother is forced to display her few belongings in the search for a missing thousand-yen note. Their shabbiness is revealed along with the few small toys she has managed to buy for her child should she be able to take him on a trip, an unlikely eventuality.

An Inn in Osaka, 1954, Gosho Heinosuke, with Otowa Nobuko and Sano Shuji.

By carefully balancing and mixing the tender, the cruel, the comic, and the pitiful, Gosho orchestrates the response he desires in a manner which places him in the tradition of the great narrators, novelists. He shows us objects and allows the emotional content of each to speak for itself. In the resulting conflict of emotion any thought of sentimentality is lost. That *An Inn in Osaka* is not based on a novel but on an original script by Yasumi Toshio indicates even more clearly the novelistic concerns of both the scriptwriter and the director.

By refusing to comment, Gosho can get away with even more. At the end of *Growing Up*, a boy gives the girl an iris. As she crosses the drawbridge into the house of prostitution, she unthinkingly throws it away. The iris, landing in a dirty canal, becomes a symbol which through careful usage manages to regain something of its original urgency. In the book by Higuchi Ichiyo, the author refused to explain. In the film, Gosho refuses to linger.

Growing Up, 1955, Gosho Heinosuke, with Yamada Isuzu, Misora Hibari.

Toyoda Shiro brought his own means to the genre. One critic describes the director's approach: "Toyoda subscribed to the principles and practices of the representational narrative, yet his . . . literary depictions are a springboard to experiences quite different from those of the printed word." [35] Often written with Yasumi Toshio, a scenarist who specialized in jun-bungaku adaptations, Toyoda's films begin from a novelistic origin, then, in subtle ways transcend this narrative.

The Mistress, 1953, Toyoda Shiro, with Akutagawa Hiroshi, Takamine Hideko.

In *The Mistress* (Gan, aka, Wild Geese, 1953), based on a Mori Ogai novella, cinematic means often take the place of verbal description. In the final scene, the young heroine walks along the pond where she first spoke with a student whom she will not meet again. She turns to watch the wild geese as they start from the marsh. Toyoda's camera turns to catch her face, and finds hope. The viewer is able to complete the story.

Marital Relations (Meoto zenzai, 1955), based on Yasumi Toshio's rendering of Oda Sakunosuke's novel, takes as its theme the compromise between traditional ideals and personal freedom. The couple—a young no-good (Morishige Hisaya) and his geisha mistress

Marital Relations, 1955, Toyoda Shiro, the michiyuki scene with Awashima Chikage, Morishige Hisaya.

A Cat, Shozo, and Two Women, 1956, Toyoda Shiro, with Kagawa Kyoko, Morishige Hisaya.

Snow Country, 1957, Toyoda Shiro, with Ikebe Ryo and Kishi Keiko.

(Awashima Chikage)—eventually, almost without knowing it, give up the benefits of traditional Japanese life in order to be together. At the end, wastrel and paramour go off in the snow together, a completely recognizable parody of the michiyuki, that kabuki convention where the traditional lovers set out into the cold, cold world. By having one genre comment upon another, Toyoda presents a wry parallel which a novel could only suggest.

Another michiyuki parody is seen at the conclusion of *A Cat, Shozo, and Two Women* (Neko to Shozo to futari no onna, 1956), the Yasumi-Toyoda adaptation of Tanizaki's novel by the same name. The callow hero Shozo (Morishige again) is much more in love with his cat than with either of his women (Yamada Isuzu and Kagawa Kyoko). Shozo's position is a familiar one. He resents tradition (the older wife), but is afraid of the anarchy of freedom (the younger one)—so he is happy only with Lili, his cat, a creature absolutely free yet reassuringly domesticated. When Shozo finds his recently runaway pet at the end, both now drenched in a summer shower, he picks her up, saying, "We'll just go away together . . . we won't go back."

In these films and many other bungei-eiga—Yasumi-Toyoda's *Snow Country* (Yukiguni, 1957), Inoue Yasushi's *Madame Yuki* (Yushu heiya, 1963), Shiga Naoya's *Pilgrimage at Night* (Anya koro, 1959),

and Nagai Kafu's *Twilight Story* (Bokuto kitan, 1960)—Toyoda turns written words into moving images. By using traditional literary material, he makes films which seriously and sensitively reflect the concerns of the authors.

Still, when turned into film, literature is invariably reinterpreted. An example is Yoshimura Kozaburo's *The Tale of Genji* (Genji monogatari, 1951), which, like every other version of *Genji*, reflects its own time as much as it does that of the Murasaki Shikibu novel. Yoshimura's *Genji* was filmed just one year before the Occupation was over, and in it we see Japan trying to redefine itself. The scenes are plainly mid-twentieth century. The court ladies

The Tale of Genji, 1951, Yoshimura Kozaburo, with Hasegawa Kazuo, Kogure Michiyo.

neglect their calligraphy lessons and, groupie-like, race to the doors to watch the sexy Genji pass. Even if Aoi no Ue dies in properly resigned and womanly fashion (as in the novel), she is played by Kogure Michiyo, who had just played the gangster's moll in Kurosawa's *Drunken Angel* (1948). Murasaki herself is Otowa Nobuko, the quintessential 1950s modern girl.

Equally of its time was Kurosawa's *Rashomon* (1950). Based on two Akutagawa Ryunosuke stories, which in turn are based on anecdotes from the Heian period (794–1194), the film famously recounts the story of a man and wife (Mori Masayuki and Kyo Machiko) set upon by a robber (Mifune Toshiro). During the trial, each gives his or her version of the incident, but the versions are so apparently variant that magistrate and spectators alike are unable

Rashomon, 1950, Kurosawa Akira, Mifune Toshiro, Mori Masayuki, Kyo Machiko.

to decide what had actually occurred. A woodcutter (Shimura Takashi), the sole witness, and an unreliable one at that, provides his tale in the framing story.

In explaining the script he wrote with Hashimoto Shinobu, Kurosawa was able to give his assistant directors some insight: "Human beings are unable to be honest with themselves about themselves . . . Even the character who dies cannot give up his lies when he speaks to the living through a medium. Egoism is a sin the human being carries with him . . . This film is like a strange picture scroll that is unrolled and displayed by the ego. Some say they can't understand this script at all, but that is because the human heart itself is impossible to understand."[36]

Akutagawa's original story was about relative truth, but Kurosawa's film is about the kind of relative reality which perhaps only film can offer. We watch each version of the story—each one as "real" as the other—all of them expressed through the amalgam of play of light and shadow created by Miyagawa Kazuo, Kurosawa's cameraman. With its psychological modernity and its postwar questioning, the film was a literal re-creation of the Akutagawa story. The seeming reality of each version makes us question that of the others. The author's original intention had been anecdotal, but the film is now considered a contemporary existential statement—each one of us invents a personal reality.

Among the many interesting facets of this multifaceted film is that, within its structure, it displays one of the Japanese cinema's defining characteristics, the opposition between a represented reality and that reality itself—a trait we have already seen in the antithesis between the presentational and the representational.

Though the producer of *Rashomon*, Nagata of Daiei, famously said that he had no idea what "his" film was about, the questioning mode of the picture appealed not only to the Japanese (it was one of the top ten moneymakers of the year) but to everyone else as well. This became apparent when the film won the Venice Golden Lion, the Academy Award for Best Foreign Film, and other prizes—becoming the most honored of all Japanese films and, for a time, the single Asian picture most viewed in the West.

Literature offered one means of expressing an individual view. From an accepted original came a new and personal interpretation. Another means was comedy. Indeed, in the postwar era, individuality was a new way of being funny. To be sure, there had been several kinds of comedy in prewar Japanese cinema, from the romps of Saito Torajiro to the social comedies of his disciple, Ozu. What was novel was an individualistic irreverence—one which resulted in satire, a new genre for Japan.

Two of the more successful of the postwar satires were both based on a prewar model. Both *The Girl Who Touched His Legs* (Ashi ni sawatta onna, 1952), directed by Ichikawa Kon, and *The Girl Who Touched His Legs* (Ashi ni sawatta onna, 1960), directed by Masumura Yasuzo, were based on the 1926 Abe Yutaka film of the same title. One reason for the remakes was that Ichikawa had been an assistant of Abe and that Masumura was an assistant of Ichikawa. Another reason was that the roots of this type of situation-comedy extended back to the Taisho days of ero-guro. The erotic element was the protagonist herself, a pickpocket who, as though unaware, would allow her shoes to graze the pant-leg of her proposed prey. The grotesque were the cartoon types she ran into: wide-eyed innocents, bumbling policemen, stuffy bureaucrats, officious housewives.

In postwar Japan, the satire was much broadened to include people in all walks of life.

This democratic approach cut across social boundaries. These films may have even been structured so as to make this possible. The original Abe movie was about the upper middle-class in a hot spring resort. Both the Ichikawa and Masumura films, however, take place in the upper lower-class milieu of trains and boats, where potentially comic social intercourse was inevitable. Likewise, Shibuya's *No Consultations Today* (Honjitsu kyushin, 1952) is about a doctor whose day off at the clinic is complicated by a wide variety of patients who just cannot wait. Ichikawa Kon's *A Crowded Streetcar* (Man'in densha, 1957)—for which the assistant director was Masumura Yasuzo—takes its story from the title—a slice of life in crowded, proletarian postwar Tokyo.

Satire even further-out (from the Japanese point of view) was shown in one of the earliest postwar comedies, *Emperor's Hat* (Tenno no boshi, 1950), directed by Saito Torajiro. The plot alone would have constituted a political crime in prewar Japan: a man working in a museum steals the emperor's hat from its display case and, with it, gets a job as a haberdashery sandwich man. The plot revolves around the reactions of the police and public to this bit of lèse majesté.

Still more controversial was Ichikawa's satire *A Billionaire* (Okuman choja, 1954), one of the writers of which was Abe Kobo. One of the characters has as her slogan "Make Atom Bombs for World Peace," and is shown in the midst of constructing just such a peace-maker. At the end of the picture she has finally completed her project and is confidently awaiting its explosion.

Among the new satirists of the 1950s, the most outspoken was Kinoshita Keisuke. His earlier debut film, *The Blossoming Port*, poked discrete fun at national policy. Two sharp confidence men deceive simple islanders into backing a fake shipbuilding company. It is the bumbling virtues of the islanders, however, not national policy that makes honest men of the crooks. The director went on to make a series of more memorable satires.

The Blossoming Port, 1943, Kinoshita Keisuke, with Higashiyama Chieko.

Here's to the Girls (Ojosan kampai, 1949), about the love affair between a low-class roughneck and a girl from an aristocratic family, herself one of the new-poor of the period, was in itself practically a burlesque of the old-fashioned Shochiku "woman's film." *The Broken Drum* (Yabure daiko, 1948) took on the Japanese father—the damaged musical instrument of the title. A construction-company father tries to run his family along feudal lines and runs into trouble when wife and children ignore him. There is an added resonance in that the famous and manly jidaigeki star Bando Tsumasaburo plays the hapless father. The cowriter of this picture was Kobayashi Masaki, who would later have more to say about authority.

The Broken Drum, 1948, Kinoshita Keisuke, with Bando Tsumasaburo, Mori Masayuki.

Kinoshita's best satires, perhaps the finest made during this period, were *Carmen Comes Home* (Karumen kokyo ni kaeru, 1951)—coincidentally Japan's first color film—and *Carmen's Pure Love* (Karumen junjosu, 1952). In the first, a striptease artist, whose stage name is Carmen (Takamine Hideko), returns to her rural hometown where her postwar manners embarrass and even frighten the simple country folk. Satirized were not only the pretensions of postwar society but also the credulity of those who clung to prewar beliefs.

Carmen Comes Home, 1951, Kinoshita Keisuke, with Takamine Hideko, Kobayashi Toshiko.

Carmen's Pure Love, 1952, Kinoshita Keisuke, with Kobayashi Toshiko, Takamine Hideko.

The "sequel," which came out one year later, was created after Kinoshita had made a trip to Europe to meet his idol, René Clair, a director who was much admired—Ichikawa Kon has also mentioned his influence on such early films as his *A Crowded Streetcar*. Again, Takamine was the stripper, but now she was also the symbol of Japan, and so all sorts of postwar types were satirized: the feudal hidebound and the ultra-Americanized, alike. The plot parodies maternal love, patriotism, marriage, and much else. The widow of an army officer tries to run her house like a barracks; an avant-garde artist's studio is so cluttered with mobiles that there is no room to move; one character blames the A-bomb for everything including stuck windows; and, in one comic sequence, a pro-militarist election candidate's procession collides with a demonstration of Mothers Against War.

Kinoshita was also one of the few postwar directors who wrote almost all of his own scripts. In this he was like Ozu and Kurosawa, though unlike them, he usually wrote his scripts by himself. He, too, had his own cinematic "family" to work with. Kusa Hiroshi was always the cinematographer, and the director's younger brother, Chuji, always wrote the music. Kinoshita also maintained a stable of actors. These included some of Japan's finest character actors along with such stars as Sano Shuji and Sada Keiji. The familial aspect was, in part, real—Kinoshita would eventually arrange the marriage between Takamine Hideko and his favorite assistant director (later himself a director), Matsuyama Zenzo.

Since Kinoshita—rather than his company or his producer—was responsible for his films, these formed a coherent whole. His oeuvre extended from the postwar satires to the family melodramas that practically defined the "Shochiku Ofuna style." This resulted in an even broader spectrum when Kinoshita eventually began interesting himself in a more conservative style of filmmaking. From the fast-cutting of Clair (who had an influence on postwar Japanese directors similar to that which Lubitsch had on the prewar group), Kinoshita turned to longer scenes and a more plainly presentational delivery.

One of the most successful films of this later style was *She Was Like a Wild Chrysanthemum* (Nogiku no gotoki kimi nariki, 1955), based on the Ito Sachio novel, where the memories of an old man (Ryu Chishu) recalling his first love affair are shown in the style of Meiji daguerreotypes.

She Was Like a Wild Chrysanthemum, 1955, Kinoshita Keisuke, with Tanaka Shinji, Arita Noriko.

One of the most popular of the later films was *Times of Joy and Sorrow* (Yorokobi mo kanashimi mo ikutoshitsuki, aka The Lighthouse, 1957). Here Kinoshita supported rather than criticized in this story of a couple (Takamine and Sada Keiji) who tend lighthouses in various parts of Japan. The end assumption is that living in relatively uncomfortable living quarters and doing one's duty pays off in all the joys and sorrows mentioned in the main title. Like Ozu's old couple in *Tokyo Story*, they have done "better than most." For this conventional story Kinoshita devised a conservative narrative style which contrasted long, placid panoramas with occasional flurries of stormy cutting.

Times of Joy and Sorrow, 1957, Kinoshita Keisuke, with Sada Keiji, Takamine Hideko.

Even more traditional-seeming was *Ballad of Narayama* (Narayama bushiko, 1958), based on the Fukazawa Shichiro novel, to be filmed again, some twenty-five years later, by Imamura Shohei. Still later, the story formed the basis for Shindo Kaneto's *Will to Live* (Ikitai, 1999). The Kinoshita version was set in a small community in the northern mountains whose custom it was to expose the aged to the elements so that there would be more food for the young. The barbarity of the custom did not move Kinoshita so much as did the weeping

Ballad of Narayama, 1958, Kinoshita Keisuke, with Takahashi Teiji, Tanaka Kinuyo.

son being forced to deposit his aged mother on top of Mount Nara. Here the son's love for his mother echoes the equally thwarted love of the mother who sees her son off to the front in *Army*. Yet, whereas the latter film provokes our indignation through implied criticism of the military, the former elicits our admiration for the traditional respect with which youngsters presumably regarded their elders in rural Japan.

Stylistically, *Ballad of Narayama* was also deliberately traditional. Though it was shot in both color and wide screen, the director relied on deliberate stage effects, choosing to frame the story in narrative and scenic devices taken from kabuki. Traditional theater was purposely duplicated, resulting in, among other things, a certain distancing of the more extreme emotions—as in the aged mother who, to impair her ability to eat and hence provide more food for the young, breaks her sound teeth on a millstone. Another result of the director's stylistic choice, however, is a blunting of social criticism in the interests of pictorial drama.

The River Fuefuki (Fuefuki-gawa, 1960), Kinoshita's last important picture, chronicles five generations of a poor farming family during the sixteenth century. Again, the film has a rich theatricality about it, emphasized by the use of color which purposely imitates Japanese woodblock prints. In addition, particularly in the battle scenes, Kinoshita uses still photographs which both halt and hold the action. Though, in 1960, this technique might have been described as innovative, it also much resembled that of the *kamishibai*, the traditional paper-slide theater to which Mizoguchi's one-shot, one-scene style had been scornfully compared.

The River Fuefuki, 1960, Kinoshita Keisuke, with (left) Takamine Hideko.

The antitraditional nature of the film's theme is merely appearance. What is apparent in the picture as a whole is that Kinoshita rejects only the worst of traditional life: the rest he now approves. The final scene shows the last remaining member of the family picking up the banner of the ruling clan, for which he and his ancestors have traditionally fought, as it floats down the river. With a gesture of rejection, he then throws it back. Nevertheless, one reason he does so is not ideological but because his mother had been killed. After all, the family is most important.

Certainly it is a blend of criticism and compassion that distinguishes Kinoshita's most popular film, *Twenty-Four Eyes* (Nijushi no hitomi, 1954). This story of the life of an elementary school teacher on Shodo Island in the Inland Sea, based on the Tsuboi Sakae novel, is once again about the inhumanity of wartime oppression. The teacher (Takamine) sees a whole generation of her pupils scarred by war. This thoroughly antiwar picture is so seemingly undemanding of emotion and yet so skillful in obtaining it that audiences all over the world have been reduced to (or ennobled by) tears.

Twenty-Four Eyes, 1954, Kinoshita Keisuke, with Takamine Hideko.

War is terrible and inhuman, with much resulting suffering, but the Kinoshita film, somewhat like shimpa itself, finds virtue in adversity. The director may present this in different ways. Some were radical. *Snow Flurry* (Kazahana, 1959), a severely fragmented story of rural giri-ninjo, full of flashbacks and ellipses, was a predecessor of the Shochiku "new wave," though never given credit for it. In the main, however, Kinoshita opts for a traditional way of presenting his narrative. Thus, even in the films whose theme is antitraditional, tradition usually informs the style. Perhaps this is because the films, which like kabuki itself find fault with authority, can only advise traditional remedies: *shikata ga nai* (can't be helped), *gambaranakucha* (you just got to put up with it). They do not offer solutions. Doing so would be within the expectations of the social-problem film.

This new genre, the social-problem film, did not even have a name until *shakai-mono* was suggested. To be sure, social criticism had long existed, but the examples had never been numerous enough to form a genre—a few social comedies (Ozu's among them) and the all-but-banned keiko-eiga.

These latter "tendency" films located social problems within Japan's political system and advocated reform, in some cases, revolution in others. All were vigorously censored, as we have seen, and it was not until the war was lost that anything like a politically committed social-problem film was possible. Among those who initially explored the dimensions of this new genre were the directors who had made keiko-eiga, such as Kamei Fumio and Sekikawa Hideo, as well as the recent socially committed directors Imai Tadashi, Yamamoto Satsuo, and Shindo Kaneto.

In an interview with Imai, Joan Mellen asked: "Would you say that the essential theme of your films is the struggle between the ruling class and the working class?" He answered: "No, not so much the class struggle. This theme is more appropriate to the works of Yamamoto Satsuo."[37] So it is. In his *Street of Violence* (Pen itsuwarazu: Boryoku no machi, aka Boryoku no machi, 1950), based on an actual attempt to suppress a journalist's investigation of collusion between a rural police chief and the local gangster bosses, Yamamoto's theme was supposedly the democratization of local government. Nevertheless, the methods used resembled those of the Communist union which produced the film. In his *Sunless Street* (Taiyo no nai machi, 1954), an adaptation of Tokunaga Sunao's proletarian novel of 1929 about a prolonged strike at a printing plant, there was a conscious application of Soviet "social realism" and noticeably idealized portrayals of the working class.

Imai's methods were much less politically motivated. In response to another of Mellen's questions, he made an attempt to pin down terms: "The word 'political' is difficult to define. It can be broad, meaning 'social,' but 'social' can also mean 'political.'" He added: "I cannot formulate the theme of my work very well, but after perusing my pictures and listening to critics talking about them, it seems to me that my work is centered on human tragedies—those created by the weight of war, poverty, and social oppression."[38] This perhaps accounts for Imai's liking for Kinoshita, a director with similar themes and one whom Imai said he most admired.

Yet, compared with Kinoshita, Imai's pictures have a decidedly more "political" orientation. Max Tessier has put it succinctly: "If Imai's options lead him at times to prefer propaganda to art and the didacticism of simple statement, his sincere humanism always protects him from the dangerous temptations of dogmatism." As for the director's methods, Tessier has said that realism functions not only as a mirror of reality but, "more importantly," as "a stone thrown against that mirror."[39] Whether this means that the higher reality of political "realism" is used to shatter the complacent realism of everyday movie life, or not, Imai's degree of political intention remained troubling (or reassuring) to his audience.

Blue Mountains (Aoi sammyaku, 1949) is about a love affair condemned by feudalistically minded elders, until teachers and fellow students join the fight on the side of young love. *Until the Day We Meet Again* (Mata au hi made, aka Till We Meet Again, 1950)—no relation to the lost Ozu film of 1932 of the same title—shows oppressed young lovers destroyed by the war: he dies at the front, she dies during an air raid. By the time Imai made *And Yet We Live*, discussed earlier, the Occupation had changed its direction, and films about the exploitation of workers were considered suspiciously leftist.

With the Occupation over, Imai went on with films of social realism, turning his attention to the recent war. The result was the immensely popular *The Tower of Lilies* (Himeyuri no to, 1953), showing the deaths of a number of combat nurses during the American invasion of Okinawa. The film was named after the monument there dedicated to them. The major blame for the tragedy was put on "traditional" Japanese "fatalism," the fact that these girls had been, in effect, trained to die. Another film about the traditional oppression of women, though under feudal society, was *Muddy Waters* (Nigorie, aka Troubled Waters, 1953), based on four stories by Higuchi Ichiyo, as scripted by Mizuki Yoko and Ide Toshiro.

Both films are examples of what the critics called Imai's *nakanai* realism (realism without tears), in contrast to both the Chaplinesque smiling-through-the-tears of, say, Gosho Heinosuke, and the shameless *namida chodai* (lots of tears, please) of the average melodrama makers. Such, however, was not Imai's major concern—social drama itself was.

Blue Mountains, 1949, Imai Tadashi, with Ikebe Ryo, Sugi Yoko.

Until the Day We Meet Again, 1950, Imai Tadashi, with Okada Eiji, Kuga Yoshiko.

The Tower of Lilies, 1953, Imai Tadashi.

Muddy Waters, 1953, Imai Tadashi, with Awashima Chikage.

One of the director's most politically sensational films was *Darkness at Noon* (Mahiru no ankoku, 1956), a film which shared nothing but the title with Arthur Koestler's well-known novel. The story is based upon an actual occurrence and assumes the innocence of the apprehended. Imai has said that it was the story of four young men who were arrested, tortured, and forced to confess to a crime which they did not commit. In reality, no political charges were made against them.

Darkness at Noon, 1956, Imai Tadashi, with Hidari Sachiko, Kusanagi Kojiro.

They were known as "bad boys" and had been marked by the police for some time. The director claimed that the young men were not anti-establishment in any way but that the police, when faced with an unsolved murder, framed them.

Written by Hashimoto Shinobu (who had scripted *Rashomon* and many other films), the picture takes a social issue and dramatizes it. That it did so when the trial for the four was still pending (Japanese justice can take long to achieve its results) caused some criticism but did nothing to affect their fate—they were sentenced to death.

Miscarriages of justice and the prevailing "feudal" thought were the stuff of Imai's later films as well. Among these was *Night Drum* (Yoru no tsuzumi, aka The Adulteress, 1958), a version of a Chikamatsu Monzaemon puppet play, written by Hashimoto Shinobu and Shindo Kaneto. In it, a samurai who does the proper feudal thing and kills both his wife's seducer and the wife herself, then realizes that by having satisfied a feudal society he has destroyed his own life.

More modern targets included, in *Kiku and Isamu* (Kiku to Isamu, 1958), the plight of mixed-

Night Drum, 1958, Imai Tadashi, with Mikuni Rentaro, Arima Ineko.

blood children in an uncomprehending and uninterested society, and, in the multipart *River Without a Bridge* (Hashi no nai kawa, 1968–70), the pathetic lives of those whom society attempts to ignore—the *burakumin* (the outcast class). All of these pictures and many more (Imai made a total of nearly fifty) were perhaps influenced by his political affiliations, though they were also distinguished by his emotional commitment.

Given such antitraditional content, one might expect the films to employ a like style: something incisive, brilliant—like the Russians in the twenties. Here, however, one would be disappointed. Imai's films are almost without style—that is, a consistent visual-aural presentation.

Unlike other directors of his generation, notably Kinoshita and Kurosawa, who underwent long apprenticeships under directors Shimazu Yasujiro and Yamamoto Kajiro, respectively, Imai entered the cinema untrained. This does not mean that his point of view is amateurish or awkward, but it explains his stylistic diffusion or, another way of looking at it, his freedom from limitations.

Imai's individuality is found in his statement, in what the film is about, rather than in a strongly individual style. Though his methods are eclectic, his content is remarkably coherent. Yoshimura Kozaburo, then an assistant to Shimazu Yasujiro, remembered early on showing Imai around the lot and then telling him, "a person like you would be better suited as a movie critic."[40]

The creation of a style depends upon a personal vision and the means to communicate it. Company directors take the house style, Communist directors use the party style, Catholic directors adopt a churchly style. Other directors move among available styles, and only a few evolve their own. In Japan, the social film seemed to demand the kind of realism that the directors had observed in the Italian neo-realist films (De Sica, for example, had a strong influence on early Imai). On the other hand, the demands of the Japanese tradition were nonrealistic. The resulting dilemma (if that is what it is) is seen in the social films of Shindo Kaneto.

Shindo was originally a scriptwriter, working most noticeably with Mizoguchi Kenji, for whom (on *The Loyal Forty-Seven Ronin*) he also served as chief assistant director. Later, he would make a film about his mentor: *Mizoguchi Kenji: The Life of a Film Director* (Aru eiga kantoku no shogai: Mizoguchi Kenji no kiroku, 1975). As a scriptwriter, Shindo was unusually eclectic, having written films as different as Shimizu's prewar *Children in the Wind*, and both *Ball at the Anjo House* and *The Tale of Genji*, by Yoshimura.

The director came to wider notice when the Japan Teachers' Union sponsored *Children of Hiroshima* (Gembaku no ko, 1952), the film version of a best-selling Osada Arata novel. By this

Children of Hiroshima, 1952, Shindo Kaneto, with Otowa Nobuko.

time, Hiroshima had become the loaded political subject that it was to remain. The Americans, who had originally banned any mention of it in Occupation Japan, were still trying to find reasons for their atrocious actions ("shortened the war . . . really saved a number of lives"), and Japan was divided into those who saw the bombing as more akin to an act of nature, just one more calamity for suffering Japan, and those who wished to use it as a political stick with which to beat Uncle Sam. This latter aim, also that of the Soviets, was reflected in the film requested by the Teachers' Union.

Though shot in the ruins of Hiroshima and using many of its inhabitants, Shindo's film was thoroughly nonpolitical, even traditional. It opens with the school-teacher heroine (Otowa Nobuko) going into the city and, in effect, acting as the viewer's benshi. "*Minasama*" (Ladies and Gentlemen), she begins, and then takes us on a guided tour. She tells us about the tragedy, and (in various flashbacks to the fatal day) she shows it to us.

The presentation is traditional and the acting is stagey—close to the standards of shimpa, though most of the actors were from shingeki. A result of the presentational stance is that we are told much more than we are shown. Hence, a demanded emotion becomes sentimentalism. One is reminded of James Joyce's phrase, "sentimentality is unearned emotion." Certainly, the film is no answer to the emotional demands earned by the subject: the annihilation of a city and its inhabitants. Though the picture was a popular success, the sponsor complained that Shindo had made a tearjerker and that all political orientation was destroyed.

Consequently, the Teachers' Union next backed a project which would, in their words, "genuinely help to fight to preserve peace." The result was Sekikawa Hideo's *Hiroshima* (1953), a film whose political orientation was obvious. Yagi Yoshitaro's script was all the Union could have hoped for, and if the results were both stage-bound and melodramatic (as the West was to see five years later in those scenes included—uncredited—in Alain Resnais's *Hiroshima, Mon Amour*), the context was politically correct.

Shindo is in the West most remembered for *The Naked Island* (Hadaka no shima, aka The Island, 1960), a documentary-like feature film about a hard-working family on an island in the Inland Sea—a film which Oshima Nagisa once called "the image foreign people hold of the Japanese."[41] Made entirely without dialogue, it escaped much of the sentimentality which conversations about how awful life is would have made inevitable. We observe the social conditions which make the islanders' labor necessary and we draw our own political conclusions.

The Naked Island, 1960, Shindo Kaneto, with Otowa Nobuko.

As in the works of Sekikawa Hideo, Yamamoto Satsuo, Kamei Fumio, and Imai Tadashi, the party line is never completely invisible in Shindo's earlier films. Yet his concerns are so humanistic that they make political distortions difficult. In any event, in time all of these directors mellowed, if that is the word. They either stopped directing or changed their direction. Among the latter, Shindo's change was perhaps the most divergent.

Onibaba (The Hole, 1964) marked the beginning of this change. This first period-film by the director was about two women (Otowa Nobuko and Yoshimura Jitsuko) who prey on samurai. Shindo returned to this theme in the less successful *Black Cat* (Yabu no naka no kuroneko, 1968). Both films might have been read as antigovernment allegories, but so filled were they with naked flesh and sex (a subject hitherto alien to the Shindo oeuvre) that no one did.

That sex and politics are bedfellows is not a new observation but, given the almost suspiciously pure nature of Shindo's pictures up until this point, the change

Onibaba, 1964, Shindo Kaneto, with Otowa Nobuko, Yoshimura Jitsuko.

came with a certain suddenness. Shindo himself, however, found the shift logical. He told Joan Mellen: "No, I am not at all pessimistic about politics [and] my idea of sex is nothing but the expression of the vitality of man, his urge for survival."[42] And indeed it is but a small step to move from the imperative of the proletariat's survival as a social class to the quest for the means of continuation of its members. Certainly, the same route is to be observed in the films of many a leftist director, as in the case of Sekikawa Hideo, who was now making pictures about the sex trade, such as *Kamo* (1965), *Himo* (1965), and *Dani* (1965).

Whatever the reason, Shindo was now making lyrical studies of sexual subjects, among them: *Lost Sex* (Honno, 1966), *The Origin of Sex* (Sei no kigen, 1967), *Hadaka no jukyusai* (aka Live Today Die Tomorrow, 1970), right up through *Owl* (Fukuro, 2003), something like a modernized *Onibaba*. Though the hero of the first film in this series loses his potency after being exposed to the atom bomb, one could not consider the picture a political statement.

Shindo's was but one example of changes in the social-problem film. There were many others. A later example is the work of Kumai Kei, who came into international prominence with his *Sandakan 8* (Sandakan hachiban shokan: Bokyo, 1974), a strong indictment of the Japanese wartime policy of providing "comfort women" for the imperial troops. One such woman, now old but still victimized (Tanaka Kinuyo), tells her sad story to a young reporter. (The only other director to make serious use of this subject was Imamura Shohei in his documentary, *Karayuki-san: The Making of a Prostitute* [Karayuki-san, 1973]). Kumai went on to create one of his most controversial shakai-mondai films in *The Sea and Poison* (Umi to dokuyaku, 1986), a disclosure of the Imperial Army's medical experiments on American POWs. The director works on, honestly disclosing. He is one of the few directors to have made a serious picture about Japan's most sensational shakai mondai—the Aum Shinrikyo, the religious cult responsible for the Tokyo subway sarin nerve gas attack in 1994. His *Darkness in the Light* (Nippon no kurai natsu: enzai, 2001) is about the "tryout" for the attack in the provincial capital of Matsumoto, where a number of people were killed and one of the injured was accused of the crime by the local authorities. Police and media connived to convict him and it was, ironically, only the Tokyo attack that led to an understanding of the man's innocence. Film directors outraged enough to make films on such subjects and brave enough to endure the resultant flak are rare.

A more famous example of the socially conscious director willing to expose problems is Ichikawa Kon. Director of eighty-six films, he worked under Ishida Tamizo—remembered for *The Blossoms Have Fallen* (Hana chirinu, 1938), scripted by Morimoto Kaoru—and was originally a house director doing what the producer wanted: His *One Thousand and One Nights* (Toho sen'ichiya, 1947) was billed as "Japan's Own *It Happened One Night*."

Later, in the 1940s and into the 1950s, Ichikawa became better known for his Daiei satirical comedies. It was not, however, until he made *The Harp of Burma* (Biruma no tategoto, aka The Burmese Harp, 1956) that he was judged a "serious" director.

The Harp of Burma, a Nikkatsu antiwar film based on a novel by Takeyama Michio, was a very serious

The Harp of Burma, 1956, Ichikawa Kon, with Yasui Shoji, Mikuni Rentaro.

picture indeed about a soldier who decides to stay behind after World War II to become a monk in order to bury the dead. The theme was right for the times and the picture was popular enough that the director remade it in 1985, using the same script. The scenarist was Wada Natto, a very talented screenwriter whom Ichikawa married. That she was responsible for many of the excellent qualities of Ichikawa's films is evident in a certain decline in their quality after her death.

Together, Ichikawa and Wada had an early interest in "social problems," as their satirical comedies witness. They found a natural subject in the rise of postwar problems with "rebellious" youth, the theme in *Punishment Room* (Shokei no heya, 1956), a picture about restless youths and their reckless ways. The novel from which Wada fashioned the script was by Ishihara Shintaro—later a right-wing politician and, however improbably, the governor of Tokyo. It is from Ishihara's novel *Season of the Sun*—itself

Punishment Room, 1956, Ichikawa Kon, with Wakao Ayako, Kawaguchi Hiroshi.

soon made into a film by the same name (Taiyo no kisetsu, 1956), by director Furukawa Takumi—that *taiyozoku* was coined as a genre.

The taiyozoku phenomenon, a true creation of the media and due in large part to Ishihara's novels, drew the public's attention to the dangerous antics of "the sun tribe"—that is, the young. The topic spawned a number of films, the one best remembered being Nakahira Ko's *Crazed Fruit* (Kurutta kajitsu, aka Affair at Kamakura, aka Juvenile Passion, aka This Scorching Sea, 1956), a picture which also propelled the career of its young hero Ishihara Yujiro, Shintaro's younger brother.

Punishment Room, though it did not star the phenomenally popular Yujiro—Yujiro belonged to Nikkatsu, while this was Ichikawa's first film for Daiei—it did do well enough to convince the company to let Ichikawa and Wada make several more literary adaptations—their best work, and to which we will return. The two were also allowed to make the war film they had really wanted to make—*Fires on the Plain* (Nobi, 1959). Unlike *The Harp of Burma*, which could be considered conciliatory, this later film was deliberately confrontational.

Scripted by Wada after the Ooka Shohei novel, *Fires on the Plain* is about the final days of a Japanese battalion in the Philippines after the defeat.

Fires on the Plain, 1959, Ichikawa Kon, with Funakoshi Eiji.

Told mainly through images (there is almost no dialogue in the first half and little throughout), the story is one of despair. Scenes remain long in the mind: the slow march through the jungle, a plane approaches, the soldiers all fall to the ground, the plane passes, only half the men rise to stagger on and not one looks back; a man tasting salt for the first time in months, an involuntary tear running down his cheek; men dead on their haunches, like animals, with even the dignity of death taken from them.

Japan had never seen a war film like this, and those responsible for such experiences had never been so indicted. There was some public concern, but the political import was muted by the honesty of the script and the appalling beauty of the images. In this sense, *Fires on the Plain* resembled *Five Scouts* (1938), a film which had begun the cycle that Ichikawa's picture now ended.

A completely different social issue was taken on by Ichikawa and Wada in *Bonchi* (1960), their adaptation of a Yamazaki Toyoko novel. The film title is untranslatable—it is an Osaka dialect word used to designate a feckless elder son. In this film the son is purposely spoiled because his merchant family is entirely run by women.

That Japan is really a matriarchy is a proposal sometimes heard, and Ichikawa would later make a comedy about women really controlling things, *Ten Dark Women* (Kuroi junin no onna, 1961). In this latter film the ladies gang up on the two-timing gent and conspire to do him in. Among its many delights is a long scene between two of the most vengeful of the women (Kishi Keiko and Yamamoto Fujiko) in which their murderous conference takes place in front of an insipid Japanese-style painting showing two kimonoed Japanese women behaving as ideal Japanese women should.

Bonchi, 1960, Ichikawa Kon, the Girls' Day scene, with Mori Kikue, Yamada Isuzu, Ichikawa Raizo.

Ten Dark Women, 1961, Ichikawa Kon, with Kishi Keiko, Yamamoto Fujiko.

In *Bonchi*, Ichikawa's women create the very situations from which the women in more traditional films are always attempting, unsuccessfully, to escape. The grandmother is a matriarch who has decided that the family needs an heir, and this means that the playboy grandson must marry and produce. What they want is a girl child so that they can later "adopt" a husband for her as a provisional head of the family—just as the boy's own father was adopted—and thus keep power among the women.

A suitable marriage candidate is found for the grandson, and the grandmother and her daughter plot the outcome—a charming scene where the two, like little girls, are sitting before the traditional doll display on Girls' Day, as seemingly innocent as the girl children they are talking about. Later, the two delve into the toilet to try to discover if the new wife's menstrual cycle has halted, thus heralding the arrival of the wanted child. After they leave, the camera regards the gleaming bowl in the half light, as beautiful as a porcelain vase.

We are shown all this with an honesty that is ruthless and, at the same time, with a beauty that transfigures everything it touches. In this film, as in the others on which they worked together, Ichikawa and his cameraman, Miyagawa Kazuo—who shot both *Rashomon* and *Ugetsu*, among many other films—insist that power and beauty are no strangers. The juxtaposition is particularly acute in the scene where, the first child being a boy, the furious grandmother sends the new wife back home. It is so quietly beautiful that one all but forgives the family its wretched self-interest. It is one long, immaculately lit, single scene: five people talking in the late summer afternoon.

In *The Sin* (Hakai, aka The Outcast, 1962), a brooding and brutal film about the discrimination directed against the outcast class, the burakumin, Ichikawa alternates scenes as black as they are bleak against backgrounds of enormous beauty. The morality of this Ichikawa-Wada film is always balanced by its aestheticism. While there were few social themes as potentially explosive as that of the marginalized burakumin, a form of discrimination which still continues in contemporary Japan, there are few black-and-white films in postwar Japanese cinema which are so compositionally perfect, so aesthetically right. The film's appearance inexorably undercuts its meaning.

The Sin, 1962, Ichikawa Kon, the final snow scene, with Ichikawa Raizo, Fujimura Shiho.

A scene in which the young school teacher "confesses" to his pupils that he is of the pariah caste—a very painful sequence—is followed by the scene in which he must leave the small mountain community. He is met by the maid at the school, the only one who cared for him. They say goodbye. Suddenly it begins to snow. The camera turns to catch this mantle of white slowly covering the black forests, the dark mountains. This lovely moment is a metaphor for the entire film—beauty covers a darker hidden truth. Aesthetics support morality—or even take its place.

Ichikawa waited for weeks in his expensive mountain location for that snowfall. Though some directors—Ozu, Mizoguchi, and Kurosawa, among them—would have gotten away with spending that much of the company's money for reasons that all film companies everywhere would regard as bad business, Ichikawa's company, Daiei, dissatisfied with the returns on his films, decided to curb the director's expensive tendencies.

Among the resultant indignities was the order to remake a venerable tearjerker. This was *An Actor's Revenge* (Yukinojo henge, aka The Revenge of Yukinojo, 1963). The original was a melodramatic scenario by Ito Daisuke which had already been filmed before—a three-part version under the same title by Kinugasa Teinosuke, released in 1935–36. It was obviously not a film for the mordant Ichikawa. Nevertheless, director and scriptwriters saw possibilities.

The film focuses on Yukinojo, a kabuki actor specializing in female roles, and this was something that interested Ichikawa. In fact, the director's very first picture was a puppet version of the similarly named doll drama *Musume Dojoji* (1946)—the maiden at Dojoji Temple being, of course, a man. The director had always been fond of the stage, puppets, cartoons, and the like. He was later to interest himself in the Italian mouse puppet, Topo Gigio, and—as he was originally a graphic artist—he had long maintained an interest in

An Actor's Revenge, 1963, Ichikawa Kon, with Wakao Ayako, Hasegawa Kazuo.

stylistic experiments, such as the artificial decor and painted sets of his *Men of Tohoku* (Tohoku no zummu-tachi, 1957) and Miyagawa Kazuo's artificially filtered color work in *Younger Brother* (Ototo, aka Little Brother/The Younger Brother, 1960), where the screen was made to look like a hand-tinted daguerreotype. Asked about the greatest influence on his work, Ichikawa answered, without hesitation, that it was Walt Disney.

The Yukinojo project also offered possibilities within the vast, uncharted realm of kitsch. Wada found the original scenario so bad it was good, and kept almost everything. Ichikawa also insisted upon the star of the original version—the aging matinee idol, Hasegawa Kazuo—and proceeded to find out, as he phrased it, "what movies can do." The resulting film is a tour de force of great virtuosity in which the director deliberately scrambled stage and screen, tried every color experiment he could think of, and created one of the most visually entertaining films of the decade.

Ichikawa being Ichikawa, he also succeeded in making a very disturbing picture. The love scenes—an elderly but dignified Hasegawa playing a man playing a woman, and the young Wakao Ayako—are both arresting and troubling. Innuendos, always to be inferred, give all of these scenes a certain edge. The spirit of camp is never far away, yet one remains uncertain whether Hasegawa is being made a fool of or is giving a great if ambivalent performance. One consequently begins to feel, little by little, the pathos and terror which must have originally lurked in this hackneyed little story. Disney would not, perhaps, have appreciated the nature of the tribute but he might have admired the presentational display.

Not only is the production self-consciously stagelike, it also shows Yukinojo himself as the final incarnation of Onoe Matsunosuke, that first actor to move from stage to screen, by means of the long, stationary shot, the frontal view, and the two-dimensions of this ideal and theaterlike world. Though much had occurred in the intervening half century, the amount of sheer presentation originally assumed by the Japanese cinema still remains in pictures such as this.

Ichikawa also experimented with more realistic representation—the documentary. He was commissioned by Toho to make a film on Little League baseball, *Youth* (Seishun, 1965); by Olivetti to make a half-hour film on the old capital, *Kyoto* (Kyo, 1968); and by the 1970 Osaka Exposition to make *Japan and the Japanese* (Nihon to nihonjin, 1970, n.s.), a half-hour documentary designed to be shown on a mammoth nine-panel screen in the Japanese Pavilion.

The first and finest of these commissions was *Tokyo Olympiad* (Tokyo Orimpiku, 1965), a documentary of the 1964 Tokyo Olympic Games. It was scripted by the poet Tanikawa Shuntaro—later to write another exceptional scenario for *The Wanderers* (Matatabi, 1973). Tanikawa created a structural space for the director to work in. Aesthetically, the picture is superb—a masterpiece of visual design. One remembers the incisive use of slow motion during the track-and-field events; the beautiful repeated shots in the pole-vaulting competition; the fast zooms in the shot-put event; and the long, brilliant climax of the marathon—the work of the director and a staff of nearly six hundred people, including sixteen cameramen led by Miyagawa.

None of this, however, was what the Olympic Organizing Board wanted. Not only had Ichikawa refused to monumentalize the games, he had humanized them. In the uncut version (never publicly screened), the camera turns time and again from the major events to capture details: the spectators; athletes at rest; those who came in, not first, but third—or last. Japanese victories are not favored. At the end, the celebrations over, the stadium is empty. A man with a ladder crosses the field; from far away comes the sound of children at play. The games were, after all, only games. They are over and life goes on. Much of this footage has never been publicly screened, and among examples of film vandalism, the case of *Tokyo Olympiad* must rank as especially regrettable. That the picture was also brilliantly presentational, rather than representational in a more documentary-like way, did not, of course, offend the Board. But what they had wanted was presumably a Leni Riefenstahl kind of aggrandizement, and this they did not receive.

In Ichikawa's single finest picture, *Conflagration* (Enjo, aka Flame of Torment/The Temple of the Golden Pavilion, 1958), these humanized aesthetics were already evident. Written by Wada after the popular Mishima Yukio novel, translated as *The Temple of the Golden Pavilion*, the film is about the acolyte who deliberately set fire to and destroyed Kyoto's famous Kinkakuji. The visuals are superb. As his ex-assistant director, Masumura Yasuzo has said:

"He possesses tremendous compositional skill, rivalled only by Kurosawa Akira. His talent allows him to create first-rate images that easily escape realism and result in superior films." [43]

Particularly impressive is the use of architecture—the theme, after all, of the film. The action is balanced by an architectural detail which, as

Conflagration, 1958, Ichikawa Kon, with Ichikawa Raizo, Nakamura Ganjiro.

one scene follows another, re-creates the temple itself. Or, another use of architecture, Ichikawa set his acolyte high on the balcony of the Nanzenji in Kyoto, then shot from far below with a telephoto lens. The result is a bas-relief of the foreshortened temple roof, the student black and tiny and lost amid the gray maze of tile and weathered wood. Ichikawa and Miyagawa use the wide-screen format as no one had before, capturing textures in the crispest black and white.

Through dialogue and controlled flashbacks, we are told the story of this boy who eventually comes to destroy what he most loves—the pavilion. These architecture-filled scenes serve to emphasize the narrative, the boy's awareness of his isolation and loneliness. Though aesthetically prodigal, the film uses beauty to envelop and to define the acolyte and his feelings, to create an atmosphere, a space to hold them.

Equally moving in its disturbing beauty is *Odd Obsession* (Kagi, aka The Key/Strange Obsession, 1959). Loosely based on the Tanizaki novel *The Key*, beauty is again linked to its opposite: the picture equates love with illness. The screen is filled with hypodermic needles, catheters, unmade beds—all filmed by Miyagawa in muted color. Erotic obsession reaches claustrophobic intensity, and the spectator is made a participant.

Odd Obsession, 1959, Ichikawa Kon, with Kyo Machiko, Nakamura Ganjiro.

A typically extraordinary scene finds the husband (Nakamura Ganjiro) making love to the wife (Kyo Machiko). For an instant we think we are witnessing his orgasm. Then we realize that he has had a stroke. Love has turned to death before our eyes. Though the film is flawed by its lazy conclusion (the maid done it), the tensions of its theme and of Tanizaki's original intentions are still there—something which is not true of Ichikawa's next Tanizaki adaptation and his last film of any note, *The Makioka Sisters* (Sasame yuki, 1983), a commercial venture which has been called "a kimono show." Critic Iwasaki Akira summarized his view of the director's shortcomings during a symposium in 1963: "Ichikawa must have thematic limits he can work in . . . The Ozu Tofu Restaurant can sell only tofu. The Ichikawa Restaurant, however, can sell both tofu and pork cutlets, but not tofu, pork cutlets, beefsteak, and tempura."[44]

The equilibrium of a film such as *Conflagration*, for many, remains typical of the fine balance which the Japanese film sometimes attains. An acute eye, tempered by a controlled and directed vision; realistic performances, particularly that of Ichikawa Raizo (who also starred in *Bonchi* and *The Sin*); and a social theme (National Treasure Burned Down) humanized—all contributing to a controlled atmosphere which, no less than in *Souls on the Road*, defines character and creates meaning.

Another director concerned with the Japanese social dilemma was Yoshimura Kozaburo. Though he worked under Shimazu Yasujiro, it was Mizoguchi Kenji whom he most admired. Nonetheless, he felt that the Japanese tradition was a poor one for making films. He once said that Japanese fiction after a thousand years still lacked dramatic construction. It was all mono no aware, and this naturally spilled over into films.

Though eclectic, Yoshimura's films are about traditional subjects, for example, the tradition of unfortunate oppression borne by Japanese women. In *Clothes of Deception* (Itsuwareru seiso, 1951), a film much like Mizoguchi's *Sisters of the Gion*, the modern ideas of the heroine (Kyo Machiko) clash with traditional behavior and get her into trouble. In *Women of the Ginza* (Ginza no onna, 1955), the geisha's life is seen as one of smiling tragedy. In *Night River* (Yoru no kawa, aka Undercurrent, 1956), a traditional Kyoto girl, played by Yamamoto Fujiko, is led astray by her modern ideas. In *Night Butterflies* (Yoru no cho, 1957), yet another version of *Sisters of the Gion*, Yamamoto Fujiko is the traditional bar mistress from Kyoto, and Kyo Machiko plays her Tokyo rival. In *The Naked Face of Night* (Yoru no sugao, 1958), however, one woman rebels: Wakao Ayako, on her way up in the world of traditional Japanese dance, pushes aside her mentor, Kyo Machiko.

All of these very successful Daiei films treat the fact of being a woman as though it is a social problem. It is women who are exploited and forced into inauthentic lives, and this problem is society's. Yoshimura's *Ball at the Anjo House* reflected criticism of Japan through the rup-

The Naked Face of Night, 1958, Yoshimura Kozaburo, with Wakao Ayako, Kyo Machiko.

tured institution of the family. The director's later films share the same theme, but the focus is women, their plight, and their occasional bravery. These themes, presented with a grace and fluidity which reveals the influence of Mizoguchi, contributed to the laconic dramatic construction which helped define the Daiei house style.

Masumura Yasuzo, a Daiei director and pupil of both Ito Daisuke and Mizoguchi as well as Ichikawa, owed much to Yoshimura as well. It was from the latter, he once said, that he learned his editing methods. These were developed in opposition to a tendency in Japanese films to play every scene out, even after it has made its necessary points. This can be salubrious, as when Ozu does it, but in lesser hands it can be tiresome, as when it arises from the so-called "realism" of shingeki, where everything should be "just like life."

Yoshimura would frequently make a direct cut right from the high point of one scene to another. This telescoping of effect—one dramatic point piled on top of another—is a method of construction which gives his films their pace. Masumura, using the same method, cut even more stringently and created an even livelier effect, something which many other Daiei directors emulated.

An example of this manner of pacing is *Warm Current* (Danryu), a picture made by Yoshimura in 1939, and remade by Masumura in 1957. Both versions are about a young doctor responsible for a small hospital who must choose between a spoiled, rich girl and a dedicated nurse. The Yoshimura version moves swiftly but is filled with careful revelation of character, sustained by a finely contrived hospital atmosphere. Masumura's version moves much faster—at a pace quite foreign to most Japanese films of its time. One scene is shoved off by another almost before it is done. Character and atmosphere may suffer, but storyline interest increases.

It is not surprising that many Japanese critics, tired of the valid but discursive styles of Ozu or Mizoguchi, should have greeted the novelty of a faster-moving film enthusiastically. The young Oshima Nagisa describes his reaction after watching the flight of the rebel couple —a sequence shot with a hand-held camera following the couple's motorbike—in Masumura's *Kisses* (Kuchizuke, 1957). Oshima recounts how he "felt that the tide of the new age could no longer be ignored; that a powerful, irresistible force had arrived in the Japanese cinema." [45] The upshot of such a style is that the director has almost no time in which to establish character, and such fast cutting is certainly not conducive to the creation of atmosphere.

The incisive nature of this style, so like a series of short, declarative sentences, fitted Masumura's adversarial stance. It was he who, upon returning from a season of study at the Centro Sperimentale in Rome, called for nothing less than the destruction of mainstream Japanese cinema. Masumura (like Yoshimura) argued that it was congruent only with Japan's literary tradition, that it advocated suppression of individual personality, that all of the characters in these films invariably submitted to a collective self, and that even in the leftist films the heroes deferred to the will of the masses.

In *Giants and Toys* (Kyojin to gangu, aka The Build-Up, 1958), Masumura exercised his theories in this fast-moving attack on the advertising racket in Japan and, by implication, on the values of a merchant-based society. A slick advertising director takes an unknown girl from the slums and turns her into a national celebrity. The sudden fame ruins her, from his point of view, since she walks out on him when he needs her most.

In such films as *Afraid to Die* (Karakkaze yaro, aka A Man Blown by the Wind 1960), a gangster film which marked the acting debut of Mishima Yukio, and *Manji* (1964), a Tanizaki adaptation featuring Wakao Ayako and Kishida Kyoko as the two women in love with each other, a certain shallowness of characterization is perhaps the price exacted by a restless camera and fast editing.

Manji, 1964, Masumura Yasuzo, with Wakao Ayako, Kishida Kyoko.

It is interesting to compare Masumura's vital, noisy *Love Suicides at Sonezaki* (Sonezaki shinju, 1978), based on a Chikamatsu bunraku play, with Mizoguchi's slow and elegiac *A Story from Chikamatsu.* Though it is a period-piece, the actors in the Masumura version were a rock star and a young "idol" starlet. After a breakneck if doomed romance, they go off onto a convoluted michiyuki which finds them as dead as the puppets they portray. But that is one of the points of the picture: it was the system that did them in.

Love Suicides at Sonezaki, 1978, Masumura Yasuzo, with Kaji Meiko.

Masumura's films critical of Japan's military past are particularly interesting. The *Nakano Army School* (Rikugun Nakano gakko, 1966) is a school for spies where the hero (Ichikawa Raizo) finds that, in serving his country, he left himself little to live for. *The Hoodlum Soldier* (Heitai yakuza, 1965) is the story of a soldier and his officer who, for

The Hoodlum Soldier, 1965, Masumura Yasuzo, the bathhouse scene, with (center) Katsu Shintaro.

entirely different reasons, hate the army. The film is so filled with blood and laughter, torture and horseplay, and is so cynical about national ideals that for a time there was talk of its not being released abroad. In Japan itself, the picture was so popular that it later became a series.

The pace of *The Hoodlum Soldier* matches the complications of the story, while the simplicity of construction fits the artlessness of the two major characters (Katsu Shintaro and Tamura Takahiko). Sometimes the action beautifully erupts (as in the celebrated fight in the bathhouse). At other times (the finale where the hapless heroes escape on the wrong train), it simmers, controlled but boiling. While such bravura could wreck a lesser story, it is just this that so distinguishes the picture and gives it its critical edge.

Masumura, ironically, never entirely revolted against the constraints of his company, Daiei, and remained the last major director on the payroll, long after others, such as Ichikawa Kon, had left. His contract gave him no control over his material, and he was continually saddled with unprepossessing scripts and hedged in with conditions from which other directors largely escaped by forming their own companies. Of the sixty-odd films he made, only a handful of these were ones he wanted to make.

But such is the way of film companies. While profits were to be made, it was not unusual for directors to be allowed to film what they wanted. When profits fell off (as they would from the mid-1960s on), directors were made to toe the line, and personal, critical, and socially minded films were discouraged.

An example is Kobayashi Masaki, who in his entire career made only twenty-two films, due in part to the lack of company support. Originally one of the Shochiku stable, he worked as assistant to Kinoshita. Interestingly, his first major film, *The Thick-Walled Room* (Kabe atsuki heya, 1956), scripted by Abe Kobo and based on the diaries of "war criminals," had a most un–Kinoshita-like theme—the idea that most of the imprisoned were innocent, while the real criminals escaped. One of the very few Japanese films to raise the question of responsibility for the war, it was not the sort of film one expected from Shochiku. Indeed, the company held up its release for several years.

Not in the least contrite, Kobayashi next made *I'll Buy You* (Anata kaimasu, 1956), about the commercialization of Japanese baseball, and followed this with the highly critical *Black River* (Kuroi kawa, 1956), which tackles the matter of corruption on American bases in Japan. The

Black River, 1956, Kobayashi Masaki, with Nakadai Tatsuya, Arima Ineko.

villain is not the United States for its presence, but Japan for permitting lawlessness to go unpunished.

Returning to World War II and those responsible, Kobayashi went on to make his most popular film, the massive three-part epic *The Human Condition* (Ningen no joken, 1958–61)—no relation to the similarly named André Malraux novel. Scripted by Matsuyama Zenzo after the Gomikawa Jumpei best-seller, the epic depicts a young soldier (Nakadai Tatsuya) who is appalled by the conditions he finds in Manchuria, particularly by the brutal military use of slave labor. He fights against it and is sent into active duty, where he is killed.

The Human Condition, 1958–61, Kobayashi Masaki, with Nakadai Tatsuya.

The enormous popularity of the film tempered Shochiku's criticisms, and Kobayashi chose to again target the system in his single finest picture *Harakiri* (Seppuku, 1962). The script, by Hashimoto Shinobu based on the Takiguchi Yasuhiko novel, concerns a samurai (Nakadai Tatsuya) who sets out to kill the official he thinks is responsible for forcing the samurai's son-in-law (Ishihama Akira) to disembowel himself with a bamboo sword—one he was wearing because he (just like the hero of *Humanity and Paper Balloons*) had sold his real one in order to eat. The father-in-law discovers

Harakiri, 1962, Kobayashi Masaki, with Ishihama Akira.

that it is not a person but the system that is responsible—a system which, then as now, is integral to the traditional Japanese way of life.

Kobayashi referred to this when answering a question posed by Linda Hoaglund regarding his theme, in terms of his ideas about history. "All of my pictures . . . are concerned with resisting entrenched power. That's what *Harakiri* is about, of course, and *Rebellion* [1967] as well. I suppose I've always challenged authority. This has been true of my own life, including my life in the military."[46]

Kobayashi has said that while making *Harakiri* he became very much aware of traditional Japanese aesthetics: "I was keenly attracted to the stylized beauty of our traditional forms. At the same time, since I felt I had come to the end pursuing realism in film, this new mode of expression [the use of traditional aesthetics] delighted me."[47] It delighted his mentor as well. When *Harakiri* won the jury prize at the Cannes Film Festival, Kinoshita told Kobayashi that the film was his masterpiece, and that if he were asked to name the five greatest Japanese films of all time, he would include *Harakiri*.

Even though the film made Shochiku a lot of money, it was perhaps thought that a director this critical of the system could no longer work for a company so much a part of it. After a few more pictures, Kobayashi had to search for work. Toho let him make the decorative and "traditional" *Kwaidan* (Kaidan, 1965)—a Mizuki Yoko script after four stories by Lafcadio Hearn—and the Hashimoto-scripted *Rebellion* (Joiuchi, aka Samurai Rebellion, 1967), another of Takiguchi Yasuhiko's traditional looks at the vengeful warrior, this one played by Mifune Toshiro.

Rebellion, 1967, Kobayashi Masaki, with Koyama Shigeru, Mifune Toshiro.

Despite box-office successes, Toho decided not to continue with the unpredictable Kobayashi, or perhaps he decided not to continue with them—the stories differ. With three other directors who were dissatisfied with their companies (Ichikawa Kon, Kinoshita Keisuke, and Kurosawa Akira), he entered into a new production company, the Yonki-no-Kai (Club of the Four Knights).

The first film, Kurosawa's *Dodes'ka-den* (1970), was a critical and financial failure, and the director's feelings of obligation toward his "club" were perhaps instrumental in his later suicide attempt. The four "knights" made no further efforts until the eventual filming of one of their scripts, *Dora Heita* (2000), directed by the sole knight still alive, Ichikawa Kon.

The last years of Kobayashi's life were spent in the construction of another large indictment of society, *The Tokyo Trial* (Tokyo Saiban, 1978–83), an independently produced, questioning, fragmented, four-and-one-half-hour film compiled from over one hundred seventy hours of documentary footage. In it, the entrenched powers of the world, that of Japan, and that of the United States, are bravely, even defiantly resisted.

The director who most particularly made the shakai-mono film his own was Kurosawa Akira. During his long career he made a total of thirty-one films, and all, in some way, are about social issues. Kurosawa's interest is in reflecting and interpreting his society. This aim, to be sure, is one quite taken for granted in other countries, but in Japan, it is not the average director who interests himself in controversial social issues. Kurosawa, Imai, Kobayashi, Oshima—directors similar only in their interest in controversy—are exceptions to the general rule of Japanese filmmaking.

Kurosawa's interest in the most pressing (and hence most controversial) social issues is seen in films such as *The Bad Sleep Well* (Warui yatsu hodo yoku nemuru, aka A Rose in the Mud, 1960), a title which might be best rendered as "The Worse You Are, the Better You Sleep." The theme is the corruption of big business, and the underlying assumption is that absolute power absolutely corrupts.

The Bad Sleep Well, 1960, Kurosawa Akira, scene from the wedding-scene sequence.

The movie opens with a brilliant sequence: in a traditional wedding reception the hero (Mifune Toshiro) is shown celebrating his marriage to the company president's daughter (Kagawa Kyoko), whom Kurosawa (and his cowriters Hashimoto Shinobu, Oguni Hideo, and Kikushima Ryuzo) made lame for the same reason that Shakespeare made Ophelia mad.

Both must provide for the hero's eventual downfall. The president (Mori Masayuki), amid his unctuous employees, his corrupt board of directors, and the full paraphernalia of traditional Japan's most telling ritual, prides himself upon the hope that his line will continue. And so it does, despite the fact that the wedding itself is interrupted and the hollow pretense it embodied is eventually exposed.

The bridegroom is really the son of a murdered company official, and Hamlet-like, he plots his revenge. He even engineers a play within a play when he makes an ostensibly dead company official observe his funeral, only to be undone by pity for his own wife and by the revenge of her Laertes-like brother. At the end of picture, after the hero's death, we see the president on the telephone telling those even higher than himself that the matter has been taken care of—an implication that public corruption goes right to the top.

Kurosawa gives his audience no easy way out. *The Record of a Living Being* (Ikimono no kiroku, aka I Live in Fear, 1955) is about a man openly obsessed by the secret fear of his time—atomic destruction. A successful factory-owner (Mifune Toshiro) is so concerned that he tries to get his family to move with him to Brazil where he believes he might find safety.

The Record of a Living Being, 1955, Kurosawa Akira, with Mifune Toshiro, Shimura Takashi.

The family, complacent and cynical, is outraged by this, and tries to have him judged insane. The last we see of him is in an asylum, looking at the sun and believing that the earth is at last on fire. At the same time, the family is shown to be responsible for his insanity. In reality, they want his factory. To deprive them of this, their last recourse, and to force them to join him, the father destroys the factory. This act is used as evidence of his insanity. Traditional society—here in the form of the family—thwarts individual will.

At the same time, the individual himself (or, more rarely, herself) must also assume responsibility. This is a theme in Kurosawa's major films, from the hero of *Sanshiro Sugata*, who learns to be accountable for his own actions, through Dr. Akahige, who teaches his intern what medical responsibility is, in Kurosawa's last major film, *Red Beard* (Akahige, 1965). It is for this reason that the morality of the Kurosawa film is rigorous, and such easy dichotomies as good and bad are not tolerated. In the finale of *Drunken Angel*, the "bad" gangster emerges white (after falling into spilled white paint) as in an apotheosis. In *Stray Dog*, the good cop captures the bad robber after an exhausting fight in the mud; the camera looks down at them and finds them, both mud-covered, indistinguishable. In *High and Low* (Tengoku to jigoku, 1963), the plate of glass separating jailed kidnapper and visiting victim, reflects and fuses their images in the final scene.

Red Beard, 1965, Kurosawa Akira, with Kayama Yuzo, Mifune Toshiro.

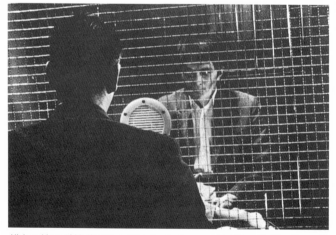

High and Low, 1963, Kurosawa Akira, the final scene, with Mifune Toshiro, Yamazaki Tsutomu.

Kurosawa's classic statement on personal responsibility and the ills of the world is found in *Ikiru* (1952), a film about the largest possible social issue—death. A petty official (Shimura Takashi) learns he is dying. For the first time in his life he realizes that he has accomplished nothing, has never enjoyed anything. He spends his savings on a spree, but this brings him only grief, as he indicates in the celebrated scene where he sings a song of his youth.

> Life is so short,
> Fall in love, dear maiden,
> While your hair is still black,
> Before your heart stops—
> For there will be no more tomorrows. [48]

Ikiru, 1952, Kurosawa Akira, the singing scene in the entertainment-district sequence, with Shimura Takashi.

The dying man returns to the office and uses all of his strength to bring to realization a petition (for months on his desk and on the desks of others), a request for a children's park. In the face of official antagonism he pushes his project through. Finally it is complete. That night, sitting on a swing in the new park, the snow falling about him, he dies.

Despite Kurosawa's criticisms—and the film, in part, is as sweeping an indictment of bureaucracy as has been filmed—*Ikiru* is not an angry movie. We are not so concerned with a bad society as we are with a good man, and Kurosawa makes us realize this by framing the latter half of the film with his wake. The tone is frankly elegiac, but there is little mono no aware. Instead, there is the statement that we are what we do. Others may be in states of self-delusion but the dead man has escaped. He created himself.

The way in which he is seen to do so is through a cinematic style which is as controlled as it is inventive, as incisive as it is subjective. All directors create their films in just this way—showing what they have learned both from life and from other pictures—but Kurosawa displays this with extraordinary panache. It is this genius for amalgamation which one may find typical of Kurosawa and very Japanese of him. All of Kurosawa's best pictures are animated by this quality, but it is seen at its best in his period-pictures, those films which, like the jidaigeki of Ito, Itami, and Yamanaka Sadao, see the past in terms of the present, making its problems and solutions ours.

The fusion of all the elements which make up the individual style of Kurosawa perhaps most convincingly occurs in *Seven Samurai* (Shichinin no samurai, 1954). Though its story is laid in the past, the picture is concerned with the present. It criticizes contemporary values, but insists that they are, after all, human values; it honestly creates the context of Japanese life but is also concerned with verities seen as timeless and attitudes viewed as universal. Through controlled realism, Kurosawa presents an absolutely believable world.

In many ways the picture is the continuation of *Rashomon*. The earlier film represents the limitations of the intellect—four stories, each

Seven Samurai, 1954, Kurosawa Akira, the final scene, with Shimura Takashi, Kato Daisuke, Kimura Isao.

intellectualized, all mutually incompatible, with reality itself becoming relative. In *Seven Samurai* we step beyond intellectualization. Only those acts which spring from the emotions are valid acts, and action thus motivated is truth. In this film, theory becomes practice. Violent physical action is what the film is made of—and the end result of all this action (and there has rarely been so violent an "action film" as *Seven Samurai*) is the distillation of a single almost unpalatable truth—one whose emotional acceptance is impossible to avoid.

The story is simple. A village is harassed by bandits. The villagers ask the aid of a masterless samurai who in turn gathers others, a group of seven—they themselves as outside society as the robbers they are asked to fight. They plan their defense and carry it out. A number die, and the villagers are grateful for the protection rendered. But it is spring planting season; they have things to do.

The final scene shows the three remaining samurai (Shimura Takashi, Kato Daisuke, Kimura Isao) stopping by the mound where their comrades are buried. The farmers, ignoring them, are busy with their planting. Shimura turns to his two fellow samurai.

> *Shimura:*   And again we lose.
> *Kato:*   . . . ?
> *Shimura:*   We lose. Those farmers . . . they are the winners. [49]

The film is a call for cooperation among men, but it also suggests why this has always been and always will be impossible. This is the theme that the director often called his "unpalatable truth."

The samurai fight side by side with the villagers yet, at the end, nothing is changed, except that the bandits are dead too. This experience turns out, not tragic, but exhilarating. One is so overcome by the vitality of the visuals that it is only later that one realizes how near tears one has been. To remember a viewing of this film is to remember a hundred images: the initial fight where the swordmaster shows us everything we need know about samurai, the series of scenes where Takashi devises a plan to test his new men; the last samurai and his death; the first attack of the bandits, their image against the sky, their slow descent through the waving grasses; the last rout and the rice-planting sequence, and then the final scene, so right, so spare, so honest that it is near catharsis.

In making this picture—it took over a year to film—Kurosawa created a new style: for the first time he used telephoto lenses to capture detail. In the attack of the bandits, men and horses pile up to create massed detailed images of solidity. The director also used multiple cameras, each taking the scene from a different angle: thus he was able to cut directly, without stopping the action, from one perspective to another. The splendid final reel, the battle in the rain, was shot in this manner. Though such a method uses a vast quantity of film, Kurosawa—who almost invariably shot at a ratio of ten to one—preferred it, even using it in the intimate conversation-filled scenes of *The Lower Depths*.

Though many critics considered Kurosawa the finest director in Japan, his own crew found him to be the best editor in the world. Perhaps this was because, as he once said, he edited his films as they demanded to be edited: "Whenever we get down to talking about editing, the issue of montage is immediately brought up, yet I cannot but feel that such a theory is a pretty strange aberration of the imagination." He added: "When it comes down to the basics of film technique, I am a naive Griffithean." [50]

The mature Kurosawa style, one which creates a realism of its own, is put to the uses of an equally realistic but personal morality. Such abstract virtues as heroism, dignity, virtue, even bravery for its own sake, do not interest him. In this his films are far from the ordinary period-film. Even a film which deliberately uses the very stuff of chambara, *The Hidden Fortress* (Kakushi toride no san akunin, aka Three Bad Men in a Hidden Fortress, 1958) is not done in the heroic manner. One of the points is that there are three bad men, though we are shown only two—the thieving, lying peasants—until we realize that General Mifune Toshiro, our hero, is just as bad.

There are equally no heros in the comic period-film *Yojimbo* (1961) and its sequel *Sanjuro* (Tsubaki Sanjuro, 1962). In both films, the hero (Mifune) is not in himself heroic. In the first picture, he cunningly pits the two opposing factions (both bad) of a town together and then sits back and watches the fun. In the latter film, he is continually worried by a group of young samurai who really believe in the supposed heroics of their profession. His concern is that their "heroic" foolhardiness will get them all killed.

The stories, both about rival politics at the end of the Edo era, are composed of the very stuff of the ordinary period-film, but Kurosawa, like Yamanaka before him, infused this common material with new life, returning to even the most notorious clichés their original values.

In *Yojimbo*, to take but one example, the old cliché of a falling fighter's crying *oka* (from *okasan*, meaning "mother") is used

The Hidden Fortress, 1958, Kurosawa Akira, with Mifune Toshiro.

Yojimbo, 1961, Kurosawa Akira, with Mifune Toshiro.

Sanjuro, 1962, Kurosawa Akira, with Mifune Toshiro, Kayama Yuzo, Irie Takako, Dan Reiko.

and reused. First, there is a short scene with a mother and her small son, where the cry is heard as it is in ordinary speech; next is a funny scene where a weak son utters the word and his mother slaps him; and, finally, there is the scene where a dying gang member cries oka and returns to the cliché all of its horror and despair.

In these three films, Kurosawa has again fitted technique to his requirements. There is greater dependence upon close-ups, a constant use of deep focus, low-key photography, and a realistic intricacy of detail. Space is outlined by right-angled shots so that shortly the locations become evident even when not seen. With this comes that sense of reality which is atmosphere—creating a home, as it were, for the believable character. One remembers *Humanity and Paper Balloons*.

Kurosawa's use of history is comparable to that of Yamanaka. The Edo period is a known historical period—1600 to 1867—but it is also a domain where the director can construct a place with its own conventions, its own laws. If the director of the historical film is a Yamanaka or a Kurosawa, he makes it completely his. In the hands of a more conventional director, the period will be reconstructed from conventions we all know, those of the period-film. When Inagaki Hiroshi made his entertaining *Samurai Saga* (Aru kengo no shogai, 1959), based on Edmond Rostand's *Cyrano de Bergerac*, for example, he used only the accent of his genre. This particular play, to be sure, already had a fairly thick accent. It was first made into a shimpa favorite, *Shirano Benjiro*, from which all its emotional posturings found their way into the film.

In transplanting Shakespeare's *Macbeth* to the middle ages of Japan in *The Throne of Blood* (Kumonosu-jo, 1957), Kurosawa made a film completely nongeneric, utterly his, and ours. Though the characters were all Japanese and the locale was obviously Japan, this was still a story of vaulting ambition. This was its appeal to the director, who saw in it the continuation of a major theme: "I keep saying the same thing in different ways. If I look at the pictures I've made, I think they ask, 'Why is it that human beings aren't happy?' Both *Ikiru* and

The Record of a Living Being are such pictures. *The Throne of Blood*, on the other hand, shows why they must be unhappy."[51] Both Shakespeare and Kurosawa agree on what the theme is—the pull of power and its inevitable corruption. However, since the story was already legend and the theme timeless, the director discarded the seeming hyper-realism

The Throne of Blood, 1957, Kurosawa Akira, with Kagawa Kyoko, Mifune Toshiro.

of his other historical films and created a film style that would conform to the necessities of his vehicle.

Using only a few components—drifting fog and smoke, a rainy forest, the glint of armor, the sheen of natural wood, cloudy skies, the dead white of skin—Kurosawa, with his cameraman, Nakai Asakazu, created a film with a definite texture. We feel the bite of swords, the thud of hooves, the leaf-filled catastrophe of the advancing forest.

There are fruitful additions to the original as well. Some examples are the scene where dozens of birds, disturbed by the destruction of their forest, fly into the banquet hall and circle around the distraught hero; the sequence where tiny nocturnal sounds form an *ostinato* to the murder of Duncan; the appearance of the ghost of Banquo where the director, disdaining trick photography, uses the actor himself, made up purely white, with lights creating a halo around him; and the climax where Macbeth is immobilized by arrows, the last one transfixing his neck.

The restrained prodigality of this film is matched in *The Lower Depths* (Donzoko, 1957), a literal film version of the Maxim Gorky play, yet one which has its own individual style. A consistent set of rules governs characters, camera movement, formal composition (those dramatic diagonals), and editing. These rules unify the film, making it a bit more consistent than life itself. They also box in the characters of this claustrophobic drama. Everything is carefully threadbare, and the only method of punctuation the director allows himself is the simple cut. In fact, Kurosawa confined himself and his actors to just two sets and permitted no star turns. Further, he kept the cast for weeks in these sets, with daily camera rehearsals, until every last reminder of the stage had been removed. Among the results was a unanimity of ensemble rare in a Japanese film.

The Lower Depths, 1957, Kurosawa Akira, with Mifune Toshiro, Kagawa Kyoko.

Likewise, for once, Kurosawa allowed little music. The music is mainly what the actors make for themselves—singing, banging on pans, and tapping bowls—this and the rhythmic sound of the *hyoshigi*, those clappers which call the audience's attention at the traditional theater. In the final scene, after the death of one of the characters, another takes a drink, turns to the camera, and says: "What a shame! Just when the party was beginning." At the same time there is a single clap from the hyoshigi, and instantly the end title glows for a second, then disappears, wresting us from what was indeed a floating world, but one which was also ours. While the picture is theatrical in the most bravura of manners, we are convinced that it is life we are watching. With its purposely shallow playing areas and its two-dimensional architectural backgrounds, *The Lower Depths* reaches back into the same kind of traditions that gave us early Japanese cinema. Its continual sacrifices for theatricality are here rewarded.

This ability to evoke the stage while denying it became even more apparent in Kurosawa's later work. *Dodes'ka-den* (1970) employed obviously painted sets, as did the dream sequence in *Kagemusha* (1980). *Ran* (1985), Kurosawa's adaptation of *King Lear*, was so purposely stagelike it became operatic, enhancing the already apparent influence of noh, long a favorite Kurosawa entertainment.

In the films following *Red Beard*, Kurosawa became more openly interested in a highly structured, even schematic presentation. Such structure was, as we have seen, always there, though the realistic style of the earlier films made it less apparent. The visual architecture of *Seven Samurai*, for example, may turn schematic (the map the samurai draw is seen as a schema for subsequent action), but the effect is softened and rendered less apparent by the realistic context. The map is there for the use of the samurai. It is only secondarily of any use to us. *Ran*, on the other hand, is neither a realistic rendition nor an illustration of the King Lear story, nor is it intended to be.

Indeed in these later films the director seems to be himself repeating that well-known pattern where the Japanese artist (Tanizaki, Kawabata, Mishima, and many others) turn to the outside world, the West, the realistic style, and then return to something we might identify as more Japanese. These later films of Kurosawa's share much with earlier Japanese cinema.

Toward the end of his life, Kurosawa said that he "watched with a detached gaze," just like the noh playwright and theorist Zeami. This meant that the director's eyes were to compass everything in detail but did not remain—as he expressed it—"glaring at the set." Indeed with the camera rolling, the later Kurosawa rarely looked at the actors. He explains it as a sort of peripheral sixth sense: "I focus my gaze somewhere else and I sense instantly when something isn't right."[52]

In the last films, *Dreams* (Yume, aka Akira Kurosawa's Dreams, 1990), *Rhapsody in August* (Hachigatsu no kyoshikyoku [rhapsody], 1991), and *Madadayo* (1993)—all of which Kurosawa scripted alone—the controlled realism which had so marked earlier films is less apparent, and more conventional views emerge. The critic who said that watching late Kurosawa was like watching the history of Japanese film backwards revealed a prejudice toward realism, but he also stated a truth.

Kurosawa's lack of accommodation to received ideas has allowed some Japanese critics to call him their "least Japanese" director. The description is understandable in that he is "Western" enough to be openly individual. Completely uninterested in the standard program film, and failing whenever he was forced to make one, he has gone beyond the accepted confines of cinematic language as the Japanese understood them and, in so doing, has broadened them. Consequently, perhaps, his films have been widely accepted in the West itself.

Kurosawa was the first Japanese director to be "discovered" abroad, and this discovery is also one of the reasons that his local critics have found him "un-Japanese." The director himself, however, was made famously furious by such criticism. He said he had not read one review from abroad that had not read false meanings into his pictures and, in any event, he would never make a picture especially for foreign audiences: "If a work cannot have meaning to Japanese audiences, then I—as a Japanese artist—am simply not interested in it."[53]

THE ADVENT OF TELEVISION AND THE FILM'S DEFENSES:
SUZUKI, NAKAHIRA, KAWASHIMA, AND IMAMURA

Television, something which damaged the Japanese film industry much more than had either the 1923 earthquake or the 1945 fire-bombings, officially commenced in Japan in 1953, but its ravages were not apparent until a decade later. Indeed, in 1958, when over one billion tickets were sold, the Japanese film industry reached its financial peak. The record for the most productions was set in 1960, with 537 Japanese movies being released in some 900 theaters. This may be compared with the figures for 2000: 282 films released in approximately 300 theaters.[1]

There are, of course, many more theaters in Japan, nearly 3,000, but the vast majority show only foreign films. By 1999, after the complete collapse of Shin-Toho, a Toho subsidiary which had been financed from 1947, and the partial collapses of Daiei and Nikkatsu, Toei had turned its Kyoto studio into a theme park—the Toei Uzumasa Eigamura, with its Haunted House ("No one has returned alive yet . . ."). One year later, Shochiku, having already closed its own theme park (Ozu House, Tora-san Street), was moving its head office, closing theaters, and selling off its Ofuna Studio.

Earlier the entertainment economy had been burgeoning. A watershed date for the period is usually given as 1964. This was the year of the Tokyo Olympics, and the event (symbolically so important for Japan, marking its reentry into "the family of nations") was distinguished by all sorts of modernizations and cleanups. There was a new system of elevated highways, strip shows and blue movies were banned, the bullet train was installed, and everyone acquired a television set in order to view the Games.

With a tube in front of every family and consequently not many families in the motion-picture houses, the film industry decided it had to do something about itself. In 1960, the peak year, there had been six major film-producing companies: Shochiku; Daiei; Nikkatsu (resumed from 1954); Toei (from 1951); Toho; and its affiliate, Shin-Toho, shortly (1961) to go bankrupt. With tickets selling and crowds remaining, these companies had been confident. But, by 1964, viewers were deserting the theaters and loss was looming.

The remaining major film companies thus attempted remedies, all under the rubric of "modernization." Having already displayed the insufficient attractions of color and various sorts of wide screens, the industry now turned to other hoped-for attractions. These included odd feature lengths, stars in heavy concentration, and diversified monsters—Honda Ishiro's *Godzilla* (Gojira, aka Godzilla, King of the Monsters, 1954) having been a hit.

The lumbering lizard went on to star in a twenty-seven-film series. Here he met with a number of other Toho monsters, including Mothra, Rodan, King Ghidorah, Ebirah, Megalon, and that famous foreign tourist, King Kong. He also continued to carefully crunch models of Tokyo, Osaka, Nagoya, and other Japanese cities. "Awakened" by the A-bomb and put to rest (again and again) by selfless Japanese scientists, Godzilla became a kind of barometer of the political mood. From punishment-figure-from-the-past he turned friendly and finally took to defending his country (right or wrong) from not only foreign monsters but also the machinations of both the U.S. and the U.S.S.R. Political ambitions did not, however, kill Godzilla. Toho did. He was no longer pulling his financial weight and so *Godzilla: Final Wars* (Gojira: fainaru uozu, 2004) marked his final appearance. During his fifty years of popularity he spawned many fellow monsters and was viewed by nearly one hundred million people.

Another audience-attention item was the double bill. Two features for the price of one had all long been a distribution ploy, and some of the examples were fairly exotic. Shochiku-Tenkatsu, for example, had earlier mixed genres. *Souls on the Road* (1921), in which no one had any confidence, had been shown on a bill, at least in some places, with a Hollywood film from 1920, *The Revenge of Tarzan*. Such miscegenation did not last long, but now, in the crisis of the sixties, it was again encouraged.

Companies also dangled lavish genre-product displays. Toei, which had begun production only five years before, pioneered wide screen, in 1957, and now routinely made all its films in that format and specialized in big, wide yakuza and prison-life series. Daiei, noting the early success of Henry Koster's *The Robe* (1953), had Misumi Kenji make *The Life of Buddha* (Shaka, 1961) in 70 mm, with every star on the lot in it. This was perhaps in emulation of Toho's earlier *The Three Treasures* (Nihon tanjo, 1959), an Inagaki Hiroshi wide-screen spectacular about the origins of Japan, with special effects from the people who brought you *Godzilla*. Hara Setsuko starred in the role of the sun goddess, and Mifune Toshiro was her unruly dragon-slaying sibling.

Among the better of those directors who specialized in genre film was Kato Tai. Beautifully crafted, filled with long, contemplative scenes, and interspersed with crisp fast action, his films seemed a return to an almost forgotten heroic cinema. He made films from scripts by

Hasegawa Shin, who forty years before had defined the jidaigeki—*Love for a Mother* (Mabuta no hana, aka Long-Sought Mother, 1962) and *Tokijiro of Kutsukake: Lone Yakuza* (Kutsukake Tokijiro: yukyo ippiki, 1966)—and revived the kyuha in movies such as his *Oiwa's Ghost* (Kaidan Oiwa no borei, 1961), a version of the kabuki play *Tokkaido Yotsuya Kaidan*.

Another genre specialist was Fukasaku Kinji, who made *Battles Without Honor or Humanity* (Jingi naki tatakai, aka The Yakuza Papers, 1973–76), a multipart series for Toei. The series criticized the yakuza and concerned itself with the extreme consequences of giri and ninjo. These pictures formed a subgenre within the major yakuza-film genre. Known as *ninkyo-eiga*, such vehicles were idealized, highly formalized elaborations, set usually in the late Meiji, the Taisho, or the early Showa eras. The hero wades into the rival gang and emerges victorious.

Though popular and profitable, the ninkyo-eiga did not last and was replaced by another subgenre called *jitsuroku* ("reporting reality") *eiga*. These films were set in gritty post–World War II times and in the brutal and amoral present. Examples would be Fukasaku's kid-killing *Battle Royal* (Batoru rowaiaru, 2000); its sequel *Battle Royal II* (2003), finished by Fukasaku's son, Kenta; some of Kitano Takeshi's films; and most of Miike Takashi's. In these, the lawless, nihilistic hero of Ito Daisuke is revived—now no longer a figure of serious moral concern but of merely fashionable violence.

There were during the period many other genre craftsmen as well. Nakamura Noboru, who had worked as assistant director on Yoshimura Kozaburo's *The Story of Tank Commander Nishizumi*, became a latter-day jun-bungaku specialist, making into persuasive films such novels as Ariyoshi Sawako's *The River Ki* (Kinokawa, 1966) and Kawabata's *Twin Sisters of Kyoto* (Koto, 1963). Oba Hideo, another Yoshimura-trained director, specialized in melodrama and created the enormously popular trilogy *What Is Your Name?* (Kimi no na wa, 1953–54) and later remade *Snow Country* (Yukiguni, 1965).

Chiba Yasuki, having early completed *Certain Night's Kiss*, went on to create superior program-pictures such as the four-part *Mr. Fortune Maker* (Oban, 1957–58) and an excellent Hayashi Fumiko adaptation, *Downtown* (Shitamachi, 1957). Also working for Toho, Okamoto Kihachi began under Naruse Mikio as assistant director on *Floating Clouds*. He later went in for spectaculars including *The Sword of Doom* (Daibosatsu toge, 1966), *Kill* (Kiru, 1968), and the star-studded *The Emperor and the General* (Nihon no ichiban nagai hi, aka Japan's Longest Day, 1967); the wry war comedy, *Human Bullet* (Nikudan, 1968); and a remake of Kurosawa's *Sanshiro Sugata* (1977).

Less generic were the ways of Nikkatsu. Having finally resumed production in 1954, the company had found (as we have seen) a money-making genre in the taiyozoku films about troubled youth. When it later discovered that this kind of picture was being patronized by troubled youth itself, directors were allowed an unusual degree of independence.

One of those who, initially at any rate, profited from this move was Suzuki Seijun, who in a relatively short period (1956–67) made over forty films for Nikkatsu. Entirely youth-oriented products, his films went further than many others. Not only was there more sex and violence, but the very manner in which they were made appealed to the young. Color, frivolity, irresponsibility—this appeals to all youth everywhere, but post-Occupation Japanese youth were particularly attracted. After the earnest postwar era and the often drab-seeming neo-realism of many Japanese films, a new brand of ero-guro-nansenu became saleable, and directors such as Suzuki sold best.

Suzuki's *The Gate of Flesh* (Nikutai no mon, 1964) was a remake of a 1948 film by Makino Masahiro, but few would recognize it. A dour review of prostitution in occupied Japan is transformed into a brightly-colored pageant all about sexual liberation. Similarly, *The Life of a Tattooed Man* (Irezumi ichidai, aka One Generation of Tattooed Men, 1965), which takes on the yakuza genre, is as stylized as kabuki: carefully aimless action is combined with a parody of giri-ninjo dedication in the underworld, and violence is lavishly aestheticized.

In *Tokyo Drifter* (Tokyo nagaremono, 1966), the hero wears a white suit throughout so that during the final massacre (which takes place in a white nightclub) the splashes of blood will nicely contrast. With every killing, the strobe lights change color, turning a deep and satisfying crimson in the end. Such aestheticism, seen now mainly in *manga* (comic) books and in *anime* (sci-fi animation) films, began in large part with the films of Suzuki and his ero-guro followers.

One of the qualities of Suzuki's pictures is that, amid all the blood and laughter, a serious point is being made. In *Elegy to Violence* (Kenka ereji, aka Elegy to Fighting/Born Fighter/Fighting Elegy, 1966), the hero is the typical close-cropped, humorless, pent-up schoolboy of the sort still seen in manga. His girlfriend is far too pure to do anything, but he hates himself for masturbating; a life of violence seems the only answer. At the end of the film, he suddenly joins the notorious militarist coup of 1936. What we had seen as simple nonsense can now be read as social comment. This is what Ian Buruma meant when he wrote: "Thus the film is literally an elegy to fighting, to the innocent violence of youth. It is a nostalgic yearning for that period in life when one can be self-assertive without

Elegy to Violence, 1966, Suzuki Seijun, with Takahashi Hideki.

being punished too severely, that time of grace before the hammer of conformity knocks the nail back in."[2]

Suzuki is also anarchic, something which made him such a popular director among the young. "I hate constructive themes . . . Images that stick in the mind are pictures of destruction."[3] And the destruction is of an aesthetically Japanese kind. When asked by J. Scott Burgeson why the boiled-rice fetish of the killer in *Branded to Kill* (Koroshi no rakuin, 1967), Suzuki replied: "It's because he's a Japanese assassin. If he were Italian, he'd get turned on by macaroni, right?" Asked about the masturbation scene in *Elegy to Violence*, he responded: "The only thing I ever think about is how to make the movie more interesting . . . Back then you couldn't show nudity in Japanese movies. So I always had to think of something else as a substitute." When asked if the actor Takahashi Hideki was embarrassed, Suzuki showed his Ozu side when he answered: "Since he was told to do it, he had no reason to be embarrassed."[4]

Suzuki's pictures are now seen as a kind of manga-esque pre–pop-art. Burgeson has said: "In the same way that Japanese woodblock prints were originally mass-produced commercial posters that only later were recognized as works of art, Suzuki's films are a triumph of style and form over impossibly restricted conditions."

Shortly the conditions were to become even more impossibly restricted. Interesting though Suzuki's films were and, despite their popularity, Nikkatsu became concerned with the "antisocial" messages these colorful and entertaining films were perceived as imparting. Also, the company was being criticized as catering to the more seditious of the young. In a pattern to become familiar industry-wide, Nikkatsu dismissed Suzuki when it became plain that his youth-oriented films were not after all, returning a major audience. His dismissal occurred in 1968 and, though a number of the youth-oriented took to the streets (around the Nikkatsu Hibiya offices), their numbers were not sufficient to convince the company otherwise.

Paradoxically, during the fifties, Nikkatsu had encouraged seditious directors. When the taiyozoku genre was a popular subject, Nakahira Ko was permitted to make what he would of the script which Ishihara Shintaro had fashioned from one of his own popular novels, *Crazed Fruit*. Though the studio wanted just another juvenile delinquency film, Nakahira made a lyric tragedy, one which sacrificed little to

Crazed Fruit, 1956, Nakahira Ko, with Ishihara Yujiro, Kitahara Mie, Tsugawa Masahiko.

sensationalism and even had an integrity of its own. In it, two boys, brothers, enjoy the favors of the same girl. Nakahira captured well the atmosphere of a second-rate summer resort, the hesitant arrogance of adolescents, the animality of the young in their setting of shining sea and sun-drenched beaches. The elder brother (Ishihara Yujiro) appropriates the girl (Kitahara Mie), not so much because he wants her as that he doesn't want his younger brother (Tsugawa Masahiko) to have her. But the youngest of the brothers gets them both in the celebrated motorboat finale, where both the girl and the elder brother are killed.

Like the young people in George Stevens's *A Place in the Sun* (1951), a film which influenced this one (there is even a shot in common: the portable radio on the pier), the youngsters are vicious because they lack the imagination to be anything else. These particular young people being Japanese, the traditionally competitive ties between the boys are much stronger than any bond that might develop between the boys and the girl.

With the success of this film behind him, Nakahira was allowed a degree of freedom. He went on to make *The Four Seasons of Love* (Shiki no aiyoku, 1958), in which he showed a fine flair for comedy at the expense of the Japanese family system. The picture illustrates how much more conservative some members of the new generation are than their parents.

The Four Seasons of Love, 1958, Nakahira Ko, with Yamada Isuzu, Nakahara Sanae.

The children of the film's family all think that Mother (Yamada Isuzu) should stay at home, giving herself over to self-sacrifice and tears. Her resolve, however, is to live her own life. The children, conservatives that they are, are ashamed of her. At the end of the film, they are assembled at the railway station. Mother, they think, has seen the error of her ways and is returning home. They prepare suitable faces, hurt but brave, as the train pulls in. Mother appears—accompanied. She is with a gentleman friend and, together, they are on their way to a hot spring resort. The children are horrified. Mother smiles sweetly, the whistle blows, and the train moves off. The final scene is of the faces of the children, who for the first time become aware that it is perhaps they who are missing something.

In 1959, Nakahira was also allowed to make *The Assignation* (Mikkai). Though it was only an hour long (Nikkatsu, like everyone else, was experimenting with lengths), it turned out to be an unusually powerful film. An indication is the opening scene—six minutes— showing a married woman and her young lover, a student, lying on the ground in a deserted park. Nakahira confines our view entirely to this single setup, both actors cut off at the waist. It is in the acting and the slow, sinuous movements of the camera that sex is suggested.

At the end, the wife, fearful of dis- closure, impulsively pushes the stu- dent under a train. Here, as in the motorboat finale in *Crazed Fruit*, Nakahira uses a convincingly impres- sionistic technique, creating the action through a number of very short shots: close-ups of the two faces, the wife's hand, the student's foot slipping, and then his body turning as he falls. At the end of the sequence we see the train overshooting the station, and

The Assignation, 1959, Nakahira Ko, the opening sequence, with Ito Takao, Katsuragi Yoko.

then we are shown the tracks. In a long-held shot, there is the student, dead, his head and shoulder at one side of the frame; at the other, at an impossible angle, his leg.

Brilliant as these films were, they attracted no real following, though other directors much admired them. Presaging the company's later treatment of Suzuki, Nikkatsu conse- quently decided that Nakahira would be better occupied making action fare. A number of these films were made, after which the unhappy director extricated himself and went to Tai- wan to direct equally undistinguished Chinese entertainment films.

Another director who had initially found freedom at the new Nikkatsu was Kawashima Yuzo, who had left Shochiku and was later to go on to Daiei and Tokyo Eiga, a small in- dependent company affiliated with Toho. Among collaborations with a number of directors, Kawashima had worked as an assistant director on Ozu's *The Brothers and Sisters of the Toda Family*. Though the first half of his fifty-odd films were standard Shochiku product, at Nikkatsu he was allowed a degree of latitude.

Imamura Shohei, who had, as he put it, a "master-apprentice relationship" with Kawashima, recalled having asked the master why he had made such "completely worthless" films at Shochiku: "He looked me straight in the eye and said: 'For a living.'"[5] Kawashima indeed did a number of things for a living, including appearing as an extra in Tasaka Tomo- taka's *Five Scouts* (1938), and working intermittently with Shimazu Yasujiro, Yoshimura Kozaburo, and Shimizu Hiroshi. He was chief assistant on Kinoshita Keisuke's debut film, he made one of the early "kissing" pictures for the Allied Occupation, and became known as the man who could direct a film a month. It was not until he went to Nikkatsu, however, that he made the kind of films he wanted to make.

With money to be made from juveniles—adolescent revolt still being a box-office draw—Kawashima was permitted to turn his attention to another segment of the population which the films had more or less ignored, but of which he himself was a member. This was what the upper classes called the lower classes. To be sure, the lower classes had been seen on the screen in both the shomingeki genre and keiko-eiga, but in the former they had been "socialized"—if that is the word—to a sometimes sentimental degree, and in the latter they were too often mere propaganda fodder.

One of Kawashima's assumptions (shared with Imamura) is that there are, in effect, two Japans. One is the "official" version—noh, tea ceremony, Mizoguchi, Ozu, late Kurosawa, along with the approved high-class virtues of fidelity and devotion. Here and there, an unhappily subservient (possibly kimono-clad) woman completes the image. This is the version which most foreigners see, the one which gets exported, and the way in which Japanese society perhaps best likes to view itself.

The other Japan is the "real" one, the one both directors chose to depict. The characters in a Kawashima or an Imamura film, as has often been noted, do not behave like "Japanese" because none of the rules of order and decorum insisted upon by the official version apply. These low-class folk do not know the meaning of fidelity. They are utterly natural, even "uncivilized," to the extent that civilization means a removal from the natural. They are selfish, lusty, amoral. All the vitality of Japan comes from their numbers.

Kawashima, Imamura, and later directors who shared this view believed that the "official" civilization had long threatened to smother the real one. Imamura has said of himself: "I happen to be more interested in the Japan that flourished before the artistic decadence fostered by the political isolation of the feudal period." It still flourishes: "The Japanese did not change as a result of the Pacific War . . . they haven't changed in thousands of years."[6] This accounts for their admirable vulgarity.

In *Suzaki Paradise—Red Light District* (Suzaki paradaisu: Akashingo, 1956), Kawashima's favorite among his own films (scripted by Ide Toshiro, better known for his Naruse scenarios), people are completely without pretensions. Though the women are all more or less fallen, no one feels terrible about it in the Naruse manner. When one of them (Aratama Michiyo) has the chance for a bit more money with another man, she simply (as she is—no luggage) climbs on the back of his motorbike and, with a big smile and a wave, off she goes. No one feels particularly bad about betraying trust or stealing a bit of cash either, and the man who eventually does return the stolen money is seen as something of a wimp.

People are depicted as people—surviving. We see this in the opening shot, a very long dolly shot (under the credits) from a high angle looking down at the customers as they pass the houses of the prostitutes who attempt to drag them in. The angle is such that it is all legs and bottoms, no one's face is seen, though a hand now and then enters and snatches. This is what their roiling world is really like, struggling to survive—and we are in its throes, like it or not.

That the real Japanese world was always like this is shown in Kawashima's most popular film, *The Sun's Legend* (Bakumatsu taiyo-den, aka The Sun's Legend at the End of the Tokugawa Period, aka After Leaving Shinagawa, aka Shinagawa Path, 1957). Written by Kawashima, Imamura, and Tanaka Keiichi and based in part on *rakugo* stories, the setting is a large and comfortable brothel, the Sagamiya, toward the end of the Edo period (ca 1850). Saheiji (Furanki Sakai) cannot pay his bill and is held hostage. In no time, native wit has led to financial solvency. He collects debts and tips, is a lovers' go-between, and even gets hold of a map of the British Embassy and sells it to a resident revolutionary so that he can burn it down.

The Sun's Legend, Kawashima Yuzo, 1957, with Ishihara Yujiro, Furanki Sakai.

Here, as always in a Kawashima film, a number of characters encounter each other, engage in mundane discourse, enjoy carnal relations, and have an overall good time. Imamura thought that the film should have showed more of "how the citizens of Edo, in spite of their proverbial frivolousness, revolted against oppression."[7] But one of the points of the picture was the unorganized and unbuttoned beauty of the uncommitted. And as for the revolt against oppression, it was simply not that kind of film.

Imamura has also noted that Kawashima "wasn't interested in the conventional grammar of filmmaking and [that] he often just jump-cuts. When I wrote [the script for this film] I left many things in the script deliberately ambiguous, but he never paid any attention to the details anyway. That's the kind of man he was."[8]

Despite his lack of grammatical interest, Kawashima was also an admirer of the foursquare geometric workmanship of both Ozu and Yamanaka. *The Sun's Legend* in some ways reminds one of *Humanity and Paper Balloons*. Kawashima, like Yamanaka, attempted to show the interaction between space and people—whether space is extraneous or not depends on the situation, what happens in it. The corridors, rooms, bath, and toilet in the single main set of *The Sun's Legend* are as articulated as are the tenement and the streets outside in *Humanity and Paper Balloons*, and for the same reasons.

Many other directors learned from Kawashima. Among them was Urayama Kirio (later an assistant to Imamura), who made *The Street with the Cupola* (Kyupora no aru machi, 1962), after a script cowritten with Imamura, and *Bad Girl* (Hiko shojo, 1963). The later "new wave" directors learned from him as well. In an essay called "My Teacher," Imamura states that "Kawashima's early revolt against Shochiku's authority is precisely the reason why young people are once again taking an interest in his work. He personified the "new wave," years before its emergence."[9]

Imamura himself learned from other directors as well. "The film that shocked and moved me most was Kurosawa's *Drunken Angel*. I found the gangster played by Mifune Toshiro incredibly real—he reminded me of people I'd met on the black market."[10] And it was with Kurosawa that Imamura—then at Toho—wanted to study, but as Toho was having strikes during this period, no admission examinations were held. He therefore went to Shochiku, where he was told to work with Ozu. Imamura worked as the older director's assistant on three of his films, including *Tokyo Story*. At the time he said he much disliked the experience.

Later, in an interview with Nakata Toichi, Imamura revealed how unbearable it had been to watch the scene where the mother in the Ozu film dies of a cerebral hemorrhage, given that his own mother had recently died of the same cause. Imamura recalls taking refuge in the bathroom, almost in tears: "Ozu followed me and came to urinate next to me. 'Mr. Imamura,' he asked, 'is that what a cerebral hemorrhage looks like? Have I got it right?' At the time I thought him incredibly cruel, but I later realized that a great filmmaker sometimes has to behave like that." Imamura later said that it was while working for Ozu that he learned most of the basics of filmmaking.[11]

Under Ozu's tutelage, Imamura also learned about the kind of film he did not want to make. While Ozu's remark was certainly enough to cause resentment, what Imamura perhaps equally disliked was what he saw as Ozu's celebration of the official version—the serene world of traditional Japanese aesthetics.

The myth of the accepting Japanese woman was another of Imamura's dislikes. As he told Audie Bock: "Self-sacrificing women like the heroines of Naruse's *Floating Clouds* and Mizoguchi's *The Life of Oharu*, they don't really exist . . . My heroines are true to life—just look around you at Japanese women." Imamura went on to define this true-to-life cinematic woman: "Medium height and weight, light coloring, smooth skin. The face of a woman who loves men. Maternal, good genitals. Juicy." [12] He was talking about the heroine of *Intentions of Murder* (Akai satsui, aka Murderous Desire, aka Unholy Desire, 1964), but the description fits most Imamura women. She is maternal yet she likes to make love.

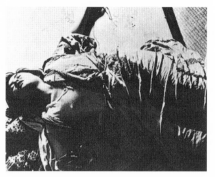

Intentions of Murder, 1964, Imamura Shohei, with Harukawa Masumi.

Most men would perhaps not make the connection between good juicy genitals and motherhood, but for Imamura this quality is necessary for a woman's full ability to nurture. This he openly shows in most of his films. In fact, an understanding of this link helps one approach the director's pictures. Imamura told critic Yamada Koichi: "I am interested in the relationship of the lower part of the human body and the lower part of the social structure on which the reality of daily Japanese life supports itself." [13]

The Imamura woman receives her first full-length portrait in *Pigs and Battleships* (Buta to gunkan, 1961), where Yoshimura Jitsuko cannot protect her innocence but closely guards her independence. In *The Insect Woman* (Nippon konchuki, 1963), the heroine (Hidari Sachiko) has the same absolute resolve as the ant we are shown attempting an up-hill climb in the first scene. In the last scene, like the insect, the protagonist struggles on: getting her stockings dirty, breaking the thong of her clog (mishaps that would make a Naruse heroine burst into tears), persevering despite these minor misfortunes.

Both this and the film which was to follow, *Intentions of Murder*, were cowritten with Hasebe Keiji, who had worked with Ichikawa Kon on both the early comedies and on *Confla-gration*, and who was particularly adept at creating an incisive, image-driven narrative. In the later film, the rape victim (Harukawa Masumi) outlives the rapist, legalizes her son, and triumphantly comes into her own in a man's world.

Imamura's women are all survivors. Within the first fifteen minutes of *A Man Vanishes* (Ningen johatsu, 1967), the female protagonist has forgotten about the missing object of her search (the vanished

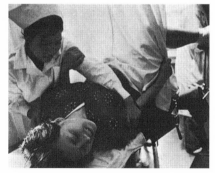

The Insect Woman, 1963, Imamura Shohei, with Hidari Sachiko.

man) and has pragmatically transferred her affections to the interviewer who is helping her find him. In *The Profound Desire of the Gods* (Kamigami no fukaki yokubo, aka Kuragejima: Tales from a Southern Island, 1968), the young shaman may be mentally disturbed but she also possesses a vitality that allows her to survive in a modern civilization which attempts to extinguish that very quality.

The Profound Desire of the Gods, 1968, Imamura Shohei, with Matsui Yasuko, Mikuni Rentaro.

Both Kawashima and Imamura find a refusal of "civilization" admirable because it is this primitive naturalness that is responsible for the wholeness which some Japanese still exhibit. It appears in various forms. In *The Pornographers* (Erogoto-shi-tachi yori: Jinrui-gaku nyumon, 1966), based on the popular Nosaka Akiyuki novel, the protagonist is a man who feels it is his duty to restore some of the things that civilization has denied. First on his list is pornography, which harms no one and pleases many. To this end he devotes himself to making blue films and manufacturing life-sized latex dolls. We watch him at work—a serious, dedicated Japanese craftsman. The film is like a documentary, an impression reinforced by the Japanese title of the film, whose literal translation is *Pornographers: An Introduction to Anthropology*. And at the end, busily, happily inserting real hair into his creation, the artisan at work does not notice that his houseboat studio has slipped its mooring line. In the calm coda of the film, we watch him drift, all unknowingly, through the canals of Osaka and out into the Pacific Ocean, presumably never to be heard of again—the end of a species.

In *The Profound Desire of the Gods*, filmed entirely on location on the southern island of Ishigakijima, much of the footage of its original three-hour length is devoted to the topography of the place, its flora and fauna, including the islanders whose ways are as primitive as they are natural. But two-thirds through, the story suddenly breaks off and a title tells us that several years have passed. The spot has been discovered by the tourist industry—planes, taxis, french fries. The final sequence—the shaman menaced by the new train—is affect-

The Pornographers, 1966, Imamura Shohei, with Sakamoto Sumiko.

ing because we have come to understand the primitive and to long for it. Now all is gone. The cry of the Coca-Cola seller is the voice of doom. It is the early Japanese, the "primitive" ones, who are real—not our rationalizing contemporaries.

Primitives are not taken in by accepted opinion. The hostess in *A History of Postwar Japan As Told by a Bar Hostess* (Nippon sengo-shi—Madamu Omboro no seikatsu, 1970) has only scorn for the official version of the Pacific War and its heroics. "It wasn't that way at all," she says. In *Eijanaika* (1981), it is the lowly showgirl (Momoi Kaori) who is the real rebel, and in *The Ballad of Narayama* (Narayama bushiko, 1983), Imamura's version of the same novel on which Kinoshita based his 1957 film, it is the mother (Sakamoto Sumiko) who imposes her will and orders her son to take her up to the mountain.

Imamura has said that he wanted to make really human, Japanese, unsettling films, thus implying that well-made, plotted, reconciling Japanese films are not really Japanese. Indeed the director has never liked the cinematically tidy. He has no more use for plot than Ozu did, though for different reasons. He prefers instead a series of stories or, if there is but one story, a chain of scenes only loosely interconnected. Imamura states his preference "for shooting true things." He elaborates: "If my films are messy, it is probably because I don't like too perfect a cinema. The audience must not admire the technical aspects of my filmmaking, as they would a computer or the laws of physics."[14]

The resulting spontaneous appearance of the films is nonetheless often the result of much planning. Even in the most documentary-like of all the films, *A Man Vanishes*, the "documentary" is a construct (cowritten with Nosaka Akiyuki) and the director's control is implicit, as in the scene where he (playing the director

A Man Vanishes, 1967, Imamura Shohei, with Hayakawa Yoshie, Tsuyuguchi Shigeru.

of this documentary they are making) and Tsuyuguchi Shigeru (playing the interviewer) talk about the woman at the center of the film, the one searching for the vanished man.

> *Imamura:* You know, she may be falling in love with you.
> *Tsuyuguchi:* That would be awful.
> *Imamura:* No, that is just what I want.[15]

So much for cinéma vérité. Imamura has in one line of dialogue openly exposed his intentions, made visible what most documentarians seek to hide: that a real-life film is as directed as any other kind, that the director still picks and chooses and thus creates his own reality.

In another such demonstration in the same film, the heroine asks, "Mr. Director, what is truth?" As though in answer, the walls of the private dining room in a small restaurant where they are sitting fall away. The lights are turned up, the camera dollies back to reveal that we are filming in a film studio, and in the midst of this enormous space sit the principals at a small table. "This is fiction," [16] says Imamura, answering the astonished woman's question. This coup de cinéma (only Imamura, not the others, knew what was going to happen) answers in the most convincing manner the somewhat *Rashomon*-like question. Reality is something we construct. As for abstract reality, it no more exists than does the abstract Japanese woman.

In Imamura's extremely tight, action-filled framing—sometimes there are smaller frames within the frames, windows, or doors, through which even more action can be glimpsed—he indicates his concerns. The director has written: "There are no shots in my films which do not contain human action. There are no empty landscapes or unmotivated cuts . . . The reason I work this way is to avoid the trap of only explaining character . . . I love all the characters in my films, even the loutish and frivolous ones. I want every one of my shots to express this love." Stasis, in the Ozu or Mizoguchi sense, would thus be a luxury his busy people cannot afford. It would also be an indication of dispassion, which Imamura himself does not possess. His explanation of this continues: "I'm interested in people, strong, greedy, humorous, deceitful people who are very human in their qualities and their failings. A reason that my fiction films sometimes look like documentaries is because I base my characters on research into real people." [17]

Likewise, Imamura cannot afford the temporal equivalent to empty spaces—free time. There are very few long, lingering, actionless shots until the late films: *Black Rain* (Kuroi ame, 1989), *The Eel* (Unagi, 1997), *Doctor Akagi* (Kanzo sensei, 1998), and *Lukewarm Water under the Bridge* (Akai hashi no shita no nurui mizu, 2001). Vitality is created through a crowded canvas and a breakneck speed.

In *The Insect Woman*, whole weeks are compressed into just three cuts. The heroine's child pulls a hot soup cauldron over and is scalded to death; cut to a detail of the child's body; cut to the crying mother, now at one of the new-religion centers—weeks have passed. Using the only punctuation that Ozu permitted himself, the straight cut, Imamura creates an equally laconic world.

Vengeance Is Mine (Fukushu suruwa ware ni ari, 1979), a study of a killer, is filled with temporal short cuts. The body of the first murder victim is found in an empty field; cut to a helicopter, then pan down to the field now swarming with police. A few scenes later, the murderer (Ogata Ken) is shown in a truck with his next victim; cut to the helicopter and the field;

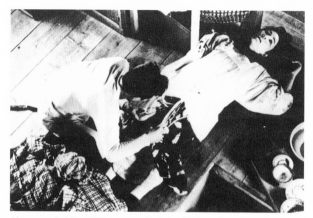

Vengeance Is Mine, 1979, Imamura Shohei, with Ogata Ken, Ogawa Mayumi.

cut to the murderer in a train looking out as the train passes the field. These scenes go by so fast and push the chronology at such a pace that one does not even notice all the scenes deliberately left out.

Sometimes, instead of cutting, Imamura will swiftly cram all we need to know into a single traveling shot—one filled with spatial variety, though the temporal value is constant. A spectacular example from the same film is composed of two end-to-end traveling shots. The first shows the murderer going to a new town. We are in the train with him. The scene is filled with passengers getting ready to get off the train. Through the windows, the station slides into view. When the murderer also alights, the camera gets off along with him, staying just behind as he traverses the platform, passes through the wicket, leaves the station, and gets into a taxi. Cut to the taxi stopping on a small street. The second traveling shot begins at once. The killer gets out, pays, walks up the street. The camera continues to follow him as he turns, opens a gate, passes through the garden, and enters an inn, through the windows of which we see the proprietress playing mahjong. Without interruption, the shot proceeds up the stairs as she leads him into the second-floor room, which will be his.

Though no time has been elided, the frame has been so filled with motion that the sequences, which are actually relatively long, seem short. They have pushed us into the film's chronology and made us feel its urgency. Like e-maki, these traveling shots have both informed and oriented, while at the same time producing an effect of overflowing vitality, one which bursts the confines of the frame. For its equal, the West would have to wait until the invention of the steadicam, as seen in the opening shot of Robert Altman's *The Player* (1992) and in the celebrated into-the-nightclub–through-the-kitchen-entry shot in Martin Scorsese's *Goodfellas* (1990).

Back in the late 1950s, when Nikkatsu was leading the way—with its new directors showing a modest profit and an enlarged, mostly young audience promising to reward its increased turnout of youth-oriented films—Shochiku, the most conservative of the companies, decided to allow its directors a bit more autonomy as well, something which it had previously accorded only Ozu Yasujiro and Kinoshita Keisuke.

Shochiku thus cautiously encouraged a number of assistant directors, among them Oshima Nagisa, Yoshida Kiju, and Shinoda Masahiro. This group was the nucleus of an identity later created by the media with the help of the studio: *nuberu bagu* (*nouvelle vague*, or "new wave"), a copy of the commercial designation used for the new French film product of the 1960s which incorporated such otherwise dissimilar directors as Jean-Luc Godard, François Truffaut, and Claude Chabrol.

That the audience was ready for a "new wave" kind of picture had already been indicated by the reception given the work of Hani Susumu, a very young director working completely outside the studio system. Hani was employed by Iwanami Eiga, the film-producing section of a publishing company, and his methods were utterly different from those who had studied filmmaking in the mainstream studios.

He had made a series of documentary shorts, most notably *Children in the Classroom* (Kyoshitsu no kodomotachi, 1954) and *Children Who Draw* (E wo kaku kodomotachi, 1956).

In 1960, Hani filmed his first feature, *Bad Boys* (Furyo shonen, 1961). Mixing documentary with fiction in this film about boys in a reformatory, Hani improvised scenes with the young delin-

Bad Boys, 1961, Hani Susumu.

quents. Starting with no story at all, he gradually built up a series of situations and, in the end, created a highly perceptive film. While the boys were sometimes told what the situation was, the dialogue was their own, as was the "acting." Hani soon discovered that the camera went largely ignored. Since the boys had all earlier spent time at the reform school, they quickly fell back into their old lives, the difference being, according to Hani, that now they were reliving their lives. This made the young actors thoughtful and gave the film a deliberate quality.

While the actors did not consider their actions, they seemed to be considering the consequences, which, of course, they already knew. This attractive ambivalence led to the ironic final scene of the film, where the protagonist, being released, thanks the institution which has formed (or perhaps deformed) him. This irony, with its implied social criticism, both made the film popular and earned it the Kinema Jumpo prize.

Hani's sense of irony was to continue into later films. His next feature was *A Full Life* (Mitasareta seikatsu, 1962). It was made for Shochiku and used well-known screen actors whom Hani continued to direct as though they were amateurs. In it, a young woman

A Full Life, 1962, Hani Susumu, with Arima Ineko.

(popular screen star Arima Ineko) wants to better herself. She tries various means: radical politics, drama troupes, a number of men. At the end, a very long close-up indicates that the woman has found happiness by behaving in the manner in which many Japanese housewives behave: subservient, repressed, feminine. But this does not lessen the irony.

She and He (Kanojo to kare, 1963) explores the same theme, a woman's attempts to discover herself, though no solution is offered here—ironic or otherwise. She (Hidari Sachiko, whom Hani had married) plays a happily married wife in the film itself; he, her husband (Okada Eiji), is a good provider. But this is not enough for her. Again, at the end, there is a long close-up as the wife lies in bed, sleepless, gazing into the darkness. She is half-afraid, half-hopeful.

She and He, 1963, Hani Susumu, with Hidari Sachiko.

The methods used in *She and He* are similar to those of *Bad Boys*. Hani and his scenarist, Shimizu Kunio, followed no script. They wrote the lines as they went along, and each set-up became a documentary-like affair. The theme of finding oneself is repeated in *Bride of the Andes* (Andesu no hanayome, 1966), a Toho production in which a mail-order bride (Hidari again), straight from Japan, feels that she must somehow find her true self, married, and in the wilds of Peru as she is.

Hani's women, well understood, well presented, are far from those of Mizoguchi Kenji or Yoshimura Kozaburo, and nearer to those of Imamura. Yet these directors would all agree that the Japanese woman is a fitting symbol of a problem which many face: how to learn to be yourself in a society that doesn't want you to. Though Mizoguchi's women largely fail, Hani's occasionally don't.

This need to realize the self is not limited to women. In the Daiei film *Children Hand in Hand* (Te wo tsunagu ko-ra, 1964), a remake of an Inagaki Hiroshi film from 1948 based on an earlier Itami Mansaku script, a backward child comes to realize his limitations and hence his possibilities. In *The Song of Bwana Toshi* (Buwana Toshi no uta, 1965), an ordinary Japanese man (Atsumi Kiyoshi, later famous as Tora-san) who never before bothered with notions as to who he might be other than a Japanese, finds himself without a clue in darkest Africa. The film is made of up documentary-like, unplotted scenes: Toshi up in a tree baying for hippopotami; the excitement and awe of the village people turning on the electric light for the first time; and the dancing finale in which we see Toshi pleased, embarrassed, happy, and very human.

Both the bride of the Andes and Toshi in Africa experience being outside Japan, away from the tradition which has so formed them. That tradition itself is by nature repressive is something which all people experience, but the Japanese experience it a bit more openly. Society wants citizens, not fully developed human beings. This theme animates much cultural expression, in Japan as elsewhere. In Hani's films, the theme of collective tradition versus freedom is an important one.

A major statement of this theme was *The Inferno of First Love* (Hatsukoi jigokuhen, aka Nanami: First Love, 1968), an independent (Art Theater Guild) film. An adolescent boy and girl meet and want to make love. She has had some experience and he has had none—but both are equally innocent. Their voyage to experience finds its central statement in the desperate sincerity of the young people and in the machinations of a society which threatens to (and eventually does) overwhelm them.

The Inferno of First Love, 1968, Hani Susumu, with Mitsui Koji, Takahashi Akio.

Sentimentality, posing an equal threat, is avoided by the harshness of the photography; by a nervous, prying camera; by the refusal of anything short of actual locations; and by the tact and grace with which the young people are directed. This thoroughly modern version of the giri-ninjo theme garnered great critical and popular acclaim, but it was also Hani's last major film.

With the "new wave" commercializing new attitudes, and the studios moving to cash in on what they perceived as a fresh, open market, Hani discovered further productions nudging him in ways he did not want to go. Since he had no commitment to the film industry, he returned to the documentary, a genre for which he is now famous in Japan: he is the fore-most director of wildlife films. In them, Hani finds a naturalness and, yes, as he recently phrased it, an innocence which he no longer finds in Japan.

Most "members" of the Japanese new wave did not even know each other, nor did they all come from the same studios. Hani was unaffiliated, as was Teshigahara Hiroshi who, son (and scion) of the founder of a very successful ikebana (flower-arrangement) school, early made experimental films and then privately financed his first feature, *Pitfall* (Otoshiana, 1962).

Pitfall, as was the case with the majority of this director's films, was scripted by novelist and playwright Abe Kobo. Their most successful film together was *Woman in the Dunes* (Suna no onna, 1964). It was, like most of their collaborations, a parable. A school teacher on an outing is imprisoned by the local folk in a large sand pit with a recently widowed woman. His attempts to escape are all unsuccessful. Eventually, he adapts to his impossible life. In discovering a way to make potable the water that seeps from the sand, he hits upon his purpose in life. When the chance to escape finally comes, he refuses it.

Woman in the Dunes, 1964, Teshigahara Hiroshi, with Kishida Kyoko, Okada Eiji.

The theme of the search for and discovery of identity shares much with the central theme of Hani's films, though Teshigahara's way of illustrating it is quite different. Early a maker of documentaries, Teshigahara combines great technical skill (extreme depth of focus, immaculate detail, elaborately choreographed camera movement) with a precise fidelity to his script, a combination which resulted in a number of interesting theme-related Abe-based films, such as *The Face of Another* (Tanin no kao, 1966) and *The Man Without a Map* (Moetsukita chizu, aka The Burned Map, 1968). In the former, a man loses his face in a laboratory accident and has a new one made for him. In the latter, a detective unwillingly assumes the identity of the missing man for whom he is searching.

Teshigahara has said that he believes his talents are those of a cameraman. It is certainly true that the documentary-like realism of his early work is striking. The two-part documentary, *José Torres* (1959 and 1965) and *Summer Soldiers* (Sama soruja, 1971), the latter scripted by John Nathan, are of a designed realism rare in Japanese films. Working closely

Summer Soldiers, 1971, Teshigahara Hiroshi, with Keith Sykes, Lee Reisen.

with photographer Segawa Hiroshi and composer Takemitsu Toru, Teshigahara created some of the most strikingly original films of the decade.

Later, having taken over as head of the ikebana school after his father's death, the director turned much more "Japanese." Interesting himself in traditional aesthetics, he made such heavily detailed historical dramas as *Rikyu* (1989) and *Princess Go* (Go-hime, aka Basara, 1992). This sudden return to an almost prewar-like monumentality was obviously predicated on the traditionalism of his new profession. It also affirmed a kind of cultural pattern we have previously encountered: a period of exploration in the various realities outside Japan, concluding with a return to Japanese tradition as it is understood.

THE "NEW WAVE": OSHIMA, YOSHIDA, AND SHINODA

C redit for the cresting of the "new wave" is usually given to Shochiku and the stable of young directors it initially sponsored. The first of these was Oshima Nagisa. A twenty-six-year-old assistant director, Oshima was given an unprecedented full-directorship under the "new-wave policy," designed to promote fresh and free films, and allowed to direct *A Town of Love and Hope* (Ai to kibo no machi, 1959). That Kido himself gave this hackneyed title to a film about neither love nor hope and which the director had wanted to call *The Boy Who Sold His Pigeon* indicated just how fresh and free the new-wave experience with the company was going to be.

Though Kido disliked the picture, calling it a "tendency film" and allowing it only restricted distribution, it got good reviews. After half a year the young director was allowed to go on and make *Cruel Story of Youth* (Seishun zankoku monogatari, aka Cruel Tales of Youth, 1960) and *The Sun's Burial* (Taiyo no hakaba, 1960). While these films could be seen as extensions of the concerns of the taiyozoku—violent youth in revolt—they were

Cruel Story of Youth, 1960, Oshima Nagisa, with Kawazu Yusuke, Kuwano Miyuki.

also found interesting by the critics for their narrative innovations and inherent social concerns. The filmmakers of the postwar era had embraced politics of a leftist humanism. Now Oshima went on to express disillusion with the organized left and a continued despair with the right.

Oshima's fourth film, *Night and Fog in Japan* (Nihon no yoru to kiri, 1960), was clearly intended as his declaration of independence. A political fable which criticizes both right and left, it was made with minimal means, many long takes, and is filled with theatricality. It is surprising that the director thought he could peacefully foist this on his studio, and it is amazing that Shochiku allowed him to make it at all. Perhaps the company was reassured by the inclusion of a wedding scene. The film, however, is not about a wedding. It is about the failure of the left to end the United States–Japan Security Treaty during the 1960 demonstrations. The film is so palpably opposite the concerns of Kido, so little in accord with the "Ofuna flavor," that one can only read its production as a challenge.

In his adversarial stance, Oshima was to Japanese cinema somewhat as Jean-Luc Godard was to the French. "I don't agree specifically with any of [Godard's] positions," Oshima told Joan Mellen, "but I agree with his general attitude in confronting political themes seriously in film . . ." [18] In Oshima's view, no one else was doing this. "My hatred for Japanese cinema includes absolutely all of it," [19] he said in a later interview. An earlier statement provides insight: "It is not a matter of good or bad. My point is that their films [Ozu's and Mizoguchi's] were made to be acceptable to the Japanese because they were based upon a familiarity with general concepts readily understandable by the Japanese—they used a narrative style long established and understood, but I am not attempting to remain within this congenial, older mode. Our generation cannot rely on the congeniality of our all being Japanese in order to communicate." [20]

If *Night and Fog in Japan* was intended as provocation, it was successful. Shochiku, provoked, shelved the film after only a few days on limited release. It used a recent political assassination as an excuse, pleading the risk of political "unrest." Oshima famously stormed out, calling for his studio to just stop using that term "new wave" once and for all. Shochiku did not, and indeed Oshima subsequently released a number of independently produced films through Shochiku.

A breach had been made, however, and film audiences now realized that there existed an alternate cinema. Oshima was even able to pinpoint its birth: "In the rip of a woman's skirt and the buzz of a motorboat, sensitive people heard the heralding of a new generation of Japanese film." [21] The reference is to *Crazed Fruit* (1956), by Nakahira Ko, one of the directors Oshima spared from his general condemnation.

Among the others thus reprieved was Masumura Yasuzo. Oshima lauded him for, as he said, turning his back on the lyricism dominant in Japanese society and cinema. He also approved of Masumura's saying that his goal was "to paint, in all their excess, the desires and passions of human beings." [22] Such a statement leads one to surmise that prior Japanese cinema did not do this, or at least not in terms that were acceptable to Oshima himself.

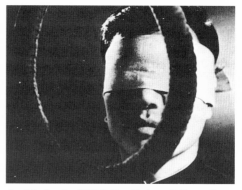

Just what the director expected of cinema is indicated in one of his most interesting pictures, *Death by Hanging* (Koshikei, 1968), based on

Death by Hanging, 1968, Oshima Nagisa, with Do-yun Yu.

a real incident which had occurred in 1958 and had already been the subject of several stories and a novel. According to Oshima, none of these prior authors had delved deeply enough to reveal what he called the core, the inside of the crime.

The plot concerns a young Korean who had presumably murdered a Japanese schoolgirl. In the resulting investigation, Oshima takes the Korean side (against which, on all issues, the Japanese are often prejudiced) and declares the youth ethically innocent. He argues that law is not possible without crime, and that policemen are unimaginable without criminals. Upon being assured that it is very bad to kill, the condemned young Korean boy observes with unassailable logic: "Then it is bad to kill me."

In order to prove to the suspect his own guilt, the police set out to re-enact the crime—each policeman playing a role. This device finds them first re-creating the rape and the murder before the uncomprehending eyes of the youth, and then going back further in time to act out the boy's earlier years, or rather, their idea of what his early years had been like. Being first and foremost Japanese and second, cops, their ideas of childhood in the Korean neighborhoods of Japan are bizarre indeed. Oshima skillfully underlines both the comedy of their lack of imagination and the horror of their lack of comprehension.

The policemen's inept pantomime is alienating to the extent that we fully feel the irony of this crime within a crime within a crime, the latter being capital punishment itself. The film accuses the police of being more obsessed with the idea of crime than any criminal is. Consequently, from a misguided wrongdoer the law literally creates a criminal.

This is brilliantly displayed when one of the policemen, carried away, attempts to kill. He is so intent upon re-creating a role that he assumes it. As Oshima has said (and in doing so explained Japan's continued failure to come to any sort of terms with its wartime past): "As long as the state makes the absolutely evil crime of murder legal through the waging of wars and the exercise of capital punishment, we are all innocent." [23]

Stylistically, the film is entirely presentational. The "realism" of Oshima's earlier films—already on its way out in *Night and Fog in Japan*—is nowhere to be seen. Those foreign critics who mention German playwright Bertolt Brecht in speaking of this film (and almost all of them do) are certainly correct in implicitly evoking the stage. Oshima was earlier interested in expressionist drama and belonged to a Kyoto troupe that specialized in it—not Brecht, however, so much as Frank Wedekind and Ernst Toler.

Just as expressionist drama is a drama of ideas, so Oshima's largely expressionist films are concerned with thought. We follow arguments in many of his pictures, and these are presented in stagelike or essay-like form. To the older generation these films appeared odd indeed.

The opinion of Kobayashi Masaki, under whom Oshima had worked as assistant director, is typical. After looking at his pupil's films, the older director said that, while they had a certain political interest, Oshima was clearly not an artist who loved the craft of film for itself.

Though some critics have sought to fit Oshima into the very mainstream he was trying to overthrow, the attempts have not been convincing. His stagelike settings and shallow playing spaces have been seen as continuations of early Japanese cinema; his expressionism has antecedents in various late-Taisho and early-Showa cinema; likewise, his staring camera—shots held for an unusually long time—is seen as something he shares with Mizoguchi Kenji.

All of this is problematical. When one sees a long-held scene in contemporary Japanese cinema, the influence of Mizoguchi is but one possibility. The influence of Michelangelo

Antonioni, of the "talking head," of the television interview—all of these are equally likely. In the case of Oshima, since words are as important to him as images, and ideas are perhaps more important than emotions, the long take is one of his most effective tools.

Oshima's style is eclectic—it becomes whatever best serves his purposes. The stagelike artificiality of films such as *Death by Hanging* is followed by the "realism" of *Boy* (Shonen, 1969). The slow pace of *Night and Fog in Japan* (only forty-three shots in the whole film) is followed by the swift pace (fifteen hundred shots) in *Violence at Noon* (Hakuchu no torima, 1966). In this sense, Oshima is like a multitude of directors, regardless of their respective political stances.

One might equally see Oshima as a more serious Suzuki Seijun. Both use popular culture, both are concerned with political ideas, both love talk for its own sake, and both share a very real renegade inventiveness.

Boy, 1969, Oshima Nagisa, with Abe Tetsuo, Koyama Akiko.

Both are also intellectuals whose films are about political sedition. This is what Imamura Shohei indicated when, comparing himself with the younger director, he said: "I'm a country farmer; Oshima Nagisa is a samurai." [24] He was implying that he was not interested in politics and that Oshima was interested in little else.

One of the most political and, at the same time, autobiographical of Oshima's pictures is *The Ceremony* (Gishiki, 1971), the story of a family as shown through their ceremonial occasions of weddings and funerals. This twenty-five-year period of postwar history, which somewhat resembles Oshima's own early years, is seen as both personal and as an allegory of postwar Japan. Each ceremony is carefully timed to coincide with a year significant in the postwar history of Japan. Each marks a stage on a downward spiral, for it is the "spiritual death" of Japan that Oshima is chronicling.

Oshima as romantic intellectual is a reading which might account for some of his extremes and much of

The Ceremony, 1971, Oshima Nagisa, with Kaku Atsuko, Kawarazaki Kenzo.

his style. "I'm very self-indulgent," he once said. "I like to do extreme things—the more enthusiastic I am, the more extreme my technique becomes." [25] *The Man Who Left His Will on Film* (Tokyo senso sengo hiwa, 1970) is an elaborately self-referential picture: a young filmmaker shoots a film about shooting a film. *Summer Sister* (Natsu no imoto, 1972) is a simple allegory about Japan's relations with its southernmost, and most recent, province, Okinawa. In it, a Tokyo girl receives a letter from an Okinawan boy claiming to be her long-lost brother. The styles of the films are so different that one would not guess they were the work of the same director.

Another new direction emerged in *In the Realm of the Senses* (Ai no korida, aka Empire of the Senses, aka The Realm of the Senses, 1976). Based on an actual occurrence, the film is about a man and a woman completely consumed with each other. Sex had always been present in Oshima's films, usually as a metaphor for political power—man over woman—but

in this picture the sexual relationship is equal. Kichizo, a real 1930s *bonchi*, is as completely enamored of Osada, the new maid in the house, as she is of him. Their love is shown in entirely sexual terms.

The film's erotic content has led it to be described as hard-core, which, in part, it is. This should not, however, be confused with pornographic. Yet the film was refused screen-

In the Realm of the Senses, 1976, Oshima Nagisa, with Fuji Tatsuya, Matsuda Eiko.

ing at the 1977 New York Film Festival. And, in 2000, when it was revived "uncut" in Japan, it was only the woman who was rendered visible—the man, whose nudity (vulnerability) is to be avoided at all costs in sexist countries, was still modestly censored. As Oshima has said, such censorship made his pure film dirty. The film certainly does not seek to excite its audience. Indeed, given its outcome, the result is just the opposite.

Ian Buruma has described one view of the film: "Sex becomes the lovers' whole claustrophobic universe and after strangling her lover during a shuddering climax, the girl cuts off his penis as the ultimate gesture of possession. It is a beautiful but frightening film perfectly expressing that anxious-sensuous ambivalence which is so much a part of the Japanese psyche." [26]

In the Realm of the Senses is also Oshima's most openly transgressive film. It attempts to break all the various "public decency" laws in Japan, and actually involved the police in a law suit. Oshima demanded that "obscene" be defined. Given this impossibility, he won the case. Notwithstanding, the "public decency" laws extant at the time remain unchanged to this day. As a political statement, the film fails. As an artistic statement of great beauty and power, it is eminently successful. And as for those in Japan who maintained that the director had sold out to the foreign porn market, he retorted: "Completely involved as I am with being a Japanese, I have no way to make films except by examining the Japanese and endeavoring to discover what they are."[27]

Given the opportunity to examine Japan's actions in World War II, Oshima directed the Japanese-British coproduction *Merry Christmas, Mr. Lawrence* (Senjo no meri kurisumasu, 1983). And, in a Japanese-French coproduction, *Max, Mon Amour* (1987), he had the chance to view sexual relations with a parodic twist: woman loves ape. Though his own sense of history continued to broaden, he confessed to Bock: "I don't feel that the age of the samurai is mine yet."

Nonetheless, after a long silence and a serious illness, Oshima finally directed his samurai film, *Gohatto* (aka Taboo/Forbidden, 1999). With *In the Realm of the Senses*, the director shows the lovers' ardor triumphing over customs, mores, and even their own deaths. *Gohatto* repeats the theme, in that love destroys. Yet, by 1999, heterosexual love on screen, through repeated exposure, had already lost its transgressive power. Oshima therefore turned to another expression of desire.

The society at the film's core is the Shinsengumi, an elite group of swordsmen commissioned in 1863 to form a police unit to counter anti-shogunate activities. They are fanatically

Gohatto, 1999, Oshima Nagisa.

loyal, think as a group, and attempt to subdue personal feelings. Into their midst is enrolled an extremely handsome youth. Passion grips the all-male Shinsengumi, discipline disappears, and death results.

In creating this beautiful and startling film, Oshima (who also wrote the script, basing it on a Shiba Ryotaro novel) is aided by his actors, film directors Sai Yoichi and Kitano Takeshi among them; by the photography of Kurita Toyomichi; and by a carefully sustained atmosphere of rigid enclosures opening into rich autumnal gardens. Beautifully styled, essentially static (despite bursts of swordplay), its anti-establishment message remains strong.

Within Shochiku, the director perhaps most resembling Oshima was Yoshida Kiju. His *Good-for-Nothing* (Rokudenashi, 1960), a juvenile-delinquent film about student crimes, could be compared with *The Cruel Story of Youth*. In *Dried Blood* (Chi wa kawaiteiru, 1960), the criminal elements are more mature but still mixed with social concern.

In *The Affair* (Joen, 1967), social concern is even more evident. A young woman (played by the director's wife, Okada Mariko) fights against her own sensual nature. She has her reasons, among which is this reaction against a mother who slept around. Nonetheless, when she gives in—with a young day laborer who had known her mother—she gives in thoroughly. The combination of well-to-do young lady and common laborer predicates society's disapproval. Yet for the daughter, these meaningless social prejudices—violate them though she will—are the only "normality" to which she can cling.

Formally shot and edited with much economy, the film ends honestly. Having settled with a proper man, we find the woman one day waiting for a train. Suddenly, and with a surge of emotion that Yoshida makes us feel, she sees the young laborer on the other side of the tracks waiting for a train going in the opposite direction. His train arrives first. She waits. When the train pulls clear he is gone. She continues to stand there. We are to infer that at this moment she realizes how false to her own nature she has been.

Later, *Eros Plus Massacre* (Erosu purasu gyakusatsu, aka Eros Plus Vengeance, 1970) and *Heroic Purgatory* (Rengoku eroika, 1970) greatly enhanced the director's reputation.

Eros Plus Massacre, 1970, Yoshida Kiju, with Kusunoki Yuko, Hosokawa Toshiyuki.

The former is a long and complicated examination of sexual and political liberation. Written by Yoshida and Yamada Masahiro, it is about love and anarchism—as its title indicates. Cutting between two stories—one set in the present, the other in the early Taisho period—it concerns two lovers who are both documentary filmmakers and student radicals. Their relationship is mirrored in the second story, that of Osugi Sakae—an early advocate of free love, abolition of private property, and women's liberation—and her lover.

Though Yoshida has called his films an "answer" to the films of Ozu, Kinoshita, Kurosawa and other traditional directors, he is not unaware of their influences. "Just as the last half of [Kurosawa's] *Ikiru* is concentrated on the . . . discussion of the deceased Watanabe, so [my film] focuses on contemporary persons who act thinking of the dead." [28] This is particularly true of *Promise* (Ningen no yakusoku, 1986)—scripted after a Sae Shuichi novel by Miyauchi Fukiko and the director himself—which might be seen as a new kind of *Tokyo Story*. Here an old man (Mikuni Rentaro) murders his elderly spouse (Murase Sachiko) because of the various horrors of old age. Through *Ikiru*-like flashbacks chronicling the stages of his confession, we are brought to understand senility and the virtues of anaesthesia.

Indeed, one of the qualities of these new films of the late 1960s was their innovative combination of both radical and traditional means though, with Western style now so much a part of the Japanese cinema, it is often impossible to determine whether the compositional decentering of a scene, for example, is to be traced to the Japanese woodblock prints, Mizoguchi, Antonioni, or modern graphic design.

Another of the Shochiku "new wave" directors, one quite different from Oshima or Yoshida, was Shinoda Masahiro. Though, like them, he came from a theatrical background (earlier directors, by contrast, such as Ozu, Mizoguchi, Kurosawa, and Ichikawa had been graphic artists), Shinoda was the only one of the group who had majored in theatrical history. This, he has said, gave him an aesthetic distance denied the others. "Reality for its own sake is not what interests me," he told Audie Bock. "If my films had to be perfect reconstructions of reality, I would not make them. I begin with reality and see what higher idea comes out of it." [29]

In his conviction that something higher than reality exists, Shinoda followed in the steps of the directors he admired more than any others: Ozu and Mizoguchi. He worked with the former as assistant on *Tokyo Twilight*, in 1958, and was deeply impressed. Ozu, the young Shinoda told Kido Shiro, was like an aloof reclining deity observing the human world, perhaps looking for and finding that higher reality.

Even the "new wave" films Shinoda made are quite different from those of the other young directors herded into the movement. The best of these films, *Pale Flower* (Kawaita hana, 1964), is really as much about ceremonial behavior as was Mizoguchi's *The Loyal Forty-Seven Ronin*, though the subject is the yakuza rather than ronin. Shinoda has said he chose this subject because the yakuza world is the only place where the Japanese ceremonial structure is sustained, where an aesthetic response to ceremony is still possible. Though the young hero stoically dies—exemplifying that "masochism" which Shinoda claims is inherent in the aesthetic impulse—there is little bloodshed, and the violence is choreographed in a traditional fashion.

Pale Flower, 1964, Shinoda Masahiro, scene from the opening gambling sequence.

The opening is particularly striking in its ceremonial presentation. The gangsters are gathered in the gaming room and—in a montage of over one hundred and forty shots that precedes the first dialogue in the film—the atmosphere of the place and its people is presented. To intensify and dramatize this, the director and his composer, Takemitsu Toru, altered the sound track. The actual sound of the cards being cut and shuffled is replaced by the sound of a tap-dancing routine. The degree of formalization which this creates is even now surprising.

It was this opening that heralded the many troubles Shinoda would experience, ones which resulted in his—like everyone else's—leaving the hapless Shochiku. When the scriptwriter for *Pale Flower* (Baba Ataru, working from a story of Ishihara Shintaro) saw his dialogue shoved aside to make room for all the audio-visuals, he was so angry he took his complaints to the company. Had he not also accused Shinoda of making an "anarchistic" film, his complaints would perhaps not have been taken so seriously. But the times were such that this accusation resulted in a nine-month delay in the film's release.

Though the film was successful according to Shinoda—he avers it served as a model for the form and appearance of Toei's yakuza genre—he went on to make more overtly Mizoguchi-like pictures. In the series of films that followed—*With Beauty and Sorrow* (Utsukushisa to kanashimi to, 1965), based on a Kawabata novel; *Clouds at Sunset*

(Akanegumo, 1967); and *Banished Orin* (Hanare goze orin, aka Symphony in Gray, 1977), photographed by Miyagawa Kazuo—the protagonists, all of them women, bear a strong family resemblance to the long-suffering heroines of Mizoguchi and, indeed, are photographed like them—long takes, distant, aesthetically balanced scenes, and camera movements which seem to lead these doomed women (usually played by the director's wife, Iwashita Shima) to their eventual destruction.

The most successful of the director's later films is *Double Suicide* (Shinju ten no amijima, 1969), based upon a bunraku play by Chikamatsu. Not only is it less "adapted" than either the Mizoguchi or Masumura Yasuzo versions of what amounts to the same material, its presentation is different as well. Both playwright and director share a fatalistic view—destiny awaits, man is incapable of escaping from it.

The film's overriding fatalism is illustrated by its use of the doll drama itself. The film opens at the Osaka bunraku theater, where all of the preparations for making the film are seen: light cables are laid, camera positions are determined, and the director himself appears, as do his technicians and his scriptwriter, Tomioka Taeko. The film begins as a doll-drama documentary, drawing attention to how each puppet is held and manipulated by the traditional three men, two of whom are masked. As the story proceeds, Shinoda substitutes actors for the puppets. The actors take

Double Suicide, 1969, Shinoda Masahiro, with Nakamura Kichiemon, Iwashita Shima.

over the telling of the story. One-shot, one-scene methods are used, and the completely theatrical artificiality of the doll drama is insisted upon.

Yet, though the dolls are now alive, the puppeteers remain. They are always there, masked by black gauze, behind which we see their faces, compassionate yet helpless as they watch the characters—now thoroughly human—find their way to their fate. Shinoda told Sato Tadao that these figures are as much a part of his film as they are of the puppet play, that they "serve as agents for the viewer who wants to penetrate the truth of the lovers' plight [their eventual double suicide]." They also represent Chikamatsu himself who, in this modern reading of the play, "created this antisocial world, tinged with the melodramatic concept of a double suicide."[30]

The story is a simple one: giri-ninjo, duty versus love in this case. The world is that of the doll drama—all flats and painted sets. When the hero gives way to despair, it is a stage set he destroys—closed, claustrophobic, inescapable. This world, as stylized and contrived as that of, say, *The Cabinet of Doctor Caligari*, is filmed as though it is realistic—there is little cutting, only two hundred and forty shots; and most of the movement is that of the turning, gliding camera.

It is also the world as theater. Shinoda returns in this film to the near beginnings of cinema, for the good reason that his story—inescapable fate—is close to those of early films. The experimental nature of the picture (little is owed to contemporary film narrative) and its beauty (art direction by Awazu Kiyoshi; photography by Narushima Toichiro; music by Takemitsu Toru, who also helped write the script) make this return to simplicity a moving experience, one which illustrates Chikamatsu's fatalistic concept of awaited destiny and the impossibility of escape.

That our destiny will catch us in the end and that love, a supposed lifesaver, will sink before anything else is again illustrated in *Assassination* (Ansatsu, 1964), a picture which Ichikawa Kon, an early supporter of Shinoda, thought his finest work. The film takes place in 1863 (with flashbacks to earlier action) and deals with the plots and counterplots which resulted in the opening of the country. Shinoda—like any period-film director—takes for granted that the audience knows the ramifications of the story and quickly draws the viewer into these

Assassination, 1964, Shinoda Masahiro, with Okada Eiji, Kimura Isao.

complications, whether he comprehends them or not. It has been said that the story is not to be understood without a précis, and if this is true it would still not bother the director.

Shinoda is not interested in the intricacies of history. They are useful only insofar as they establish the kinds of action necessary for the disclosure of the director's main concern—an exclusively aesthetic one—namely, the shape of men's lives, the patterns they make. This interest accounts for both the director's cursory treatment of history and for the structure of the film itself.

In the first reel we believe that we are being introduced to the heroes and that their talk is about the villains. By the time the second reel is over, however, we have learned enough to know that those we first thought were heroes may very well be villains, and vice versa. As the film progresses, we are led to question the ethical moves of everyone in the picture. Nothing is certain.

At the same time, a strongly realistic presentation encourages our belief. Yamada Nobuo's script, based on the Shiba Ryotaro novel, is as prosaic of fact as it is baroque of gesture; Kosugi Masao's black-and-white photography is purposely grainy, with strong contrasts, looking like a feudal newsreel; and Takemitsu's music is spare and evocative of the period. Shinoda, as was to become his custom when making historical films, shows us as many authentic structures as he can find. The result is a film in which uncertainty is tempered by an apparent reality. Shinoda said that he wanted to see what "higher idea" could come out of reality. This is just what he attempts in *Assassination*. In this regard, he was much like Mizoguchi, who would sometimes tell an understated story through the most definite of realistic means. Shinoda once said of a Mizoguchi scene: "The portrait of Oharu's despairing flight through the bamboo grove [in *The Life of Oharu*] conveys as much of the tragedy of the human condition as any film ever made." [31] We don't know where she is going or even exactly why, but the woman and the grove are as real as life itself.

Sometimes, however, Shinoda's delicately balanced aestheticism may be an end in itself. Examples are his "kabuki" film, *The Scandalous Adventures of the Buraikan* (Buraikan, 1970), based on a Terayama Shuji script; a later bunraku film (also after Chikamatsu), *Gonza the Spearman* (Yari no Gonza, 1986); an evocation of old Edo, *Sharaku* (1995); and the spectacular chambara, *Owl Castle* (Fukuro no shiro, 1999)—all beautifully mannered exercises in the Mizoguchi mode, with mannerist finish taking the place of character interest.

Indeed, this heightened aestheticism is to be observed in others of the "new wave." Oshima Nagisa's aesthetic concerns in *Gohatto* had critics comparing the film to the late Mizoguchi pictures of forty years before. Yoshida Yoshishige's *Wuthering Heights* (Arashigaoka, 1988), the Emily Brontë novel done in a period setting, is concerned almost entirely with art for its own sake. These films also indicate a Japanese characteristic— a return to a self-conscious Japaneseness after a period of foreign-inspired experimentation.

AFTER THE WAVE

Following the innovations of the 1960s and the gradual accommodation of the "new wave" directors, it would have been appropriate if—had the finances of the motion picture industry made it possible—another new wave of young directors were to have appeared in the 1980s. They did not.

The majority audience, debauched by television, vanished forever. Despite occasional visits to movie houses for pictures about dogs left behind in the Antarctic and the like, a regular audience would never return. The later story of the Japanese film industry (as distinguished from the later story of the Japanese cinema) is one of decline and bankruptcy. Thus far in this account, we have followed a number of industrial ups and downs—always against a background of general audience availability. Now there was no general audience available.

Genre products kept some companies afloat for a time. Yamada Yoji's *Tora-san: It's Tough Being a Man* (Otoko wa tsuraiyo, 1969–96) series, which continued its success until the death of its star (Atsumi Kiyoshi as the beloved "Tora-san"), kept Shochiku solvent for decades.

Genre as such, however, could no longer command a market. What happened to the yakuza film is instructive. With the jidaigeki fading into television, this modern descendant of the *matatabi-mono* became, for a time, the leading action-film genre. Yakuza etiquette is really a parody of the samurai code, and its expression is actually a continuation of what one critic called the "Chushingura mentality." With such "Japanese" virtues as loyalty, dedication, and subservience inculcated, one might have thought that a lasting popularity was assured.

Stylistically conservative, the yakuza genre was further a "rationalized" product in that it was constructed of standard units: the "return" scene, the "identification" scene, the "reconciliation" scene. These were shot, from film to film, in more or less identical fashion. Like many traditional Japanese cultural products, the films were constructed of modules, one attached to another. Not only did they resemble the chambara in this way, they even reflected Onoe Matsunosuke's methods—one duel per reel. Such rationalization also means a product which is cheaper to make and easier to distribute, thus reducing the unit price.

Yet the popularity of the yakuza film lasted only a decade, from about 1963 to 1973. Film yakuza, models of submission, were quite unlike the modern gangsters with which audiences were now familiar from crime films. What is more, the sacrifice of individuality for the sake of the group (giri-ninjo again), the message inherent in the ritualistic yakuza film, was of little interest to a more permissive, younger audience. As a result, though producers forced directors to keep churning out the product, the genre itself died.

Many genres died along with the yakuza film, including the "youth film," a product whose directors were now said to have reached an average age of sixty-five. Eventually, in the eighties and nineties, the yakuza film became just another vehicle for violence, along with films about fast cars, aliens, and natural disasters. As has been mentioned, there was some attempt to rethink the genre, notably in the films of Kitano Takeshi, Miike Takashi, and others, but it never again attained an audience-wide popularity.

In 1971, Daiei turned turtle, carrying down Chairman Nagata with it. Later, other companies tried to stay afloat by turning to the production of *roman-porno*, a soft-core pornographic genre which was to take the place of clandestine blue films, themselves victims of the pre-Olympic Games cleanup. Among the first was Takechi Tetsuji's *Day Dream* (Hakujitsumu, 1964), a Shochiku picture after a story by Tanizaki Jun'ichiro. Though it was a simple exploitation picture, filled with rising breasts and open thighs, it aroused some public dismay, including a protest from the Japan Dental Association since the crazed hero who has his way with the ample heroine is a dentist. There was private dismay as well. Tanizaki, who had wanted so much to raise the standards of early Japanese cinema, was publicly furious at this example of their decline.

Director Takechi got into deeper trouble with *Black Snow* (Kuroi yuki, 1965). This picture, about an impotent young man who makes love with a loaded pistol (instead of the more usual weapon), was highly critical of that safe target, the American bases in Japan. Nonetheless, the Metropolitan Police Board sued. Though Takechi and Shochiku won and a higher court upheld the verdict, the director shortly went back to the stage, from whence he had come.

There was now precedent for others to build on. Roman-porno buoyed up Nikkatsu, at least for a time. *Roman* comes from "romantic," the idea being that this somehow made the product respectable. In French the word means "novel" (as in the literary genre), lending the results a jun-bungaku–like luster. For years, Nikkatsu made nothing but these films. Their novelty, while it lasted, was enough to ensure a kind of audience and to generate competition as well. Many new talents emerged, among them Kumashiro Tatsumi, a director with literary pretensions. *The World of Geisha* (Yojohan fusuma no urabari, 1973) was based on a jun-bungaku Nagai Kafu story.

Other, smaller companies began to issue plain, if soft-core, blue films, with no romantic or literary embellishments. Japan has a category for everything, and so such pictures were called *erodakushon*, a portmanteau word derived from "erotic productions." Though never hard-core, their intent was titillation. In this, they were successful, since they made up in numbers what they lacked in everything else. For a time, almost half of the annual film production figures released in Japan were composed of these hour-long minifeatures.

Usually arranged into a triple bill, the pictures were produced by small independent companies (such as Okura) and projected in the companies' own theaters, which never showed anything else. One of their Matsunosuke-like rules was that a stimulating scene should occur every five minutes. As the genre became more established, the films became more pretentious, with room for artistic and political self-importance—as in the films of Wakamatsu Koji.

Though the product was too severely rationalized to permit anything like creative filmmaking, the roman-porno studios did provide a training school once the major studios had declined to the point where the master-apprentice system ceased to exist. These smaller studios served as a training ground for many younger directors.

The larger film companies began diversifying when it became apparent that making films was no longer a viable business. Handicapped by heavy studio costs and by a relentless double-bill distribution which demanded over one hundred films a year from each of the producing companies, other means of making money seemed the only solution. Thus occurred the anomalies of Shochiku bowling alleys; Daiei supermarkets; and heavy investments in railroads, all-girl dancing troupes, and baseball teams.

The collapse of the film industry (a phenomenon observed in every country that had one) did not, of course, mean the collapse of film—as entertainment, art, or both. It merely indicated that one unrealistically expensive way of making a formula product was no longer operative. There was still an enormous movie audience, but it was a minority one. At the same time, this smaller audience was not attracted to an industry where the producers were afraid of the new and the original, and where directors had little say in the kind of work they produced. In Japan, as in other countries, one answer was independent film—pictures made outside of the studio system. This had revitalized cinema in both Europe and America, and it would now benefit the home front as well.

An initial problem for the independents was not only the exclusive nature of the ruling majors but also the fact that the latter had a cartel on almost all of the theaters. At the same time, each major had to keep its houses filled with expensive double-billed features. In these trying times, a company sometimes did not make enough product and had to acquire a hopefully profitable picture from outside its purviews. An independent film such as Shindo Kaneto's *The Naked Island* (1960) remained unshown. No theater was willing to take it, that is, until it won the Moscow Prize in the same year of its production, thereby enhancing its attractiveness to theaters back in Japan. A Toei theater was found for it, and shortly other directors discovered that their productions could find a home within the beleaguered majors themselves.

Perhaps attracted by the title, Shochiku released *The Body* (Ratai, 1962), an independent debut film from Narusawa Masashige, who had scripted Toyoda Shiro's *The Mistress* and worked on the later Mizoguchi films. This delicate and understated comedy is based on a Nagai Kafu story, about a young girl (Saga Michiko, daughter of Yamada Isuzu) who becomes aware of her charms and proceeds to use them—not Shochiku's kind of film at all, but in these times you took what you could get.

The company also released *Tokyo Bay* (Hidarikiki no sogekisha: Tokyo wan, 1962), an excellent chase-thriller about cops and robbers in Japan's capital, directed by Nomura Yoshitaro, son of company old-timer, Nomura Hotei. For its part, Nikkatsu allowed *Black Sun* (Kuroi taiyo, 1964), Kurahara Koreyoshi's serious film about the bond between a Japanese jazz-loving youth and an AWOL GI.

The Body, 1962, Narusawa Masashige, with Saga Michiko, Nagato Hiroyuki.

There were, in addition, a growing number of noncommercial experimental films. These would eventually be collected in the archives of Tomiyama Katsue's Image Forum, but originally they were individual efforts which showed wherever they could—rarely in motion-picture theaters, though the independent Sasoriza screened a number. Among these noncommercial experimental films were those of Terayama Shuji, a poet and playwright whose theatrical troupe, the Tenjo Sajiki, produced some of the most interesting theater of the period. His film *Throw Away Your Books, Let's Go into the Streets* (Sho wo suteyo, machi e deyo, 1971) is a playfully anarchist call which could never have found its way into a commercial motion-picture theater.

The first major attempt to produce independent commercial films and encourage their screening was the Art Theater Guild (ATG), backed by a consortium which had some Toho money but which was mainly the work of Towa (headed by Nagamasa and Kawakita Kashiko), the foremost importer of foreign films. Originally, ATG's theaters were for foreign art films (they were the first to show Ingmar Bergman, Robert Bresson, and Luis Buñuel in Japan). Later, ATG offered half the production costs for new Japanese films, a welcome move, particularly to the survivors of the "new wave," nearly all of whom had lost their jobs.

Thus, such important films as Oshima's *The Ceremony*, and Hani's *The Inferno of First Love* were ATG pictures. In addition, the company helped fund the films of independent filmmakers such as Higashi Yoichi. With ATG's help he made *Third* (Sado, aka A Boy Called Third Base, 1978), based on a Terayama Shuji script, and went on to direct the prize-winning *Village of Dreams* (E no naka no boku no mura, 1996). Jissoji Akio's *This Transient Life* (Mujo, 1970) and Matsumoto Toshio's *Funeral Parade of Roses* (Bara no soretsu, 1969) also benefitted from ATG assistance. Kuroki Kazuo was given his first directorial opportunity by ATG and later went on to make *The Assassination of Ryoma* (Ryoma ansatsu, 1974), *Ronin-gai* (1990)—a remake of the 1928 Makino Masahiro film of the same name—and the autobiographical *A Boy's Summer in 1945* (Utsukushii natsu Kirishima, 2003). Though it only lasted ten years, ATG was responsible for sustaining Japanese cinema during its most difficult period.

When the crunch was over, toward the end of the 1970s, Japanese film had found an audience, a much smaller one, and though income from foreign-film showings now far surpassed that from Japanese-film showings, there were at least a number of independent companies and theaters that could carry on a tradition.

Though three of the major companies— Toho, Shochiku and Toei—are still somehow surviving as of this writing, it has long been apparent that they are being kept alive by means other than simple filmmaking. The film industry, in Japan, had gone the way of all others. And here, as elsewhere, the death of the industry allowed new forms of cinema to emerge.

Third, 1978, Higashi Yoichi, with Nagashima Toshiyuki.

MAKING AUDIENCES

Just as new forms of cinema require new audiences, new spectators require new kinds of movies. Among the many innovative changes in the media during the last decades of the twentieth century, diverse technologies created different kinds of audiences. These, in turn, made possible both divergent means of viewing and fresh genres to view. Once again, a local shift could be observed in which a "pattern of initial Western influence [was] followed by the development of 'purely' Japanese forms, [a pattern] which has been repeated again and again, not only in individual careers but throughout the culture."[1] In a way, the end of the century was like the Taisho era all over again.

Japan, always technologically adept, soon found new ways to create and augment this newly segmented audience. Just as earlier Japanese film had successfully divided the field, so too had it sought to create its audiences. During the early postwar years, the industry even allocated its spectators: Daiei and Toho appealed to the urban young, Shochiku sought the family, and Toei had the rurals and whatever Japan possessed of the lower classes.

When the large audience and the enormous profits disappeared, it seemed only natural to exert audience control over what was left, though in a considerably simplified manner. As always, the controlling power was the producing company.

To be sure, producers (usually representing the film company itself) have always ordained product—it is after all their money that is being invested. Hitherto, however, certain films had made enough money that some directors—Mizoguchi Kenji, Ozu Yasujiro, Kinoshita Keisuke, and for a time, Kurosawa Akira—were allowed to make what they wanted. Their box-office record was good, and occasional losses could be written off. There were also a large number of producers who desired fine films just as much as the directors did.

Kikushima Ryuzo, for example, one of Kurosawa's writers, was the producer not only of *Red Beard* but of Naruse Mikio's fine film, *When a Woman Ascends the Stairs*. Even the policies of Daiei's Nagata (who was concerned mainly with money) and Toho's eclectic

Tanaka Tomoyuki (who produced everything from *Yojimbo* to *Mothra*) allowed fine films to slip through.

As movie attendance declined, such a state of affairs could not continue. Kurosawa, at the end of his career, said: "One reason why we had so many good directors is that Japanese studios gave talented people the freedom to make the movies they wanted. Now, however, the people in the marketing department are in charge—and all they think about is the box office. [So] they keep remaking the same kinds of pictures. If a movie about a cat does well, they make one about a dog." [2]

Indeed, both feline and canine films made money at the box office. *Milo and Otis* (Koneko monogatari, aka The Adventures of Chatran, 1987), assistant-directed by, of all people, Ichikawa Kon, and *The Story of the Loyal Dog, Hachiko* (Hachiko monogatari, 1986), with a script by, of all people, Shindo Kaneto, were successful financially. The animals were rigorously controlled—there was even a rumor that quite a number of similar-appearing cats had to be used in filming the feline's dangerous adventures. Carefully controlled, as well, was the audience.

Subjected to what were, at the time, unprecedented levels of advertising hype, the curious flocked, money was made, and a precedent was created. The pictures, of course, were unexceptional. As Umberto Eco has observed, mass media insists upon repetition, redundancy, and iteration as well as obedience to a schema. This means that the film is fit only as product, and soon only product fits the audience.

In this cycle, since the cultural traffic is all in one direction, any cultural creativity that is not mainstream will be neglected. Whole visual cultures, many venerable, will disappear, along with the personal vision of the artist and the apprehension of all that is different— since these are contrary to the expectations of mass media.

The growing control of producers and the marketing people was not the only reason for change, however. Japan's new directorial talent was not interested in the values that Kurosawa and his contemporaries had been interested in. These larger issues—the collapse of prewar Japan, the Western "invasion," the problems of the new individuality—did not concern young directors, all born after World War II and nurtured by a then-burgeoning economy.

Kurosawa Kiyoshi (no relation to Kurosawa Akira), from this new generation, refers to directors such as Ozu and Kurosawa as "masters of the studio system." Yet, he says, they have little meaning: "Sometimes when I watch their pictures on television they seem like foreign films to me. Even though I'm a fan of Ozu, they are so different from our time and our films now." [3]

One of the differences is that the new product is mostly genre oriented. This is partially due to what the new forms, such as computer games, music videos, anime, and a wealth of special effects, can accomplish. Pictures tend to exploit the latest means. Easy morphing means monsters; inexpensive explosions means violence.

To be sure, Japan had always devoted itself more to genre than had many other countries. There was jidaigeki, gendaigeki, haha mono (about mothers), tsuma mono (about wives), the tendency film, and a myriad of others. But at the same time, there were also a large number of films which were not generic in inspiration.

By the end of the century, however, a majority of the product were determined by genre. As Kurosawa Kiyoshi saw it, after the studio system collapsed and production ceased, genres actually grew fewer in number, while those that remained became ubiquitous. "The dominant genre today is the yakuza genre. I think the reason for this is that the Japanese audience likes Hollywood films. That is why the main genres are mysteries and thrillers and yakuza films. And, of course, one of the most important names here is Kitano Takeshi."[4]

Genre is certainly one of the ways in which the remaining audience is funneled into theaters, but there are many others. Just as we saw the attempt to counter the threat of television by introducing monsters, sex, and wide screen, so we now see an audience wooed back with genre, spectacle, and the promise of a product to be viewed in a theater only. These films were made independently, were unaffiliated with whatever major studios remained, and were able to offer something more sophisticated in the way of entertainment at a significantly lower cost to the producers.

While the West is familiar with this way of making films, it was relatively unknown in Japan. A picture could be made for comparatively little since a recently formed company would not be burdened with the cost of a full-time studio and staff. And, as not much was spent, a major audience was not needed to realize a profit. Financial gain, though limited, could still be considered sufficient if it managed to finance another film.

The term "independent film" in the West at that time usually indicated an independent attitude as well. It was the kind of film the major production companies could not make, given what was considered its narrow audience appeal. This was initially the reading of the term *dokuritsu purodakushon* in Japan as well. In time, however, as in America, the independent film gradually turned mainstream.

Maverick films became box-office hits, the avant-garde turned up on big-theater screens, new filmmakers were awarded government prizes. With the expansion and later contraction of Japan's economy, a new conservatism—compared to the relative liberalism of the 1950s and 1960s—became evident. In film this was seen in the slow backing away from the style of modern realism to something which could be labeled as "postmodern"—a mixing of high and low, art and commerce, which posited that culture had never been as pure as assumed, the notion that all culture is syncretic, hybridized. Postmodernism called for a definite return to the presentational quality which had always defined the Japanese dramatic ethos, bringing about the emergence of that completely presentational film genre, anime. This return to the presentational implies a return to open control (as opposed to the covert control implied by the representational), and it operates on many levels.

One such level is the open presentational character of the film itself. Another is the hands-on and openly controlled manner of selling the product. Like film merchants worldwide, the Japanese became adept at playing the market. Japanese films might not rake in much money at home, but their appeal could be enhanced by prizes won at foreign film festivals. Eventually, Kitano Takeshi, Kurosawa Kiyoshi, Aoyama Shinji, Miike Takashi, and many other younger directors were winning prestigious awards abroad which resulted in larger sales (cassettes, discs, rentals, direct money from television showings) in Japan.

Film production methods at the beginning of the twenty-first century have in some ways returned to those prevalent at the beginning of the twentieth: many small production companies, all more or less unaffiliated, all seeking to purvey sensation and novelty. The masterless ronin is now the nearly anarchic yakuza and his postmod posturings are not far from the kabuki-esque posings of Matsunosuke.

THE NEW INDEPENDENTS

The breakup of the studio system meant more freedom for directors. Beginning in the 1980s there were a number of attempts to attract those audiences which were not satisfied with corporate fare, those who still took film seriously, and also those who had the greatest amount of disposable income in their pockets—the young.

Toho, having seen that investing in ATG had proved profitable, tied up for a time with PIA publications to launch YES (Young Entertainment Square) which was to produce low-budget films by young directors and distribute them in Toho theaters. Shochiku answered with its Cinema Japonesque which had much the same aims.

Both eventually foundered after each had released several pictures. The differences between entrenched authority and young filmmakers were too great. This way of financing was completely different from the old studio system, which was all that the company bureaucrats knew. Toho simply backed out. The Shochiku board preferred to ax its Cinema Japonesque people—despite the fact that two of their films—Imamura Shohei's *The Eel* and Ichikawa Jun's *Tokyo Lullaby* (Tokyo yakyoku, 1997)—had won awards.

More successful were those independent companies that attempted to enter the field without major film-industry partnership. Argo Project, a consortium of independent producers backed by Suntory, sought to break the monopoly on both production and theaters, and for a time was able to attract a number of viewers. Software-maker Pony Canyon joined advertising agency Hakuhodo to make independent films; WOWOW, a major television satellite station financed the J-Movie-Wars series under Sento Takenori, and so on.

Many of the resulting products have the youth market in mind and are often relentlessly cool, modish, and filled with various special effects. They are, almost by definition, given to dispersing what is new—techniques, styles, attitudes. Whatever its minority beginnings, the "independent film" has thus become mainstream fare. Nevertheless, these independent production units have often also been responsible for the best of recent Japanese cinema.

In the international breakdown of consolidated film production and distribution, the proliferation of new production companies, and the emergence of a variety of distribution circuits one senses something like the beginnings of film all over again. Once more we have a cinema of views and scenes, of raw sensation and rudimentary narrative. The music video is the new nickelodeon, the early *Sinking of the Lusitania* (1918) becomes the late *Titanic* (1997). In Japan, *Armed Robber* (1899) turns into the criminal confrontations in Miike Takashi's *Rainy Dog* (Gokudo kuro shakai reini doggu, 1997). And, again, as a century before, we have the merchandizing of the self-proclaimed new.

While history is not necessarily cyclical, similar stimuli sometimes produce similar results. The original "opening" of Japan to foreign media a century ago was indeed like that even greater opening post-World War II, and this corresponds, again fifty years later, to the buying sprees of the 1980s and the consolidation of purchases in the 1990s.

The independents of today are displaying a new kind of Japanification. The divergence between traditional and nontraditional is much less marked. Whether something is tradi-tionally Japanese or not is no longer a concern—no one can tell and no one cares. Tradition is not to be guarded. It is to be augmented as the riches of the rest of the world are assimi-lated.

At the same time, the distance between styles has grown. On the one hand, the most representational of means, the documentary and its new practitioners; on the other, the most presentational, those directors heavily influenced by manga and manga-like anime. Both have been so far neglected in this account of the Japanese film but they—and their implications—will be considered later. In truth, there are so many crossovers in independent production that no amount of generalization can account for the variety.

This said, one must nevertheless remark upon the new importance of genre. To be sure, as we have seen, genre films have been more common in Japan than in many other countries. There was the major division between jidaigeki period film and gendaigeki contemporary film; and there were many subdivisions, the haha-mono, about mothers, the tsuma-mono, about wives, the yakuza film, and so on. This genre menu has now widened and though there are still many films which defy genre, a new majority readily succumbs.

There are a number of reasons for this. Audiences like to know the kind of film they are going to see before they see it. Most people want to know the perimeters of their entertainment. This is particularly true in Japan. Also, category works as a kind of brand name. If one film diverts then maybe the next one from the same genre will too.

Also genre is as reassuring as it is entertaining. As Martin Scorsese has observed: "For better or worse, story as entertainment is saddled with conventions and stereotypes, formulas and cliches. All of these limitations are codified into specific genres."

For film producers, genre is product with its own shape, its own mold. Each genre product costs about the same, and directors are expected to confine themselves to its specifications. And for those directors who do not wish to conform to this rigid pattern there is the challenge of enlarging or subverting it at little extra cost.

Among the most successful of recent genres has been the horror film. Though the genre is not new in Japan, its popularity has been hitherto among children—films about ghosts, monsters, or such local products as giant felines and footless phantoms. It is only recently that major audiences have made such fare profitable.

Perhaps the first horror film to make big money was *The Mystery of Rampo* (Rampo, 1994). It was released by its production company in two competing versions, one by its director, Mayuzumi Rintaro, the other by its producer Okuyama Kazuyoshi. Much of the publicity which surrounded the films, and perhaps accounted for the financial success of Okuyama's film, was due to the falling out between director and producer which occasioned the two versions. Both, however, were based on a story by Edogawa Rampo, a local master of the horror story who even took the name of a famous predecessor, Edgar Allan Poe. This literary touch argued for a kind of respectability. Imitations followed and a genre was revitalized.

With a similar revival of interest in horror in the United States (evidenced by the popularity of Stephen King films, for example), Japanese companies jumped aboard the bandwagon and the Japan-gothic genre began to appear. Among the first films in this genre was Ishii Sogo's prescient *Angel Dust* (Enjeru dasuto, 1994). A new religion convert is supposed to be deprogrammed but is instead turned into a serial killer—all this a year before the serial attacks of the followers of the Aum Shinrikyo cult. There is also a menacing Mount Fuji, and mass mind control.

Perhaps the most famous of the resulting nouvelle horror flicks was *Ring* (Ringu, 1998, Nakata Hideo), followed by *Ring 2* (Ringu 2, 1999) by the same director, both based on a novel by Suzuki Koji and later treated to an American remake. Among others who also later sold their scripts to Hollywood was Shimizu Takashi whose *The Grudge* (Ju-on, 2000) was, said the ads, about that popular horror staple "the curse of one who dies in a powerful rage."

The director who gave the genre whatever creditability it has achieved was Kurosawa Kiyoshi (no relation to Akira). A protégé of Itami Juzo, he had a small role in Itami's *The Funeral* (Ososhiki, 1984), and Itami himself played the monster in the younger director's

Sweet Home (Suito homu, 1989). From there Kurosawa opened up the genre—fewer monsters and more social criticism. *Cure* (Kyua, 1997) is about a young man cursed with socially conscious evil power. *Barren Illusion* (Oinaru gen'ei, 1999) is set in the awful future. The director called it a film "about two people who are trying to live between eternal love and the horror that is modern life."

Equally allegorical in intent, and just as much about the horrors of modern life, is *Charisma* (Karisuma, 1999)—a large, mysterious, and eponymous tree is killing an entire forest: is the individual then more than important than society? In *Kairo* (2001), the dead come out of computers to attack the living; in *Bright Future* (Akarui mirai, 2003) the threat is poison jellyfish, and yet another kind of doom is the coming of the clones in *Doppelgänger* (Dopperugenga, 2003).

Or perhaps the clones are already here. One of the indications is the new activity of the generic film. Spectators go clone-like to see the same thing at the same time; they all seem to have the same opinions of these popular entertainments. A favorite is Tsukamoto Shinya who has made such youth-cult pictures as *Tetsuo: The Iron Man* (Tetsuo, 1989) and *Tetsuo II: Body Hammer* (1992). Here, flesh and fabrication are united in the cyborg hero and the

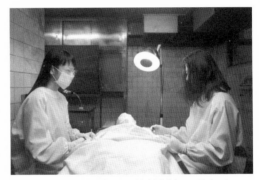

Vital, 2004, Tsukamoto Shinya, with (right) Asano Tadanobu.

pounding pace is both welcome and familiar to those who have long watched television. Tsukamoto received most of his media training in commercials, and made promotion videos before turning to film. Later pictures find him more conventional. There is only one mechanical-serpent torture device in *A Snake of June* (Rokugatsu no hebi, 2002). *Vital* (Vitaru, 2004) finds him preoccupied with mere scalpels.

Sensational violence, injury, varyingly horrid forms of death—such things have long made up much of popular cinema. Perhaps a contemporary difference is the reputability that such excess has achieved. Rape, torture, murder are there to be viewed in a manner not only non-judgmental, but detached. It is cool to do so.

Since this quality—being cool—has come to play such a leading role in contemporary Japanese film (as well as in modern Japanese life) one might examine it. First, to be cool, or hip, or whatever word is used, is to exhibit a style that defies the mainstream, whatever that may be at the time. The young wish to believe that they are "with it" and are hence more empowered than they actually are. Dissent becomes a means. Most young persons, however, will settle for something less time-consuming than real counterculture alienation. They are satisfied with adopting a look, a style, an attitude. To be cool means to have lots of attitude.

This phenomenon is by no means restricted to Japan and is, at any rate, not new to it. Back in the repressive Edo period, to be hip was to show some *iki*, to be square was to be *yabo*, and no one wanted to be that. Extreme stage fashions (and morals) were imitated, the "prostitute look" was in, and Edo had its own distinctive trendy take which we can see in such chroniclers as Hokusai and Utamaro.

Again, in the Taisho period, the popular ero-guro-nansensu genre (combining erotic, grotesque and farcical elements) was in its own manner antiestablishment and, as we have seen, its expression of dissidence ran against the grain of increasingly repressive government. To extol violence was perhaps too anarchic—though many a samurai film of the period did just that. To claim nansensu, however, was to suggest that it was mainstream culture which was the more nonsensical. The attitude itself was also discovered to be a marketable item. Nansensu stories and novels became nansensu movies, and ero-guro could be translated into smart outfits (cloche hats, bobbed hair, plus-fours for the men) and marketed accordingly.

Cool is nonverbal. It does not explain itself, nor can it. Hence its means of communication are purposely limited. In this it resembles manga construction, a storyboard-like assemblage of discrete boxes, each containing its grain of information, affording nothing further than chronology as linkage. There is little explanation, much is assumed, and the reader or viewer is encouraged to do no more than register each event. His or her emotions are beside the point, since to be with it is to be out of it. This is cool—or, in Japanese parlance, not the despised *uetto* (wet), but its desired opposite, *dorai* (dry).

This uninvolved and uninvolving dryness which the manga or anime format famously affords probably accounts for much of its popularity in both printed and filmed form. A majority of new non-anime (live-action) films are now constructed like manga, since this is the only narrative form that most young people know. Bite-sized boxes means that one need not feel, and rarely even think, since the chronology is self-propelling. It is fast, it is familiar, and it affords a safe way to view dangerous life.

Violence, institutionalized, is thus a cool item, whether purveyed by Quentin Tarantino, Kitano Takeshi or Miike Takashi. The viewer is uninvolved, that is, untouched. Consequently, it is danger that these safely insulated manga narratives revolve around.

The films of Kitano "Beat" Takeshi, a television personality who is now something of a social force, may be seen as an illustration of this fondness for danger at a distance. Originally a standup comedian, Kitano made his film debut as an actor—he was the brutal sergeant who says "Merry Christmas, Mr. Lawrence," at the conclusion of Oshima's film, thus giving the picture its title.

Oshima gave the role to Kitano, a relative unknown, because he had seen him playing a psychotic killer in a 1983 television serial *The Crimes of Okubo Kiyoshi* (Okubo Kiyoshi no hanzai). Kitano later said that the reason he accepted was that Oshima's earlier films were just about the only Japanese cinema he had seen, and that he admired the director's treatment of casual violence. He agreed to appear not only in *Merry Christmas, Mr. Lawrence* but also in the director's later *Gohatto*.

Kitano's expertise in violence led to his being offered the lead in *Violent Cop* (Sono otoko kyobo ni tsuki, 1989), a picture scheduled to be directed by Fukasaku Kinji, master of the yakuza genre. Fukasaku became ill, however, and the project was postponed. After some thought, and perhaps some fear that hiring a lesser director might mean losing a promising actor, producer Okuyama Kazuyoshi asked Kitano to also direct.

The actor-director has said that, though he was perhaps influenced by such films as Fukasaku Kinji's *Battles Without Honor or Humanity* series, he knew that there was no way for a single yakuza (like Takakura Ken) to take on a rival gang with a wooden sword (as in the ninkyo-eiga). Aestheticized violence has no interest for him. He believes violence should be used for entertaining dramatic purposes—the jitsuroku-eiga ideal.

Consequently Kitano reworked the plot of his debut film. Now it was about a cop who has reason to be violent. Not only was he up against really depraved yakuza, he was also locked in conflict with the truly corrupt officers in his own department. At the same time he recast the script. As Robert Schwartz has described it: "He insisted on a static camera that stood stoic, like Takeshi himself and many of the characters he would play . . . an unmoving camera would capture quiet, pensive stretches that served to build tension and the eye would be equally unblinking to the ruthless and relentless violence."[5]

Having played a cop too violent for his department, he next played—in *Boiling Point* (San tai yon ekkusu jugatsu, 1990)—a gangster too furious for his gang. These roles would be alternated throughout his career. In *Sonatine* (Sonachine, 1993), the last of the old-time gangsters (Kitano) is sent on a hit mission to Okinawa. At the end, the expressionless gangster machine-guns the opposition, not a facial muscle moving. Such scenes stud the oeuvre. As the director commented at the time: "Really tough guys don't experience a lot of tension—by nature they're cool."

The finale of *Hana-bi* (aka Fireworks, 1997) is a revenge scene almost Jacobian in its blood-bath excess, but, like *Sonatine*, singularly detached, and therefore cool. But coolness can also generate a kind of manga-like sentimentality. In *Hana-bi* the two cop buddies share a deep affection. One (Osugi Ren) is paralyzed in a shootout when the other (Kitano) ought to have been there but was actually visiting his wife in hospital. Osugi finds peace in

Hanabi, 1997, Kitano Takeshi, with Kishimoto Kayoko, Kitano Takeshi.

learning to paint (the pictures are by Kitano himself who, like Ozu, Kurosawa, Ichikawa and many others, is a part-time painter) but Kitano, filled with a familiar macho-romanticism, himself discovers tranquility only in "delivering" his ailing wife and then himself as well, while the camera turns and looks elsewhere—a gesture made popular by *Reservoir Dogs* (1992). Good buddies though they were, we are invited to remain uninvolved.

The film also offers some indication as to how Kitano obtains his effects. In the script, Osugi Ren was supposed to die in one of the early scenes but Kitano so liked his performance that he kept him in the film until the end, and indeed made his character one of the points of the plot. When Kitano doesn't like something, however, he is famous for rarely reshooting the offending scene. Usually he cuts it out entirely.

This way of making a film certainly does not argue for the necessity of a shooting script. In a way, we are back in the days before Makino Shozo thought the better of carrying around a single sheet of paper and shouting his instructions to the waiting actors. Kitano's static camera, and his one-shot-one-scene style of narration may owe more to manga than to Mizoguchi but it has resulted in a highly viewable product, where simple contrast rules. There is good (no matter how bad it looks) against bad (no matter how good it looks) and there is the violent contrast between static scenes and scenes madly mayhem-filled.

An example would be *Brother* (2000), shot in Los Angeles, about an ex-yakuza boss who visits the United States to help a gang brother lay out the locals. All of the stylistic elements are in place: simmering silence, carefully timed bursts of trademark violence, an insistence upon gangster chic (costumes by designer Yamamoto Yoji) and a hero (played by Kitano) who is so explosive that he is too combustible for the gang. There is also (as is common in Kitano's films) minimal acting by the director and over-the-top melodramatics by everyone else.

This formula never sold better than in *Zatoichi* (2003), Kitano's remake of Misumi Kenji's 1962 hit *Zatoichi: The Life and Opinions of Masseur Ichi* (Zatoichi monogatari). Kitano himself plays the blind swordsman with a slow and thoughtful dignity, a true artisan, dedicated to his craft of cutting and slicing—always reluctant to begin the mayhem but always determined to see it through. Against his somber and restrained rendering of the title character is the frenzied behavior of the rest of the cast—leading up to the famous all-singing, all tap-dancing finale.

———————

Kitano's influence on other filmmakers is considerable, since it was he who made manga-like violent spectacle respectable. Ishii Sogo had been experimenting with cartoon-like violence in *High School Panic* (Koko dai panikku, 1978) and *The Crazy Family* (Gyakufunsha kazoku, 1984), but it was not until *Angel Dust*, the year after Kitano's *Sonatine* appeared, that he perfected the opposition of movement and stillness, of "goodness" and "badness" which is typical of these manga-influenced films. The action is stop-and-go, posed tableaux-vivants and hyperactive violence.

Ishii Takashi (no relation to Ishii Sogo) was himself a manga artist before entering films. He consequently knew the technique even before he stepped behind the camera. His debut film, *The Guts of an Angel* (Tenshi no harawata, 1988) was a success, and he followed it with *Night in Nude* (Nudo no yoru, 1993) and his best-known films, *Gonin* (1995) and *Gonin 2* (1996).

The misadventures of five members (*gonin*) of a gang involved with another yakuza group makes up the *Reservoir Dogs*-like story of this film. Cut like a music video, noir details piled up, sensation is achieved in every shot. Design happy, each frame is distinguished by its lighting, its colorization, its composition, by zooms and fast or slow motion.

An apogee in presentational technique is reached in the many films of the intensely prolific Miike Takashi, formerly an assistant to both Higashi Yoichi and Imamura Shohei. A typical example is *Dead or Alive* (Deddo oa araibu: hanzaisha, 1999), which opens with a drug-induced leap off a rooftop, goes on to the buggery of a gang punk in a toilet, the explosion of the shot-up (if digitalized) stomach of a gangster just after he has eaten a lot of Chinese noodles, and a close-up of a call-girl drowned in her own excrement—all of it shot with a nervous camera, lots of flashpans, and other handheld gymnastics.

Audition (Odishon, 2000) is about a middle-aged widower looking for love but encountering unmitigated evil in the form of his intended bride—or is it all a dream? Based on a Murakami Ryu novel, and scripted by Tengan Daisuke (son of Imamura Shohei), the film is, like most of Miike's pictures, misogynist to a degree. Like the rest, it is also expertly tailored and delivers the advertised goods with a dead-faced indifference which meets all the demands of contemporary cool. Since these films are built like manga they are hence several times removed from feeling.

There is some Kitano influence in all the super commotion. There is however, no balancing stasis, and certainly no idea that violence should only forward dramatic complications. Rather, since nothing in a Miike film is believable, nor intended to be, we are invited to regard it as spectacle, a kind of anime with real folks. Indeed, we are back in the world of pure flash—the realm of Ito Daisuke at his most frenetic, of Tanaka Tsuruhiko and the swish-pan samurai action of the early thirties. The resemblance is particularly noticeable in *Izo* (2004), which begins as a sword-swinging chambara. Not that Miike has ever seen anything by these directors. Rather, this kind of calculated embroidery is part of an original Japanese accent—and influenced too, of course, by lots of permissive examples from the United States.

Another reason for the form and content of the Miike film is the intended venue. He has made many more OVs ("original videos") for the video shops and the small screen than he has made feature films for the theater chains. Made on the cheap, using new talent and young directors, such OVs fill many a shop shelf. Miike's work represents a lucrative comeback for the nearly moribund yakuza film, a genre which has more or less had its day in the theaters but still appeals to youthful tube-gazers and to those who find all the laid-back excess cool.

Among others pushing this quality is Aoyama Shinji, who played a black-shirted fascist in Kurosawa Kiyoshi's *Barren Illusion*, and who well reflects the kind of world young people think they live in. As Aaron Gerow wrote, "it is commonplace [for such young directors] to mourn the inability of contemporary youth to communicate. Lost in their virtual realities of video games and cellular phones they seem unable to handle people of flesh and blood—other than perhaps through random violence. It is as if they cannot establish contact because they don't even acknowledge the existence of their conversation partner." [6]

Such autism is typical of the young hero of Aoyama's debut film, *Helpless* (1996), a self-scripted melodrama which the director said was inspired by the work of Arthur Rimbaud, a poet often identified as the original rebel. While this is not otherwise evident in the film (a buddy-movie about a young gangster just out of jail taking up with a rebellious classmate), both of the principals seem to find murder a satisfying fashion statement.

The even more violent *Wild Life* (Wairudo raifu, 1997), again a yakuza picture, is at the same time cooler. A pachinko pinball "fixer"

Helpless, 1996, Aoyama Shinji.

has his easy life enlivened by even more lawless invaders. As in the films of Quentin Taran-tino, which Aoyama, along with a number of young directors admires, the one-cut one-scene method is filmed with lots of violent action within the frame, manga-like, and when things become too awful the camera looks away. Technique becomes decoration, violence is a kind of stylistic crocheting, a venerable Japanese tradition. One remembers Tanaka Tsuruhiko's *The Red Bat* (1931), a film made sixty-six years before but little different from Aoyama's in its dependence on flash, dazzle, and gore. Another resemblance to the crowd-pleasers of the thirties is that in Aoyama's picture action is all, and characterization is kept to a minimum, the better to display it.

The couple in *Shady Grove* (Sheidi gurobu, 1999) are so characterless that they seem barely to know each other. In *Eureka* (Yuriika, 2000) the young people, one of whom is a serial killer, cannot communicate—and this, indeed, constitutes the plot of this nearly four-hour film. Still, victims of a bus-jacking, they make the most of it, victimization being in fashion among the young. In *EM—Embalming* (Ii emu embamingu, 1999) everyone is even more alienated. One critic said that "even the bang-bang scenes feel deadened. Blasting away at one another, both the good guys and the bad guys stand straight and expressionless as shooting gallery targets—a steal from Kitano Takeshi's *Sonatine*." In *Lakeside Murder Case* (Reikusaido mahda keisu, 2005), the alienation is extended to the murder-mystery genre and most of the suspects.

Equal justification for antisocial ways is found in the films of Iwai Shunji, a music-video director who made his first picture in 1995. *Love Letter* is about a young woman who writes a letter to a dead lover and gets a reply. Its television-like romanticism and music-video–like editing drew a large audience and provided the director with funds to make *Swallowtail* (Suwaroteiru, 1996), a manga-inspired vision of the future set in Yen City, a junk-chic place owing much to Ridley Scott's *Blade Runner* (1982).

Iwai himself has said that his young audience knows nothing of Ozu or Mizoguchi nor anything of the society they portrayed in their films. Consequently, he concludes, "we have to make movies that appeal [to younger movie-goers] and reflect the world they live in."[7] One result is that the filmmaker becomes a "visual artist" (*eizo sakka*) who makes no distinction between the forms of film, television and music video, and whose "message" is the stylish nihilism which has remained a favored youth-oriented mannerism since the early days of expressionism in Japanese cinema.

There are other takes on crime as a youth specialty, however. Isaka Satoshi, a former assistant of Higashi Yoichi, had something new to say about the crimes of the young in his first film, *Focus* (Fokasu, 1996), which he both wrote (with Shin Kazuo) and directed, and in which he revealed the manipulativeness of the Japanese media. A television director deliberately exploits a young and solitary computer nerd (Asano Tadanobu) who lives his life only through his electronic eavesdropping devices. Eventually the nerd hijacks the television-exploitation feature they are making and gives the director a true adventure. The film is taken entirely from the viewpoint of the television photographer—one cut, one scene (actually the work of cameraman Sano Tetsuro) and looks like a documentary, but one which eventually includes us, the audience, as its target. It was produced by Hara Masato, one of Japan's most innovative producers—who also helped make both *Merry Christmas, Mr. Lawrence* and *Ran*.

Isaka, in his later works, went on to further explore the themes he introduced in *Focus*. *Doubles* (Daburusu, 2001) was about the collision between how the young want to be seen and how they really are, and *G@me* (2003) shows a young couple embroiled in identity pranks with the grown-up world—pointing to new and interesting directions in genre films.

This pandering to youth, anarchy and the box office is not, however, the only way to make a film. Another is to drop hard-core cool and attempt to show something of the reality of being young in a disciplinary society. One such possibility was early indicated by the late Somai Shinji. He first came to attention with *Typhoon Club* (Taifu kurabu, 1985), directed after a Kato Yuji script, about a group of high-school juniors and the four days they spend together at their country school waiting out a storm. The teenagers are shown as they really are, not as "youth" pictures would have them. In the grip of their glands, they are moody, contradictory, either at the heights of enthusiasm or in the depths of despair. The title—certainly an echo from

Typhoon Club, 1985, Somai Shinji.

Thomas Kurihara's long lost "youth" comedy *Amateur Club*—insists upon unity, but everything we are given shows only dissent: an older girl nearly drowns a young boy, another youth is carried away by his budding sexuality, and yet another lectures his friends on the purposelessness of their lives and then kills himself.

Somai is not interested in solving educational problems—he wants to reveal how difficult it is to understand adolescents, and to show what they go through. In this he is notably successful. As Sato Tadao has said: "Somai is able to capture this precarious psychological state of early adolescence in which joviality and morbidity became hard to distinguish." [8] Somai uses long takes, usually with the actors far from the camera. The climactic dance scene in the eye of the typhoon is taken from very far away and is held for a long time. One remembers similar scenes from early Japanese cinema—the films of Murata Minoru, or Tanaka Eizo.

This long shot as a technique to isolate and to locate the character in his or her world is also memorably demonstrated in the coda of Somai's *Moving* (Ohikkoshi, 1993). A little girl (Tabata Tomoko) wanders through the remains of the festival after everyone has left—the camera following, keeping its distance, isolating her, distant against the last of the festivities. Actor and narrative are fused through atmosphere, and something which we have all experienced—the end of childhood—is suggested.

Moving, 1993, Somai Shinji, with Tabata Tomoko (left).

To show things as they are is to show them as Japanese. Real Japanese life is not about guns and dope, yakuza and crooked cops, car chases and lovingly crafted explosions. Thus to reflect something of an actual reality is to return, even if inadvertently, to something Japanese.

Other young directors are also moving in different directions. One example is Nakahara Shun, who started on the dissident edge by working in the soft-core porn industry at Nikkatsu, an experience which taught him much. "Porno is very simple, easy to understand. But people aren't animals, so you start to think about their feelings, to look deeper into human behavior. Porno is the best way to learn how to make films about human beings." [9]

Nakahara's *The Cherry Orchard* (Sakura no sono, 1990), after a script by Jinno Hiroaki loosely based on a manga by Yoshida Akio, is about four members of a girls' high-school drama club and their annual production and performance of the eponymous Chekhov play. In the two hours before the curtain goes up (film time and actual time being the same) we observe the relationships which hold the girls together, the forces which will drive them apart, and come to understand the characters much more deeply than is common in a youth-oriented Japanese film.

The Cherry Orchard, 1990, Nakahara Shun, with Nakajima Hiroko, Tsumiki Miho.

Nakahara acknowledges a general lack of character depth in Japanese films and attributes it to the American influence: "Japanese movies have lost the kind of feeling that [earlier] directors had . . . Japanese directors stopped being Japanese, [they] wanted to be like Americans. They threw away their own drama and went off to Hollywood." Now, he feels, "we're relaxed enough that we can again remember the past. We don't have to go to Hollywood anymore."[10] An example of this return is his *The Gentle Twelve* (Juninin no yasashii nihonjin, 1991) an expert comedy about how a Western concept, in this case the jury system, might work in Japan (where there are no juries, only judges) and how a very "Japanese" accommodation would be finally worked out.

Another director to show something more than the cool edge is Suo Masayuki, best known abroad for *Shall We Dance?* (Sharu ui dansu, 1996), the film which became the most popular Japanese film abroad since Kurosawa Akira's *Rashomon*. A charming comedy about the daily grind of a salaried man (Yakusho Koji) and his dreams and hopes, it resonated with young audiences both in Japan and abroad. Suo is also admired in Japan for his absurd and loving parodies of Ozu. The first, a soft-core porn film, is a pink remake of *Late Spring* called *An Abnormal Family: My Brother's Wife* (Hentai kazoku: Aniki no yomesan, 1983). The second was a television drama series segment, *A Businessman's Schoolroom* (Sarariman kyoshitsu, 1986). Both use the celebrated Ozu method for ends which the older director would not perhaps have envisioned but might well have approved.

Mochizuki Rokuro, who also learned his craft making soft-core porn, created his first critical hit with *Skinless Night* (Sukinresu naito, 1991), about the dilemmas encountered by those working in the marginalized business of making porn. This theme of social exclusion was further explored in *The Fire Within* (Onibi, 1997) and *Kamachi* (2003), the latter a youth-film about a pop painter and poet who died young.

Nagasaki Shun'ichi's major theme is also the socially excluded, as seen in *The Enchantment* (Yuwakusha, 1989), a feminist statement with teeth in it. In *The Drive* (Saigo no doraibu, 1992) a woman (Muroi Shigeru) murders a girl and implicates her lover (Tamaki Koji). In *Some Kinda Love* (Romansu, 1996) a flaky young woman (Mizushima Kaori) has an unwelcome effect on her friends—one of whom is played by Tsukamoto Shinya.

A fine portrait of the teenager grown older but still cherishing her revolt was given by Fujiyama Naomi in Sakamoto Junji's *The Face* (Kao, 2000). Now fat and frumpy, she resents her popular, pretty sister, and kills her. On the run she begins to find a new life. This discovery (or creation) of self is a theme now seen more frequently, particularly in such Sakamoto films as *Boxer Joe* (1995) and the explosive *Knockout* (Dotsuitarunen, 1989).

The real problems of real young people is a dominant theme among young directors as they move further from cool genre and into particular rather than general statements. Yukisada Isao in *Go* (2001) shows what it is like to be of Korean ancestry in an all "Japanese" high school. In *Poisonous Insects* (Gaichu, 2002) Shiota Akihito gives us a seventh-grade girl who is ostracized at school but finds freedom on the street. In *Canary* (Kanaria, 2004), a young boy runs away from a religious cult. That freedom can be dangerous is indicated in Ishioka Masato's documentary-like *Scoutman* (aka Pain, 2000), which is about a teenage couple who fall straight to the bottom—he into pimpdom, she into the awful world of "compensated companionship." A painful rebellion which succeeds is found in Furumaya Tomoyuki's *Bad Company* (Mabudachi, 2001) where a high-school boy and his friends turn against their tyrannical teacher's idea of what "a real human being" should be. They reflect, then rebel, and make a real moral choice for themselves.

Among these independent directors who refuse genre and try to make some sense of society, the best known is the late Itami Juzo. Son of the director Itami Mansaku, who died when Juzo was twelve, he was originally well known as an essayist and an actor before becoming a director.

Itami sometimes said that his theme was "what it means to be Japanese," a subject upon which he elaborated to Vincent Canby: "Americans, because of their ethnic, economic and educational differences, share far less in the way of common experience than do the Japanese. Living in Japan is like living in a nation of twins."[11] This presupposes more similarity than difference and supports a perceived need for a tradition to guide.

Yet, despite or because of his interest in what it means to be a Japanese, Itami also maintained that he was strongly influenced by American movies, saying that he learned how to construct stories and develop characters by studying American films. Like many before

The Funeral, 1984, Itami Juzo, with (rear) Sugai Kin, Miyamoto Nobuko, Yamazaki Tsutomu.

him—Ozu leading the way—his goal was to connect the new means to the old ways.

In *The Funeral* he satirizes the Japanese for forgetting their traditions: they no longer know the proper way to hold a funeral. The characters even have difficulty sitting in traditional style, feet tucked under them. Yet the way in which this is shown is learned from the West. The funeral-instruction tape is viewed as a film within a film in the manner of the *Our-Gang*–like home-movie scene in Ozu's *I was Born, But. . . .* Another parallel is the long revealing dolly—a technique used on several occasions in the Ozu film and, before that, in the films of René Clair—which reveals the funeral guests having trouble sitting in the required formal position. The final scene, the widow's formal speech, is filmed as a lengthy single shot. The camera moves slowly forward into close-up, a way of filming—seen at the end of many a Hollywood women's film, seen also in the final shot of Mizoguchi's *Sisters of the Gion*—which might be defined as traditional.

To be sure, influences exist on a sliding scale. No matter how novel at first appearance, eventually, everything becomes traditional. What we identify as once derived from Ernst Lubitsch is no longer that—it has become a part of the Japanese tradition. As I write, other influences (let us say those of Quentin Tarantino) are already being subsumed into Japanese contemporary film and will shortly become "traditional" as well.

In the expertly carpentered films of Itami, the demands of tradition and of modernity are meshed in a highly structured narrative. In the two-part *A Taxing Woman* (Marusa no onna, 1987–88), and in later pictures, the director claimed to be creating essays. He called *Supermarket Woman* (Supa no onna, 1996) a lesson on how to make a success of a poorly run store; and *Minbo or the Gentle Art of Japanese Extortion* (Mimbo no onna, 1992), "a kind of essay on how to stand up to the Japanese mob."

As for *Tampopo* (1985), it was, said the director, a sociological essay based on a Western—Howard Hawks' *Rio Bravo* (1959). The film wasn't really about Japan at all. Indeed, the film was much more popular in the United States than it was in its home country.

Itami, though a true independent in that he himself financed his first film, *The Funeral*—mortgaging everything he owned in order to do so—soon established distribution then production ties with Toho. Before long, efforts were being made to "improve" the purchased product, to turn it into something like formula fare, an "Itami production." Among the subsequent failures (both

Tampopo, 1985, Itami Juzo, with Watanabe Ken, Miyamoto Nobuko, Yamazaki Tsutomu.

commercial and artistic) was *A Quiet Life* (Shizukana seikatsu, 1995), based on the life and works of his brother-in-law Oe Kenzaburo. Concerned producers became even more interested in "fixing" the Itami product and among the many reasons put forward for Itami's unexplained suicide in December 1997 was the suggestion that he felt he had lost the impetus necessary to carry on making his films. On the other hand, Oe—in his 2000 novelization of the event, *The Changeling* (Torikaeko)—suggests that the director's death was related to his having stood up to the mob and other rightist, nationalistic organizations.

Morita Yoshimitsu's very popular *The Family Game* (Kazoku gemu, 1983), a picture which won the Kinema Jumpo prize for that year, and one which starred his mentor, Itami in the role of the feckless father, shows how satire can be used to express criticism. In it, a tutor hired to instruct a backward boy takes over the family and teaches them a lesson in modern living. The film proved one of the most influential of its decade.

The Family Game, 1983, Morita Yoshimitsu, the "last supper," with Yuki Saori, Itami Juzo, Matsuda Yusaku, Tsujita Jun'ichi, Miyagawa Ichirota.

Sato Tadao said that *The Family Game* "wreaks vengeance on the Japanese home-drama tradition." He goes on to compare the Ozu family with the Morita family. Just as Ozu often seated his family members facing the same direction, thus giving unity to their feelings, so Morita in the final family meal, lines up the father, mother, two brothers and the family tutor. But the composition no longer means accord and, indeed, this last supper turns into a food fight. "Morita makes use of the Ozu style to indicate how the Japanese family of today, with its weakened bonds of kinship, is different from the Japanese family Ozu described."[12]

It was not until fifteen years later that Morita had another comparable hit, with a picture that was neither satirical nor particularly contemporary. *Lost Paradise* (Shitsurakuen, 1997), was based on a best-selling novel and a later television series—an example of movie-TV "synergy." If *The Family Game* could be said to deconstruct Ozu, *Lost Paradise* reanimated Mizoguchi Kenji. One critic has said: "Though love suicide (*shinju*) has been a favorite device of Japanese drama dating back to Chikamatsu and beyond, its use [in the Morita film] struck many Japanese moviegoers, especially those of the same generation as the film's couple, as excitingly romantic rather than regrettably retrograde." Since then, however, the demands of television have been paramount, resulting in a kind of apogee with *Like Asura* (Ashura no gotoku, 2003), a film adaptation of a popular daytime television serial.

A director who continues to use satire as a tool is Sai Yoichi, an assistant director on Oshima's *In the Realm of the Senses*, and an actor in the same director's *Gohatto*. Sai first gained critical attention as a director with *All Under the Moon* (Tsuki wa dotchi ni dete iru, 1993).

Sai, a second-generation Korean, is one of the few directors to concern himself with the many minorities in Japan. In *All Under the Moon*, Chung (Kishitani Goro), is a Tokyo taxi driver. Although he was born in Japan, the fact that his parents were born in Korea makes their family a target of Japanese prejudice. "I

All Under the Moon, 1993, Sai Yoichi, with Kishitani Goro, Ruby Moreno.

hate Koreans," one of the other drivers tells Chung. "They're dirty, they stink and they're stingy. But you're all right. I like you. Lend me some money."

Though stigmatized, Chung gets along. He puts up with the prejudice and has a whole stock of stories about how bad it makes him feel. These he uses for picking up impressionable young Japanese women. But it is a Filipina (Ruby Moreno) he falls for. His colleagues are puzzled and ask "Why would you want to go out with such a dark-skinned person?" His mother displays reverse racism with: "I absolutely forbid you to marry any except our own folk." But Chung chugs on, a happy loner who has learned not to expect too much—a more socially integrated Tora-san. He knows that prejudice makes prejudice and that victims make victims, but all the same he longs for some happiness himself.

Sai's people are loners but they are rarely losers—usually they find a way to fit in and learn how to live under the most extreme conditions. Examples of such resilience are the convicts in *Doing Time* (Keimusho no naka, 2002). A mixed lot, they are distinguished by their ability to go along with the authorities and to make sense of the meaningless rules under which they live. The resulting comedy is a satire which cuts two ways. The rigid prison system is exposed, but so are the craven ways of the prisoners. Seen as allegory, something which the director perhaps intended, it is an indictment of a double-edged hypocrisy, but— as an elderly internee (Yamazaki Tsutomu) discovers—adversity also teaches.

Sai's major minority statement is in *Blood and Bones* (Chi to hone, 2004), a nearly three-hour saga about a first generation Korean family in an unfriendly Japan. The fortunes of the brutal head of the household (Kitano Takeshi) are followed from his arrival to his lonely death in North Korea. Filled with violence, the film does not attempt to take sides—it merely shows the awfulness of both. What emerges is an admiration for sheer endurance.

Another director using comedy and satire is Obayashi Nobuhiko. *Beijing Watermelon* (Peikin no suika, 1989) is about a Japanese greengrocer who befriends a group of Chinese students. It was shot without a completed script and the dialogue was supplied by the actors or amateurs playing the roles. Often the camera simply stands and watches for almost all of its ten-minute load, while the frame is varied by all the entertaining comings and goings of the cast.

When the story demands that the grocer and his wife go to Peking at

Beijing Watermelon, 1989, Obayashi Nobuhiko.

the invitation of the returned Chinese students, Obayashi suddenly abandons the realistic picture he has begun. The reason was that it was June 1989, and he and his cast would not go to film in China because of the Tiananmen Square incident. Instead, Obayashi staged the airplane trip, the visit to Beijing, the trip to the Great Wall of China all in the studio, making this staginess clear to the viewer with cardboard mock-ups and painted sets. This enormous and calculated rift in the style—from Lumière to Méliès in mid-scene—also serves as a comment on the enormity of the massacre itself.

Riyu, 2004, Obayashi Nobuhiko, with Kishibe Ittoku.

An example of Obayashi's style—light, satirical, purposely incongruous—is seen in his popular *Transfer Students* (Tenkosei, aka, Exchange Students, aka I are You, You am Me, 1982), a very funny picture about two students, boy and girl, who somehow come to occupy each other's bodies. In *The Discarnates* (Ijintachi to no natsu, 1988) a man meets his dead parents just as they were when he was a child. In *Chizuko's Younger Sister* (Futari, 1991), the elder sister returns from death to look after the younger. In *Nostalgie* (Haruka, nosutaruji, 1993), a failed writer meets a girl who strongly resembles a childhood sweetheart. He looks on as she meets an adolescent student who turns out to be the writer himself when young. In *Riyu* (aka The Motive, 2004), a murder mystery becomes a cross section (over one hundred speaking parts) of post-bubble Japanese life.

Shinohara Tetsuo, a younger director, uses the built-in incongruities of manga to make his satirical points. In *The Big Collection of Showa Era Songs*, (Showa kayo daizenshu, 2002) he has a bunch of punks battling spoiled middle-aged women to the death. Shimizu Hiroshi, a Kitano disciple, also finds the comedy in violence. In *Chicken Heart* (Chikin hato, 2002), his hero is a man who makes a living by being publicly beaten up for money. Shimizu finds in his professional *nagurareya* ("human punching bag") a metaphor for modern Japan.

Gentler, but just as satirical is Hayashi Kaizo, best known abroad for his take-off of Japanese noir in his *Mike Hammer* (Maiku Hama) series, which includes such titles as *The Most Terrible Time in My Life* (Waga jinsei saiaku no toki, 1994). His first film, however, is his best remembered. *To Sleep so as to Dream* (Yume miru yo ni nemuritai, 1986) is a loving pastiche of early Japanese film (detectives in caps, girls in cloche hats and spit curls, the Victor dog, sepia toning) which affectionately parodies modern foibles as well.

Among the best directors of this comic satire genre is Hirayama Hideyuki, and in *Turn* (2001) he created a completely commercial Japan with no one in it. The heroine has entered another time level and lives in a Tokyo filled with things to buy and no people. In *Laughing Frog* (Warau kaeru, 2002) he takes on the ordinary marriage and what happens when it goes wrong.

The film which made Hirayama's reputation, however, was *Out* (2002), a mordant satire about four women who work in a box-lunch factory and must get rid of the body of an abusive husband. Having successfully dismembered his corpse and dumped it, the four start a lucrative business in the disposal of the bodies of murder victims. Gruesome and funny, the picture is a study of behavior at its most extreme, beautifully captured by the ensemble performance of veteran actresses Harada Mieko, Baisho Mitsuko, Muroi Shigeru, and Nishida Naomi.

Making the picture you want and then managing to control it is, of course, the goal of any film director. If your subject is not instantly saleable, usually to a young audience, then this is much more difficult. And if you work for a large company, independent or not, you then turn into a company hack—neither creating nor managing what you want.

Many Japanese films get made but are never released. Others are tailored for release but go straight to the tube. Others are designed for the tube from the first. Still others are scheduled as just for the spool stores. Where a given film will go is now figured into the balance sheets of new productions.

Kurosawa Kiyoshi's *Charisma*, for example, played in only one small Tokyo theater, though it lasted a number of weeks. The rest of the money was made on DVD and video sales and rentals. The pictures of a popular director such as Miike Takashi will be shown at a theatre in the suburbs simply so that they will have had an opening date, and the money will be made at the video stores.

At the same time much film funding comes from television itself. All the big box office movies of 2004 owed their success to network backing of what were the networks' own films. And the films themselves were often expanded versions of television programming, a phenomenon that Aaron Gerow has described as "the film projector as an extension of the cathode-ray tube."[13]

Director Shinoda Masahiro has estimated that now only thirty percent of current income comes from movie theaters and that seventy percent comes from television broadcasting and video rentals. He also believes that this meager thirty percent will be further eroded by the Internet[14], so different has "distribution" in Japan become.

An example of a director who still manages to work successfully within this system is Ichikawa Jun (no relation to Ichikawa Kon). Since 1987, he has made a series of films which have established him as one of the most serious recent filmmakers. Though he is also Japan's leading director of television commercials—which is how he makes his money—his feature pictures are distinguished by a laconic structure and a quiet dignity, both of which have recalled to some the work of Ozu.

In *Tokyo Siblings* (Tokyo kyodai, 1995), the resemblance to Ozu was intentional on the part of the director. Though the style is not Ozu's—no consistent sitting-on-tatami shots, no ban on pans—the world we are shown is that of Ozu. A brother and sister, orphaned, live together in an old Japanese-style house in downtown Tokyo. The same red Ozu coffee pot sits there while night after night, the sister prepares tofu for her brother. When the sister finds a boyfriend, her brother resents it and the family falls apart in the finest Ozu tradition.

Tokyo Siblings, 1994, Ichikawa Jun, with Awata Urara, Ogata Naoto.

Ichikawa himself calls the picture an "Ozu homage," adding that he never tires of seeing the older director's films. The reason, he told Mark Schilling, is that "today kids may have TV games and the world may seem to be different but really nothing has changed. The feelings between parents and children, between brothers and sisters, between husbands and wives are still the same. That's why Ozu's films never become dated."[15]

Ichikawa considers his "real" Ozu film to be *Dying at a Hospital* (Byoin de shinu to iu koto, 1993). "I didn't want close-ups of doctor's faces or suffering patients such as you usually find in hospital films . . . Death is an equalizer. All the six patients in those six wards were main characters. I didn't want to focus on one at the expense of others. I wanted to view them all equally. That's why I kept the camera in one place. The camera itself has no

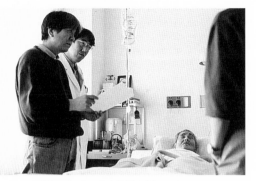

Dying at a Hospital, 1993, Ichikawa Jun.

emotion—it is simply a neutral observer. I wanted to maintain that neutrality."[16]

The film, an essay in severity and compassion, is made of very little: a few hospital rooms, and a number of patients—a young father slowly dying, an elderly couple in separate hospitals who want to be together, a woman who fights against her death. The imposed distance from the camera, coupled with the empathetic subject, finds the spectator trying to get closer but unable to—the position most of us assume when visiting the afflicted in hospitals. Lest the strain become too great, Ichikawa intercuts these scenes with lyric documentary sequences of life outside the hospital: random, inconclusive, beautiful scenes that the terminally ill will never again see.

Another community-focused film is *Zawa-zawa Shimokitazawa* (2000), about a neighborhood in a Tokyo suburb. As in many of the director's films, what begins as a group portrait turns into a character study. Nothing much seems to happen, but as we watch we begin to understand something about life. The seasons change from the heat of summer to the cold of winter, and with them, the people change. What began as nothing becomes everything.

In *Tokyo Marigold* (Tokyo marigorudo, 2001), the purposeful indirection is even more extreme. In this story of an ordinary, aimless young girl and her emotional disappointments, the narrative is not about what is shown but what is missing. The dialogue gets the viewer no further than it gets the inarticulate young people—the story is elsewhere.

In films such as this one, Ichikawa may easily be perceived as a true maverick, for he turns against his times and celebrates the old, refusing to sell out to violence as a panacea for emptiness, and, in so doing, defies the mainstream.

Oguri Kohei, like Ichikawa, has also retained his independence. His first film, *Muddy River* (Doro no kawa, 1981), a deliberate return to black-and-white shomingeki, is set in 1956

Osaka and is about kids growing up to learn the disillusioning facts of life, a scenario that makes one think of Ozu's children, and of Shimizu Hiroshi's. A little boy, son of a lower middle-class family, makes friends with two other children who live on a houseboat. The little boy comes from a poor but loving family and does not know that his new friends have no conventional family at all, and that their mother prostitutes

Muddy River, 1981, Oguri Kohei.

herself to provide for them. Of *Muddy River*, Sato Tadao asked: "Why is it that the best Japanese films about children are so sorrowful?" He then answered his own question. "It may be because of the authoritarian nature of Japanese society . . . and the need to prepare children from early on to endure the repressiveness of that authoritarianism."[17]

Oguri went on to make *For Kayako* (Kayako no tame ni, 1984) about the minority group most discriminated against in Japan: ethnic Koreans, most of whom have been born in Japan. Though the film was condemned by some for avoiding social criticism and depicting only passive suffering, this was obviously how the director viewed the problem.

Even more passive is the storyline of *The Sleeping Man* (Nemuru otoko, 1996). A young man, hurt in an accident, lies in a coma—he dies six months later. This is all that happens so far as the story goes. But this event, like a stone cast in water, makes little waves of life which affect everyone else in the picture. The months move on, the seasons pass, and the man asleep becomes a presence, a nucleus for his family, his friends. When he dies the picture implodes.

As is fitting with such subject matter, Oguri works very slowly, and fills his films with long takes. The scenes in *The Sleeping Man* purposely exceed what might be called their informational quotient. Like Mizoguchi's they are beautiful and, like Antonioni's, they are expressive. Unlike both directors, however, Oguri has always experienced financial difficulties making his films. *Muddy River* was financed by a factory-owner film fan. *The Sleeping Man* was financed by Gumma Prefecture, where it was filmed. It is not often, in Japan as elsewhere, that civic endeavor is rewarded with art, but this time it was.

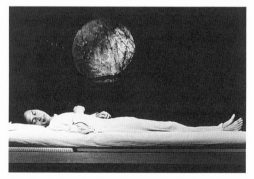

The Sleeping Man, 1996, Oguri Kohei, with Ahn Sung-ki.

An equally innovative director is Yanagimachi Mitsuo. Though he has made only seven films he has, nonetheless, created a body of work whose serious independence is rare in contemporary Japanese cinema. The first of the seven was *God Speed You! Black Emperor* (Burakku empera; goddo spido yu, 1976), a documentary about a Japanese bike gang. Of it the director has said that each society has its own rational laws but these have no relevance to bike gangs. Yet, that is for him no problem. Nothing needs justification because "society versus the individual is a false equation."[18] It is false because, as society changes its nature, it is constantly being rephrased.

Though all of Yanagimachi's films are about the erosion of traditional values, this is not something he deplores. *The Nineteen-Year-Old's Map* (Jukyusai no Chizu, 1979), based on a Nakagami Kenji novel, a would-be ter-  rorist newspaper boy is filled with thoughts of violence. The director has said that "I don't mean to make it [violence] legitimate, I mean to make it visible, to show it for what it is."[19]

A Farewell to the Earth (Saraba itoshiki daichi, aka Farewell to the Land, 1982) is about the breakdown of the rural Japanese family through the story of a junkie truck

The Nineteen-Year-Old's Map, 1979, Yanagimachi Mitsuo, with Okiyama Hideko, Homma Yuji.

driver and the havoc he creates. Of this film Yanagimachi said: "It's not that I believe the extended family is a good thing. I can't make a judgment. But, whether for good or bad, the balance has been destroyed."[20]

Again, this destruction of traditional balance is the theme of Yanagimachi's finest film, *Himatsuri* (aka Fire Festival, 1985), also based on a Nakagami novel. The director has said that he wanted to develop further "the relationship between nature and man." His modern macho Japanese man, a lumberman in  the forest of Kumano, comes up against ancient deities—palpable, if invisible— in a remarkable series of scenes where nature becomes manifest: a storm, then sudden stillness and sunlight in the sacred forest. One of the most extraordinary sequences in contemporary Japanese cinema, it is composed of kleig lights, wind machines,

Himatsuri, 1985, Yanagimachi Mitsuo, with Kitaoji Kinya.

rain makers, Tamura Masaki's calculated color photography, and Takemitsu Toru's magical score. Everything works in perfect balance to create five minutes of transcendental wonder. Here the false equation of society versus the individual is resolved. It is really society (transient humans), versus nature (the way things permanently are).

It is also typical of the way things are that most of Yanagimachi's films have had to be privately financed and produced, and that he has often found himself unable to work. His last feature film was *About Love, Tokyo* (Ai ni tsuite Tokyo, 1993), concerning illegal Chinese immigrants in Japan's capital. After that he directed only *Shadow of China* (1990) for Warner Brothers, and a made-for-television film, *The Wandering Peddlers* (Tabisuru Pao-Jiang-Hu, 1995). Yanagimachi's first film was a documentary about Tokyo bike gangs and he has remained true to fine-grained realism. In *The Wandering Peddlers* he returned to the documentary format to explore the subject of the medicine peddlers of Taiwan—a vanishing breed who share much with other Yanagimachi characters. The director and his cameraman (again Tamura Masaki) roamed all over the island, making friends and taking pictures.

In these detailed, descriptive films, there is nothing prescriptive; nothing is being sold, and there are no obvious agendas. One thinks of the films of Robert Bresson and, indeed, the younger Japanese acknowledges the influence of the older French director. At the same time he mentions another influence: "I much admire Mizoguchi Kenji . . . he had a very cold, objective, almost documentary style of filming. Bresson's films are different, but both directors share that cool, detached point of view with which I can identify."[21]

The objective and detached point of view is very close to that of the documentary and, indeed, many of these young directors have worked in this format. One such director is Shinozaki Makoto, whose first film, *Okaeri* (1996), is about a seemingly typical young married couple, getting along, living an ordinary life—like in some latter-day Naruse film. But one day the wife runs away, steals a car, becomes someone her husband does not know. He is pulled out of his placid two-dimensional existence and dropped into three-dimensional life. Yet this is not a domestic tragedy because it is her "madness" which saves them both from the true madness of a meaningless existence.

At the end they stand together on the brow of a suburban hill, a place where she has often stood, and they both hear the wash of the invisible (and, in the middle of Tokyo, nonexistent) sea. We can only infer that they are at last feeling something authentic. This irony is nowhere directly expressed but everywhere shown. At the same time something eternal is suggested.

Okaeri, 1996, Shinozaki Makoto.

Many films only celebrate the status quo, just as some new directors are only concerned with saying what everyone already knows. Shinozaki, more famous as an essayist, knows how to think for himself. Also a projectionist (this is how he supports himself) he knows film, including—the largest influence on his work—Robert Bresson. The ghost of *Une Femme Douce* (1969)—another "mad" woman—hovers just above the surface of *Okaeri*, though Shinozaki's heroine does not kill herself. She shows us that socially structured life is not the real one, a theme explored in the work of many contemporary Japanese directors, such as Kurosawa Kiyoshi, Kitano, and Yanagimachi.

Kawase Naomi also made something like a documentary with her first feature film, *Suzaku* (Moe no Suzaku, 1997). It depicts fifteen years in the life of a family in a remote rural area. It is a place where the young leave and the old die. The remnants of a family—a young girl, an older boy—stay on. She is attracted to him, he is drawn toward the wife of his dead uncle. But there are no melodramatic complications. The attentive camera (Tamura Masaki) looks at the beautiful mountain village and observes those people still there.

Suzaku, 1997, Kawase Naomi.

Unlike many younger directors, Kawase was not inspired by other films. Born in a suburb of Nara, she says that she grew up seeing almost no movies or television. This, she believes, makes her more like filmmakers fifty years ago, whose films are much more realistic than those she now finds her contemporaries making. She creates movies based on what she has actually seen and felt, not on genres or trends. Her films, she says, are formed by the environment in which she grew up.

In making her first feature, she studied the village where she intended to film for three years. She and her staff then lived there for three months prior to shooting. During this time they repaired the old farmhouse where she would shoot. She cast all the parts, except that of the father, from amateurs, including a number of local people.

For her next film, a more conventional documentary, *The Weald* (Somaudo monogatari, 1997), Kawase returned again to the village to record the lives of nine of the old people still living. Talking with them more as a close relative than as a filmmaker, she records their past and, in extreme close-ups, their limited present. *Sharasoju* (Shara, 2003) is again set in Nara. It deals with the theme of the absence of family through the story of a boy who loses his twin brother and is still dealing with the pain. Though the boy comes to terms with his loss, the film is no affirming fantasy. Rather it is a docu-drama; simple, apparent, devastating.

A similar docu-drama approach was Suwa Nobuhiro's debut film, *Duo* (2/Duo, 1997), produced by Sento Takenori who, in addition to a number of more commercial films, also produced *Suzaku*. In this picture, Yu lives with Kei. She works in a shop and he wants to be an actor. Theirs is a common dilemma: they cannot live with each other and they cannot live without each other. He thinks marriage will solve the problem; she is not so sure. One day she leaves. It is a banal story which happens every day, but that is the point.

Suwa, earlier a documentarist, has made a common situation extraordinary in this movie. His methods are radical. He asks his actors to read the treatment and then forget about it. Through rehearsals he molds their version of the forgotten script—all movement, all dialogue their own. The cameraman (again, Tamura Masaki) is as much a part of the action as they are, watching, always in control, always generously relinquishing it.

In 1999, Suwa made *M/Other* (Emu-maza), again an ensemble film, about the love between a divorced man and a younger female office worker. When the man's ex-wife falls

Duo, 1997, Suwa Atsuhiko.

ill, he must assume the responsibility of looking after their son. He brings the boy to the home he shares with his lover without even asking her. This story and its complications were arrived at through discussions between the director and the performers—actors Miura Tomokazu and Watanabe Makiko. Suwa believes that this Cassavetes-like way of filming reflects a deeper reality, and it is true that such believable spontaneity would not occur in a scripted picture.

To allow room for this, cameraman Inomoto Masami, known mainly for his documentary work, maintained a certain distance, always shooting the action in long takes, and often in long shots. What we are not shown becomes almost as important as what remains unsaid. The result is a kind of believability very rare in more conventionally constructed films. Upon winning a Cannes award for this picture, Suwa commented that the honor might have been because he described ordinary people and not some exotic breed called "the Japanese." At any rate, he affirmed that this was why he shot it the way he did.

In *H Story* (Eichi sutori 2001), Suwa made another kind of "documentary," a new version of Alain Resnais' *Hiroshima, Mon Amour* (1959), which shows the film (a reconstruction) being made while the relationship between a French woman and a Japanese man is being explored.

Another documentarist, Kore'eda Hirokazu, made his first feature film in 1995, *Maboroshi* (Maboroshi no hikari). A young Osaka woman loses her grandmother, then her husband inexplicably commits suicide and she is left alone. Eventually she remarries. Her new husband is a fisherman in a coastal village, and without our having been told (we are far from any authoritative voice) we understand that she believes she somehow causes deaths. The children (his and hers, one each from previous marriages) return late after a sudden storm, and she broods. After the funeral of an acquaintance, her husband, sensing her feelings, tells

Maboroshi, 1995, Kore'eda Hirokazu, with Esumi Makiko.

her what his father told him, that everyone is tempted by such illusions (*maboroshi*) as hers, that she is not alone—and she is consoled.

From a slender story by Miyamoto Teru (who wrote Oguri Kohei's *Muddy River*), Kore'eda created a film filled with light and shadow (cinematography by Nakabori Masao), unstressed parallels, and a regard for people in their surroundings now rare in Japanese cinema. In it the director rejects not only contrived storylines and editing tricks, but also the media-driven consumer madness of urban Japan. The pace is deliberate, the colors muted, and the actors seem to blend modestly into the background, as though the film were a new kind of shomingeki.

In addition, many scenes were shot from far away. Though we know that the people in this film are warm, understandable, just like us, we cannot reach them—distance imposes a kind of coldness. All we can do is watch. At the same time, as one carefully composed scene follows another, the power of the sheerly quotidian is felt. We notice details, patterns—both in the storyline and in the mise-en-scène, each with its carefully prepared echoes and repetitions.

The respect radiated in Kore'eda's work is now rare in any film, let alone one made in modern Japan. Kore'eda's camera waits, just like Ozu's, for people to leave the room before it shows us the next scene. Sometimes it waits for a long time. At the end of *Maboroshi* there is a distant, long-held scene which shows only a far away procession of mourners, the wife at the very end. This we watch as it slowly inches its way across the screen. Two-and-a-half minutes is the length of this scene—an enormous amount of time if there is "nothing" to watch but just the right amount if there is everything to feel.

Ozu-like too is a method of construction where objects are given a kind of storyline autonomy—as in the scene where the young husband leaves to go to work which cuts to a laundry-holder in the rain which then cuts to the wife bathing the baby. The holder acts as a kind of enjambment, both to separate time and to suggest water affinities.

Another influence, one which has done much to illuminate contemporary Japanese film, is the highly popular cinema of Abbas Kiarostami, whose extremely distant shots force the same kind of curiosity and eventual empathy. There is in *Maboroshi* a scene where the young widow and her child wait for the train at a provincial station. And wait, and wait. Yet this time is necessary, as is having the two characters at a great distance, if we are to feel as Kore'eda wants us to. Context, atmosphere, nexus as narrative.

At the end of the film, after the widow has finally shed her black dress and is wearing a white blouse, the camera looks out of the window . . . and sees the calm and ceaseless sea. Just what we were shown at a like moment at the end of Ozu's *Late Spring*.

In his second feature film, *After Life* (Wandafuru raifu, 1998), Kore'eda returned to a theme he had first treated in his television documentary *Without Memory* (Kioku ga ushinawareta toki, 1996), about a man suffering from brain damage who, robbed of his memory, lives in an eternal present. In *After Life*, the setting is an ordinary-looking limbo where the recent dead gather, and it is explained to them by the staff that they will take their most precious memory with them into eternity. If they cannot or will not choose, then they have no eternity. This is a problem the staff know well, as they

After Life, 1998, Kore'eda Hirokazu.

are there (like the bodhisattva of the Buddhist cosmology) precisely because they were unable to choose, and their task is now to help those who can.

To make the picture, Kore'eda interviewed nearly five hundred people (men, women, old, young) and from these chose ten for his picture. These ten were interviewed on film by actors playing the staff whose duty it was to help reconstruct each person's most precious memory. Although the staff had scripted lines, the ten amateurs did not. There is thus a strong storyline but no written dialogue.

Just as loosely scripted is *Distance* (Disutansu, 2001), a dark and disturbing film about a cult very like Aum Shinrikyo, the religious organization responsible for the sarin-gas poisonings in both Matsumoto and Tokyo. It has been a year since the perpetrators of a similar poisoning incident were killed by their fellow cult members, and a group of relatives and friends drive to the distant lake where the executions occurred. Slowly and subtly, Kore'eda creates from the deserted cottage, the empty groves, the still lake, a world of regret and fear.

Distance, 2001, Kore'eda Hirokazu.

Filmed documentary-style, using handheld cameras, the picture is explicit about nothing. Rather it leaves us to infer the full horror of what these people did and what happened to them.

In *Nobody Knows* (Dare mo shiranai, 2004) the horror is explicit. A feckless young mother abandons her own children. We watch as they try to cope, and fail. The electricity is turned off when no one pays the bill, they wash their clothes in the park, try to live on junk food bought at the convenience store, and the house gets dirtier as the kids get filthier. The injustice of this is apparent but there is no one to blame. The mother is more childish than her children, and for them society—irresponsible or not—does not even exist. Something is bound to happen and something overwhelmingly does.

Nobody Knows, 2004, Kore'eda Hirokazu.

Kore'eda the documentary-maker has learned that the truth is in the details. The son quietly asks the errant mother if he can't please go to school; doggedly the children try to keep an account book of what they have to spend; they forage in the neighborhood, turning feral and not knowing it. Without any ostensible comment, Kore'eda piles one observation on top of another until the weight crushes all this innocence.

By displaying the children alone, the writer-director is saying something about what is missing—the family. As with Ozu, from whom Kore'eda has learned much, the decomposition of the Japanese family is the major theme. The abandoned children try to make their own family. They fail. And in the process they show us that the world they live in is ours—and our fault.

"I'm strongly interested in the line between fiction and documentary, between real and unreal," Kore'eda told Itakura Kimie. "In this film I want to capture that moment in between these two."[22] When Aaron Gerow asked the director why he initially chose television documentaries, Kore'eda said that it was because he had no other way to start. "We knew that the majors were finished, so hardly anyone of my generation was thinking of working in the studios." He did go to Iwanami Productions, which had first encouraged Hani Susumu, but they were now only making public relations films. Kore'eda summarizes his options: "Thinking of how I could get behind a camera, a television production company was the next choice."[23]

It was for television that Kore'eda made the series of documentaries which eventually led him to feature-film production. In this he is like other directors of his generation: the techniques of the documentary continuing into his commercial films. These younger filmmakers have thus given the documentary style a more apparent realism, a definite place in the films of the turn of the millennium.

DOCUMENTARY AND *ANIME*

As we have seen, a major motif in the history of the Japanese film has been the oscillation between representation and presentation, between the perceived poles of an apparent reality and a highly controlled if realistic fiction. One of the effects of this duality is that the documentary, that most realistic of film genres, has not had in Japan anything like the influence it has had in other countries.

All film begins as documentary. Early scenes of Tokyo streets and of geisha dancing were quite apparently real. Later films continued what Abé Mark Nornes has phrased as "the shift from the general to the specific in the documentary's vicarious, virtual experiences of reality."[24]

The Russo-Japanese War of 1904 produced an enormous amount of filmed material, some of it authentic, which informed a clamorous public and at the same time ensured that this public thought as the government wanted it to. We have earlier in this book looked at some of this material in an attempt to define Japan's idea of presentation. Here, in this short survey of the Japanese documentary, we will notice that though this popularization of newsreel reality allowed the acceptance of that kind of fiction which is based on appearances, that is, realism, it also left the documentary as a film form with no place to go.

Some critics, Sato Tadao among them, hold that the first Japanese documentary of any significance was *The Japanese Expedition to the South Pole* (Nippon nankyoku tanken), made in 1910 and released in 1912. Others, however, have maintained that this film achieved this distinction only because it was the first to resemble the foreign "documentary."

In any event, the genre matured slowly in Japan, without many role models. Robert Flaherty's 1922 *Nanook of the North*—regarded by most film historians as the first feature-length documentary—was far in the future, and even when the foreign documentary film achieved its definite form in other countries, few examples were shown in Japan. Paul Rotha's book, *Documentary Film*, was as near as the Japanese got to the important British school of documentary.

Much closer in influence was the German kultur-film, imported as early as 1930, and widely available locally because of the growing political ties between Japan and Germany.

These pleasant pictures were popular and were usually safely apolitical, unlike say, Russian documentaries of the same period.

Russian documentaries themselves went unseen. Though the writings of Vsevolod Pudovkin, Sergei Eisenstein and Dziga Vertov were translated into Japanese in the early 1920s, such films as Eisenstein's *Potemkin* (1925) and Aleksandr Dovzhenko's *Earth* (1930) were not screened until after World War II. Even though Eisenstein's *Old and New* (1929) and Pudovkin's *Storm over Asia* (1928) were permitted screenings before the war, they were heavily censored.

Russian writings had their influence, however. In the fiction film this is seen in the works of Ito Daisuke, Itami Mansaku, and even Ozu Yasujiro. The Russian influence vitalized and for a time defined the nascent Japanese documentary. As Iwasaki Akira said: "All arts are vessels of ideology, and cinema is ideology in the form of an *obi* made of 35 mm film." [25]

As the Japanese government became more repressive during the 1930s and 1940s, dissident opinion became more difficult to voice. Film was seen as a way of showing dissent and, from 1927 onward, the organization Prokino, known as the "proletarian film movement," attempted to use the documentary (as had Eisenstein and others) as a means of protest.

The government fought back with film as its own ideological means and we have already seen here some of the results. Among these were documentaries which were the first Japanese attempts at long-form, large-scale, non-fiction films. Most of these documentaries pushed a militaristic agenda, with mixed results—as in Kamei Fumio's 1939 *Fighting Soldier*.

Others, like Ishimoto Tokichi's *Snow Country* (Yukiguni, 1939) attempted more. This film reflected the reality of rural Japan, actuality rather than aspiration, and in so doing achieved what is implied in John Grierson's definition of documentary as "a creative treatment of actuality." Most did not reach this level, however, and until the end of the Pacific War the documentary was seen mainly as a weapon.

But when peace has been achieved, weapons are no longer useful. Helping hands are needed. These were offered by the Allied Occupation of Japan, America leading, and the role of documentary as an instructional (and often indoctrinating) tool was acknowledged.

The American-inspired documentaries of the Occupation period were also propaganda, to be sure, and carried their own ideological load. At the same time, different issues were approached by other documentary makers. The diet of the Japanese was examined by Okuyama Dairokuro, while films about infectious diseases were made by Onuma Tetsuro and Sugiyama Masami. These were seen by large numbers of people since the Occupation's Civil Information and Education Section (CI & E) had lent the Ministry of Education over a thousand 16-mm projectors, making "movie classrooms" popular.

Political issues were approached in the films of Yoshimi Yutaka, Noda Shinkichi and Kamei Fumio, though these appeared mostly after the Occupation was over. Around this time the Iwanami publishing house created its own film unit, Iwanami Eiga. Among the educational films it produced were those of Kyogoku Takahide, Haneda Sumiko and Hani Susumu.

The Hani pictures were of great importance in the emergence of the postwar documentary. Just as his feature films defined "new wave" freedoms in independent commercial production, so his early documentaries freed the documentary form and enlarged the field. *Children in the Classroom* (Kyoshitsu no kodomotachi, 1954) and *Children Who Draw* (E wo kaku kodomotachi, 1956) inspired a whole generation of filmmakers. They proved that documentary did not have to be paternalistic and essay-like. Rather, one could, as did Hani, set up a camera and simply record what occurred—sorting it out could come later. Before the term existed, *cinéma verité* was in Japan and would yield spectacular results—as in the documentaries of Kore'eda Hirokazu.

Documentary, however, continued to fulfill its role as a vehicle of political dissent. The protest movement against the United States–Japan Security Treaty of 1960, though it ended in failure, gave further impetus to the genre. Matsumoto Toshio, Noda Shinkichi, and others made their first films around this time and these led to the protest films of Ogawa Shinsuke, one of Japan's most original documentarists.

Ogawa most famously made a long series (some ten hours) of films focusing on the protests against the construction of Narita International Airport. Acting with arbitrary authority, the government had requisitioned land and, for once, the farmers rebelled. They were joined by various sympathizers (including Ogawa), and the resulting ruckus became one of the most celebrated social upheavals of the decade. Among the titles in the Ogawa series are *Sea of Youth* (Seinen no umi, 1966) and *Summer in Narita: The Front Line for the Liberation of Japan* (Nihon kaiho sensen: Sanrizuka no natsu, 1968).

Ogawa has said that while they were making the Narita series, they gradually became aware of the "inner spirit" of the farmers—perhaps a bit like Uchida Tomu and his crew when they were making the contraband *Earth* (1939) many years earlier. This awareness resulted in a later series of documentaries by the same director on farm life, among them the prize-winning *A Japanese Village: Furuyashiki* (Nippon koku Furuyashiki-mura, 1982).

This kind of political statement was new to the documentary genre in Japan. Usually more akin to an anodyne kultur-film, or else obviously propaganda for either the United States or the Soviet Union, such a strong personal bias was rare, and showing the resulting product was difficult. Oshima Nagisa's television documentaries were relegated to odd hours; Imamura Shohei's, even though sponsored by the television company itself, were aired only at three or four in the morning.

Some documentaries were initially not shown at all, such as Tsuchimoto Noriaki's important *Minamata: The Victims and Their World* (Minamata: Kanja-san to sono sekai,

1972) about the mercury poisoning of an entire community by a nearby chemical company, and the scandal occasioned by the efforts of those responsible to escape. Tsuchimoto went on to make a number of other socially responsible documentaries—many more on the Minamata pollution tragedy, as well as other like disasters on the Shimokita Peninsula and in Korea. This line of documentary still continues in the ecological pictures of Sato Makoto and Himeida Tadayoshi.

In addition, the documentary was finding an audience other than in the classroom and on the television screen. From the 1970s on, a number of small theaters began to specialize in the genre. One such was Iwanami Hall, which has shown the documentaries of Haneda Sumiko, Miyagi Mariko and many others. In 1989, the Yamagata Documentary Film Festival was inaugurated, and in 2000 a similar festival was started in Yufuin, in Kyushu. By showing both local and foreign works, these festivals have not only stimulated a real interest in documentary, but have been able to bring controversial films to a wider audience. Without such venues and such support, a film such as Matsui Minoru's brave *Japanese Devils* (Riben guizi, 2001), for example, would not have been possible. The film is a series of statements by fourteen former imperial army soldiers who fought in China and who on camera tell exactly what they saw and did. The making and marketing of a film which challenges Japan's amnesia regarding its wartime atrocities was an act of real conscience and courage.

Among the younger documentarists, the strongest—though still least likely to be shown on prime-time television—is Hara Kazuo. As a student of the Tokyo Academy of Photography he worked part-time in a school for children with disabilities, where he discovered the theme of his first film, *Goodbye CP* (Sayonara CP, 1972), about adults with cerebral palsy and how they are regarded (or disregarded) by the Japanese. It deliberately challenges taboos about the shame of physical difference and refuses any facile empathy. As one of the afflicted says in the film: "Pity, I can do without it."

Hara's next film, two years later, caused even more of a stir. *Extreme Private Eros: Love Song* (Kyokushiteki erosu: Koiuta 1974) is about Hara and his estranged wife, a radical feminist, in Yokosuka, a Japanese port town which, as in Imamura's *Pigs and Battleships* (1961), is "corrupted" by the American naval presence. Hara's real subject, however, is the Japanese family and its insular structure. "I thought that if I could put my own family under the camera, all our emotions, our privacy, I might break taboos about the family."[26]

With *The Emperor's Naked Army Marches On* (Yukiyukite shingun, 1987), Hara created his strongest and his most controversial film. Not since Ichikawa Kon's *Fires on the Plain* had a Japanese film dealt so frankly with the facts of World War II, and none since Kamei Fumio's banned 1946 *A Japanese Tragedy* had so confronted the responsibility of the emperor. The picture focuses on a man who obstinately implicates Emperor Hirohito, denouncing him as "the most cowardly man in Japan."

Like the hero in Kurosawa's *Record of a Living Being*, the protagonist of Hara's film, Okuzaki Kenzo, is obsessed with his theme. Like the earlier hero, he, too, comes to use the very means he is criticizing. The man is a champion for righteousness and he is at the same time much given to violence—he attacks those he interviews and at the end of the film he is in prison yet again for attempted murder. The paradoxes are so much like those in Imamura Shohei's *A Man Vanishes* that one is not surprised to learn that the entire project was origi-nally conceived by him. He gave it to Hara while the younger director was working as an assistant cameraman on *Vengeance Is Mine*.

The film itself, with Hara and his camera much in evidence, transgresses a number of Japanese social norms—so many, indeed, that no one wanted to touch the picture once it was made. Everyone was afraid of retaliation by rightist thugs and their yakuza counterparts. But Hara persevered. As he has said of himself: "My outlaw complex is very strong."[27] Finally the documentary and experimental film archive, Image Forum, was brave enough to show it.

This film was followed by *A Dedicated Life* (Zenshin shosetsuka, 1994), produced in-family by Kobayashi Sachiko, where again motivation is unveiled and Hara himself is part of the picture. He has said that this film continued his interest in the dividing line between the documentary and the fictional film and that he had featured firebrand Okuzaki Kenzo because "he was something like an action star."[28] Fact and fiction are seamlessly closed in Hara's first "feature film," *Chika* (Mata no hi no Chika, 2005).

Many younger Japanese documentary makers are similarly interested in the line between the real and the fictional. Kore'eda Hirokazu once told Aaron Gerow that he had always believed that the filming person and the filmed subject occupied two separate dimensions, as it were, but that in his first documentary he became aware that this was not what he wanted. Hara would agree in that he is continually experimenting with a form which will include both real and fictional. This is one of the reasons that *A Dedicated Life* has many "memories" reconstructed for the camera, and why Hara is now devoting all of his energies to fictional films.

If the documentary traditionally represents one pole of the representation-presentation axis, the animated film, that most presentational of film forms, can be seen as the other. Here photographic realism does not exist. Rather, a created actuality is presented and the realism is that of the artist—the person who draws the images.

The presentational style has been variously described, but the term usually implies that images are created for the camera rather than found by it, and that these have a stylistic unity, or a controlled stylization missing from representational styles—variously controlled though they may be. One of the liveliest defenses of this presentational quality occurs in one of its famous fictional celebrations—André Gide's novel *Les Faux-Monnayeurs.*

Here Gide has Edouard, his protagonist, state that the creator should absolutely not be "a slave to resemblance." Rather, he ought to cultivate "that deliberate avoidance of life which gave style to the works of the Greek dramatists," whose works are "deeply human only in their depths; they don't prize themselves on appearing so—or, at any rate, on appearing real. They remain works of art."[29]

This is the appeal of any presentational work—it is a work of art, unified in vision, singular in style, and subject to none of the vagaries of actuality. In Japan, as elsewhere, the cinematic form which most satisfies such criteria is the animated cartoon, the anime. Its growth parallels that of the Japanese feature film. It, too, had its beginnings on the stage and has long exhibited this debt; it, too, was subjected to various political and economic pressures; and finally, it, too, continues to narrate in a distinctive Japanese accent.

Projected, animated images were seen early, in the *utsushi-e* of the nineteenth-century. These were, essentially, lantern slides with movable parts (hands, feet, heads) which could be manipulated during the showing. An outgrowth of even earlier shadow plays, in which images were manipulated by hand while their shadows were projected on a screen, these utsushi-e began to be adapted to film shortly after the first foreign animated pictures were shown in Japan, around 1909. Among those experimenting with the new form were Kouchi Sumikazu, Shimokawa Oten, and Kitayama Seitaro. The means were several: single moving parts taken from the utsushi-e, blackboard drawings which were erased and modified for each succeeding exposure, and traditional stencil-cut shadow play.

One of Kouchi's pupils, Ofuji Noburo, was to become famous for his popular *chiyogami-eiga,* made from animated paper cutouts. Inspired by Lotte Reiniger's similar work, widely seen in Japan, he devised his own animation board and went into production. His first film, *The Whale* (Kujira), was completed in 1927, a year before Disney released its first Mickey Mouse feature, *Steamboat Willie.* Ofuji remade *The Whale* in color in 1952 and went on to create *Ghost Ship* (Yureisen, 1956), his best-known film. In 1940, Arai Wagoro made his popular *Fantasy of Madam Butterfly* (Ocho-fujin no genso) in a similar style.

All these films used stop-frame animation in addition to manipulation of the images while the camera was running. The technique of drawing directly on celluloid "cels"—the accepted method of early animation in the West—was seen in Japan only after 1929, and was not widely used until much later.

In the West, the animated-cel pioneer was Walt Disney, and his pictures, in Japan as elsewhere, soon established a hegemony. When sound film became feasible in the early 1930s there were a few Japanese animated talkie films, mainly those of Masaoka Kenzo, but Disney's were thought superior, and many animators were put out of jobs.

Wartime Japan offered a new role for animated pictures, however, since these could be used to inculcate a young and malleable audience. In 1936, the J. O. Studios produced a short about Momotaro, the redoubtable Japanese Peach Boy, versus Mickey Mouse. In it, the popular rodent is quickly dispatched. Momotaro made further appearances in Seo Mitsuyo's *Momotaro's Sea Eagle* (Momotaro no umiwashi, 1943) and *Momotaro—Divine Troops of the Ocean* (Momotaro: Umi no shimpei, 1945). In both of these the Peach Boy goes to war. "Momotaro makes a leap onto the stage of the Greater East-Asia War!" said the press release.[30] The evil demons speak English (with Japanese subtitles) and Momotaro finds a plaque which reads, "On a night when the moonlight is bright, there will come from an Eastern land of the Son of Heaven a divine soldier on a white horse who is destined to liberate the people."[31]

After World War II was lost, there was little need for this sort of animation, or indeed any animation at all. Just as the documentary had been somewhat compromised by wartime use, so the propagandization of animation worked against postwar acceptance. In addition, animation was expensive to make, and the times were inclining toward a new realism. Consequently there was little animated film. Ichikawa Kon managed to finish his kabuki-based puppet picture, *Musume Dojoji* (1946), only to have it banned by the Occupation. Another animated film, this one safely non-feudal, Masaoka Kenzo's *Cherry Blossoms— A Fantasy of Spring* (Sakura, aka Haru no genso, 1949), featuring butterflies and girls under the blossoms of Kyoto, and synchronized to the music of Karl Maria von Weber's "Invitation to the Dance," was approved and shown. Besides, the director had already had some success with a rare non-propaganda wartime musical animation, *The Spider and the Tulip* (Kumo to churippu, 1943).

All these works—prewar, wartime and postwar—defined the aesthetic limitations of the Japanese animated product. Seen now, they indeed demonstrate that their graphic spatial assumptions are those one associates with early Japanese cinema and with the print artists of a century before. Composition remains a major concern, and the regard for balance, as seen in the work of master printmakers Hokusai and Hiroshige, is taken for granted. Likewise there is little attempt at any three-dimensional illusionism—two dimensions are enough— and there are equally few attempts at depth. And the action (even by the evolving international standards of the time) is still limited.

Until computer animation became a possibility, Japanese cellular animation limited itself to eight frames a second. The Western standard was and remains twelve frames a second. At a film speed of twenty-four frames per second, this meant that the Japanese anime presented each frame three times, while the Western films offered a new image every two frames. The result is that American and European animation appeared slightly more lifelike. Jerky Japanese animation of this period is called "limited animation" and indeed it is.

The standard adopted by the Japanese, however, saved time as well as money, and made weekly television animation series possible. It fit the budgets of the producers. Eventually, thanks not only to limited animation (which in some cases was so jerky it seemed to revert to the earlier slide-show format), but also due to the low wages of Japanese animators—and the even lower wages of subcontractors in Taiwan, China and Korea—making an animated film became cheaper than making an ordinary picture. As Sato Kenji has said: "Animation offers a means of producing slick, stylish films without spending much money." [32] Since natural-appearing movement was not one of the concerns, it was also not considered inappropriate to be unrealistically jerky in motion.

Indeed, the halting poses of much Japanese animation have been compared to the series of still poses which supply the continuity of *nihon buyo*, Japanese classical dance. This kind of dance differs from, say, Western ballet, in that the moments of rest are considered the high point, while in ballet it is the dynamic movement itself (from one moment of rest to another, as it were) which defines the strength of the choreography. Anime pauses in a way reminiscent of nihon buyo, and in both instances naturalistic movement is not a considered alternative.

Lifelike representation is largely missing because it is rarely attempted. Rather, all manga and most anime are considered as opportunities for presentation. Just as the comic-book manga, overwhelmingly popular in Japan, is in reality a series of storyboards, so the anime retains the storyboard effect. This effect is seen at its purest in Oshima Nagisa's *Band of Ninja* (Ninja bugei-cho, 1967), which consists of photographed stills—the original drawings which Shirato Sampei made for the comic strip of the same title. The storyboard effect is also evident in Ichikawa Kon's *Shinsengumi* (2000), where comic-strip cutouts are manipulated in the most purposely elementary manner.

The strong structural connection between manga and anime is logical, since most Japanese animated features are based upon best-selling manga series. An example would be Tezuka Osamu's *Astroboy* (Tetsuwan Atomu). It made its debut as a manga comic book in 1951, was instantly popular, and in 1963 was made into Japan's first animated TV series. The turbo-charged youth with searchlight eyes, and ears a thousand times sharper than ours, proved equally prevalent on the screen, and the series' theme song became ubiquitous: "There you go, Astroboy, on your flight into space! Rocket high, through the sky, what adventures you'll face!"

Tezuka, sometimes called "the Walt Disney of Japan," not only pioneered the animated feature but also created the first animation factory. The Disney resemblance continued in that such works as *Pictures at an Exhibition* (Tenrankai no e, 1966) and the unfinished *Legend of the Forest* (Mori no densetsu, 1988) may be thought of as homages to Disney's *Fantasia* (1940).

The compliment was returned when Disney derived its *Lion King* from the Tezuka anime, *Jungle Emperor Leo* (Janguru taitei, aka Kimba the White Lion, 1997) and its predecessors, released in Japan from 1965 to 1967 and later frequently televised in the United States.

Jungle Emperor Leo came from a comic-book manga. Tezuka's original version ran from 1950 to 1954 in a boys' magazine. It was animated and televised as a series from 1965 to 1967. Theatrical versions were made in 1965, 1989 and 1997. All of these metamorphoses argue for an enormous audience. It was reported that in 1995 an average of fifteen comic books and magazines were annually purchased by every man, woman and child on the Japanese archipelago.

In designing manga (the word was apparently first used by Hokusai in 1814 to mean "spontaneous pictures," as applied to his series of humorous sketches), the artist remains in complete control, unlike in the West where the artists are often part of a team composed of scriptwriters, inkers, letterers, and so forth. Animators such as Tezuka are thus in the position of directors like Mizoguchi and Kurosawa who assumed full control over and responsibility for everything. This means that personal style (rather than house style) becomes apparent.

Tezuka's style is straightforwardly manga-esque, but his less commercial work reveals definite personal characteristics, particularly in such experimental works as *Jumping* (Jampingu, 1984), a seven-minute conceit made in a single shot with over four thousand cel drawings, and *Broken-Down Film* (Omboro firumu, 1985), where Tezuka deliberately stained and slashed his work in order to create the feeling of "primitive" silent-period animated movies.

Just as manga influenced anime in its storyboard-like construction, so cinema has also influenced comic-book manga. Tezuka's 1947 comic-book *Shin Takarajima* (New Paradise Island) was considered a pioneering work because, in showing a driver speeding along a road, an action taking place over several comic-book frames, different visual ("camera") angles were used. Previously, Japanese manga comics had, like the first films of half a century before, showed action only from fixed positions. Tezuka's varying perspective offered something new to printed manga, and now can be regarded as a presage of animated manga to come.

In the succeeding decades, anime has achieved an enormous popularity and many new cartoonist-directors have emerged. During the late 1970s, more than forty new series were produced yearly, as well as special weekly ninety-minute-long animated programs. Matsumoto Reiji's famous television series *Space Battleship Yamato* (Uchu senkan Yamato,

1974–75) was edited into a series of five feature films, all directed by Masuda Toshio. Even established directors tried their hand at the new form, such as Imai Tadashi with *Yuki* (1981).

With so many works creating a field so wide, one that is still proliferating, only a few can be cited here. One might mention Sugii Gisaburo's popular *Night of the Galaxy Railroad* (Ginga tetsudo no yoru, 1985); Otomo Katsuhiro's *Akira* (1988), based on his four-volume comic book about neo-Tokyo in the year 2030 which, as Tony Rayns noted, was "paced like a machine-gun: hardly any image is held on screen for longer than a few seconds"[33]; Otomo's *Steamboy* (Sutimu boi, 2004), the Tezuka-influenced homage to Atomboy; Oshii Mamoru's *Ghost in the Shell* (Kokaku kidotai, 1995), based on manga by Shiro Masamune; *The Wolf Brigade* (Jinro, 1999) by Oshii's protégé, Okiura Hiroyuki; and Anno Hideaki's 26-episode *Neon Genesis: Evangelion* (Shin seiki evangerion, 1995) which was later repackaged into several feature films.

Important too, is the work of Studio Ghibli. Miyazaki Hayao directed *My Neighbor Totoro* (Tonari no Totoro, 1988); *Kiki's Delivery Service* (Majo no takkyubin, 1989); and the elaborate and eco-friendly *Princess Mononoke* (Mononoke-hime, 1997), which became in Japan the highest grossing film of its time. Miyazaki won international renown for his award-winning *Spirited Away* (Sen to Chihiro no kamikakushi, 2002), before moving on to *Howl's Moving Castle* (Hauru no ugoku shiro, 2004), both of which broke *Princess Mononoke*'s box-office record.

Princess Mononoke, 1997, Miyazaki Hayao.

Recent anime developments have seen various tie-ins among manga publications and computer games, and inroads into the toy market. One such manga-computer-toy tie-in is the *Pocket Monsters* (Pokémon, 1998) anime series which began as software for portable game machines made by Nintendo. An animated version was first shown on television, and then went into theaters as a series of features. With it went the various spin-offs common to such genres.

This pattern duplicates that of early cinema, where the first scenes and spectacles were recycled among various venues. New technical developments (the kinescope peep-show, the early kinemascope projector, the first movie halls) permitted the product—still in its original state—to pass through these more advanced viewing phases. The movement is visible in other film industries as well. The earlier faking of the sinking of the Lusitania and the latter faking of the sinking of the Titanic have much in common.

One thus sees in Japan's latest films many of the assumptions of its earliest cinema. Though the technology is now more or less on the cutting-edge of whatever technological advance is being made, the surmises are often ones we are familiar with from the traditional arts of Japan. There is no real contradiction. Japanese hardware is usually advanced, Japanese software seldom is.

As the animated field grows, genres proliferate and distinctions, such as that between *animeishon* (animation) and anime, are beginning to be observed. Miyazaki Hayao made this differentiation in the documentary interview which precedes the American English language dubbed version of *Princess Mononoke* (1999). Here he voices his dislike of anime, saying that it "simply uses manufactured images instead of reality." (Since the images in both animation and anime are manufactured, Miyazaki presumably means by this that Otomo and the other anime people are not realistic in the way he believes himself to be.)

Nonetheless, amid all such painted "realism," one rarely forgets the presence of the Japanese animator and his guiding hand. He has, with realistic detail or not, created an enormous body of work, the conventions of which now influence many other forms: advertising, design, narrative structure in the novel, and the commercial "live-action" feature film itself.

One ought perhaps to attempt to account for the enormous popularity of both manga and anime since they have come to dominate all visual markets and even (in box-office figures) to represent Japanese filmmaking as a whole. It is maintained that manga accounts for a third of all books sold in Japan, and that anime accounts for half of all Japanese movie tickets sold.

In explaining this phenomenal popularity, Sato Kenji has said that "for animation to push aside live-action films, a growing number of people had to prefer the thin, insubstantial reality of animation to the flesh-and-blood world of live-action."[34] This, indeed, is precisely what occured during the 1990s.

The flight to anime, says Sato, is the inevitable result of the ethnic self-denial that has suffused Japanese society ever since the Meiji era, and especially since the end of World War II. Bent on achieving the goals of modernization and Westernization, the Japanese, in rejecting their own history and traditions, have sought to become *nihonjin-banare* (de-Japanized)—generally a complimentary term, implying that one looks and acts more like a Westerner than a Japanese.

Toward the end of the twentieth century, many were the attempts to Westernize. There were not only Western clothing fashions to be acquired and exhibited, there was also mass hair-dying among the young (blond being preferred) and eccentric make-up for girls which rounded the eyes and built up the bridge of the nose, as well as towering platform shoes to achieve a hopefully Western height.

Only manga and anime, however, could convincingly meld Japanese and Western attributes into a natural-looking human being. Here one can have enormous round eyes and long legs. "This is because," continues Sato, "the upside of these genres' inherent lack of realism is their unique ability to exploit the appeal and fascination of the unreal. And this is why manga and anime have attained such a high status in the popular culture of Japan . . . These are the only two media capable of portraying reality the way Japanese feel it should be."[35]

Though this thesis would seem at odds with tradition-bound Japan, a moment's reflection suggests that this concern for the way things should be rather than the way they are is in itself a tradition—and not only in Japan, though perhaps, as so often, it is more visibly so there.

Despite the many exceptions, a general apathy to realism as a style is one explanation for the enormous popularity of manga and anime. Another is that the attractions of "virtual" reality are to be seen more strongly in Japan than in most other countries, perhaps because "reality" itself is regarded in so tenuous a fashion. After all, one of the comforts of virtual reality is that, even when it concerns itself with gunmen and monsters, it is not dangerous. Reality itself, on the other hand, is traditionally perceived as perilous. Indeed, a part of the education of any Japanese child is being told many times a day (usually by Mother) that this or that is *abunai*—dangerous. Virtual reality is also enormously tractable. One can control a virtual landscape or a virtual person much more easily than can one the real thing.

Japan is historically very familiar with this. It early perfected, for example, a classical garden style that is "virtual" in that it was entirely "programmed." The differences between the seventeenth-century garden of the Katsura Rikyu Imperial Villa in Kyoto and the computer game Dragonball are manifest, but their similarities should not be overlooked. Three of these are the taming of nature, the idealizing of the environment, and the making of everything into what it ought to be rather than what it actually is.

Such a conclusion might then explain Japan's perhaps otherwise puzzling lack of interest in realism as a style, and its corresponding lack of respect—if that is the term—for reality itself. It might be argued that there is no reality—that is, everything that we call by that name is really programmed somewhere down the line and hence has become something it was not. The flaw in that line of thought, however, is that it fails to particularize, which is something that this book has attempted to do.

CONCLUSION

In describing the history of earlier Japanese film I have often oscillated between the two ideas of the traditional and the modern. This is fitting because the Japanese themselves used to do so. We have thus searched for and found much living tradition within a contemporary context, many a tradition remaining in modern guise.

In the pictorial compositions of both the earliest and the latest films, I have traced connections and found ratios of empty and full which we can view as typical; have viewed the screen in the first *Loyal Forty-Seven Ronin* and even the later *Neon Genesis: Evangelion* as a two-dimensional field, something to look at rather than see through, and have read a narrative structure which retains the assumptions of the theme rather than the promptings of the plot.

A similar search of contemporary Japanese film would find much less evident tradition. Such is the erosion experienced by any tradition. Notwithstanding, these various means do metamorphose and emerge in different form. That the Japanese cinematic accent is now much closer to that of the West is apparent. What is not so obvious, and this I have attempted to describe, is that it is still there.

The lowering sky defines character in *Maboroshi* (1995) just as it did in *Souls on the Road* (1921). The narrow depth of image is as apparent in the adventures of Akira as it was in the adventures of Matsunosuke, and young directors find the long shot just as necessary as did those now long dead. Kitano, Aoyama and Iwai find it cool, Naruse and Mizoguchi found it non-involving, and the shot is the same, though the contexts in which it is used are different indeed.

This living tradition (unseen, accepted, even unconscious); this amalgam of supposition, of conjecture, surmise and accepted assumption; this aesthetic celebration of pattern and composition; this extreme angle from which life is to be viewed; this need for an authoritative and Japanese voice—that is what this book has been about.

II

A SELECTIVE GUIDE
TO DVDs AND VIDEOS

Japanese film for home use is presently found in two formats: DVD and VHS (videocassette). In Japan and the Americas the system is NTSC, while much of Europe relies on PAL. France and Russia use SECAM. All these systems are mutually exclusive. In addition, DVDs are often designed to be playable in a single zone and to be unplayable in others. A DVD designed to be played in the USA (Zone 1), for example, cannot be played in Japan (Zone 2) without a "universal" DVD player. This messy state reflects the economic ambitions of both hardware and software producers.

The films listed below are almost all English titled (with the exceptions plainly indicated) but may not all be obtainable (and will be distinguished with OP for out-of-print). These OP titles are nonetheless included since this listing aims to show whatever is or once was available. Many of the out-of-print films are available at rental shops or sold as collector's items at popular online sites or in specialty stores. Most titles included have already been mentioned in the pages of this book. Films of major directors, if available, are also included even if they have not been mentioned earlier. And, of course, many mentioned in the text cannot be included in this guide since they were never issued in tape or disc format. American-made discs and videos are given preference, those from other countries being listed only if there is no American-made product.

The title under which each film is listed is usually that preferred by the issuing company, but it is also cross referenced with its alternative titles. In the matter of film lengths there is little agreement. I use the Japanese reference standard, which is sometimes different from that supplied by foreign video and disc manufacturers. There is also the matter of quality. This is generally good, but can vary, depending on the original printing materials and the amount of care taken in the transfer.

Of course, all versions are less perfect than the original projected film version. My listing of these tape and disc versions does not imply that I endorse the results. The experience of watching *Seven Samurai* on television is nothing approaching that of seeing the film on a theater screen. But in most countries (including Japan itself) tape and disc are now the only ways to view these films.

Finally, in commenting upon each, I have tried to give an indication of general critical opinion by including some listing of awards. The reader will be familiar with most of these, but perhaps not with the *Kinema Jumpo* award for best film. This is important in Japan and is awarded by a body of film critics, thus making it similar to the New York Film Critics' Award. I have designated these as KJ#1. There is also a Japan "Academy Award" panel operating in much the same inner-industry manner as does its Hollywood counterpart.

In making this list I am extremely grateful to Marty Gross, Lalu Danzker, and Stuart Galbraith IV, all of whom were generously helpful in finding for me which Japanese films were available. I would also like to thank Racha Abazied for help in locating French sources. Any oversights are mine, not theirs.

A

Actor's Revenge, An (Yukinojo henge, 1963), Ichikawa Kon. A kabuki female impersonator takes revenge for the forced suicide of his parents. Veteran Hasegawa Kazuo plays a double role as both male actress and the thief who befriends him, and Wakao Ayako is the girl who falls in love with the cross-dressing actor. Kitsch and camp meet dedication and true love. 114 mins. DVD/VHS, British Film Institute (UK).

Affair at Kamakura. See *Crazed Fruit.*

Afraid to Die (Karakkaze yaro, aka A Man Blown by the Wind, 1960), Masumura Yasuzo. A gangster film with famous author Mishima Yukio in the leading role. The script was written by Kurosawa scriptwriter Kikushima Ryuzo, but the results are more curious than believable. 96 mins. DVD, Fantoma Films.

After Life (Wandafuru raifu, 1998), Kore'eda Hiro-kazu. A thoughtful elegy in which the dead line up to be processed into the next world. In order to enter, they have to choose a single memory to take with them. This memory is then filmed by the dedicated staff—comprised of those who could not or would not themselves choose a memory. 118 mins. DVD/VHS, New Yorker Films.

Akira (1988), Otomo Katsuhiro. The animated feature that, for a time, defined Japanese anime. Based on a popular Otomo comic-book, it is set in Tokyo after World War III with Akira, the apocalypse personified, pitted against young biker Tetsuo. Characterization is minimal; special effects are over the top. 124 mins. DVD, Pioneer Video.

Akira Kurosawa's Dreams. See *Dreams.*

All Mixed Up. See *Manji.*

Angel Dust (Enjeru dasuto, 1994), Ishii Sogo. Among the first of the nouvelle horror flicks. A new-religion convert is supposed to be deprogrammed but is turned into a serial killer. Our heroine catches on, with terrible results. 123 mins. DVD, Panorama Entertainment (Hong Kong); VHS, New Yorker Films.

Antonio Gaudi (1984), Teshigahara Hiroshi. The director of *Woman in the Dunes* visits the best known buildings of his favorite architect, including houses in Barcelona and its environs and the famous Sagrada Familia Cathedral. With a score by Takemitsu Toru. 45 mins. DVD, New Yorker Films.

Auberge à Tokyo, Une. See *Inn in Tokyo, An.*

Audition (Odishon, 2000), Miike Takashi. A video producer finds the girl of his dreams and it is a nightmare. He (Ishibashi Ryo) holds a fake audition for a new bride. She (Eihi Shiina) holds a real audition for a new victim. Maybe. Is it a dream or isn't it? Little boy paranoia about creepy girls. 115 mins. DVD/VHS, Ventura Distribution.

Autumn Afternoon, An (Samma no aji, 1962), Ozu Yasujiro. The last film of a great director. Again, and more poignantly than ever, the family falls apart. Widower (Ryu Chishu) arranges for his loving daughter (Iwashita Shima) to be married, though it means a life of loneliness for him. Again, an Ozu/Noda Kogo script and luminous color photography by Atsuta Yuharu. 112 mins. DVD, Panorama Entertainment (Hong Kong).

Autumn of the Kobayagawa Family, The. See *End of Summer, The.*

Avalon (Abaron, 2000), Oshii Mamoru. Though just a "game" movie at heart, this real-life "animation" is so beautifully made and so astonishing to watch that it leaves its genre far behind. Shot in Poland, and in Polish (with English and French titles), it is wonderfully photographed by Grzegorz Kedzierski. 106 mins. DVD/VHS, Miramax Home Entertainment.

B

Bad Company (Mabudachi, 2001), Furumaya Tomoyuki. A high-school student rebels against a repressive school system and asks us to make a moral choice—his individuality is called delinquent but the teacher's discipline is shown as authoritarian. 106 mins. VHS (Dutch titles), Tiger Releases, Holland.

Bad Sleep Well, The (Warui yatsu hodo yoku nemuru, aka A Rose in the Mud, 1960), Kurosawa Akira. A finely made melodrama, highly critical of the ties between big business and government, with Mifune Toshiro in the Hamlet-like role of the man who must avenge his murdered father. Mori Masayuki is the Claudius-like boss and Kagawa Kyoko is the Ophelia-like crippled daughter. 151 mins. DVD/ VHS, Home Vision Entertainment.

Ballad of Narayama (Narayama bushiko, 1958), Kinoshita Keisuke. The first version (Imamura's film in the following entry was the second) of the Fukazawa Shichiro novel about a village where the sons were by custom forced to leave their aged parents to the elements of Mount Narayama. Here Tanaka Kinuyo is the determined mother and Takahashi Teiji is the reluctant son. The director presents his story in quasi-kabuki fashion with revolving scenery, tableaux and a traditional score. KJ#1. 98 mins. VHS, Kino.

Ballad of Narayama, The (Narayama bushiko, 1983), Imamura Shohei. The second version of the Fukazawa Shichiro novel about life in the village where the aged are taken to Mount Narayama to die. (The first was Kinoshita Keisuke's version in the above entry.) Imamura's is the more realistic, with

Sakamoto Sumiko doing her preparations with dispatch and some humor, and Ogata Ken as the unwilling son. Cannes, Grand Prix; Japan Academy Award, Best Film. 130 mins. VHS, Home Vision Entertainment.

Battle Royale (Batoru rowaiaru, 2000), Fukasaku Kinji. The government, tired of juvenile delinquency, rounds up the kids and orders them to kill each other. This they do at great length and in full detail. Grim and earnest, it sports a few ironic touches, one of which is having Kitano Takeshi as the home-room teacher. There is a "director's cut" version (2001) and a *Battle Royale II* (2003) as well. 113 mins. DVD/ VHS, Tartan (UK).

Battles Without Honor and Humanity (Jingi naki tatakai, aka The Yakuza Papers, 1973), Fukasaku Kinji. The first of a multi-part series devoted to chivalrous yakuza and their honor-bound way of life, as contrasted to the smarmy ways of the common criminal. 99 mins. DVD, Home Vision Entertainment.

Being Two Isn't Easy (Watashi wa nisai, 1962), Ichikawa Kon. A *coup de cinéma*, the whole movie seen from the viewpoint of a two-year-old. It is he whom we hear on voice-over and through whom we learn that the ways of adults are strange indeed. The bemused parents are Yamamoto Fujiko and Funakoshi Eiji. The script is by Wada Natto. KJ#1. 88 mins. VHS, Home Vision Entertainment.

Black Lizard (Kuro tokage, 1968), Fukasaku Kinji. Mishima Yukio adapted this Edogawa Rampo story and Narusawa Masashige wrote it up. It stars transvestite Miwa Akihiro, with a bit part for Mishima himself. It could have been a lot campier than it is. Fukasaku did not know he was creating a cult classic. 86 mins. VHS, Facets Multimedia (OP).

Black Rain (Kuroi ame, 1989), Imamura Shohei. After the atom bomb, the black rain, and after that, radiation sickness. Imamura's version of Ibuse Masuji's famous novel about the Hiroshima disaster is made with warmth, sincerity and compassion. In sober black-and-white and with a Takemitsu Toru score. Cannes, Critic's Prize; Japan Academy Award, Best Film; KJ#1. 123 mins. DVD/VHS, Image Entertainment.

Boiling Point (San tai yon ekkusu jugatsu, 1990), Kitano Takeshi. Baseball teammates go to Okinawa to buy guns to avenge a murdered coach but fall into the hands of psychopathic yakuza. Kitano Takeshi plays himself (pop media idol, Beat Takeshi), and the cast includes people with names like Bengal and Johnny Okura. 98 mins. DVD/VHS, Fox Lorber.

Born Fighter, The. See *Elegy to Violence.*

Branded to Kill (Koroshi no rakuin, 1967), Suzuki Seijun. An inventive and ultimately anarchic take on gangster thrillers. Guryu Hachiro's script flounders midway and Suzuki tries on the bizarre for its own sake. All very interesting but the company didn't think so. This is the film that got Suzuki fired. 91 mins. DVD/VHS, Criterion.

Build-up, The. See *Giants and Toys.*

Burmese Harp, The. See *Harp of Burma, The.*

C

Charisma (Karisuma, 1999), Kurosawa Kiyoshi. A large tree seems to be sucking life from the forest. Which is most important—the individual or society? This problem is not solved but obliterated by all the graphic violence at the end. With Yakusho Koji. 103 mins. DVD (English titles), King Records (Hong Kong).

Chikamatsu Monogatari. See *Story from Chikamatsu, A.*

Children of Hiroshima (Gembaku no ko, 1952), Shindo Kaneto. Otowa Nobuko as the young teacher who takes care of the homeless young after the bombing of Hiroshima. More broadly humanistic than narrowly political. 97 mins. DVD (English titles), Asmik Ace (Japan).

Chushingura (aka The Loyal Forty-Seven Ronin, aka Forty-Seven Samurai, 1962), Inagaki Hiroshi. The most lavish of the many screen adaptations of the famous kabuki classic. This one, here formatted as a two-part version, contains all the famous scenes but takes for granted a certain acquaintance with the story line. An all-star cast with a new subplot for Mifune. 204 mins. DVD/VHS, Image Entertainment. (See also: *Loyal Forty-Seven Ronin, The.*)

Conflagration (aka Enjo, aka Flame of Torment, aka The Temple of the Golden Pavilion, 1958), Ichikawa Kon. Yukio Mishima's *The Temple of the Golden Pavilion* (scripted by Wada Natto and Hasebe Keiji) becomes the finest of Ichikawa's literary adaptations. A young monk destroys that which he most loves by setting fire to Kinkakuji, the Golden Pavilion. With action-hero Ichikawa Raizo splendid as the inarticulate priest, extraordinary black-and-white widescreen photography by Miyagawa Kazuo, and a fine score by Mayuzumi Toshiro. 98 mins. VHS, New Yorker Films.

Crazed Fruit (Kurutta kajitsu, aka Affair at Kamakura, aka Juvenile Passion, aka This Scorching Sea, 1956), Nakahira Ko. One of the seminal films of the fifties, a well-made atmospheric picture which gave respectability to the taiyozoku flaming-youth genre. Older and younger brother (Ishihara Yujiro and Tsugawa Masahiko) are both involved with the same girl (Kitahara Mie) with disastrous results. Takemitsu Toru's first film score as well. 86 mins. DVD, Criterion.

Crazy Page, A. See *Page Out of Order, A.*

Crépuscule à Tokyo. See *Tokyo Twilight.*

Crucified Lovers, The. See *Story from Chika-matsu, A.*

Cruel Story of Youth (Seishun zankoku mono-gatari, aka Cruel Tales of Youth, 1960), Oshima Nagisa. A teenage tough pimps his girl friend then extracts dough from the middle-aged buyers. Shot through with Oshima's somehow sentimental nihilism. With Kawazu Yusuke and Kuwano Miyuki as pimp and product. 96 mins. VHS, New Yorker Films.

Cure (Kyua, 1997), Kurosawa Kiyoshi. Pop gothic-horror hit. Detective Yakusho Koji is baffled by spaced-out punk Hagiwara Masato's seemingly irrational powers, which include mind control, and making murderers of the innocent. 111 mins. DVD, Home Vision Entertainment.

D

Daylight Demon. See *Violence at Noon.*

Death Japanese Style. See *Funeral, The.*

Dernier Caprice. See *End of Summer, The.*

Dersu Uzala (1975), Kurosawa Akira. Based on Vladimir Arseniev's accounts of early exploration in Siberia (amongst the director's favorite books) this film shows how Arseniev encountered Dersu, child of nature, intrepid hunter and noble savage. Filmed mainly on location in Russia. Academy Award, Best

Foreign Film. Original, 141 mins; US version, 137 mins. DVD, Kino International. Also anamorphic ver-sion, (Russian and English titles), Ruscico (Russia).

Désir Meurtrier. See *Intentions of Murder.*

Diary of Chuji's Travels, A (Chuji tabi nikki, 1927), Ito Daisuke. One of the most famous films of the twenties. A few segments are included on the CD-ROM, "Masterpieces of Japanese Silent Cinema," which contains excerpts from forty-five other silent Japanese pictures. CD-ROM (Windows only), Urban Connections, Inc., (Japan).

Distance (Disutansu, 2001), Kore'eda Hirokazu. A mysterious and powerful elegy centered around four people who are family of members of a religious cult killed for having attempted genocide. When the four visit the scene of the tragedy, their car goes mysteriously missing, and they are forced to spend the night. 164 mins. DVD (English titles), Bandai Visual (Japan).

Dodes'ka-den (1970), Kurosawa Akira. A decora-tive, highly colored slice-of-life served in a contem-porary Tokyo slum. Various characters interact with others to indicate that though life is certainly diffi-cult, it is none the less worth living. Kurosawa's first color film, music by Takemitsu Toru. 140 mins. VHS, Home Vision Entertainment.

Double Suicide (Shinju ten no amijima, 1969), Shinoda Masahiro. The Tomioka Taeko script, retaining the plot of the Chikamatsu original, also preserves the conventions of the bunraku puppet theater for which the play was originally written. The story revolves around a married merchant's infatuation with a geisha. The result (actors attended by puppeteers) lends a fatalistic compassion which much benefits the film. With kabuki actor Nakamura Kichiemon, and Iwashita Shima in the double role of wife and courtesan. Music by Takemitsu Toru. KJ#1. 103 mins. DVD/VHS, Criterion.

Dreams (Yume, aka Akira Kurosawa's Dreams, 1990), Kurosawa Akira. Eight episodes based on dreams of the director: a foxes' wedding, the atomic end of Japan, a meeting with van Gogh (Martin Scorsese), and five others. Lots of fantasy and special effects, coupled with the moral message that we ought to be nicer to each other. Kurosawa meets Spielberg. 119 mins. DVD/VHS, Warner Home Video.

Drifting Weeds. See *Floating Weeds*.

Drunken Angel (Yoidore tenshi, 1948), Kurosawa Akira. The angel of the title is a doctor (Shimura Takashi) who believes in healing, yet cannot stop drinking. Among those he tries to save is a death-obsessed gangster (Mifune Toshiro). The first of Kurosawa's morality plays and a brilliant evocation of postwar Tokyo. KJ#1. 98 mins. VHS, Home Vision Entertainment.

E

Early Spring (Soshun, 1956) Ozu Yasujiro. A nine-to-five officer worker (Ikebe Ryo) is dissatisfied with both his job and his wife (Awashima Chikage). He has a fling with the office flirt (Kishi Keiko) but eventually takes a provincial post and decides to start over again with his wife. Filled with character insight and implicit social criticism. 144 mins. DVD Criterion.

Early Summer (Bakushu, 1951), Ozu Yasujiro. One of the director's finest films—the Japanese family slowly, beautifully, inevitably falls apart. Hara Setsuko is the daughter who leaves to marry, Sugimura Haruko is the grateful mother of the groom, and the rest of the Ozu troupe (including Ryu Chishu as the disapproving elder brother) have never been better. KJ#1. 125 mins. DVD, Criterion.

Eclair, L'. See *Lightning*.

Eijanaika (1981), Imamura Shohei. Celebrating the anarchy of the last days of the Tokugawa shogunate, Imamura juggles a number of plots, all of which memorialize civil disobedience. Momoi Kaori is the stripper, pop-star Izumiya Shigeru is the recent returnee from the USA, and production designer

Satani Akiyoshi created the enormous Ryogoku Bridge set and adjoining fairgrounds. Everything is big, sprawling and vital. "What the hell!" as the title says. 151 mins. DVD (English titles), Panorama (Hong Kong).

Elegy to Violence (Kenka ereji, aka Fighting Elegy, aka The Born Fighter, 1966), Suzuki Seijun. In the militarist 1930s a student represses his urges and turns fascist. Suzuki sees this as a comedy, though a serious one. With a style more realistic than usual, he and his scriptwriter, Shindo Kaneto, turn growing up into social comment. With Takahashi Hideki as the gland-gripped youth. 86 mins. DVD, Criterion; VHS, Home Vision Entertainment.

Empire of Passion. See *In the Realm of Passion.*

Empire of the Senses. See *In the Realm of the Senses.*

End of Summer, The (Kohayagawa-ke no aki, aka The Autumn of the Kohayagawa Family, aka Dernier Caprice, 1961), Ozu Yasujiro. An older man, alone but for his three daughters, decides to marry his former mistress. This upsets the entire family, a disturbance which is settled only by his death. With Nakamura Ganjiro, Aratama Michiyo, Hara Setsuko, Tsukasa Yoko. 103 mins. DVD (French titles), Arte Video (France).

Enjo. See *Conflagration.*

Eureka (Yuriika, 2000), Aoyama Shinji. A bus hijack changes a number of lives, including that of driver Yakusho Koji. A serial killer emerges and is eventually unmasked as one of the hijacked young. All of this is told simply and unsensationally but at great length. 217 mins. DVD/VHS, Artificial Eye (UK).

F

Face of Another, The (Tanin no kao, 1966), Teshigahara Hiroshi. Abe Kobo fashioned the script after his novel, the story of a man who dons a life-

like mask after his face is horribly scarred in an accident. Nakadai Tatsuya is the man, Kyo Machiko is the unsuspecting wife seduced by her masked husband. Art direction is by Awazu Kiyoshi. Both director and writers had already created *Woman in the Dunes* and so pure claustrophobia is an intended and brilliantly attained result. 122 mins. DVD (English Titles), Asmik Ace (Japan).

Family Game, The (Kazoku gemu, 1983), Morita Yoshimitsu. Mordant satire on the Japanese family. To cram sonny into the right school, mama and papa hire a tutor (Matsuda Yusaku) with appalling results. Consumerism, social status, filial devotion—all receive hilarious treatment, culminating in a final dinner which turns into a food fight. The original manga-like novel by Honma Yohei was scripted for film by Kobayashi Yoshinori and Morita himself. Itami Juzo, later to become the celebrated director, plays the awful father. KJ#1. Japan Academy Award, Best Film. 107 mins. VHS, Circle Releasing/Sony (OP).

Femme de Tokyo, Une. See *Woman of Tokyo.*

Femmes de la Nuit, Les. See *Women of the Night.*

Fighting Elegy. See *Elegy to Violence.*

Fires on the Plain (Nobi, 1959), Ichikawa Kon. The most powerful of Japanese antiwar films. Based on the Ooka Shohei novel, scripted by Wada Natto, this film tells the devastating story of a platoon lost in the Philippines at the end of World War II. The single survivor (Funakoshi Eiji) wanders the jungle and finally finds what it is that sustains those fellow soldiers he meets. With impeccable photography by Kobayashi Setsuo and a moving score by Akutagawa Yasushi. 105 mins. VHS, Home Vision Entertainment.

Fireworks. See *Hana-bi.*

Five Women around Utamaro. See *Utamaro and His Five Women.*

Flame of Torment. See *Conflagration.*

Flavor of Green Tea over Rice, The (Ochazuke no aji, 1952), Ozu Yasujiro. A middle-aged, middle-class couple experience a crisis in their marriage. Their routine lives have lost their meaning. Both attempt to change, and over a simple meal of green tea over rice they begin to succeed. 115 mins. VHS (English titles), Panorama Entertainment (Hong Kong).

Floating Weeds (Ukikusa, aka Drifting Weeds, 1959), Ozu Yasujiro. The head of a troupe of traveling players (kabuki actor Nakamura Ganjiro) returns to the island where a former flame (Sugimura Haruko), who is the mother of his son, waits for him. His present companion (Kyo Machiko), jealous, pays the ingenue (Wakao Ayako) to seduce the boy (Kawaguchi Hiroshi). That is all there is to the story and Ozu, who never liked plot, has turned his tale into a light idyll in which narrative parallels are reflected in the superb color photography of Miyagawa Kazuo and the summer-tinted score of Saito Ichiro. A "remake" of his 1934 *Story of Floating Weeds.* 119 mins. DVD, Criterion.

Flowing (Nagareru, 1956), Naruse Mikio. Based on a Koda Aya story, beautifully scripted by Tanaka Sumie and Ide Toshiro, this is one of the director's finest films. The story of the decline of a geisha house in Tokyo's downtown, it displays the splendid ensemble talents of Japan's finest actresses: Yamada Isuzu, Tanaka Kinuyo, Takamine Hideko, and Sugimura Haruko. 117 mins. DVD, Criterion.

Focus (Fokasu, 1996), Isaka Satoshi. First-rate mockumentary, an intrusive TV-tells-all program

that goes wrong. A fine script by Shin Kazuo and a beautiful performance by Asano Tadanobu as the nerd that turns. 73 mins. DVD (English titles), Asmik Ace (Japan).

Forbidden. See *Gohatto.*

Forty-Seven Ronin, The. See *Loyal Forty-Seven Ronin, The.*

Forty-Seven Samurai. See *Chushingura.*

Frère et Soeur. See *Older Brother, Younger Sister.*

Funeral, The (Ososhiki, aka Death Japanese Style, 1984), Itami Juzo. The director's first and finest film—a satire on the passing of old Japan. The bereaved no longer even know to hold a proper funeral: they can't sit on the floor in the traditional manner, don't know how much to pay the priest, and have to watch a video to learn the etiquette. Though often edged into farce by its large and lively cast, the comic premise holds and it all comes together when, finally, with dignity and devotion, death is itself addressed. KJ#1. Japan Academy Award, Best Film. 114 mins. DVD/VHS, Fox Lorber.

G

Gate of Flesh, The (Nikutai no mon, 1964), Suzuki Seijun. The most stylish of the various film versions of this popular post–World War II play by Tamura Taijiro about political togetherness among prostitutes, a solidarity wrecked by love. Here the story is told with knowing melodrama and intentional artifice. Glaring color and over-the-top design support the antics of a lead whore (Nogawa Yumiko) who just won't stop. 90 mins. VHS, Home Vision Entertainment.

Gate of Hell, The (Jigoku mon, 1953), Kinugasa Teinosuke. Weak Kikuchi Kan period play made into limp film with flaccid performances by Hasegawa Kazuo and Kyo Machiko as the lovers forbidden to love. If anyone paid attention to this film it was because of Sugiyama Kohei's superlative color photography, a quality which is not captured on tape. 86 mins. VHS, Home Vision Entertainment.

Geisha, A (Gion bayashi, aka Gion Festival Music, 1953), Mizoguchi Kenji. Based on a Kawaguchi Matsutaro story, scripted by Yoda Yoshikata, this film tells the sad story of two geisha (Kogure Michiyo and Wakao Ayako) and their attempts at a better life. Filled with sentiment, rather than with sentimentality, the picture earns concern—particularly when everything is so persuasively photographed by Miyazawa Kazuo, and the performances are so perfect. 95 mins. VHS, New Yorker Films (OP).

Ghost in the Shell, The (Kokaku kidotai, 1995), 82 mins. Oshii Mamoru. More anime from the creators of *Akira*—this one from a manga by Shiro Masamune. It is now 2029 and the cybercop heroine chases after a villainous brain-hacker. Big special effects, small plausibility and little attention paid to character. Beware of English-dubbed version. 83 mins. DVD/VHS, Manga Video.

Giants and Toys (Kyojin to gangu, aka The Build-Up, 1958), Masamura Yasuzo. The building up and tearing down of a young television "idol" (Nozoe Hitomi) in the cut-throat world of entertainment. A bright script by Shirasaka Yoshio based on a Kaiko Ken novel. 95 mins. DVD, Fantoma.

Gion Festival Music. See *Geisha, A.*

Godzilla, King of the Monsters (Gojira, 1954), Honda Ishiro. The first appearance of Godzilla who, like Tora-san, went on to make countless sequels in which the lovably cheesy monster, in his rubber suit, carefully steps on models of famous cities. In this one it is Tokyo through which he cuts his swath. The U.S.-released version deletes much and adds Raymond Burr. The success of this monster spawned others—Rodan, Mothra, Gamera, Daimajin, and so on—most of whom also made it to English-titled video but will not here be listed. 98 mins. DVD, Simitar Video (OP).

Gohatto (aka Taboo, aka Forbidden, 1999), Oshima Nagisa. It is the end of the Edo period (ca. 1865) and the Shinsengumi army, all military macho, is defending its lost cause when in comes a new, beautiful, willing seventeen-year-old recruit. Military formations collapse in the face of passion. Lots of killing but lots of love-making as well. 100 mins. DVD/VHS, New Yorker Films.

Gonin (1995), Ishii Takashi. A group of amateurs, five in all (*gonin*), set out to take a lot of dough from a yakuza outfit. An implacable gunman (Kitano Takeshi) is hired to gun them down, which he does—one by one. Gore galore. With Sato Koichi, Nagashima Toshiyuki and Motoki Masahiro. 109 mins. DVD, Leo Films.

Gonza the Spearman (Yari no Gonza, 1986), Shinoda Masahiro. The Chikamatsu play as scripted by Tomioka Taeko, made into a visually beautiful film which shows both lord and retainer caught in their vengeful roles. The handsome Gonza is played by pop-singer Go Hiromi, and the lord's spouse with whom he falls in love by Iwashita Shima, the director's wife. It is all very classy and refined and a little slow. Berlin, Silver Bear. 126 mins. VHS, Kino.

Good Morning (Ohayo, 1959), Ozu Yasujiro. A very amusing satire on suburban ways. Two small boys rebel at the banality ("Good morning") of adult small talk. Something of an update of the 1932 *I Was Born, But . . .* , this film has the boys' refusal to say good morning exposing just those social gaps which such small talk usually bridges. 94 mins. DVD/VHS, Criterion.

Gosses de Tokyo. See *I Was Born, But . . .*

H

Hana-bi (aka Fireworks, 1997), Kitano Takeshi. Over-the-hill cop (Kitano) feels dreadful at having let down a police buddy and at the same time neglected a dying wife. He robs a bank to get some money to make amends, scrubs out a gang in the process, and at the conclusion puts a bullet both in her and in himself. Kitano's aesthetic take on trendy anarchy has here been turned into something like an art form. KJ#1; Venice, Golden Lion. 103 mins. DVD/VHS, New Yorker Films.

Harakiri (Seppuku, 1962), Kobayashi Masaki. The finest of the director's films, the story (based on

a Takiguchi Yasuhiko novel, scripted by Hashimoto Shinobu) of a former samurai (Nakadai Tatsuya) who avenges the cruel death (harakiri with a bamboo sword) of his beloved son-in-law (Ishihama Akira). He succeeds but the reigning lord (Mikuni Rentaro) orders him killed and his acts left unrecorded. In this way the samurai code remains enshrined. Photographed by Miyajima Yoshio, music by Takemitsu Toru. Cannes, Special Jury Prize. 135 mins. DVD, Home Vision Cinema.

Harp of Burma, The. (Biruma no tategoto, aka The Burmese Harp, 1956), Ichikawa Kon. The first (and better) of Ichikawa's two versions of the Take-yama Michio novel. A Japanese soldier is so saddened by the carnage of war that he stays behind to bury the dead. Resolutely pacifist, the film manages its message without too much recourse to sentimentality. Venice, San Giorgio Prize; Academy Award, Best Foreign Film. 116 mins. VHS, Home Vision Entertainment.

Herringbone Clouds. See *Summer Clouds.*

Hidden Fortress, The (Kakushi toride no san akunin, 1958), Kurosawa Akira. A delightful parody on the ordinary samurai film, with a dethroned princess, hidden gold, two greedy peasants, an impossibly heroic hero (Mifune Toshiro) and lots of swordplay. A wonderful finale where—joined by an erstwhile enemy (Fujita Susumu), and aided by the roaming, roving camera of Yamazaki Kazuo and the exhilarating score of Sato Masaru—gold, horses and cast gallop to freedom. Berlin, Best Director and International Critics' Prizes. 139 mins. DVD, Criterion.

High and Low (Tengoku to jigoku, 1963), Kurosawa Akira. A morality play in the form of a thriller—written by Kurosawa and others after the Ed McBain novel, *King's Ransom*. A self-made man (Mifune Toshiro) is ruined by a jealous nobody (Yamazaki Tsutomu in his first important screen role) but goes on to do the right thing and in the end the camera observes more similarities than differences. With a memorable mid-film climax on a high-speed bullet train. 143 mins. DVD, Criterion.

Himatsuri (aka Fire Festival, 1985), Yanagimachi Mitsuo. A strong Nakagami Kenji novel made into an equally powerful film. A modern macho lumberman faces vengeful nature—but such a one-line précis cannot begin to communicate the enormous potency of the film. With luminous photography by Tamura Masaki, a ravishing score by Takemitsu Toru, Kitaoji Kinya as the lumberman and Nakamoto Ryota as his shifty sidekick. Locarno, Silver Leopard. 120 mins. VHS, Kino.

History of Postwar Japan As Told by a Bar Hostess, A (Nippon sengo-shi: Madamu Omboro no seikatsu, aka Histoire du Japon Racontée par

une Hôtesse de Bar, 1970), Imamura Shohei. A splendidly ironic documentary which cuts through the cant and gives us Madam Omboro's version of World War II and the resulting occupation. Accepted truths blasted and many holy cows put out to pasture. 105 mins. VHS (French subtitles), Films sans Frontières (France).

Hole, The. See *Onibaba*.

Human Condition, The (Ningen no joken, 1958–61), Kobayashi Masaki. Long, powerful anti-war trilogy written by Matsuyama Zenzo and Kobayashi after the Gomikawa Jumpei novel. It is 1943 and an idealistic young inspector (Nakadai Tatsuya) is sent by his company to report on the mines of Manchuria. He finds the exploitation of the workers extreme, complains, and is punished. Drafted, he discovers the Japanese army to be even worse. Extremely critical of authoritarian mentality, the film became one of Japan's most controversial—over nine hours inside the military mind. The three parts of the film are given the titles of *No Greater Love,* 200 mins., (Venice, San Giorgio Prize); *The Road to Eternity,* 180 mins.; and *A Soldier's Prayer*, 190 mins. DVD, Image, Entertainment.

Humanity and Paper Balloons (Ninjo kamifusen, 1937), Yamanaka Sadao. One of the great Japanese films—Mimura Shintaro's adaptation of a Kawatake Mokuami kabuki play, in which something like the true life of the people under the Tokugawa regime is revealed. Yamanaka (in this, his last film) illuminates his claustrophobic theme through a construction where the spatial concerns echo the needs of the story. 86 mins. DVD, Criterion.

I

I Live in Fear. See *Record of a Living Being, The.*

I Was Born, But . . . (Umarete wa mita keredo, aka Gosses de Tokyo, 1932), Ozu Yasujiro. An early masterpiece. Two little boys begin to grow up when they learn something of the ways of the adult world. Why can't they beat up their father's boss's kid when they are stronger? they ask. A very amusing comedy and at the same time the darkest of social commentaries, the picture is both funny and devastating. A silent film with dialogue titles. KJ#1. 91 mins. DVD (French titles), Arte Video (France).

Idiot, The (Hakuchi, 1951), Kurosawa Akira. The director adapts his favorite novelist, Dostoevsky. St. Petersburg becomes modern Hokkaido, and the Russians become provincial Japanese. A wildly uneven film to begin with, it was further damaged by the fact that Shochiku cut its running time nearly in half prior to its release. Still there is a certain charm in seeing Mori Masayuki (nobleman in *Rashomon,* company president in *The Bad Sleep*

Well) as Prince Myshkin, and in watching all the rest (Mifune Toshiro, Hara Setsuko) overact. 165 mins. DVD (English titles), Panorama Entertainment (Hong Kong).

Ikiru (1952), Kurosawa Akira. A city government bureau chief learns he has cancer, will not live long, and realizes that he has done nothing with his life. He sets out in his last months to accomplish something—to build a local park. This anecdote becomes an enormously moving saga as we follow this modern pilgrim through his progress, to a final achievement. It is simultaneously an existential exploration (man is solely what he does) and a devastating indictment of bureaucracy. KJ#1. Berlin, Silver Bear. 143 mins. DVD, Criterion.

In the Realm of Passion (Ai no borei, aka Empire of Passion, 1978), Oshima Nagisa. A rickshaw driver is murdered by his wife and her ex-soldier lover. They are haunted by their crime and finally pay for their passion. A film not to be compared to the magisterial *In the Realm of the Senses* (1976), though Oshima's scorn for authority here reaches similar heights. With Fuji Tatsuya, last seen bleeding on the mattress in the 1976 film. Cannes, Best Director Award. 105 mins. VHS/DVD, Fox Lorber.

In the Realm of the Senses (Ai no korida, aka Empire of the Senses, aka The Realm of the Senses, 1976), Oshima Nagisa. Based on a real 1936 occurrence, a couple lose themselves in each other with enormously erotic results. Though banned as obscene in both Japan (where it still cannot be shown uncensored) and, initially, elsewhere, the film is really a serious study of possessive love and is not in the least pornographic. With Matsuda Eiko and Fuji Tatsuya. 100 mins. DVD/VHS, Fox Lorber.

Inferno of First Love, The (Hatsukoi jigoku-hen, aka Nanami: First Love, 1968), Hani Susumu. One of the seminal films of the sixties. Terayama Shuji's script about innocence in a time of corruption, is beautifully realized by Hani at his most documentary-like. Tokyo's Shinjuku nightspots have never been more fascinatingly displayed, and amateurs Takahashi Akio and Ishii Kuniko as the young lovers are consummately directed. The original length is 107 mins. This US release, however, hacks the film about. VHS, New York Film Annex (OP).

Inn in Tokyo, An (Tokyo no yado, aka Une Auberge à Tokyo, 1935) Ozu Yasujiro. A beautifully observed film about a transient man and his two young sons finding companionship with a widow and her little girl. With Sakamoto Takeshi and Okada Yoshiko. 80 mins. VHS (French titles), Ciné Horizon (France).

Insect Woman, The (Nippon konchuki, 1963), Imamura Shohei. Superlative saga of a poor country woman who sets out to conquer the world on its own terms. With all the determination and energy of the ant seen in the opening sequence, she succeeds in materially bettering herself though her means are whoring, pimping and blackmailing. A joyous and affirming film (written by Imamura and Hasebe Keiji) with Hidari Sachiko transcendent as the heroine. KJ#1. Berlin, Best Actress. 123 mins. DVD/VHS, Connoisseur (UK).

Intentions of Murder (Akai satsui, aka Murderous Desire, aka Unholy Desire, aka Désir Meurtrier, 1964), Imamura Shohei. A slow, lazy, but very determined wife gets her own way: she outlives her rapist, legitimizes her son, and triumphs over her creepy husband. A deep, black, glorious film. Written by Imamura and Hasebe Keiji after the Fujiwara Shinji novel. 150 mins. VHS (French titles), Films sans Frontières (France).

Island, The. See *Naked Island, The.*

J

Japanese Tragedy, A (Nihon no higeki, 1953), Kinoshita Keisuke. A mother in wartime Japan strives to raise her child, only to be met with indifference and ingratitude. The nascent sentimentality of the theme is offset by the neo-realism of the filming, the inclusion of actual wartime and postwar footage, and the performance of Mochizuki Yuko as the mother. 116 mins. DVD (English titles), Panorama Entertainment (Hong Kong).

Joy Girls. See *Story of a Prostitute.*

Judo Saga. See *Sanshiro Sugata.*

Juvenile Passion. See *Crazed Fruit.*

K

Kagemusha (1980), Kurosawa Akira. A thief is spared if he will impersonate a warlord. The latter has been killed but the enemy still has to be fooled. Lots of production values and a great final battle but the thief's role was written for Katsu Shintaro, and Nakadai Tatsuya, who stepped in, is miscast. In addition, Kurosawa had so much time (no initial funding) that he predesigned and color coordinated just about everything, lending a certain staginess to the production. Cannes, Grand Prix. 180 mins. DVD, Criterion.

Key, The. See *Odd Obsession.*

Kwaidan (Kaidan, 1965), Kobayashi Masaki. Four of the stories which Lafcadio Hearn originally transcribed are here scripted by Mizuki Yoko and directed for all their aesthetic worth by Kobayashi. Gorgeous pageant-like entertainment, all of it paper thin. Cinematographer Miyajima Yoshio and art director Toda Shigemasa arrange for a brilliant naval battle in the third story, for which Takemitsu Toru wrote his now famous *biwa* (lute) score. Cannes, Special Jury Prize. 164 mins. DVD, Criterion.

L

Lady Musashino (Musashino fujin, aka The Lady of Musashino, 1951), Mizoguchi Kenji. Minor Mizoguchi but elegantly done. A Yoda Yoshikata script crafted from an Ooka Shohei novel, with Tanaka Kinuyo in the leading role. 88 mins. DVD, Artificial Eye (UK).

Late Autumn (Akibiyori, 1960), Ozu Yasujiro. A daughter is reluctant to leave her widowed mother, even though it is time for her to marry. The story could be seen as a "remake" of *Late Spring*—and though more autumnal, it is just as moving. Hara Setsuko plays the mother and Tsukasa Yoko is the daughter. 125 mins. DVD (English titles), Panorama Entertainment (Hong Kong).

Late Chrysanthemums (Bangiku, 1954), Naruse Mikio. A fine adaptation of several Hayashi Fumiko stories (scripted by Tanaka Sumie and Ide Toshiro) about middle-aged geisha facing an uncertain future. Beautiful performances by Sugimura Haruko, Mochizuki Yuko, Hosokawa Chikako and Sawamura Sadako. Cannes, Special Jury Prize. 101 mins. VHS, World Artists.

Late Spring (Banshun, 1949), Ozu Yasujiro. A daughter lives with her widowed father. He wants her to have a life of her own and get married. She wants to stay and look after him. That is all there is to the story, but the sad understanding and rigorous beauty shown in this film make it unforgettable. Scripted by Ozu and Noda Kogo after a novel by Hirotsu Kazuo, with Ryu Chishu as the father and Hara Setsuko as the daughter. KJ#1. 108 mins. DVD, Criterion. VHS, New Yorker Films.

Life of Oharu, The (Saikaku ichidai onna, aka Life of a Woman by Saikaku, 1952), Mizoguchi Kenji. Based on a picaresque novel by the seventeenth-century writer Saikaku, the film takes a more serious view of the decline and fall of the heroine from court lady to common whore. Yoda Yoshikata's script, Tanaka Kinuyo's performance as Oharu, Mizutani Hiroshi's art direction and Saito Ichiro's score—using Japanese instruments—help make this one of Mizoguchi's most elegant films. Venice, International Prize. Originally, 148 mins. US version, 133 mins. DVD, Artificial Eye (UK); VHS, Home Vision Entertainment.

Lightning (Inazuma, aka L'Eclair, 1952), Naruse Mikio. An unhappy young bus conductor (Takamine Hideko) makes a new family for herself in this Tanaka Sumie scripted version of a Hayashi Fumiko story. 87 mins. VHS (French titles), Les Films de Ma Vie (France).

Lower Depths, The (Donzoko, 1957), Kurosawa Akira. Gorky's famous play moved to an Edo slum, its humanist message enlarged and its melodrama muted by a remarkable ensemble performance from the large cast—Mifune Toshiro, Yamada Isuzu, Nakamura Ganjiro, Kagawa Kyoko, Hidari Bokuzen, and others. Sato Masaru's "music" (all of it made by the actors) is extraordinarily right. 137 mins. DVD, Criterion.

Loyal Forty-Seven Ronin, The (Genroku chushingura, aka The Forty-Seven Ronin, 1941–2), Mizoguchi Kenji. This two-part version of the kabuki classic is based on a wartime reworking by Mayama Seika. The slow dignity of the film is much aided by the sober aesthetics of the presentation and the gravity of the cast: Kawarasaki Chojuro, Nakamura Gan'emon, Ichikawa Utaemon. Stately camerawork by Sugiyama Kohei and a grave score by Fukai Shiro. 111 mins./106 mins. DVD, Image Entertainment. (See also: *Chushingura*.)

M

Maboroshi (Maboroshi no hikari, 1995), Kore'eda Hirokazu. A deeply troubled young woman (Esumi Makiko) fears that she brings death. She has lost her grandmother and then, to suicide, her husband. Though she has happily remarried she remains afraid. Her fear is explored with extraordinary tact and her

despair is redeemed through understanding. Miyamoto Teru's novel, finely scripted by Ogita Yoshihisa, is perfectly directed by Kore'eda in this, his first feature film. 109 mins. DVD/VHS, New Yorker Films.

Madadayo (aka Not Yet, 1993), Kurosawa Akira. The master's last film, a tribute to Uchida Hyakken, a Japanese Mr. Chips, who gathers his adoring students about him for an annual party. Nostalgic and sometimes maudlin, it is acted out by such remaining Kurosawa favorites as Kagawa Kyoko and Matsumura Tatsuo. 134 mins. DVD/VHS, Wellspring.

Mademoiselle Oyu. See *Miss Oyu*.

Makioka Sisters, The (Sasame yuki, 1983), Ichikawa Kon. The third film version of the Tanizaki novel and no better than the others. The original plot is hacked out of shape by Hidaka Shinya and Ichikawa himself, and the holes are filled with cherry blossoms. Also something of a kimono show, it features model-actresses Sakuma Yoshiko, Yoshinaga Sayuri, and Kotegawa Yuko. 140 mins. VHS, MCA-Universal.

Man Blown by the Wind, A. See *Afraid to Die*.

Manji (aka All Mixed Up, aka Passion, 1964), Masumura Yasuzo. The Tanizaki novel about a three-cornered love affair (husband, wife, another woman—Funakoshi Eiji, Kishida Kyoko, Wakao Ayako) rendered fairly faithfully in Shindo Kaneto's script with lots of love scenes intimately arranged by director Masumura. 90 mins. DVD, Fantoma.

Max, Mon Amour (1987), Oshima Nagisa. Though often deemed a flop, this film is actually a wonderfully outrageous farce. Married Charlotte Rampling falls in love with a large chimpanzee, and both Oshima and scriptwriter Jean-Claude Carrière gleefully subvert bourgeois pretensions and extend Oshima's anarchic ambitions. Why did you choose *him*? asks the husband. To which Rampling replies, in the cultured tones of the boulevard-comédie tradition: "He chose *me*." 98 mins. DVD, Cinema Club.

Men Who Tread on the Tiger's Tail, The.
See *They Who Step on the Tiger's Tail.*

Merry Christmas, Mr. Lawrence (Senjo no meri kurisumasu, 1983), Oshima Nagisa. One of Japan's few accounts of its own POW camps. David Bowie is horribly disciplined, Sakamoto Ryuichi falls in love with him, and Kitano Takeshi gives us the final line. Through it all Oshima continues exploring his major theme of social constructions (like armies) undermined by love. 122 mins. VHS, Artisan Entertainment.

Minbo or the Gentle Art of Japanese Extortion (Mimbo no onna, 1992), Itami Juzo. In this courageous comedy, Itami takes on the Japanese mafia—not the gentle knights of the yakuza film but the horrible real thing. Miyamoto Nobuko is the lawyer who gets rid of these truly bad baddies. Itami's take on them is that they are manga-like clowns, but dangerous ones. It was to this that the real yakuza most objected and they consequently hacked up the director. 125 mins. VHS, Home Vision Entertainment.

Miss Oyu (Oyu-sama, aka Mademoiselle Oyu, 1951), Mizoguchi Kenji. Based on Tanizaki's 1932 novel *Ashikari*, scripted by Yoda Yoshikata, and meticulously photographed by Miyagawa Kazuo, but it is really a showcase for Tanaka Kinuyo. 95 mins. VHS (French subtitles), Les Films de Ma Vie (France).

Mistress, The (Gan, aka Wild Geese, 1953), Toyoda Shiro. Narusawa Masashige's beautiful adaptation of the Mori Ogai novel about a young woman who, forced to be the mistress of a moneylender, falls in love with an idealistic student. Miura Mitsuo's photography reflects the elegiac days of the late Meiji period when the old ways were falling away. Takamine Hideko as the pathetic heroine. 104 mins. VHS, Janus Films.

Miyamoto Musashi. See *Samurai.*

Most Beautiful, The (Ichiban utsukushiku, 1944), Kurosawa Akira. An "everyday documentary" about a group of women giving their all as they make optical instruments for the war effort. Though the director had no control over the script, he did his best to create a group of real characters. With Shimura Takashi and Irie Takako. 86 mins. DVD (English titles), Mei Ah (Hong Kong).

M/Other (Emu-maza, 1999), Suwa Nobuhiro. A divorced man brings his son back to live with him and his girlfriend. Filmed without a script, the dialogue arrived at by director and actors, it has a spontaneity that would not be possible in a scripted film. 147 mins. DVD (French titles), Arte Video (France).

Mother (Okasan, 1952), Naruse Mikio. Based on a girl's prize-winning school essay on the subject of "My Mother," Mizuki Yoko fashioned one of her most moving scripts. Upon the death of her husband the mother (Tanaka Kinuyo) runs the family laundry by herself. She is helped by her first daughter (Kagawa Kyoko) but must send her second daughter to live with relatives because she cannot afford to keep her. A real shomingeki with lots of heart. Venice, Silver Lion. 98 mins. VHS, Facets Multimedia (OP).

My Neighbor Totoro (Tonari no Totoro, 1988), Miyazaki Hayao. Sweet, good-tempered animated film about a group of children and their friendly monster neighbors. Lots of nice effects—like the wildcat bus. For children of all ages. Adults should avoid the dubbed version. KJ#1. 86 mins. VHS, Twentieth Century Fox.

Murderous Desire. See *Intentions of Murder.*

N

Naked Island, The (Hadaka no shima, aka The Island, 1960), Shindo Kaneto. A film made entirely without dialogue (music by Hayashi Hikaru) about a family struggling for existence on a small island in the Inland Sea. The leftist message is certainly there as we watch the little people lead their awful lives. Moscow, Grand Prize. 92 mins. DVD, Asmik Ace (Japan).

Nanami: First Love. See *Inferno of First Love, The.*

Narayama bushiko. See *Ballad of Narayama.*

New Tales of the Taira Clan. See *Tales of the Taira Clan.*

Night and Fog in Japan (Nihon no yoru to kiri, 1960), Oshima Nagisa. One of Oshima's most advanced films. Flashback-filled saga of leftist manipulation, involving a wedding, student riots, and general mayhem. This is the picture that got Oshima fired from Shochiku—and gave him his freedom. With Watanabe Fumio, Kuwano Miyuki and Koyama Akiko. 107 mins. DVD (English titles), Panorama Entertainment (Hong Kong).

No Regrets for Our Youth (Waga seishun ni kui nashi, 1946), Kurosawa Akira. A deeply felt meditation on wartime Japan. A university professor (Okochi Denjiro) is suspected of liberal views and one of his pupils (Fujita Susumu) is arrested as a spy. His wife, the professor's daughter (Hara Setsuko), stands by him and after he is dead goes to his parents'

farm and endures the worst of wartime suspicion. Kurosawa's major feminist statement and an answer to the criticism that he did not understand women. 110 mins. VHS, Home Vision Cinema; DVD (English titles), Mei Ah (Hong Kong).

Nuages d'Eté. See *Summer Clouds.*

O

Odd Obsession (Kagi, aka The Key, 1959), Ichikawa Kon. Tanizaki Jun'ichiro's splendid novel, *The Key,* doubly traduced. First, by the inane English title given the film, second, by a script (Hasebe Keiji and Wada Natto) which ridiculously simplifies the original. In this version the maid done it. This said, the film boasts luminous photography by Miyagawa Kazuo and fine performances by Nakamura Ganjiro and Kyo Machiko as the kinky couple. Cannes, Special Prize; Golden Globe Award. The original version is 107 mins. The U.S. version is 96 mins. VHS, Home Vision Entertainment.

Okaeri (1996), Shinozaki Makoto. Writer-director Shinozaki in his debut film tells the arresting story of a typical young couple, who are brought to sanity

through the wife's madness. Beautiful, laconic film-making with a splendid performance by amateur Uemura Miho as the wife. Berlin, Wolfgang Staudte Award. 99 mins. VHS (French titles), K Films (France).

Older Brother, Younger Sister (Ani imoto, aka Frère et Soeur, 1953), Naruse Mikio. One of the director's best remembered films. A brother and sister (Mori Masayuki and Kyo Machiko) are involved in a love/hate relationship of an almost suspicious intensity. The Muro Saisei story as scripted by Mizuki Yoko. 86 mins. VHS (French titles), Les Films de Ma Vie (France).

One Wonderful Sunday (Subarashiki nichiyobi, 1947), Kurosawa Akira. A sunny, sentimental comedy written by the director and his old school friend, Uekusa Keinosuke. Boy and girl on a date find romantic magic when he tries to conduct the Schubert "Unfinished" in an empty band shell and she tearfully implores us to believe in him—and, sure enough . . . 108 mins. VHS, Home Vision Cinema; DVD (English titles), Mei Ah (Hong Kong).

Onibaba (aka The Hole, 1964), Shindo Kaneto. Mother and daughter (Otowa Nobuko and Yoshimura Jitsuko) survive by killing samurai and selling their armor. Kuroda Kiyomi's finely textured photography and Hayashi Hikaru's experimental score create a sensual atmosphere, but the film is also given to portentous allegorizing. 104 mins. DVD, Criterion.

Osaka Elegy (Naniwa ereji, 1936), Mizoguchi Kenji. An Okada Saburo magazine serial ennobled by Yoda Yoshikata's script, Yamada Isuzu's perfor-

mance and Mizoguchi's direction. To keep her job as a telephone operator a woman has to become her employer's mistress and after he gets rid of her has no recourse but prostitution. Mizoguchi said that he finally found his true direction with this film. Original length, 89 minutes. US release, 71 mins. VHS, Home Vision Entertainment.

P

Page Out of Order, A (Kurutta ichipeji, aka A Crazy Page, aka A Page of Madness, 1926), Kinugasa Teinosuke. A purposely scrambled script by Kawabata Yasunari at his most modernist about a man who gets a job in an insane asylum in order to be near his inmate wife, this film is a welter of expressionist experiments in which narrative is questioned at every turn. This version contains the score which Kinugasa commissioned in 1970 (after the rediscovery of the negative) and then repudiated. 60 mins. VHS, Facets Multimedia (OP).

Pain. See *Scoutman*.

Pale Flower (Kawaita hana, 1964), Shinoda Masahiro. A seminal yakuza film and one that helped form the Toei genre. A young hood makes bad, based on an Ishihara Shintaro story, with lots of rhetoric and a Takemitsu Toru score. The punk is Ikebe Ryo and his girl is Kaga Mariko. 96 mins. DVD, Home Vision Cinema.

Passion. See *Manji*.

Pleasures of the Flesh, The (Etsuraku, aka Les Plaisirs de la Chair, 1965), Oshima Nagisa. A dry run, as it were, for *In the Realm of the Senses*. A deal made between the criminal, the cops and the yakuza with sex as the currency. With Nakamura Katsuo and Kaga Mariko. 90 mins. VHS (French titles), Films sans Frontières (France).

Pornographers, The (Erogoto-shi-tachi yori: Jinrui-gaku nyumon, 1966), Imamura Shohei. Nosaka Akiyuki's finely mordant novel, scripted by

Numata Koji and Imamura himself. The hero (Ozawa Shoichi) quite seriously believes that being a pornographer is a way to satisfy one of society's most deeply felt needs. Very funny and quite moving by turns, with Sakamoto Sumiko grotesque and touching as the fish-obsessed lady of the house. 128 mins. DVD, Criterion.

Princess Mononoke (Mononoke-hime, 1997), Miyazaki Hayao. Eco-friendly animated feature about the middle ages in Japan, wolf-riding princesses, noble spirits of the forest, and so on. This is the English dubbed US version, the whole affair rendered even less likely by the broad American accents. Japan Academy Award, Best Film. Original length, 134 mins. DVD/VHS, Miramax/Disney.

Princess Yang Kwei Fei, The (Yoki-hi, 1955), Mizoguchi Kenji. Slow and stately film set in eighth-century China about the Emperor Huan Tsung and his mistress Yang Kwei Fei (Mori Masayuki and Kyo Machiko). Beautiful photography by Sugiyama Kohei (who filmed the colorful *Gate of Hell*) and a lovely "Chinese" score by Hayasaka Fumio. Otherwise, formal cinema with an almost exclusive emphasis upon aesthetics. 98 mins. VHS, New Yorker Films (OP).

Q

Quiet Duel, The (Shizukanaru ketto, 1949), Kurosawa Akira. Mifune Toshiro is the virgin doctor who gets syphilis from a scalpel cut and has to explain things to his fiancée. The script, by director Taniguchi Senkichi, is based on an otherwise forgotten play by Kikuta Kazuo. Even given such unpromising material, Kurosawa still manages to make us care, if only for the time being. 95 mins. VHS, Facets Multimedia.

R

Ran (1985), Kurosawa Akira. Kurosawa's version of *King Lear* with three sons, a transvestite fool, lots of

heart, and superb battle scenes. Also slow, stately and color coordinated within an inch of its life. Shakespeare is deconstructed by Oguni Hideo, Ide Masato, and Kurosawa himself. Nakadai Tatsuya is very grand and stagy as the lord and there is a splendidly Mahleresque score by Takemitsu Toru. New York Film Critics' Award, Best Foreign Film. 162 mins. DVD/VHS, Wellspring.

Rashomon (1950), Kurosawa Akira. Two Akutagawa Ryunosuke stories scripted by Hashimoto Shinobu and the director form this famous multi-faceted film which questions not only truth but reality itself. A warrior (Mori Masayuki), his lady (Kyo Machiko), a bandit (Mifune Toshiro) and a spying woodcutter (Shimura Takashi) each give very different accounts of a rape and a murder. A fascinating, even magical film. Venice, Golden Lion; Academy Award, Best Foreign Film. 88 mins. DVD, Criterion.

Realm of the Senses, The. See *In the Realm of the Senses*.

Rebellion (Joiuchi, aka Samurai Rebellion, 1967), Kobayashi Masaki. Scripted by Hashimoto Shinobu, who also worked with Kobayashi on *Harakiri*, a film which has a similar message: the feudal system is inhuman and those under it must revolt. In this case, the lord wants back Mifune Toshiro's daughter-in-law (Tsukasa Yoko), and that spells trouble. With an elegant corpse-filled finale as Mifune finally has enough of his brutal overlord. KJ#1. Original version, 128 mins. US release version, 121 mins. VHS, Home Vision Entertainment.

Record of a Living Being, The (Ikimono no kiroku, aka I Live in Fear, 1955), Kurosawa Akira.

The aging head of the family (Mifune Toshiro), worried about the atomic threat, tries to convince everyone to emigrate with him to Brazil, which he hopes is safer. They respond by finding him insane—which he eventually becomes. The script (written by Hashimoto Shinobu and Oguni Hideo, as well as Kurosawa) is somewhat melodramatic, and—given the didactic aims of the director—a bit sententious as well. 103 mins. DVD (English titles), Mei Ah (Hong Kong); VHS, Home Vision Entertainment.

Record of a Tenement Gentleman, The (Nagaya shinshi-roku, 1947), Ozu Yasujiro. The director's first postwar film. A little boy is most reluctantly given a home by a childless woman and is then much missed when his father finally turns up. One of Ozu's most perfect domestic comedies with Iida Choko as the put-upon samaritan. 72 mins. VHS, New Yorker Films (OP).

Red Beard (Akahige, 1965), Kurosawa Akira. An adaptation of Yamamoto Shugoro's humanistic novel about a doctor (Mifune Toshiro), his young assistant (Kayama Yuzo), and the worth of human beings. Long, affecting, and beautifully paced, with a splendidly affirming score by Sato Masaru, it is a lesson in both fellow feeling and film making. KJ#1; Moscow, Film Union Prize; Venice, Best Actor Award and San Giorgio Prize. 185 mins. DVD, Criterion.

Red Light District (Akasen chitai, aka Street of Shame, 1956), Mizoguchi Kenji. The director's final film, as well as his last statement on Japanese women and repressive society, based on a script by Narusawa Masashige after a Shibaki Yoshiko short story. A group of prostitutes go about their business as the government is passing the anti-prostitution legislation which will officially do away with them. Fine ensemble performances by Kyo Machiko, Kogure Michiyo, Wakao Ayako and others. 94 mins. VHS, Home Vision Entertainment.

Rhapsody in August (Hachigatsu no kyoshikyoku, 1991), Kurosawa Akira. An American relative (Richard Gere) returns to the Nagasaki homestead and hears about the atom bombing from his aged aunt (Murase Sachiko.) He apologizes, is forgiven, and the children are pleased. The sententiousness is somewhat minimized by the wonderful five minutes at the end. 100 mins. DVD, MGM.

Rikyu (1989), Teshigahara Hiroshi. Long, solemn spectacle with a script by Akasegawa Genpei and Teshigahara after the Nogami Yaeko novel, and Mikuni Rentaro in the title role of the famous teamaster. Beautiful Momoyama-period sets and costumes (the work of Nishioka Yoshinobu and Shigeta Shigemori) but nowhere are we reminded that this is the work of the director of *Woman in the Dunes*. The original version is 135 mins. The US version is 116 mins. DVD, E-Realbiz.com; VHS, Capitol Entertainment.

Rose in the Mud, A. See *Bad Sleep Well, The*.

S

Samurai (Miyamoto Musashi, 1954–56), Inagaki Hiroshi. The Toho trilogy (there is a "rival" Toei trilogy, 1961–63) based on the popular Yoshikawa Eiji potboiler. Part one (*The Legend of Musashi*,

92 mins.) introduces the young warrior (Mifune Toshiro), who decides on a career as a samurai. Part two (*Duel at Ichijoji Temple*, 102 mins.) shows him honing his fighting skills. Part three (*Duel on Ganryu Island*, 115 mins.) finds him using them against his lifelong nemesis, Sasaki Kojiro (Tsuruta Koji). All three parts are heavily edited in their U.S. versions but the first part nonetheless won an Academy Award for Best Foreign Film. DVD, Criterion.

Samurai Assassin (Samurai, 1965), Okamoto Kihachi. A Hashimoto Shinobu script based on a story by Gunji Jiromasa about a masterless samurai (Mifune Toshiro) who plots to assassinate the emperor in order to further his own career. Wild and entertaining chop-'em-up. With Sugimura Haruko and Fujita Susumu. 122 mins. DVD/VHS, Animeigo.

Samurai Banners (Furin kazan, aka Under the Banner of Samurai, 1969), Inagaki Hiroshi. Rousing chambara based on an Inoue Yasushi novel as scripted by Hashimoto Shinobu, with Mifune Toshiro and Nakamura Kinnosuke as the swordsmen, with music by Sato Masaru, 166 mins. VHS, British Film Institute (UK).

Samurai Rebellion. See *Rebellion*.

Samurai Saga (Aru kengo no shogai, 1959), Inagaki Hiroshi. Entertaining version of Rostand's *Cyrano de Bergerac*, set in the Momoyama period, with Mifune Toshiro as the long-nosed Cyrano and Tsukasa Yoko as his enchanting Roxanne. Elegant production design by Ito Kisaku and a big thumping score by Ifukube Akira. 111 mins. VHS, New York Film Annex.

Sanjuro (Tsubaki Sanjuro, 1962) Kurosawa Akira. A kind of a sequel to *Yojimbo*, and just as good. Here Sanjuro (Mifune Toshiro again) cleans up local corruption, while having to put up with a band of boy-scout samurai. There are many funny parodies of the ordinary period film and a most impressive blood-letting finale. 96 mins. DVD, Criterion.

Sanshiro Sugata (Sugata Sanshiro, aka Judo Saga, 1943), Kurosawa Akira. The director's debut film (based on the Tomita Tsuneo book) and still quite impressive. It is about cocky judo champ Sanshiro (Fujita Susumu) and his learning that discipline is more important than prowess. 79 mins. DVD (English titles), Mei Ah (Hong Kong); VHS, Home Vision Entertainment.

Sanshiro Sugata, Part Two (Zoku Sugata Sanshiro, 1945), Kurosawa Akira. A rather crude sequel foisted off on the director by the producers. The closest to a propaganda film that Kurosawa ever made. 83 mins. DVD (English titles), Mei Ah (Hong Kong).

Sansho the Bailiff (Sansho dayu, 1954). Mizoguchi Kenji. Written by Yoda Yoshikata after a Mori Ogai novel, this pensive, cruel, and beautiful film contrasts the solitary fate of the exiled mother (Tanaka Kinuyo) with the brutalization of the exiled son. Nothing is explicit and everything is searingly apparent in this memorable picture. Venice, Silver Lion. 132 mins. VHS, Home Vision Entertainment.

Scandal (Shubun, 1950), Kurosawa Akira. A minor picture based on a Kikushima Ryuzo script about a young man (Mifune Toshiro) and his female acquaintance (Yamaguchi Yoshiko) libeled by the yellow press. Just as earlier Kurosawa films were about the excesses of the wartime military so this picture is about the excesses of the peacetime media. Both tend to be didactic. 104 mins. VHS, Home Vision Entertainment; DVD (English titles), Panorama Entertainment (Hong Kong).

Scoutman (aka Pain, 2000), Ishioka Masato. The best of the sex-biz films, photographed like a documentary and distinguished by fine performances from first-time actors Matsumoto Miku and Nakaizumi Hideo. Nakaizumi is the "scoutman," out stopping girls on the street to try to get them into the sex industry. 114 mins. DVD (English titles), Winson (Hong Kong).

Seven Samurai (Shichinin no samurai, 1954), Kurosawa Akira. Six unemployed samurai and a farmer's son agree to protect a village from the depredations of a group of bandits. They win but, as the memorable final scene demonstrates, they also lose. Superb action sequences, fine performances (particularly Shimura Takashi as the head samurai), and a final reel which is one of the glories of world cinema. 200 mins. Venice, Silver Lion; Academy Award, Best Foreign Film. DVD, Criterion.

Shall We Dance? (Sharu ui dansu, 1996), Suo Masayuki. A charmingly slight comedy about a man (Yakusho Koji) who finds himself—or tries to—through the local social-dancing club. With Takenaka Naoto as the equally dance-crazed colleague. Much hyped in the USA where it became the largest-grossing Japanese film until then—though none of the hype mentioned that it was Japanese. Original version, 136 mins. US version, 119 mins. DVD, Walt Disney Home Video; VHS, Miramax Home Entertainment.

She and He (Kanojo to kare, 1963), Hani Susumu. She is a housewife who is not yet dehumanized by the typical suburban life. He is a proper upwardly-mobile office-worker who doesn't like her being interested in a group of local rag-pickers. With Hidari Sachiko (who won several Japanese prizes for this role) and Okada Eiji in a beautifully understated script written by Hani and Shimizu Kunio. Berlin, Best Actress. 114 mins. VHS, Facets Multimedia .

Shin Heike Monogatari. See *Tales of the Taira Clan.*

Sisters of the Gion (Gion no kyodai, 1936), Mizoguchi Kenji. Two geisha sisters—one of them

traditonal and faithful to her patron, the other modern and fickle—get to the end of their respective ways of life. Mizoguchi in this film consolidated his mature style and positively illuminates the Yoda Yoshikata script through the controlled acting of Umemura Yoko and Yamada Isuzu as the sisters. KJ#1. 69 mins. VHS, Home Vision Entertainment.

Snow Country (Yukiguni, 1957), Toyoda Shiro. The first, and best, of a number of screen versions of the Kawabata Yasunari novel. Ikebe Ryo is the feckless artist and Kishi Keiko is the troubled country geisha. Yasumi Toshio's script inserts some incidents not in the novel, but the feeling is very close to the original. All of this was subverted when the U.S. version was released (by Toho) with many cuts and a running commentary. Original release, 124 mins. VHS, Facets Multimedia.

Sonatine (Sonachine, 1993), Kitano Takeshi. The artist also known as Beat Takeshi directs his own script and plays the star role in this picture about gangsters going to settle old scores in Okinawa and getting carried away by the sun and sea. Not exactly a comedy (lots of guts flying at the end) but definitely soft-core violence by hoods who have heart. 94 mins. VHS, Miramax; DVD (English titles), Panorama Entertainment (Hong Kong).

Story from Chikamatsu, A (aka Chikamatsu monogatari, aka The Crucified Lovers, 1954), Mizoguchi Kenji. A Chikamatsu puppet-play (*Daikyoji Mukashi Goyomi*), scripted for the screen by Yoda Yoshikata and photographed by Miyagawa Kazuo, becomes a sober, serious and beautiful film about a merchant's wife (Kagawa Kyoko) accused of adultery with one of her husband's apprentices (Hasegawa Kazuo). It is only after they flee that they finally become lovers, are caught, and crucified. 102 mins. VHS, Facets Multimedia.

Story of Floating Weeds, The (Ukikusa monogatari, 1934), Ozu Yasujiro. The leading actor of an itinerant group (Sakamoto Takeshi) returns to the town where he left a woman (Iida Choko) and a son (Mitsui Hideo). Scripted by Ikeda Tadao after, apparently, an American film by George Fitzmaurice. The original is forgotten but Ozu's version lives on and was even remade in 1959 as *Floating Weeds*, with Mitsui Hideo playing one of the actors. KJ#1. 86 mins. DVD, Criterion.

Story of the Last Chrysanthemum, The (Zangiku monogatari, 1939), Mizoguchi Kenji. Osaka, 1885, and a kabuki actor offends his family's dignity by loving a woman of a lower class. She realizes she must sacrifice herself. Melodrama (the original is the Iwaya San'ichi stage-play based on the popular novel by Muramatsu Shofu) wedded to the most refined of cinematic means; sentimentality ennobled by precision. 143 mins. VHS, Home Vision Entertainment.

Story of a Prostitute (Shumpu den, aka Joy Girls, 1965), Suzuki Seijun. Lots of sexy goings-on with Nikkatsu star Nogawa Yumiko and others. The Takaiwa Hajime script is based on a Tamura Taijiro story, the whole transformed into another in-your-face, over-the-top entertainment by a master of the genre. 96 mins. VHS, Home Vision Entertainment.

Stray Dog (Nora inu, 1949), Kurosawa Akira. Detective Mifune Toshiro searches Tokyo for his stolen pistol while supervisor Shimura Takashi lends moral support. A documentary-like chase film (filmed in downtown Tokyo) which magically turns into a morality play when we see that hunter and quarry are more similar than different. 122 mins. DVD, Criterion.

Street of Shame. See *Red Light District*.

Summer Clouds (Iwashigumo, aka Herringbone Clouds, aka Nuages d'Eté, 1958), Naruse Mikio. A Hashimoto Shinobu script about postwar farm life. An idealistic city newspaper reporter (Kimura Isao) gets to know a poor rural widow (Awashima Chikage). 128 mins. VHS (French titles), Les Films de Ma Vie (France).

Sun's Burial, The (Taiyo no hakaba, 1960), Oshima Nagisa. Urban violence as political allegory. Rival gangs, pimps, prostitutes, cast long social shadows. With Kawazu Yusuke setting up solid citizens with the charms of Honoo Kayoko. 87 mins. VHS, New Yorker Films (OP).

Suzaku (Moe no Suzaku, 1997), Kawase Naomi. A splendidly atmospheric feature film, made like a documentary, follows the life of a rural family, ghosts and all. Kunimura Jun is the only professional actor in an otherwise amateur cast. 94 mins. DVD (English titles), Edko Films (Hong Kong).

Sword of Doom, The (Daibosatsu toge, 1966), Okamoto Kihachi. Based on the popular novel by Nakazato Kaizan, scripted by Hashimoto Shinobu, and directed by one of the better period-film specialists, this samurai saga (with fine widescreen photography by Murai Hiroshi) is about a warrior gone bad. With Nakadai Tatsuya as the samurai, Mifune Toshiro as his teacher, Aratama Michiyo and Kayama Yuzo. 119 mins. DVD, Criterion. VHS, Home Vision Entertainment (OP).

T

Taboo. See *Gohatto*.

Tales of the Taira Clan (aka Shin heike monogatari, aka New Tales of the Taira Clan, 1955), Mizoguchi Kenji. Minor if colorful excursion into parts of Yoshikawa Eiji's popular novel—with a number of Daiei stars (including Ichikawa Raizo and Kogure Michiyo) making appearances. Nice Miyagawa Kazuo photography and Hayasaka Fumio music. 108 mins. VHS, British Film Institute (UK).

Tampopo (1985), Itami Juzo. A calculated and amusing send up of Japan's passion for the West (the director said it was a "remake" of the Western, *Rio Bravo*, set in a noodle shop). The shop is named Tampopo (Dandelion) and the cast includes Miyamoto Nobuko, Yamazaki Tsutomu, and such old-time stars as Okada Mariko, Nakamura Nobuo and Kubo Akira. Smart, glib, satirical and when funny, very funny. KJ#1. Japan Academy Award, Best Film. 114 mins. DVD/VHS, Fox Lorber.

Taxing Woman, A (Marusa no onna, 1987), Itami Juzo. Fast, amusing satire on the Japanese passion for money—and their unwillingness to hand it over to the National Tax Bureau. This institution is personified by its star inspector (Miyamoto Nobuko). Tax-evader king (Yamazaki Tsutomu) finally meets his mistress. 127 mins. DVD, Fox Lorber.

Taxing Woman's Return, A (Marusa no onna zoku, 1988), Itami Juzo. Tax inspector Miyamoto Nobuko on the trail again. This time she runs into a holy tax evader, bogus high priest Mikuni Rentaro. The formula of *A Taxing Woman* is repeated, but the film is distinguished by Itami's lightness and the straight-faced humor he so expertly engineers. 127 mins. VHS, New Yorker Films (OP).

Temple of the Golden Pavilion, The. See *Conflagration*.

Tetsuo: The Iron Man (Tetsuo, 1989), Tsukamoto Shinya. Pop fantasy about the joys of being a cyborg. Flesh turns into machinery and the other way around. 67 mins. DVD, Image. Part two, *Tetsuo II: Body Hammer* (1992), is in color and a bit less home-movie and a bit more hi-tech. The director himself stars in both. 81 mins. DVD/VHS, Tartan (UK).

They Who Step on the Tiger's Tail (Tora no o wo fumu otoko-tachi, aka The Men Who Tread on the Tiger's Tail,1945), Kurosawa Akira. A slyly subversive wartime version of the kabuki play *Kanjincho*. Though the noble drama is uncut, it is considerably undermined by the comedian Enoken's playing of a new character: a very common, very human porter. Banned by Japanese army authorities as too democratic, then again banned by U.S. army authorities as too feudal, it was released only in 1953. 58 mins. VHS, Home Vision Entertainment.

This Scorching Sea. See *Crazed Fruit.*

Throne of Blood, The (Kumonosu-jo, 1957), Kurosawa Akira. Scriptwriters Hashimoto Shinobu, Oguni Hideo, Kikushima Ryuzo and Kurosawa himself move *Macbeth* to the foggy slopes of Mount Fuji. In the process they preserve and even further illuminate Shakespeare's saga. Called the best screen adaptation of the Bard ever made, it may be just that. With Mifune Toshiro as the general, Yamada Isuzu as his power-possessed wife, and superlative black-and-white photography by Nakai Asakazu. 110 mins. DVD, Criterion.

Tokyo Drifter (Tokyo nagaremono, 1966), Suzuki Seijun. Really just another yakuza film but all decked out with bright color, stagy sets, songs, jokes and a minimal plot. Delight in mayhem is its only message, but this film delivers deliriously well. Film noir meets spaghetti Western. With Watari Tetsuya. 83 mins. DVD, Criterion.

Tokyo Olympiad (Tokyo Orimpiku, 1965), Ichikawa Kon. All that is left of a masterful documentary. The remains are carefully reconstructed, with the director focusing on the human rather than on the super-human. This may disappoint sports fans (and Olympic committees) but it results in the most beautiful, attentive, and moving sports-film ever made. Cannes, International Critics' Prize; Moscow, Sports Union Prize. 170 mins. DVD, Criterion.

Tokyo Story (Tokyo monogatari, 1953), Ozu Yasujiro. A provincial couple go to visit their children in Tokyo. Upon their return the mother dies and the children come for the funeral. This is the sole and symmetrical narrative but Ozu and his co-scenarist Noda Kogo find in it an entire world of wisdom. The clear observation which makes the film such a formal delight also accounts for its emotional power, which is unforgettable. One of the great films of all time. 135 mins. DVD, Criterion.

Tokyo Twilight (Tokyo boshoku, aka Crépuscule à Tokyo, 1957), Ozu Yasujiro. A young woman discovers that her mother, whom she thought dead, is really living nearby, having deserted her husband. The discovery upsets everyone and the young woman eventually kills herself. With Hara Setsuko, Yamada Isuzu, Arima Ineko. 140 mins. VHS (French titles), Le Siècle des Lumières (France).

Twenty-Four Eyes (Nijushi no hitomi, 1954), Kinoshita Keisuke. Adapted by Kinoshita from the Tsuboi Sakae novel, this is one of the most beloved of all Japanese films. It follows the life of a first-grade school teacher (Takamine Hideko) from her beginnings in 1928 through the years of World War II and after. At the same time the film is powerfully anti-war. The combination of gentle contemplation and fierce opposition make viewing this film as unsettling as it is rewarding. Those who do not like to be so disturbed have called it sentimental. KJ#1. Original version, 154 mins. DVD (English titles), Panorama Entertainment (Hong Kong); VHS Janus/Sony (OP).

U

Ugetsu (Ugetsu monogatari, 1953), Mizoguchi Kenji. Two Ueda Akinari ghost stories linked by scriptwriter Yoda Yoshikata into one of the director's most accomplished films. With its beautifully atmospheric camera work (by Miyagawa Kazuo), all long shots, long takes, and graceful movements, this story of a potter and the two ghosts who love him becomes an emotional saga. With Mori Masayuki, Tanaka Kinuyo, Kyo Machiko and a score by Hayasaka Fumio. Venice, Silver Lion.

96 mins. DVD, Criterion; VHS, Home Vision Entertainment.

Under the Banner of Samurai. See *Samurai Banners.*

Unholy Desire. See *Intentions of Murder.*

Utamaro and His Five Women (Utamaro wo meguru gonin no onna, aka Five Women around Utamaro, 1946), Mizoguchi Kenji. The director's first postwar film, scripted by Yoda Yoshitaka after the novel by Kunieda Kanji. Though Mizoguchi got permission from Occupation censors to make this film by telling them that the script was about the emancipation of women, it is really a kind of meditation on the role of the artist in society. 94 mins. VHS, New Yorker Films (OP).

V

Vengeance is Mine (Fukushu suruwa ware ni ari, 1979), Imamura Shohei. A powerful, complex, and intricate study of a cold-blooded killer (Ogata Ken), and how he got that way. Baba Masaru adapted Saki Ryuzo's book which was based on the crimes of a real murderer. With Mikuni Rentaro as the father and Baisho Mitsuko as the wife. KJ#1. Japan Academy Award, Best Film. 128 mins. VHS Home Vision Entertainment; DVD (English titles), Panorama Entertainment (Hong Kong).

Vibrator (Vaibureita, 2003), Hiroki Ryuichi. A distressed woman meets a lonely truck driver and they take off to faraway Niigata. After sex is gotten out of the way they begin to get to know each other, though they both suspect that their affair is leading nowhere. A subtle, beautifully acted, honest film. The title, incidentally, refers to the cell phone which vibrates rather than rings. 95 mins. DVD (English titles), Happinet Pictures (Japan).

Vital (Vitaru, 2004), Tsukamoto Shinya. The director and star of *Tetsuo: The Iron Man* displays forensic skills, as a medical student (Asano

Tadanobu) regains his lost memory while dissecting, and bonds with the dead girlfriend. As one critic put it, "lyricism with formalin." Sitges Film Festival New Visions Section, Best Film. 86 min. DVD (English titles), Happinet Pictures (Japan).

Violence at Noon (Hakuchu no torima, aka Daylight Demon, 1966), Oshima Nagisa. One of the director's most experimental films, this is a purposely fragmented account of rapist-murderer through whom Oshima attempts to implicate contemporary society. As in *Death by Hanging*, there is no clear-cut guilt—we are all guilty. Berlin, Silver Bear. 99 mins. VHS, Kino.

W

When a Woman Ascends the Stairs (Onna ga kaidan wo noboru toki, 1960), Naruse Mikio. Beautiful, pensive film about the sad life of the manageress of a Ginza bar. The stairs she ascends are those which lead to her bar on the second floor, and it is a daily struggle. With Takamine Hideko at her most persuasive, and a cool jazz score by Mayuzumi Toshiro. 110 mins. VHS, World Artists Home Video.

Wild Geese. See *Mistress, The*.

Woman in the Dunes (Suna no onna, aka Woman of the Dunes, 1964), Teshigahara Hiroshi. Abe Kobo's allegorical novel about a man who finds himself caught with a woman, both shovelling sand for the rest of their lives to keep from being buried alive. The performances of Okada Eiji and Kishida

Kyoko as the couple, Segawa Hiroshi's sharply focused photography, and Takemitsu Toru's wonderfully scratch-filled score help make this a memorable and claustrophobic experience. KJ#1; Cannes, Special Jury Prize. 123 mins. DVD Image Entertainment; VHS, British Film Institute (UK).

Woman of Tokyo (Tokyo no onna, aka Une Femme de Tokyo, 1933), Ozu Yasujiro. A woman works hard to put her younger brother through school only to have him kill himself when he learns that she has financed his education by becoming a prostitute. A romantic melodrama, perfectly put together. 70 mins. VHS (French titles), Ciné Horizon (France).

Women of the Night (Yoru no onna-tachi, aka Les Femmes de la Nuit, 1948), Mizoguchi Kenji. Postwar prostitutes and their miseries. A Yoda Yoshitaka script, Mizoguchi at his most noir, and Tanaka Kinuyo at her most pathetic. 96 mins. VHS (French titles), Les Films de Ma Vie (France).

Y

Yakuza Papers, The. See *Battles Without Honor and Humanity*.

Yojimbo (1961), Kurosawa Akira. The irresistible action comedy that became the director's greatest hit. Jobless samurai Mifune Toshiro strides into an awful little town and cleans out the bad guys—or, rather, encourages them to clean out each other. An elegant, poised, balletic, remorseless, and deeply amusing picture, beautifully photographed (in

widescreen black-and-white) by Miyagawa Kazuo, with a great score by Saito Masaru. Venice, Best Actor. 110 mins. DVD, Criterion.

Youth of the Beast (Yaju no seishun, 1963), Suzuki Seijun. Shishido Jo takes on rival gangs to avenge the murder of a friend. Actually, however, the storyline is just an excuse for this joyous send-up of violence. Lots of color, lots of laughs. 91 mins. DVD, Criterion.

Z

Zatoichi (2003), Kitano Takeshi. Beat Takeshi's remake with himself in the title role. Lots of violence, naturally, but at the same time a kind of noble pathos, which shortly becomes tiresome. The all singing, tap-dancing finale is welcome but it is rather too short. 116 mins. DVD, Buena Vista Home Video.

Zatoichi: The Life and Opinions of Masseur Ichi (Zatoichi monogatari, 1962), Misumi Kenji. The blind masseur who is also a sensational swordsman (Katsu Shintaro) became one of the most durable of late period-heroes. Daiei made some twenty-six sequels, several of them directed by the star himself. It is critically agreed that Misumi (who directed six of them) got the most out of the material. 96 mins. DVD/VHS, Facets Multimedia.

JAPANESE HISTORICAL PERIODS

ANCIENT
Nara 710–94
Heian 794–1185

MIDDLE AGES (MEDIEVAL)
Kamakura 1185–1333
Northern and Southern Courts 1333–92
Muromachi 1392–1573
Warring States 1482–1573

PREMODERN
Momoyama 1573–1600
Edo (Tokugawa) 1600–1867

EARLY MODERN / MODERN
Meiji 1868–1912
Taisho 1912–26
Showa 1926–1989
Heisei 1989 to present

N O T E S

CHAPTER 1

Beginnings and the *Benshi*

1. Komatsu Hiroshi and Frances Loden. "Mastering the Mute Image: The Role of the *Benshi* in Japanese Cinema," in *Iris: A Journal of Theory on Image and Sound*, 1996, p. 34.

2. Tanizaki Jun'ichiro. *Childhood Years: A Memoir*, 1988, p. 97.

3. Komatsu and Loden. Op. cit., p. 49.

4. Kirihara, Donald. "A Reconsideration of the *Benshi*," p. 48, cited in Keiko I. McDonald, *Japanese Classical Theater in Films*, 1994, p. 26.

5. Anderson, Joseph. "Spoken Silents in the Japanese Cinema," in *Reframing Japanese Cinema*, 1992, p. 285.

6. McDonald. *Japanese Classical Theater*, p. 31.

7. Sato Tadao. *Nihon Eiga-shi (Le Cinéma Japonais)*, Vol. I, p. 59.

8. Anderson. Op. cit., p. 194.

Film, Theater, and Actors

9. McDonald, Keiko I. *From Book to Screen: Modern Japanese Literature in Film*, 2000, p. 7.

Realism and Reality

10. Sontag, Susan. "Theatre and Film," in *Styles of Radical Will*, 1966, p. 100.

11. Burch, Noël. *To the Distant Observer: Form and Meaning in the Japanese Cinema*, 1979, p. 147.

12. Sato Tadao. "Nihon eiga no seiritsushita dodai ni," in *Nihon Eiga no Tanjo*, Vol. I of *Koza: Nihon Eiga*, 1985, p. 33, cited in Joanne Bernardi, *The Early Development of the* Gendaigeki *Screenplay*, 1992, p. 24.

Western Influences

13. Ozu Yasujiro. *Kinema Jumpo*, March 1952, cited in Leonard Schrader, ed., *The Masters of the Japanese Film*, 1972, p. 219.

14. Kurosawa Akira. *Something Like an Autobiography*, 1983, p. 36.

15. Sato Tadao. *Study of History of Film*, No. 13, 1979, unpaginated.

16. Sontag, Susan. *On Photography*, 1977, p. 23.

The *Gendaigeki*

17. Bernardi, Joanne. *The Early Development*, p. 52.

18. Yamamoto Kajiro, pp. 31–33, cited in Bernardi, *Writing in Light: The Silent Scenario and the Japanese Pure Film Movement*, 2001, pp. 80–81.

19. Shindo Kaneto. "Shinario Tanjo Zengo," in *Eiga no Tanjo*, ed. Sato Tadao, Vol. I, p. 213, cited in McDonald, *Japanese Classical Theater*, p. 37.

20. Anderson, Joseph L. and Donald Richie. *The Japanese Film: Art and Industry*, 1982, p. 41.

21. Bordwell, David. "A Cinema of Flourishes," in Nolletti and Desser, ed., *Reframing Japanese Cinema*, 1992, p. 334.

22. Anderson and Richie. Op. cit., p. 44.

CHAPTER 2

Taisho Democracy and Shochiku

1. Komatsu Hiroshi. "Japan—Before the Great Kanto Earthquake," in *The Oxford History of World Cinema*, 1996, p. 177.

2. Kido Shiro. *Nihon Eiga Den*, cited by Marianne Lewinsky and Peter Delpeut, eds., in *Producer of Directors: Kido Shiro*, 1995, unpaginated.

3. Ibid., unpaginated.

The New *Gendaigeki*: Shimazu, Gosho, Shimizu, Ozu, and Naruse

4. Ozu Yasujiro. *Carnets 1933–1963*, 1996, p. 87.

5. Nolletti, Arthur, Jr., "Woman of the Mist and

Gosho in the 1930s," in Nolletti and Desser, pp. 31–32.

6. Kishi Matsuo. *Nihon Eiga Yoshiki-ko* (On Japanese Cinema Style), cited in McDonald, *Japanese Classical Theater*, p. 19.

7. Ibid., p. 19.

8. Stanbrook, Allen. *Sight and Sound*, Spring 1988, cited in Lewinsky and Delpeut, unpaginated.

9. Bordwell, David. *Ozu and the Poetics of Cinema*, 1988, pp. 23–24.

10. Ozu. *Carnets*, p. 26.

11. "Ozu on Ozu," in *Kinema Jumpo*, June 1958 and February 1964, cited in Schrader, p. 177.

12. Sato Tadao. *Ozu Yasujiro no Geijutsu*, Vol. 2, p. 57, cited in Bordwell, *Ozu and the Poetics of Cinema*, p. 6.

13. Ozu. *Carnets*, p. 100.

14. Sato Tadao. *Ozu*, p. 159.

15. Bock, Audie. *Japanese Film Directors*, 1978, p. 102.

16. Anderson and Richie. Op. cit., p. 364.

17. "Naruse on Naruse," in *Kinema Jumpo*, December 1960, cited in Schrader, p. 354.

18. Bock, Audie. "The Essential Naruse," in *Mikio Naruse: A Master of the Japanese Cinema*, 1984, unpaginated.

19. Naruse Mikio. "On Japaneseness," from Kishi Matsuo's *Collected Film Writings*, 1955, cited in Schrader, p. 393.

20. Kurosawa. *Autobiography*, p. 113.

21. Bock, Audie. "Naruse," unpaginated.

22. Iwasaki Akira. "Naruse and Japanese Tradition," in *Studies of Japanese Filmmakers* (Nihon Sakka-ron), cited in Schrader, p. 425.

The New *Jidaigeki*: Itami, Inagaki, Ito, and Yamanaka Sadao

23. Suzukita Rokuhei. Quoted in Tanaka Jun'ichiro, *Nihon Eiga Hattasu-shi*, cited in Peter B. High,

"Japanese Film and the Great Kanto Earthquake of 1923," 1985, unpaginated.

24. Sato Tadao. *Currents in Japanese Cinema*, 1982, p. 34.

25. Thorton, Sybil. *The Japanese Period Film: Rhetoric, Religion, Realism*, 1989.

26. Kirihara, Donald. *Patterns of Time: Mizoguchi and the 1930s*, 1992, p. 62.

27. Hasumi Shigehiko. "Sadao Yamanaka or the New Wave in the 1930s in Kyoto," in *Cinemaya*, No. 2, Winter 1988–89, p. 47.

28. Sato Tadao. *Currents*, p. 222.

29. Ibid., p. 222.

30. Petric, Vlada. "Vselvolod Pudovkin," in Richard Roud, ed., *Cinema: A Critical Dictionary*, 1908, p. 800.

31. Richie, Donald. "Humanity and Paper Balloons: Some Remarks on Structure," *Cinema*, Vol. 2, Winter 1988–89, p. 54.

Nikkatsu and the *Shimpa*: Mizoguchi Kenji

32. Masumura Yasuzo. "My Film Apprenticeship," in *Kinema Jumpo*, July–August 1967, cited in Schrader, p. 142.

33. Mizoguchi Kenji. *Kinema Jumpo*, from an interview with Kishi Matsuo, April 1952, cited in Schrader, p. 35.

34. Yoda Yoshikata. "Souvenirs sur Mizoguchi," *Cahiers du Cinéma*, August 1965, p. 34, translated and cited in Kirihara, *Patterns of Time*, p. 66.

35. Masumura Yasuzo. Op. cit., cited in Schrader, p. 142.

36. Richie, Donald. "Kenji Mizoguchi" in Roud, p. 699.

37. Yoda Yoshikata. *Kinema Jumpo*, April 1961, cited in Schrader, p. 9.

38. Shinoda Masahiro. "Far from Mizoguchi," *Kinema Jumpo*, in Schrader, p. 20.

39. Sato Tadao. *Currents*, p. 181.

40. Ibid., p. 181.

41. Ibid., p. 183.

42. Shinoda. In Schrader, p. 118.

43. Kirihara. *Patterns of Time*, p. 136.

44. Mizoguchi. *Kinema Jumpo*, October 1956, cited in Schrader, p. 21.

Expressionism, Kinugasa Teinosuke, and the Leftist Film

45. Auerbach, Erich. *Mimesis: The Representation of Reality in Western Literature*, 1953, p. 6.

46. Fowler, Roger, ed. *A Dictionary of Modern Critical Terms*, 1987, p. 84.

47. Miyoshi Masao. *Accomplices of Silence*, 1974, p. 96, cited in Audie Bock, *A Page Out of Order*, 1975, p. 17.

48. Rajakaruna, D. A. *Kinugasa Teinosuke's "A Crazy Page" and "Crossroads,"* 1998, p. 6.

49. Iwasaki Akira. *Kinema Jumpo*, October 21, 1926, cited in Rajakaruna, p. xvi.

50. Kinugasa Teinosuke. *Nihon Eiga Shinario Koten Senshu. Kinema Jumpo-sha*, 1952, Vol. I, p. 144, cited in Rajakaruna, p. xvi.

51. Oshima Nagisa. *Taikenteki Sengo Eizo Ron* (A Theory of Postwar Film Based on Personal Experience), 1975, cited in Hirano Kyoko, *Mr. Smith Goes to Tokyo: Japanese Cinema Under the American Occupation: 1945–1952*, 1992, p. 15.

Criticism and Crackdown: World War II

52. High, Peter B. *The Imperial Screen: A Social History of the Japanese Film: 1897–1945*, unpublished, Chapter 10, p. 18.

53. Davis, Darrell William. *Picturing Japaneseness: Monumental Style, National Identity, Japanese Film*, 1996, p. 6.

54. Ibid., p. 108.

55. Yamamoto Kajiro. *Katsudoya Suiro*, cited in High, *The Imperial Screen*, Chapter 1, p. 12.

56. Kamei Fumio. *Kinema Jumpo*, April 1939, cited in Abé, Mark Nornes and Fukushima Yukio, *The Japan/America Film Wars: WWII Propaganda and Its Cultural Contexts*, 1994, p. 259.

57. Kamei Fumio. *Fighting Movies—A Documentarist's Show History* (Tatakau Eiga—Dokyumentarisuto no Showa-shi), 1989, cited in Abe and Fukushima, p. 260.

58. Iwasaki Akira. *Asahi Shimbun*, April 4, 1939, cited in Abe and Fukushima, p. 260.

CHAPTER 3

The Occupation of Japan

1. Hirano. *Mr. Smith Goes to Tokyo*, p. 54.

2. Dower, John. *Embracing Defeat: Japan in the Wake of World War II*, 1999, p. 432.

3. Kurosawa. *Autobiography*, p. 144.

4. Sato Tadao. *Currents*, pp. 121–22.

5. Mellen, Joan. *Voices from the Japanese Cinema*, 1975, p. 105.

6. Hirano. Op. cit., p. 143.

7. *The New York Times*, Aug. 19, 1948, cited in Hirano, p. 237.

Postwar Developments

8. Nolletti. "Woman of the Mist" in Nolletti and Desser, p. 7.

Ozu and Naruse

9. Richie, Donald. *Ozu: His Life and Films*, 1974, p. 27.

10. Shochiku, publicity brochure, 1962, in Schrader, p. 249.

11. Sakamura Ken and Hasuji Shigehiko, eds. *From Behind the Camera: A New Look at the Work of Director Yasujiro Ozu*, 1998, p. 10.

12. "Ozu on Ozu," in *Kinema Jumpo*, June 1958 and February 1964, in Schrader, p. 186.

13. "Conversations with Iwasaki Akira and Iida Shinbe," in *Kinema Jumpo*, June 1958, cited in Schrader, p. 193.

14. Shochiku press release for the film *An Autumn Afternoon*, 1962, in Schrader, p. 249.

15. Ryu Chishu. "Reflections on My Mentor," *Kinema Jumpo*, June 1958, in Schrader, p. 263.

16. Shinoda Masahiro. *The Living Ozu*, Shochiku pamphlet, 1972.

17. Ozu and Noda. *Tokyo Story*. Trans. by Donald Richie and Eric Klestadt, in Howard Hibbet, *Contemporary Japanese Literature*, 1977.

18. Sato Tadao. *Ozu Yasujiro no Geijutsu*, 1971, in Schrader, pp. 298–99.

19. Naruse Mikio. "Portraying Humanness," in *Kinema Jumpo*, April 1965, in Schrader, p. 343.

20. Naruse Mikio. "Naruse on Naruse," in *Kinema Jumpo*, December 1960, in Schrader, p. 366.

21. Ibid., p. 369.

22. Mizuki Yoko, *The Naruse Retrospective*, 1970, in Schrader, pp. 408–09.

23. Naruse Mikio. Interview with Shimizu Chiyoda and Hazumi Tsuneo, *Kinema Jumpo*, December 1952, in Schrader, p. 400.

24. "Ozu on Ozu," interviews from 1951 and 1961, *Kinema Jumpo*, June 1958 and February 1964, in Schrader, pp. 176–77.

25. Naruse. "Portraying Humanness," p. 344.

Mizoguchi and the Period-Film

26. Shinoda Masahiro. "Far from Mizoguchi," in *Kinema Jumpo*, June 1969, in Schrader, p. 126.

27. Mizoguchi Kenji. *Kinema Jumpo*, October 1956, in Schrader, p. 23.

28. Mizoguchi Kenji. Interview with Kishi Matsuo, *Kinema Jumpo*, April 1952, in Schrader, pp. 29–30.

29. Shinoda Masahiro. "Far from Mizoguchi," p. 113.

30. Ibid., in Schrader, p. 112.

31. Kurosawa Akira. *Kinema Jumpo*, April 1964, in Schrader, p. 135.

32. Masumura Yasuzo. *Kinema Jumpo*, April 1964, in Schrader, p. 143.

New Means: *Jun-bungaku*, Comedy, and Social Issues

33. Kurosawa. *Autobiography*, p. 171.

34. Richie. *Japanese Cinema: An Introduction*, 1990, pp. 123–24.

35. Johnson, William, "Toyoda and the Challenge of Representation," in *Film Quarterly*, Vol. 50, No. 2, Winter 1996–97.

36. Kurosawa. *Autobiography*, p. 183.

37. Mellen. Op. cit. p. 106.

38. Ibid., p. 107.

39. Tessier, Max. *Dossiers du Cinéma* (Cinéastes II), cited in Mellan, p. 99.

40. Richie. *Japanese Cinema: An Introduction*, p. 128.

41. Mellen. Op. cit., p. 88.

42. Mellen. Op. cit., p. 110.

43. Masumura Yasuzo, "Kon Ichikawa's Method," in James Quandt, ed., *Kon Ichikawa*, 2001, p. 99.

44. Mellen. Op. cit., p. 118.

45. Sato Tadao. *Currents*, p. 213.

46. Hoaglund, Linda. "A Conversation with Kobayashi Masaki," in *Positions 2–2*, 1994, p. 393.

47. Ibid., p. 382.

48. Kurosawa Akira. *Ikiru*, Donald Richie, trans., 1960, p. 45.

49. Kurosawa Akira. *Seven Samurai*, Donald Richie, trans., 1960, 1992, p. 225.

50. Iwasaki Akira. Cited in Sato Tadao, *Nihon Eiga Rironshi*, 1977, partial, unpublished translation, Peter B. High.

51. Richie, Donald. *The Films of Akira Kurosawa*, 1965, p. 244.

52. Ibid., p. 233.

53. Ibid., p. 242.

CHAPTER 4

The Advent of Television and the Film's Defenses: Suzuki, Nakahira, Kawashima, Imamura

1. *Japanese Film: 2000*, 2001. Tokyo: Uni Japan Film.

2. Buruma, Ian. *A Japanese Mirror: Heroes and Villains of Japanese Culture*, 1984, p. 149.

3. Sato Tadao. *Nihon Eiga Shisoshi*, 1970, p. 391.

4. All three quotes from Burgeson, J. Scott. *Bug*, Vol. 3, 1998, unpaginated.

5. Imamura Shohei. "The Sun Legend of a Country Boy," in *Japanese Kings of the B's*. Uitgave, Film Festival Rotterdam, 1991.

6. Bock. *Japanese Film Directors*, p. 287.

7. Imamura Shohei. "The Sun Legend."

8. Nakata Toichi. "Imamura Interview," in *Shohei Imamura*, ed. James Quandt, 1997, p. 113.

9. Imamura Shohei. "My Teacher," in *Japanese Kings of the B's.*, p. 11.

10. Nakata Toichi. "Imamura interview," p. 111.

11. Ibid., p. 111.

12. Bock. *Japanese Film Directors*, p. 288.

13. Yamada Koichi. "Les cochons et les dieux," in *Cahiers du Cinéma*, No. 166, Mai–Juin, 1965, p. 31.

14. Imamura Shohei. "Traditions and Influences," in *Japanese Kings of the B's*, 1991, p. 131.

15. Richie, Donald. "Notes for a Study on Shohei Imamura," in *Partial Views*, 1995, p. 157.

16. Ibid., p. 25.

17. Imamura Shohei. "My Approach to Filmmaking," in *Japanese Kings of the B's*, 1991, p. 126.

The "New Wave": Oshima, Yoshida, and Shinoda

18. Mellen. Op. cit., p. 261.

19. Turim, Maureen. *The Films of Oshima Nagisa*, 1988, p. 18.

20. Mellen. Op. cit., p. 264.

21. Mellen. Op. cit., p. 12.

22. Turim. Op. cit., p. 33.

23. Bock. *Japanese Film Directors*, p. 323.

24. Tamaya Rikiya. *Nihon no Eiga Sakkatachi*, 1975, cited in Bock, p. 309.

25. Bock. *Japanese Film Directors*, p. 322.

26. Buruma. Op. cit., p. 50.

27. Mellen. Op. cit., p. 254.

28. Yoshida Kiju. Quoted by Sato, in *Kurosawa Akira Eiga Taikai*, cited in Keiko I. McDonald, *Cinema East: A Critical Study of Major Japanese Films*. Rutherford, N.J., 1983, p. 172.

29. Bock. *Japanese Film Directors*, pp. 341–43.

30. Shinoda Masahiro. Quoted by Sato, in *Nihon Eiga Shishoi*, 1970. Partial, unpublished translation, Peter B. High.

31. Quoted, Schrader, p. 25.

CHAPTER 5

Making Audiences

1. Schilling, Mark. *Encyclopedia of Japanese Pop Culture*, 1997, p. 10

2. Schilling. *Contemporary Japanese Film*, 1999, p. 59.

3. Doraiswamy, Rashmi. "Kiyoshi Kurosawa," in *Cinemaya*, Nos. 47–48, Summer 2000.

4. Ibid.

The New Independents

5. Schwartz, Robert. "The Beat and the Auteur," *The East*, Vol. XXXVI, No. 6, 2001.

6. Gerow, Aaron. "Shinji Aoyama," *Daily Yomiuri*, August 21, 1999.

7. Schilling, Mark. *Contemporary Japanese Film*, p. 30.

8. Sato Tadao. "Rising Sons," *American Film*, December 1985.

9. Ibid.

10. Ibid.

11. Canby, Vincent. "Juzo Itami," *The New York Times Magazine*, June 18, 1989.

12. Sato Tado. "Rising Sons."

13. Gerow, Aaron. "TV and Globalization Tighten Grip on Film," *Daily Yomiuri*, December 23, 2004.

14. Shinoda Masahiro. "Shinoda Speaks on the Future of Japanese Film," Japan Society Newsletter, January-February 1998.

15. Schilling, Mark. *Contemporary Japanese Film*, p. 16.

16. Ibid., p. 156.

17. Sato Tadao. "Rising Sons."

18. Richie, Donald. Yanagimachi interview, Australian School of Film and Television, Sydney, May 17, 1994. For seminar on Yanagimachi, unpublished.

19. Richie, Donald. "On Yanagimachi," *The Toronto Star*, November 22, 1990.

20. Gardner, Geoffrey and Leslie Stern. "Interview: Mitsuo Yanagimachi," *Film News*, June 1982.

21. Richie, Donald. "Notes on Mitsuo Yanagimachi: A New Japanese Director," *Film Criticism*, Vol. III, No. 1, Fall 1983.

22. Itakura Kimie. "Kore'eda Interview," *Asahi Evening News*, May 12, 1999.

23. Gerow, Aaron and Tanaka Junko. "Kore'eda Hirokazu, Documentarists of Japan, No. 12," Yamagata Film Festival, *Doc Box*, No. 13, 1999, p. 1.

Documentary and *Anime*

24. Abé, Mark Nornes. *Japanese Documentary Film: The Meiji Era through Hiroshima*, 2003.

25. Ibid.

26. Ruoff, Jeffrey and Kenneth. *The Emperor's Naked Army Marches On*, 1998, p. 6.

27. Ibid.

28. Richie, Donald. "Remarks on Hara Kazuo," International House of Japan Film Program Series, 1998.

29. Gide, André. *The Counterfeiters*.

30. Abe, Mark Nornes. *The Japan/America Film Wars*, p. 191.

31. Dower, John. "Japanese Cinema Goes to War", in *Japan in War and Peace: Selected Essays*, 1995, p. 53.

32. Sato Kenji. "More Animated Than Life," *Kyoto Journal*, No. 41, 1999.

33. Rayns, Tony. *Tokyo: Film Festivals*, 1989, pamphlet.

34. Sato Kenji. Op. cit.

35. Sato Kenji. Op. cit.

anime generic term for futuristic/sci-fi Japanese animated film. See also *manga-anime*.

bakufu Edo-period (1600–1867) shogunate government.

benshi film narrator, commentator, lecturer—a master of ceremonies whose appearance was an assumed part of early Japanese film showings.

blue film earlier American term for hard-core pornographic film.

bungei-eiga films based on literary novels. See also *jun-bungaku*.

bunraku the Japanese puppet drama which attained artistic maturity in the eighteenth century.

bushido the "way of the samurai"; the ethical code through which this military elite was expected to comport themselves.

chambara sword fights in plays and films, later a generic term for low-class samurai pictures.

Chikamatsu Monzaemon Edo-period playwright (1653–1724) somewhat facilely called "the Shakespeare of Japan."

chiyogami-eiga early form of lantern-slide show using paper cutouts.

dokuritsu purodakushon an independent production.

e-maki painted or drawn picture scrolls.

eizo-sakka something like "artistic director."

ero-guro a style (in illustration, fashion, film) which combined the erotic with the grotesque.

gendaigeki generic term for films about contemporary life, as opposed to *jidaigeki*; also *gendai-mono*.

gidayu a narrative chant (*joruri*) that greatly influenced kabuki music, though it originated with bunraku.

giri-ninjo personal inclination versus duty, often in opposition and used as a prime plot-mover in conventional Japanese dramaturgy.

haha mono generic term for films about mothers.

haiku a 17-syllable verse form consisting of three metrical units of 5–7–5 syllables respectively.

hogaku traditional Japanese music.

iemoto the "grand master" of a traditional school: noh, Japanese dance, ikebana, and so on.

ikebana "living flowers"; Japanese flower arrangement.

jidaigeki generic term for historical films, mainly those of the Edo period (1600–1867); also *jidaimono*.

jitsuroku-eiga realistic, often anarchistic yakuza films much given to entertaining violence.

joruri narrative commonly associated with bunraku.

jun-bungaku literature, as distinguished from "popular reading." See also *bungei-eiga*.

kabuki one of the three major classical Japanese theaters (with noh and bunraku) which matured in the eighteenth century.

Kabuki-za a theater showing kabuki, usually referring to the Tokyo Kabuki-za.

kagezerifu "shadow dialogue"; an earlier kind of film narration, later transformed by the benshi.

kamishibai "paper theater"; slide-show.

kanji ideographs, Chinese in origin, appropriated by the Japanese to form one component of the written language.

kata the way of doing things: the chains of movement in Japanese dance and martial arts; the discrete units of noh, kabuki, and other forms of drama; the graduated techniques of using the brush in Japanese-style painting; and so on. Traditional and/or conventional forms.

katarimono recitations, spoken narratives, etc.

keiko-eiga films with definite (usually leftist) political aims, sometimes loosely translated as "tendency films."

kimaru the name for the poses in Japanese

classical dance when action is stopped in order to admire the tableau.

kishotenketsu narrative organizing principle.

kodan didactic storytelling, much of whose material is drawn from Confucian interpretations of medieval war tales and historical events.

kokusaku-eiga "national-policy films."

kowairo the live "dubbing" of lines with full emotional emphasis—"voice-coloring"—used in early film presentations.

kultur-film pre–World War II import from Germany, a form of documentary film.

kyogen comic plays, originally interludes in the noh, now evolved into a separate dramatic form.

kyuha "old school," meaning kabuki and used in opposition to *shimpa* ("new school"); the latter term became generic for a particularly post-kabuki kind of theater.

ma aesthetic term designating an artistically placed interval in time or space. Originally a musical term indicating silence.

manga originally a generic term for a category of woodblock print. Now a generic term for Japanese illustrated "comic" books.

manga-anime a generic term for animated films. See also *anime*.

matatabi-mono movies about itinerant gamblers, ruffians, yakuza.

michiyuki the "journey," a set piece in bunraku and kabuki; the travellers are usually lovers.

mono no aware an empathetic appreciation of the transient beauty manifest in nature, including human nature.

mu a Buddhist term meaning "nothingness."

nagaya early (Edo-period) house or group of row houses.

***nakanai* realism** realism "without tears"; a realism which does not stress the more dire aspects of life as it is.

naniwabushi popular form of narrative ballad based on traditional narratives; also *rokyoku*.

nihon buyo Japanese classical dance.

Nihonjin-ron studies on the uniqueness of being Japanese.

ninjo see *giri-ninjo*.

ninkyo-eiga idealized, formalized yakuza films of a purportedly serious moral concern.

nogaki advertising, hype.

noh Japan's oldest extant theater, a form of dance-drama originated in the fourteenth century.

Nuberu Bagu the "Nouvelle Vague," i.e., New Wave.

obi kimono sash.

oyama male actresses; i.e., men acting the part of women.

PCL Photo-Chemical Laboratories, 1930s Japanese film studio.

pinku-eiga "pink movie"; soft-core pornographic film.

rakugo a popular form of comic monologue.

rensageki an early twentieth-century form of drama, part film, part stage presentation.

rokyoku see *naniwabushi*.

roman-porno soft-core pornography made mainly by Nikkatsu in the 1960s.

ronin masterless samurai, "floating men."

samisen three-stringed banjo-like musical instrument. Also *shamisen*.

SCAP Supreme Command(er) of the Allied Powers.

setsumei précis or explanation.

sewamono a kabuki genre: "modern" plays as distinguished from historical drama; usually about the lives of ordinary people rather than gods and heroes.

shakai-mono films with "social" themes.

shimpa "new school," in opposition to the "old school" of kabuki; an intermediate theatrical form, partly Western.

shingeki "new theater," comparable to that in Western countries; opposed to classical Japanese theater and distinct from *shimpa*.

shinju double (or multiple) suicide, usually that of lovers.

shinkokugeki "new National drama," an off-shoot of shingeki and mainly concerned with historical drama.

shinsei-shimpa a later form of *shimpa* which purported to be a bit more realistic.

shishosetsu autobiographical novel.

shomingeki films about the lower-middle classes, the "little people." More strictly, serio-comedy about the salaried classes. Also known as *shoshimingeki*.

suibokuga literally, "water-ink–painting," mono-chrome use of black ink on plain silk or paper.

suji "plot"; story, narrative, sequence.

tachimawari kabuki-style sword fighting.

taiyozoku "sun tribe," a late 1950s phenome-non; the "juvenile delinquent" in fiction and films about rebellious youth.

tanka a 31-syllable poem consisting of five lines in the pattern 5–7–5–7–7.

tasuke a technique (now usually used for TV advertising) in which the same scene is shown several times.

tatami reed-covered straw matting used as floor-ing in the traditional Japanese room.

tateyuki "standing role"; male lead, often macho.

tsuma mono generic for films about wives.

Tsuruya Namboku kabuki playwright (1755–1829).

ukiyo-e "pictures of the floating world"; wood-block prints usually of the Edo period.

utsushi-e an early form of lantern slide.

waka formally identical with the *tanka*, the *waka* is often considered the more colloquial.

yakuza generic for gangster, gambler, thug, etc.

Zeami Motokiyo early playwright and aestheti-cian (1363–1443).

BIBLIOGRAPHY

Abé, Mark Nornes. *Japanese Documentary Film: The Meiji Era Through Hiroshima*. University of Minnesota Press, 2003.

Abé, Mark Nornes and Fukushima Yukio. *The Japan/America Film Wars: WWII Propaganda and Its Cultural Contexts*. Chur, Switzerland: Harwood Academic Publishers, 1994.

Anderson, Joseph. "Spoken Silents in the Japanese Cinema; or, Talking to Pictures: Essaying the *Katsuben*, Contexturalizing the Texts." In *Reframing Japanese Cinema*. Eds. Arthur Nolletti, Jr. and David Desser. Indiana University Press, 1992.

———— and Donald Richie. *The Japanese Film: Art and Industry*. Princeton University Press, 1982.

Anonymous. *Japanese Film: 1997–1998*. Tokyo: UniJapan Film, 1999.

Auerbach, Erich. *Mimesis: The Representation of Reality in Western Literature*. Princeton University Press, 1953.

Bernardi, Joanne. *The Early Development of the Gendaigeki Screenplay: Kaeriyama Norimasa, Kurihara Tomas, Tanizaki Jun'ichiro and the Pure Film Movement*. Dissertation. Columbia University, unpublished, 1992.

————. *Writing in Light: The Silent Scenario and the Japanese Pure Film Movement*. Detroit: Wayne University Press, 2001.

Bock, Audie. "The Essential Naruse." *Mikio Naruse: A Master of the Japanese Cinema*. Chicago: Art Institute Film Center Publication, 1984.

————. *Japanese Film Directors*. Tokyo: Kodansha International, 1978.

————. *A Page Out of Order*. Unpublished, 1975.

Bordwell, David. *Ozu and the Poetics of Cinema*. Princeton University Press, 1988.

Burch, Noël. *To the Distant Observer: Form and Meaning in the Japanese Cinema*. Berkeley: University of California Press, 1979.

Burgeson, J. Scott. *Bug*, Vol. 3, Seoul, 1998.

Buruma, Ian, *A Japanese Mirror: Heroes and Villains of Japanese Culture*. London: Jonathan Cape, 1984.

Cremin, Stephen,. ed. *The Asian Film Library Reference to Japanese Films—1998*. Two volumes. London: The Asian Film Library, 1998.

Davis, Darrell William. *Picturing Japaneseness: Monumental Style, National Identity, Japanese Film*. New York: Columbia University Press, 1996.

Doraiswamy, Rashmi. "Kiyoshi Kurosawa." New Delhi: *Cinemaya*, Spring-Summer 2000, pp. 47–48.

Dower, John. *Embracing Defeat: Japan in the Wake of World War II*. New York: Norton/Free Press, 1999.

————. *Japan in War and Peace: Selected Essays*. New York: New Press, 1995.

Dym, Jeffrey A. "*Benshi* and the Introduction of Motion Pictures to Japan." Monumenta Nipponica, Vol. 55, No. 4, Winter 2001.

Fowler, Roger, ed. *A Dictionary of Modern Critical Terms*. London: Routledge & Kegan Paul, 1987.

Galbraith, Stuart IV. *The Japanese Filmography: 1900 through 1994*. Jefferson, North Carolina: McFarland & Co., 1996.

Gardner, Geoffrey, and Leslie Stern. "Interview: Mitsuo Yanagimachi," Sydney: *Film News*, June 1982.

Gerow, Aaron and Tanaka Junko. "Kore'eda Hirokazu, Documentarists of Japan #12." Yamagata Film Festival, *Doc Box*, No. 13, 1999, p. 1.

Gide, André. *The Counterfeiters* (Les Faux-Monnayeurs). Trans., Dorothy Busy, New York: Knopf, 1927.

Hasumi Shigehiko. "Sadao Yamanaka or the New Wave in the 1930s in Kyoto." New Delhi: *Cinemaya*, No. 2, Winter, 1988–89.

Hibbett, Howard, ed. *Contemporary Japanese Literature*. New York: Knopf, 1977.

High, Peter B. *The Imperial Screen: A Social History of the Japanese Film: 1897–1945.* Unpublished ms.

———. "Japanese Film and the Great Kanto Earthquake of 1923." Nagoya: Nagoya Daigaku Press, 1985.

Hirano Kyoko. *Mr. Smith Goes to Tokyo: Japanese Cinema Under the American Occupation: 1945–1952.* Washington, D.C.: Smithsonian Institution Press, 1992.

Hoagland, Linda. "A Conversation with Kobayashi Masaki." *Positions 2–2,* Duke University, 1994.

Imamura Shohei, et. al. *Japanese Kings of the B's.* Uitgave, Film Festival Rotterdam, 1991.

Iwasaki Akira. "Naruse and Japanese Tradition." *Studies of Japanese Filmmakers* (Nihon Sakka-ron). Tokyo: Chuo Koronsha.

Japanese Film, 2000. Tokyo: UniJapan Film, 2001.

Johnson, William. "Toyoda and the Challenge of Representation." *Film Quarterly,* Vol. 50, No. 2, Winter 1996–97.

Kirihara, Donald. *Patterns of Time: Mizoguchi and the 1930s.* Madison: University of Wisconsin Press, 1992.

———. "A Reconsideration of the *Benshi.*" *Film Reader,* No. 6., 1985.

Kishi Matsuo. *Collected Film Writings.* Tokyo: Ikeda Shoten, 1955.

———. *Nihon Eiga Yoshiki-ko* (On Japanese Cinema Style). Tokyo: Kawade Shobo, 1937.

Komatsu Hiroshi. "Japan—Before the Great Kanto Earthquake," in *Oxford History of World Cinema,* ed. Geoffrey Nowell-Smith. Oxford University Press, 1996.

——— and Frances Loden. "Mastering the Mute Image: The Role of the *Benshi* in Japanese Cinema." In *Iris: A Journal of Theory on Image and Sound,* No. 22, Autumn, 1966.

Kurosawa Akira. *Ikiru.* Trans. by Donald Richie. London: Lorrimer, 1960.

———. *Seven Samurai.* Trans. by Donald Richie. London: Lorrimer, 1960.

———. *Something Like an Autobiography.* Trans. by Audie E. Bock. New York: Knopf, 1983.

Larimer, Tim. "The Beat Goes On." *Time,* February 12, 2001.

Lewinsky, Marianne and Peter Delpeut, eds. *Producer of Directors: Kido Shiro.* Amsterdam: Nederlands Filmmuseum, 1995.

McDonald, Keiko I. *From Book to Screen: Modern Japanese Literature in Film.* Armonk: M. E. Sharpe, 2000.

———. *Japanese Classical Theater in Films.* Associated University Presses, 1994.

Mellen, Joan. *Voices from the Japanese Cinema.* New York: Liveright, 1975.

Mes, Tom and Jasper Sharp. *The Midnight Eye Guide to New Japanese Film.* Berkeley: Stone Bridge Press, 2004.

Miyoshi Masao. *Accomplices of Silence.* Berkeley: University of California Press, 1974.

Mizuki Yoko. *The Naruse Retrospective.* Tokyo: Film Library Bulletin, Aug. 1970.

Nolletti, Arthur, Jr. and David Desser, eds. *Reframing Japanese Cinema.* Indiana University Press, 1992.

Nowell-Smith, Geoffrey, ed. *Oxford History of World Cinema.* Oxford University Press, 1996.

Oshima Nagisa. *Taikenteki Sengo Eizo Ron* (A Theory of Postwar Film Based on Personal Experience). Tokyo: Asahi Shimbunsha, 1975.

Ozu Yasujiro. *Carnets: 1933–1963.* Trans. from the Japanese by Josiane Pinon-Kawataké. Paris: Editions Alive, 1996.

Quandt, James, ed. *Kon Ichikawa.* Toronto: Cinémathèque Ontario, 2001.

———. *Shohei Imamura.* Toronto: Cinémathèque Ontario, 1997.

Rajakaruna, D. A. *Kinugasa Teinosuke's "A Crazy Page" and "Crossroads."* Translated with an introduction. Kandy, Sri Lanka: Kandy Offset Printers, 1998.

Richie, Donald. *The Films of Akira Kurosawa.* Berkeley: University of California Press, 1965.

———. "Humanity and Paper Balloons: Some

Remarks on Structure." *Cinema*, Vol. 2, Winter 1988–89.

————. *Japanese Cinema: An Introduction.* Oxford University Press, 1990.

————. *Japanese Cinema: Film Style and National Character.* New York: Doubleday, 1971.

————. *Japanese Film: Art and Industry* (with Joseph Anderson). Princeton University Press, 1982.

————. "Notes for a Study on Shohei Imamura," in *Partial Views*. Tokyo: Japan Times Publications, 1995.

————. "Notes on Mitsuo Yanagimachi: A New Japanese Director," in *Film Criticism*, Vol. III, No. 1, Fall 1983.

————. *Ozu: His Life and Films.* Berkeley: University of California Press, 1974.

————. "Remarks on Hara Kazuo." International House of Japan Film Program Series, Tokyo, 1998.

Roud, Richard, ed. *Cinema: A Critical Dictionary.* London: Secker & Warburg, 1908.

Ruoff, Jeffrey and Kenneth. *The Emperor's Naked Army Marches On.* Trowbridge, England: Flick Books, 1998.

Sakamura Ken and Hasuji Shigehiko, eds. *From Behind the Camera: A New Look at the Work of Director Yasujiro Ozu.* Tokyo: University of Tokyo, 1998.

Sato Kenji. "More Animated Than Life." Kyoto: *Kyoto Journal,* No. 41, 1999.

Sato Tadao. *Currents in Japanese Cinema.* Trans. by Gregory Barrett. Tokyo: Kodansha International, 1982.

————. *Nihon Eiga-shi* (A History of Japanese Film). Tokyo: Iwanami Shoten, 1995, four volumes. Translated as *Le Cinéma Japonais.* Paris: Centre George Pompidou, 1998, two volumes.

————. *Nihon Eiga Shisoshi.* Tokyo: Tokyo Shoten, 1970. Partial, unpublished translation by Peter B. High.

————. "Rising Sons." *American Film,* December 1985.

————. *Study of History of Film.* Privately printed (English only), unpaginated.

————, ed. *Eiga no Tanjo.* Tokyo: Iwanami, 1985.

Schilling, Mark. *Contemporary Japanese Film.* New York: Weatherhill, 1999.

————. *Encyclopedia of Japanese Pop Culture.* New York: Weatherhill, 1997.

————. *The Yakuza Movie Book: A Guide to Japanese Gangster Films.* Berkeley: Stone Bridge Press, 2003.

Schrader, Leonard, ed. *The Masters of the Japanese Film,* unpublished ms., 1972.

Schwartz, Robert. "The Beat and the Auteur," *The East,* Vol. XXXVI, No. 6, 2001.

Sontag, Susan. *On Photography.* New York: Farrar, Straus & Giroux, 1977.

————. "Theatre and Film," *Styles of Radical Will,* New York: Farrar, Straus & Giroux, 1966.

Tanizaki Jun'ichiro. *Childhood Years: A Memoir.* Trans. by Paul McCarthy. Tokyo: Kodansha International, 1988.

————. *Nihon Eiga Hattatsu-shi.* Tokyo: Chuo Koronsha, 1975.

Tayama Rikiya. *Nihon no Eiga Sakkatachi.* Tokyo: David-sha, 1975.

Thorton, Sybil. *The Japanese Period Film: Rhetoric, Religion, Realism.* Work-in-progress, unpublished ms., 1989.

Turim, Maureen. *The Films of Oshima Nagisa.* Berkeley: University of California Press, 1988.

Washburn, Dennis and Carole Cavanaush. *Word and Image in Japanese Cinema.* Cambridge University Press, 2001.

Yamada Koichi. "Les cochons et les dieux." Paris: *Cahiers du Cinéma,* No. 166, Mai-Juin, 1965.

The majority of film stills in this book are taken from Donald Richie's *The Japanese Movie* (Kodansha International, revised edition). Many of these were in turn obtained from the Donald Richie collection of Japanese film stills in the Museum of Modern Art, New York; those added for *A Hundred Years of Japanese Film* were supplied by Bitters End, *Okaeri*; Gunro Productions, *Fire Festival*, *The Plan of a Nineteen-Year-Old*; Ichikawa Jun, *Dying at a Hospital*, *Tokyo Siblings*; Itami Productions, *The Funeral*, *Tampopo*; Oguri Kohei, *The Sleeping Man*, *Muddy River*;Oshima Productions/Shochiku, *Gohatto*; Shochiku, *Beijing Watermelon*; Somai Shinji, *Moving*, *Typhoon Club*; Studio Ghibli, *Princess Mononoke* © 1997, Nibariki-TNDG; The Kawakita Memorial Foundation, *The Cherry Orchard*, *Duo*, *Hanabi*, *Japanese Girls at the Harbor*, *The Sun's Legend*, *Suzaku*, *After Life*, *Maboroshi*; There's Enterprise, Inc., *Vital* © 2004 SHINYA TSUKAMOTO/KAIJYU THEATER; TV Man Union, Inc., *Distance* © *Distance* Project Team All Rights Reserved, *Nobody Knows* © 2004 *Nobody Knows* Production Committee All Rights Reserved; WOWOW, *Helpless* © WOWOW and Bandai Visual, *Riyu* © WOWOW and Bandai Visual.

（改訂新版）日本映画ガイド
A Hundred Years of Japanese Film /Revised and Updated

2005年5月27日　第1刷発行

著　者　ドナルド・リッチー
発行者　畑野文夫
発行所　講談社インターナショナル株式会社
　　　　〒112-8652 東京都文京区音羽1-17-14
　　　　電話　03-3944-6493（編集部）
　　　　　　　03-3944-6492（営業部・業務部）
　　　　ホームページ　www.kodansha-intl.com
印刷・製本所　大日本印刷株式会社

落丁本・乱丁本は購入書店名を明記のうえ、小社業務部宛にお送りください。送料小社負担にてお取替えします。なお、この本についてのお問い合わせは、編集部宛にお願いいたします。本書の無断複写（コピー）、転載は著作権法の例外を除き、禁じられています。

定価はカバーに表示してあります。